War, Politics, and Philanthropy

The History of Rehabilitation Medicine

Richard Verville

UNIVERSITY PRESS OF AMERICA,® INC.

Lanham • Boulder • New York • Toronto • Plymouth, UK

Copyright © 2009 by
University Press of America,® Inc.
4501 Forbes Boulevard
Suite 200
Lanham, Maryland 20706
UPA Acquisitions Department (301) 459-3366

Estover Road
Plymouth PL6 7PY
United Kingdom

Library of Congress Control Number: 2009925798
ISBN: 978-0-7618-4594-2 (paperback : alk. paper)
eISBN: 978-0-7618-4595-9

∞™ The paper used in this publication meets the minimum
requirements of American National Standard for Information
Sciences—Permanence of Paper for Printed Library Materials,
ANSI Z39.48-1992

This book is dedicated to the inspiring and committed rehabilitation professionals and persons with disabilities who were the pioneers and leaders in this field from WWI to date. A few in particular inspired and educated me with their sense of humanity and compassion and their love of rehabilitation: Ed Lowman, Bill Spencer, Justus Lehmann, Fritz Kottke, Henry Betts, John Ditunno, Lex Frieden, Justin Dart and Judy Heumann. I worked closely with and was a friend of most of them from the 1970's through the 1990's. To the extent I am recognized as a person with a dedication to improving rehabilitation medicine and programs and rights for persons with disabilities, I owe that recognition to them and their colleagues.

Contents

Foreword

In this most remarkable work, Rehabilitation Medicine is traced from its roots of physical restoration and vocational guidance pioneered by physicians, together with other advocates in the private and public sectors. The author identifies the three most significant factors in the development of the field in the subtitle of War, Philanthropy and Politics. Although oversimplified, War equates with the three medical pioneers who established restorative care in military hospitals, Henry Kessler, Frank Krusen and Howard Rusk, while Philanthropy and Politics were led by Bernard Baruch and Mary Switzer respectively. In the first two thirds of the book (Chapters 1 through 10), which spans four decades from the 1920s through the 1960s, we learn how each came to their own appreciation of the needs of persons with disability; fought against the traditional establishment, and then passed the baton to the next generation.

Krusen and Rusk faced resistance to acceptance in an era where diagnosis and acute care was all that mattered in medicine. What was successful for our wounded veterans had to be translated into civilian practice. To achieve that result, Krusen formed the Society of Physical Therapy Physicians (the American Academy of Physical Medicine, today) in 1938 to plan for board certification, which required a minimum of 100 members (this was not achieved until 1947).

Bernard Baruch, whose wisdom was valued by all presidents of our nation starting with World War I, was able to leverage his influence and wealth to establish the initial capacity of scientific research and training of specialists. He was able to influence organized and academic medicine at the highest levels to recognize that Rehabilitation Medicine had merit and supported the formation of medical specialty status. Mary Switzer continued to grow this capacity for research and training in all rehabilitation professions through her recognition of need of integrating medical rehabilitation with vocational training. She established the first funded Research and Training centers in 1962.

These five giants individually and most often collectively established the form and structure in the professional, private and public arenas, which fostered the fulfillment and maturation realized in the 1980s and 1990s described in the latter one third of the book. The generation of leaders that followed included Kottke, Lehmann, Spencer, Johnson and Betts. They built on the groundwork the founders had laid by developing nationally recognized centers of academic and clinical excellence. This facilitated the attraction of dynamic leaders (the third generation), who would be in a position to expand the manpower and facilities necessary to meet the demand of increased health coverage to all our citizens; the severely disabled and elderly alike, in the years to follow. However, the author points out from his special perspective, the influence of other factors in our society, such as the growth of the disability movement and the response of elected officials to consumer needs. He indicates that it no longer was sufficient just to have strong individual leaders impact government like Krusen and Rusk, but depended also on the growth of professional organizations in medicine and the other rehabilitation professions. These included such groups as the American Physical Therapy Association and analogous ones for Occupational Therapists and Vocational Counselors and the American Academy of Physical Medicine and Rehabilitation and the American Congress of Rehabilitation Medicine. The professional organizations joined with consumer organizations in the 1970s to lead the movement for disability rights and rehabilitation . Access of disabled persons and the elderly to health care through Medicare and Medicaid programs enacted in the 1960s placed additional demands on the field; and the rehabilitation momentum accelerated in the 1980s to reach a mature status at last.

With society's acceptance of medical rehabilitation, the stage was set for the recognition of rights for the disabled. This became an important issue to champion, and the story of the American Disabilities Act (ADA) is thoroughly described in Chapter 14. Drs. Betts and Spencer had long advocated that the field of Rehabilitation Medicine had to emphasize the universal access for person with disabilities.

It is not a coincidence that the ADA legislation was signed into law in 1990 at the same session of Congress that authorized a new center for rehabilitation research at the National Institutes of Health (NIH). This crowning achievement of scientific recognition advocated over 40 years ago by Kessler, Krusen and Rusk was established by the creation of the National Center for Medical Rehabilitation Research (NCMRR) in the Institute for Child health and Human Development (NICHHD) of the NIH. In the words of the author "Research in the field (Rehabilitation Medicine) was finally recognized by the NIH leadership as worthy of significant attention and investment."

Never before has the rehabilitation movement and the Rehabilitation Medicine profession been so thoughtfully and thoroughly reviewed. It deserves the attention of any serious student or practitioner of the field. The author has not only given new insights to this remarkable medical approach, but brings a unique perspective that only he could provide.

He brings a legislative perspective, because of his involvement with rehabilitation medicine organizations and his advocacy for the needs of consumers and professionals for over 35 years. The author graciously fails to mention his pivotal role in many of the legislative and regulatory achievements that he describes with an insider's detail, and which were often crossroads for the field. In addition, he brings passion and understanding, because of his dedication to the cause, not unlike that so eloquently stated in the epilogue by Dr. Kessler.

"The rehabilitation idea has taught me that there is a miraculous biological safety factor in every human being. Resources that lie dormant can be called upon to remold a personality physically and mentally. I have learned also that there is a safety factor for civilization. It is that powerful fraternity of men and women who believe that the object of all help is to make help superfluous."

Finally, he has worked much of his professional career with the leadership of the rehabilitation medical professions, the legislative bodies and the congressmen, who have advocated for the sentiment expressed above. It has been a labor of love and is a living testament to his dedication to our specialty. As an expression of our gratitude he has been honored by many of our professional organizations; such as the American Congress of Rehabilitation Medicine, the Academy of Physical Medicine and Rehabilitation, and the Association of Academic Physiatrists. But he is appreciated by all of us who have had the privilege of his association, counsel and friendship. Perhaps the awards that he cherishes most are the Human Dignity Award from Kessler Institute in 1997 and the Citation for Distinguished Service from the AMA in 2004 ("In recognition of outstanding contributions to the growth of the field of PM&R and to the advancement of disability rights"). The former links him to the roots of the rehabilitation medicine movement and the latter recognizes his contribution to our discipline by the most representative body of organized medicine in the nation.

John F. Ditunno, Jr. M.D.
Professor of Rehabilitation Medicine, Former Chair (1969–1997)
Jefferson Medical College
Regional Spinal Cord Injury Center of the Delaware Valley
Thomas Jefferson University

Acknowledgments

I am especially indebted to John Ditunno M.D. and Randall Braddom M.D., M.S. for their assistance in producing this manuscript. John Ditunno encouraged me throughout the 5 years of research and writing. He gave me ideas, sources and invaluable facts about the field from the inception of this project. He has been a leader in the rehabilitation medicine field since the 1970s and is a lover of history; both of which added to the value of his comments. He read the entire manuscript in its early stages and his perspectives were always creative and his encouragement essential.

Randall Braddom committed his many skills as writer, editor, rehabilitation medicine leader and story teller to this project when I was seeing no light at the tunnel's end. In mid-2007 he agreed to serve as Editor of the final manuscript. He was then serving on the Board of the Foundation for Physical Medicine and Rehabilitation to which I had sent the manuscript. The Foundation, to which I am also indebted, wished to be of assistance and Randall offered on its behalf, and his own, his editing and writing skills. His editing work has made the text much more readable and clear. He has also added facts about the field to my store of information. Most important, he has encouraged me to keep at the project and he has lightened the times of dreariness which writing produces for me with his wonderful wit.

Linda Gans also was an important reviewer of the first draft of the manuscript and her editorial changes were readily adopted by me. Her interest in the project also kept me going. Betsy Sandel reviewed an early draft and supplied me with valuable material on the history of the Permanente Medical Group and Henry Kaiser, both of whom were deeply involved in the history of rehabilitation medicine.

I want to acknowledge all those who allowed themselves to be interviewed by me or who responded to my email questions about rehabilitation. They are listed in the bibliography. In particular, Henry Betts M.D. was always available to discuss the field's history in which he is so well versed, and he encouraged me to stick to writing this history. I am looking forward to reading his memoirs. Joel DeLisa M.D. is another who not only discussed issues of the field's history with me, but frequently sent materials he thought relevant and encouraged me to stick to the project.

Chapter One

Setting the Stage

The history of rehabilitation medicine in the USA revolves around the stories of five courageous lay and medical leaders and their colleagues who built a new field of medicine by taking advantage of the opportunities available as a result of war, politics and philanthropy.

Rehabilitation medicine deals with the problems of impairment and disability. An impairment can be defined as an abnormal condition or disease that causes a reduced ability of the affected individual to function in society. Some of the most common impairments seen in the practice of rehabilitation medicine include brain injury, spinal cord injury, amputations, stroke, paralysis of any kind, arthritis, and many other conditions. The impairment can be congenital, or acquired at some point after birth. A disability can be defined as what a person cannot do for him or herself as a result of an impairment. For example, a person with a spinal cord injury in the thoracic or lumbar region typically would have difficulty managing the bowel and bladder (which are usually not functioning normally); would be unable to walk due to paralysis of the lower extremities; would have numbness of the abdomen and pelvis and lower limbs, would have difficulty dressing and bathing; etc. Rehabilitation medicine practitioners concentrate on eliminating disability, whether or not the impairment itself can be cured.

The person with spinal cord injury described above would need the interdisciplinary services of most members of the rehabilitation team (physician, nursing, physical therapist, occupational therapist, social worker, recreation therapist, vocational counselor, psychologist, and orthotist) to be able to learn to do the things necessary to function independently. Such a person, with appropriate rehabilitation, should be able to bathe and dress, practice skin care that would prevent breakdown, learn practical methods of compensating for

1

the dysfunction of the bowel and bladder, use a wheelchair, and even ambulate short distances with braces and crutches. This person should be able to care for him or herself completely, live alone in the community, hold down a job, and drive a car. Such a person would still have the impairments induced by the condition of spinal cord injury, but would have much less disability. Rehabilitation medicine practitioners attempt to reduce a person's level of disability, and often refer to themselves as "disability busters."

Rehabilitation medicine has often been referred to as the "third phase of medicine," with Phase I being preventive care and Phase II being acute care. It took pioneering efforts to establish it as an accepted form of medicine and health care, since its focus was not on cure or prevention. Rehabilitation medicine also suffered from having perhaps too little emphasis on traditional medical diagnosis and treatment, at a time when medicine itself was seeking legitimacy during the first half of the 20th century. The early advocates of rehabilitation were often considered quacks and charlatans. They were discouraged by organized medicine from focusing on the function of patients rather than just on their disease state; and pursuing the rehabilitation of persons with disabling conditions rather than just the treatment of disease.

One of the major reasons for the success of rehabilitation medicine, however, has been the fact that it is not narrowly medical. It focuses on the function of a person with a disability, rather than just the diagnosis of a disease state. It believes that "freedom follows function." It takes into account the social, psychological, economic, and environmental factors that can affect function and impact the likelihood of obtaining a positive health outcome.

Rehabilitation medicine is a comprehensive clinical service, which also commonly includes the use of physical agents such as heat, water, light, electricity and exercise to restore movement to body parts. In addition, it includes physical and occupational therapies, rehabilitation nursing, speech therapy, prosthetics, orthotics, specialized medical equipment, psychological, social and vocational services. The exact mix of services provided depends on the nature and severity of the disability and attendant medical complications of each case. "Patients" initially receive rehabilitation services in a hospital inpatient setting. (The terms "patient" and "client" are used in this book because they are in common use in rehabilitation medicine. They are meant only in their most positive sense, and are not meant in any way to be pejorative. They are intended to denote a therapeutic relationship between and among equal partners in care in which the patient's own functional and life goals are paramount). Upon discharge from the inpatient program, services can be rendered in a nursing facility, outpatient setting, or in the home. The goal is to return affected persons to their own homes and back to their usual activities and to employment. A team of rehabilitation medicine professionals provides the services, and the rehabilitation medicine physician generally provides the specialized medical care needed and coordinates the effort. The disabling conditions of each patient are usually accompanied by ongoing acute and chronic medical problems. Examples of such conditions include paralysis from stroke or spinal cord injury, joint pain and immobility from arthritis or injury, cognitive dysfunction or seizures from brain injury, amputations of limbs, and chronic lung and cardiac impairments. The spinal cord injured person mentioned above might have many medical problems and complications; such as bladder infections, osteoporosis of bones below the level of injury, pressure ulcers of the skin below the level of injury, and even the development of atherosclerotic heart disease from the lack of use of the lower limbs in daily exercise.

Rehabilitation medicine is also a system for delivering health care, since it utilizes the services of multiple professionals whose efforts require the integration of multiple facilities and agencies (such as hospitals, outpatient facilities, and home care agencies). The person getting care in this system has to have a seamless transition from each level and type of care to the next.

Rehabilitation medicine, with its team approach and use of varied levels and types of care, has always been a novel way to provide medical care. During most of its early development, rehabilitation medicine was primarily a hospital-based system of comprehensive care focused primarily on inpatient services. In recent years, the focus shifted more on outpatient services, since hospital stays have been reduced and the nature of disabling conditions has changed. Although comprehensive in scope, the services must be focused specifically to provide the best functional outcome for each individual patient. For example, patients with stroke can require specific training and strengthening to walk safely, feed and dress themselves, and may also benefit from assessment and counseling that fosters social reintegration with the family and on the job.

Rehabilitation medical care is provided by an interdisciplinary team that involves many health professionals. Each of these professionals has, over the years, developed its own professional association. These associations have played a prominent role in the growth of rehabilitation medicine through their advocacy, education, and efforts to enhance the quality of their work. Rehabilitation medicine involves physicians specializing in the field of Physical Medicine & Rehabilitation, who are referred to as physiatrists (there are two common pronunciations of this name: fiz e at' trist and fiz i' a trist (rhymes with psychiatrist). Physicians of other specialties such as orthopedic surgery and neurology are also extensively involved in the rehab process. The medical professionals on the team include physical therapists, occupational therapists, speech pathologists, rehabilitation nurses, prosthetists (trained to replace missing body parts with artificial limbs), orthotists (specialize in the fitting and fabrication of braces and splints), rehabilitation nurses, social workers, recreational therapists and respiratory therapists. The extent of the involvement of each professional depends upon the type and complexity of the disabling condition. The development of the field involved both professional and political interaction among these disciplines. While tensions relative to professional turf have existed throughout the past 90 years of growth and development in the field of rehabilitation medicine, there has clearly been more cooperation than conflict.

The economic outcome of vocational productivity through employment was the original emphasis that gave rehabilitation medicine its credibility. Returning an injured military person to active duty or a disabled civilian to employment were (and still are) viewed as highly valued results by the general public and the government.

Unlike other early forms of medical care, rehabilitation medicine did not evolve from within the medical enterprise. It also did not develop as the result of new breakthroughs in medical science or theory. It has a history in which factors outside of medicine, such as war, politics, and philanthropy played the major role. The field developed and was accepted largely because the public and governmental leaders saw rehabilitation medicine as necessary for the public good. They viewed it as necessary because of the positive social and vocational results it achieved. That feeling of public necessity was itself premised on humanism and pragmatism, important factors in American thought and politics during the first half of the 20th century. The leaders of our nation at that time responded to the field to a large extent because of the efforts and influence of five extraordinary individuals, who along with their colleagues and allies, organized the field and pressed its case at the highest levels of government and society.

The foundation and initial development of rehabilitation medicine were the result largely of the leadership of three physicians and two lay leaders. The physicians were Doctors Henry Kessler, Frank Krusen and Howard Rusk, who often battled with their medical colleagues for recognition of the field. The two lay leaders were Bernard Baruch and Mary Switzer, who were both the patrons and partners of the three physicians.

In the early days of American medicine, physician leadership was common in health care in general as medicine sought to establish itself and its sovereignty. In his book *The Social Transformation of American Medicine*, Paul Starr argued that that the "Progressive Era" politicians supported science and medicine and entrusted to it the management of medical care.[1] This power arguably existed until about 1970 when government and employers took the controls as costs rose. These leaders initially had to battle with medicine itself to achieve recognition for rehabilitation medicine. This was because rehabilitation was not prominent in the power structure of medicine, and medicine itself controlled medical care and medical education. They resorted to involving interested philanthropists, politicians, governmental administrators and other lay leaders in achieving their goals, since the structure of organized medicine was slow to respond and the numbers of rehabilitation medicine practitioners were few in the first half of the twentieth century. The vision, intelligence, and courage of these five leaders in the face of major obstacles were at the heart of this story of the rise of a new field of heath care. All were of the same generation except Baruch. It should be noted, however, that although Baruch was born a generation before the others, he lived until he was 95 and became a colleague of the other founders from 1945 until 1965.

The development of rehabilitation medicine owes a special debt to the change in thought and politics that took place during its formative years from approximately 1900 to 1950. These changes shaped the views of the five founders and the positive responses to rehabilitation medicine of politicians and philanthropists in both times of war and times of peace.

It was at the end of the 19th century and during the first two decades of the 20th century that journalists, politicians, and the public began to define progress more broadly than just industrial progress; and looked to government and science to provide that progress. The social and economic problems created by the extraordinary industrial growth of the late 19th century became focal points for action by these progressive forces. The emphasis on the then novel use of empirical approaches and experimentation to solve problems led to their application to social problems; including labor practices, unsafe products, unhealthy living and working conditions, and recognition of the existence of populations unable to share in the gains of industrial progress. As a result, the early 20th century saw the creation of the first major governmental programs to deal with social and economic problems: Workers' compensation including medical coverage, veterans' benefits and services, food and drug regulations, child labor laws, laws dealing with hours and other conditions of work, and the vocational rehabilitation program of services to persons with disabilities to enable them to be employable. The movement that produced these changes in governmental policies was referred to as "Progressivism."

Progressive thinking during the period of 1900 to 1920 laid the foundation for the nation's efforts during the depression years and during the Second World War to improve the economic and social condition of civilians, soldiers, and veterans through the Social Security Act, collective bargaining legislation, and military and veterans' hospitals. This was also a period of major growth for rehabilitation medicine. The social legislation that followed in the next 40 years was often an expansion of the programs of the 1930s and 1940s and rehabilitation medicine flourished and steadily grew to maturity during this span of time.

NOTE

1. Starr, The Social Transformation of American Medicine, Basic Books Inc., New York, 1982, 140.

Chapter Two

In the Beginning:
The Early Years of the Founders of
Rehabilitation Medicine

SIMON AND BERNARD BARUCH

Simon Baruch arrived in the United States from Posen, then part of Germany, at the age of 15. Seven years later, he graduated from the Medical College of Virginia in Richmond in 1862. After his graduation, he returned to his home in Camden, South Carolina, and enlisted in the Confederate Army. He received an appointment as an assistant surgeon despite his lack of surgical experience. He noted that he received this appointment: "Without even having lanced a boil."[1] As an immigrant who had achieved success, Baruch felt a strong sense of duty to his adopted state. It is reasonably clear, however, that he was not a supporter of slavery; the institution at the heart of the tension leading to the Civil War. Simon's brother, Herman Baruch, who also arrived in South Carolina from Germany, likewise enlisted in the Confederate Army.[2]

The second Battle of Manassas marked Simon Baruch's initiation into medical practice as a battlefield surgeon. His performance of an amputation earned praise from the supervisory surgeon, a battlefield veteran. He was a prisoner of war on two occasions, at Antietam and again at Gettysburg. He had been ordered by General Lee to remain at the Confederate battlefield hospital at Gettysburg to care for the many wounded, and as a result was captured by the advancing Union Army. When the war ended in 1865, Simon (now age 25 years), returned to Camden, South Carolina and began a successful medical practice.[3]

Simon Baruch was one of the most successful medical practitioners in South Carolina during the 15 years he practiced there. At age 33, he was elected President of the South Carolina Medical Association. He was also a prominent civic leader and humanist. It was said of him that: "He treated

Negroes and whites alike for all of their ailments." He was a committed supporter of the community in which he practiced.[4]

Soon after his return from the Civil War Simon married Isabelle Wolfe, known as Belle, and began a family. Isabelle and Simon had two sons, Bernard, the eldest, and Herman. Bernard was born in 1870. Simon Baruch often stressed to his family the importance of moral values and working for the good of the community, and their relative priority over pecuniary rewards (which his son Bernard would nevertheless reap). This advice ultimately had a major impact on Bernard. During the 1870s Isabelle urged Simon to consider the possibility of moving north to city life where opportunities for medical practice might be better. The oppressiveness of the Reconstruction Era in the South added impetus to their decision to move northward. In the winter of 1880, the Baruch family sold their home and Simon's medical practice and moved to New York City.[5]

Simon Baruch's talents soon led to success in both his medical practice and his involvement in community affairs in New York City. His concern for community and moral values resulted in efforts to stop the terrible sanitary practices of many urban dwellers. This condition was prevalent in most of America's large cities, due to rapid immigration into the cities and failure to plan for this explosive growth. Dr. Baruch once described Manhattan as a body of land surrounded by sewage. He began a long-term project to bring public baths to the needy of New York City. He found the tenement conditions of New York City appalling, since there was typically only one faucet to supply four families. He felt a strong need to protect the public from health problems and the baths were one answer. He was also named Commissioner of Public Hygiene for the city and was placed in charge of the city's Juvenile Asylum. This facility housed youths with various forms of disease; many of which were the result of environmental factors such as poor sanitation. Due to his interest and achievements in this area, Simon Baruch was appointed Chair of the New York Medical Society Hygiene Committee.

By the early 1900s Simon Baruch was recognized as one of the nation's experts on medical hygiene and hydrotherapy, including the beneficial use of water at various temperatures on the treatment of illness. He taught hydrotherapy at Columbia College of Physicians and Surgeons in 1892, and published the first English language text on the subject: *The uses of water in modern medicine*. He held the chair of Hydrotherapy at the Columbia College of Physicians and Surgeons from 1907 until 1913, and was actively involved in both teaching and research throughout the early 1900s. Simon Baruch was one of the earliest practitioners and teachers of rehabilitation medicine; since hydrotherapy was, and still is, one of the methods used to treat patients in rehabilitation medicine. It involved the use of a physical agent (water and its temperature), to bring about relief from illness. In addition to his prodigious work on hydrotherapy, Dr. Baruch had also been appointed Physician-in-Chief at the Montefiore Home for Chronic Invalids in 1884. Montefiore at that time was comparable to today's rehabilitation hospital, although it did not offer active rehabilitation therapy (since such programs had not yet been developed). It housed individuals with chronic illness, to whom such therapies as hydrotherapy could be applied. As Frank Krusen wrote:

> *In time, out of his compassion and determination to heal the sick and disabled, no matter how grave the illness or seemingly hopeless the disability, he became one of the earliest practitioners of that phase of medicine, which has come to be known as physical medicine and rehabilitation. While rehabilitation medicine, utilizing the services of physical therapy, occupational therapy, speech therapy, psychology and vocational counseling for persons with disabilities was not developed in Simon Baruch's time, he used the available agents which he believed would assist in healing persons who had disabilities.*[6]

Isabelle and Simon Baruch brought up and educated Bernard and Herman to be humanists, and to feel a responsibility for improving the lot of others in society. Herman became a physician. Bernard became a financier and political advisor to Presidents. He repaid his father for his many gifts of education, love, and support by financially assisting him in 1900 to give up the active practice of medicine and undertake research and writing in his chosen field, hydrotherapy and medical hygiene. Bernard Baruch enjoyed life in New York City, and made it his home for 85 years.

Bernard enrolled in City College of New York (CCNY) in 1884 when he was only 14 years of age. His heart had been set on attending Yale University, but his mother felt he was too young to be away from home. Consequently, he enrolled in CCNY, which at the time was a small municipal university. Bernard was handsome, athletic, academically talented and a natural leader (as demonstrated by his being elected class president). He graduated from CCNY in 1889 at the age of 19, an age when most of today's youth are just entering college.[7]

Bernard had great respect for his father and his father's work. Later in his life, he even came to regret not having chosen medicine as his vocation. But in 1889 he was anxious to be active in the financial and industrial growth that was at the heart of America's development in the late 19th century. His first job was working with Julius Kohn, a banker and member of the New York Stock Exchange (NYSE). Later he worked with Arthur Houseman, who served as J.P. Morgan's broker. He then began to successfully invest his own funds. By 1897, when he was only 27 years of age, Bernard purchased his own seat on the New York Stock Exchange. In 1903, he was elected to the

Board of the NYSE. Baruch was a very forceful and self-confident individual. He was ambitious and yearned to expand his influence.[8]

By the early 1900s, although tremendously successful, Bernard Baruch was tired of investing other people's money. He considered becoming a lawyer for people's rights, and eventually established his own investment business. He became a venture capitalist and traded for his own account on the floor of the NYSE. He also became very involved with the ownership and development of large industrial companies. The Guggenheim family, John D. Rockefeller, Senator Nelson Aldrich, and Bernard were owners of Continental Rubber. Bernard was also actively involved in mining, particularly the copper industry.[9]

Because of his father's concern for social responsibility and his own ambition and instinct for power, he became involved in politics. He was an avid supporter financially and otherwise of fellow Southern-born Progressive Democrat Woodrow Wilson. Baruch considered himself a Democrat and a Progressive. He became acquainted with Colonial House, President Wilson's Chief of Staff, and assisted a relative of House in becoming President of his alma mater at the City College of New York. With the advent of WWI, Wilson appointed Baruch to be a Trustee of the War Preparedness Board and then to the Administrations Defense Council. Baruch's intimate knowledge of the economics of American industry and its leaders made him a natural to lead the war mobilization effort. His tenure as Chair of the War Mobilization Board was marked by great success. His goal was to transform the American economy from one of peace to one of war. When he left the War Mobilization Board Chairmanship he had garnered widespread respect for his ability to get things done.[10]

By 1917, Bernard Baruch's personal wealth reached 10 million dollars. It reached 16 million dollars by the end of the stock market crash of 1929. He personally assisted Winston Churchill to help him survive the crash. During the first term of President Franklin Delano Roosevelt (FDR), Baruch was an active supporter of the National Recovery Act and a close friend of its administrator, Hugh Johnson. Baruch and FDR were on close enough terms that during WW II, in need of a respite from the demands of being Commander in Chief, Roosevelt vacationed at Hobcaw, Baruch's South Carolina retreat.[11]

Baruch's formal role in rehabilitation medicine did not begin until 1943 when, in collaboration with Dr. Frank Krusen, he established a national Committee on Physical Medicine. This group developed and financed a plan to establish the field of Physical Medicine and Rehabilitation. Baruch was led into this involvement with rehabilitation because of his wealth, progressive politics and dedication to his father. This plan guided the development of rehabilitation medicine in general, and the medical specialty of Physical Medicine and Rehabilitation in particular, from 1944 to 1970.

THREE PHYSICIANS AND A CIVIL SERVANT

Henry Kessler, Frank Krusen, Howard Rusk, and Mary Switzer were all born from 1896 to 1901. All but Rusk were Easterners and city dwellers. By 1950, the four had become colleagues in an effort to dramatically expand the field of rehabilitation medicine. They knew little of each other before World War II and had no collegial interaction. Their lives had actually taken very different turns until World War II, which provided the impetus for rehabilitation medicine's development. Kessler and Krusen were involved with rehabilitation medicine as early as 1919 and 1925 respectively, while Rusk and Switzer were exposed to rehabilitation medicine only during World War II, some 20 years later.

Henry Kessler

Henry Kessler was the oldest of four children, and was born in 1896 in Newark, New Jersey. He was raised by his mother, who worked as a hat trimmer and her father, an émigré from Romania and a butcher in Newark. Kessler noted: "Like many immigrant Jewish mothers, my mother was determined that her son should be a doctor." That profession was one with which he had no quarrel.[12] His family was poor and Kessler worked while attending school from high school through college and medical school. He attended Dewitt Unitary High School in New York City and boarded with a cousin of his mother. An excellent student, Kessler graduated at the age of 16 and qualified for a scholarship to Cornell University. As a pre-med student at Cornell, he worked as a waiter and night chef to pay for his room and board. Kessler graduated from Cornell at age 19 after three years of pre-med and entered Cornell Medical School in New York City. He needed to find work to assist with his living expenses, so Kessler requested assistance from the New Jersey Department of Labor. This began a relationship that would lead him to his first contact with rehabilitation.[13]

Kessler graduated from Cornell Medical School in 1919 at age 23. He had attended classes during the day and worked at night. By his own admission, sleep was a pleasure he seldom experienced, although he often napped out of necessity during classes. Upon graduation from medical school he began an internship in surgery at New York City Hospital. True to his sense of responsibility, Kessler went to the New Jersey Department of Labor to thank the staff who had assisted him in his medical education by helping find him employment. He indicated that he would like to repay the Department for its generosity to him. At this point, Dr. Kessler was introduced to Dr. Fred Albee, an orthopedic surgeon, who was in the process of beginning a new program in rehabilitation for the New Jersey Department of Labor and its Workmen's Compensation program. This program was based on one Albee had developed during World War I. Dr. Kessler began as a part-time employee of the government clinic during his hospital internship and Dr. Albee became his mentor. Albee was not only a renowned orthopedic surgeon, especially in the field of industrial accidents, but was also an innovator and humanitarian. He introduced Dr. Kessler to international health issues in the late 1920s during a trip to Europe that involved the International Congress of Industrial Accidents. Later in his career, Dr. Kessler, like Dr. Rusk, became an international missionary for rehabilitation.[14]

Kessler was a very cultivated and erudite man, and both of these qualities are apparent in his artful autobiography. Kessler was very interested in learning as much as he could, not only about his profession, but about other matters related to it as well. After his graduation from medical school, he successfully pursued a Masters degree in legislation from Columbia University.

Frank Krusen

Frank Krusen, unlike Henry Kessler, had an influential father and mother. Krusen was born in Philadelphia, Pennsylvania in 1898. His father was a professor of obstetrics and gynecology at Jefferson Medical College, and served as the Director of Public Health for the City of Philadelphia. Coincidentally, Krusen's father may have served as Director of Public Health for Philadelphia at the same time Simon Baruch was in charge of Public Hygiene for the City of New York. Krusen attended Quaker grammar and high schools before entering Jefferson University in 1915. He attended Jefferson Medical College after his undergraduate education and graduated from medical school in 1921. Krusen began a surgical internship at Jefferson Hospital in 1921, saw patients in his father's office, and served as medical director of a taxicab company. Krusen's interest in academic medicine was influenced by his father, who served as his role model and by his surgical mentor, Dr. J. Chalmers DaCosta. DaCosta impressed upon him the importance of academic discipline, close analysis, research and writing in medical journals.[15]

During his residency training in the mid-1920s, Dr. Krusen contracted tuberculosis. Having been married upon graduation from medical school and already having purchased a home, the onset of tuberculosis was a terrible setback for his economic situation as well as his health. Affording treatment was a problem. Luckily, the medical director of the sanitarium in which he was treated was a friend of Krusen's father and appointed Frank to the sanitarium medical staff, which assisted in paying for his care. The experience of serving on the medical staff of the sanitarium led to Frank Krusen's lifelong journey to rehabilitation medicine. Krusen observed that patients with tuberculosis became physically deconditioned and unable to resume active vocations. He became convinced that the use of physical agents to restore health and vocational rehabilitation to engage the patient in activity were part of a necessary new approach to medical care. Frequently in his academic life he continued to pursue and write about treatments for tuberculosis. He attributed his ultimate cure from TB to the use of heliotherapy, which is the treatment of disease by use of light and specifically by sunlight. He had read the work of the Swiss physician, Dr. Rollier, on the value of sunlight in the treatment of tuberculosis. At the sanitarium, he was encouraged to undertake clinical research on the Rollier method. It was shortly after this that Krusen began to seek the development of a scientific basis for a field in medicine that utilized physical agents.[16]

Krusen's experience as both a patient and a physician in the sanitarium started him on his career in physical medicine and rehabilitation. He became convinced that if he got well he would: ". . . do something to help people like these. Maybe this is God's will for me." When he learned that he would be unable to continue in his surgical training due to having had tuberculosis, he decided to focus on physical medicine. He remembered the patients he had seen at the sanitarium and their need for assistance of all types; including medical, spiritual and vocational. He concluded that: "There ought to be some place where they could be rehabilitated".[17]

Coincidentally, at almost the same time that Krusen was hospitalized with tuberculosis, Henry Kessler contracted the same disease and had to leave his active practice in New Jersey. Kessler was also at that time the medical director of the state Workers' Compensation program and an attending physician at Newark General Hospital. Both Kessler and Krusen had the benefit of seeing medicine from the viewpoint of the patient with a serious and often incapacitating disease.[18]

Howard Rusk

Howard Rusk was born in the small town of Brookfield, Missouri in 1901. He was the only one of the leaders in the development of rehabilitation medicine who was not born and raised in the East. His uncle and his maternal grandfather were physicians and his father wished to be one, but could not afford medical school. Rusk's first exposure to the practice of medicine was working in his uncle's office as a boy. The family was badly hit by the depression of 1919-20 and Howard had to work his way through the University of Missouri after his admission there in 1919. One of his jobs was at the State Colony for the Feeble Minded and Epileptic. At about the same time he also had his first taste of politics, as he organized a successful campaign for his father as Clerk of the County Court. Rusk was already showing his obvious talent for adapting to new people and situations and taking leadership in all environments. He was a tall, handsome and charming young man with extraordinary self-confidence.[19]

In his third year at the University of Missouri, Rusk entered the Medical School. His family tradition of medicine and his own caring nature and social consciousness led him easily to this career choice. For his last year of medical school, Rusk transferred to the University of Pennsylvania, from which he graduated in 1925. He returned to Missouri and did his internship at St. Luke's Hospital in St. Louis in internal medicine. In 1926, he began a medical practice in St. Louis. Rusk's captivating personality attracted many patients, and his patients often became his friends. He was on the staff of Barnes Hospital, and taught at Washington University School of Medicine, which was and still is a prominent medical school with a major focus on research. One of his patients provided him with funds to conduct research, a portent of things to come as Rusk's charm and dedication were quite convincing in persuading patients and philanthropists to make donations to his work. His paper on uticaria, (hives), was far removed from his later focus on traumatic injury, but was published in the prestigious Journal of the American Medical Association. Unlike Kessler and Krusen, Rusk's practice and career had not begun with a focus on rehabilitation of persons with disabilities. It was not until his service in World War II, some 15 years after his practice began, that he became involved in what would become an all-encompassing life in medical rehabilitation.[20]

Mary Switzer

Mary Switzer was perhaps the most unique of the creative leaders who founded rehabilitation medicine. She was an Easterner, and her background was probably more like Kessler's than that of Baruch, Krusen or Rusk. She was born in 1900 of Irish immigrant parents, Julius Switzer and Margaret Moor, in Newton Falls, Massachusetts (near Boston). Julius Switzer boarded with Michael Moor in the tenements of Upper Newton Falls. Both were tradesmen and part of a very close Irish immigrant community. Michael brought his mother and sisters from Ireland and his sister Margaret married Julius Switzer. Margaret died of consumption in 1911, to some extent caused by the poverty in which the family lived. Mary's grandmother and aunt moved to obtain custody of Mary and were successful. Her father never forgave them and left for New York with Mary's brother, never to return. The major influence on Mary's life was her intellectual and very political uncle, Michael Moore. It was during Switzer's formative years that the Irish were at the height of their rebellion against the English, almost 150 years after American Colonists had rebelled. But the Easter Rebellion of 1917 failed and the Irish suffered scorn not only in the British Isles, but also in New England. Uncle Mike was an active advocate for Irish independence from Britain and much of his idealism and intellect rubbed off on Mary.

Mary Switzer was a very bright and idealistic young woman who entered Radcliff College in Cambridge Massachusetts in 1917. She received a scholarship and boarded at home in order to afford the elite women's school. One of her mentors while she attended Radcliff was Scott Nearing, who lectured frequently at the Liberal League, a debating society. Nearing had formerly taught at the Wharton School of the University of Pennsylvania. He had been fired from Wharton for his criticism of Presidents Coolidge and Harding.[21]

One of Mary's best friends at Radcliff was the daughter of Justice Louis Brandeis, a Bostonian, who was appointed to the Supreme Court by President Wilson. Justice Brandeis was one of the leading intellectuals of the Progressive Politics of the early 20th century. His focus was often on correcting the abusive economic practices of the large, powerful and independent corporations of late 19th- and early 20th- century America. In many of his cases and decisions, his ultimate goal was to protect the rights of working people and more generally, to establish rights for the individual. He was known as a protector of the rights of the little man and the underprivileged against corporate America. It was his opinion that the laws at that time were weighted in favor of the corporations. Uncle Mike referred to Brandeis as the "People's Lawyer." Brandeis was Jewish and identified closely with the Irish immigrants in their plight to become socially accepted and economically independent in Brahmin Boston. Switzer spent considerable time with the Brandeis family and was very much affected by the views of Justice Brandeis. It was the influence of Brandeis, Scott Nearing, Radcliff, College, and her Uncle Mike, which shaped her idealism and progressive political views. This led to a career in government in Washington upon graduation from Radcliff in 1921.[22]

While Mary Switzer did not become actively involved in federal health, social and rehabilitation programs until the early 1930s, she was blessed by her friendships during the 1920s with a number of women active in social movements. These women also influenced her views about government's role in dealing with social problems. Among these early friends whom she met in

Washington was Jane Adams, who was already a well known social worker and social activist. She had started Hull House, a Chicago Settlement experiment to assist the poor. Another close friend in these days was Tracy Copp, who had worked for the Wisconsin Rehabilitation and Workers Compensation agencies. Tracy Copp came to Washington and became staff to the Federal Vocational Rehabilitation Program that was created in 1920.

Mary's own work was at the Treasury Department, where her skills resulted in her progressing from a secretarial position to an assistant in the Treasury Secretary's office. Her organizational skills in creating a news clipping service for the Treasury Secretary led to a position in the White House analyzing and organizing press for President Hoover. But her first real professional interests in health and rehabilitation developed later during the presidency of FDR and the arrival in Washington of another mentor, Josephine Roche, who became very involved in health insurance.[23]

While the careers of these five extraordinary individuals began on very separate paths, by the 1940's, their paths would begin to cross and rehabilitation medicine would be the end result.

NOTES

1. Baruch, B: *My Own Story*, Buccaneer Books, 1957, 5.

2. Baruch, 5, 6.

3. Baruch, 5.

4. Baruch, 1, 2; Grant, Bernard M. Baruch, Wiley and Sons, 1997, 7.

5. Baruch, 1, 21, 39.

6. Krusen, Archives of Physical Medicine and Rehabilitation (hereinafter cited as Arch Phys Med Rehabil), Vol. 46, 550; Baruch, 10.

7. Grant, 13.

8. Grant, 19-34.

9. Grant, 70–83.

10. Grant, 127–30; Baruch, 307–08.

11. Grant, Bernard Baruch, 247–49; Baruch, 271–73.

12. Kessler, *The Knife is Not Enough,* Norton and Company, 1968, 31.

13. Kessler, 31–37.

14. Kessler, 37–39.

15. Opitz, Krusen Diaries Arch Phys Med Rehabil, Vol. 78, 442.

16. Opitz, Diaries, Arch Phys Med Rehabil, Vol. 78, 443; Robison, *Frank H. Krusen M.D., Pioneer in Physical Medicine*, T.S. Denison and Company Inc., 1963, 52–56.

17. Robison, 52 and 53.

18. Kessler, 48.

19. Rusk, *A World to Care For, The Autobiography of Howard A. Rusk, M.D.*, Readers' Digest Press, Random House, 1972, 30–41.

20. Rusk, 45–50.

21. Walker, *Beyond Bureaucracy, Mary Elizabeth Switzer and Rehabilitation*, University Press of America, Inc., University Press of America, Inc., 15–24.

22. Walker, 24.

23. Walker, 26–28.

Chapter Three

The Roots of Rehabilitation Medicine in the Progressive Era, 1900 to 1920

The first programs in rehabilitation medicine grew out of the need for services to injured soldiers and workers during the early years of the twentieth century. These programs involved physician services that were specialized in rehabilitation, physical and occupational therapy, prosthetics, and vocational training. The government was a sponsor of these programs, and private philanthropy responded likewise.

The late eighteen hundreds and the first decades of the twentieth century have been characterized as the "Progressive Era." Industrial growth dominated the post Civil War era in the United States; but by the late eighteen hundreds discontent was prevalent among workers, farmers, social critics and journalists. They complained about the damaging social and economic effects of unrestrained economic growth, as well as the dramatic influx of immigrants to American cities that led to increasing slums and poverty. Simon Baruch had observed the terrible plight of the poor immigrant population of New York City, which led him to begin a crusade for improved public health for the city's slum dwellers. At that time, private economic interests were in control of social and economic policies, and the "practices of the managers of that power operated to the disadvantage of workers, farmers and small entrepreneurs".[1]

The individual seemed at risk in a world in which large corporations dominated power at all levels of government. The government had failed to act on such problems as abuse of workers and farmers, the disabilities of those wounded in war, and the public health problems of the cities. Into the breach came politicians like Republicans Theodore Roosevelt and Robert LaFollette; and Democrats Louis Brandeis and Woodrow Wilson. They led efforts to ameliorate the social and economic problems causing public discontent. Their leadership and thinking strongly affected the development and attitudes of the founders of rehabilitation medicine.

Simon Baruch was encouraged by reform politics and government to undertake his preventive health efforts and his hydrotherapy for the disadvantaged citizens of New York City. His son, Bernard, became a major supporter of Woodrow Wilson and his progressive politics, and Wilson made him one of his Executive Branch leaders in the economic reforms related to the war effort. Henry Kessler received his first exposure to the need for medical rehabilitation and his training in this field as a result of his work with the New Jersey Workers Compensation Program. Like other workers compensation programs, the New Jersey Workers Compensation Program was the result of state legislation advocated by President Roosevelt and Governor Lafollette. Mary Switzer was mentored by Louis Brandeis, father of her best college friend and the intellectual leader of progressive politics. Howard Rusk's indomitable optimism, idealism and support for the individual disadvantaged by a disability were also a reflection of the philosophy of the times in which he grew to adulthood.[2]

Another important aspect of the Progressive Era was its emphasis on experimentation, empiricism and science. The views of leading intellects of the times like William James, John Dewey and Oliver Wendell Holmes stressed the need to think empirically and try new ways to solve the problems of the age. Their thinking shaped what has become known as America's first philosophy, "Pragmatism." It was Pragmatism and not Metaphysics that was the intellectual force of the day. There was also a belief in the notion that science and professionals with training in social and physical science could change the problems of the day, including the problems of injured workers and injured soldiers. There was a sense of optimism about the world and man's ability to change it through rational, empirically driven policies and behavior. There was a belief that nothing was beyond the reach of dedicated, professional people who were well trained.[3]

Medicine should have been at a great advantage in such an era, since it was a profession whose roots were in the physical sciences. French scientific breakthroughs had led to the development of many medical advances, and with them the development of the hospital laboratory and the beginnings of clinical science. But in the late nineteenth century and very early twentieth century medical education and medicine had not kept up with scientific advances. Medical schools were not university based, but rather physician owned or controlled. Medical schools were not positioned to benefit from university based science and research. Medicine was not of even quality and had no mechanisms for policing itself. This changed dramatically with the advent of the Flexner Report on medical education that was commissioned by the American Medical Association (AMA). At the same time, there was an interest in the field of medicine in state licensing laws to facilitate self-policing through state medical boards. The Flexner report urged the integration of the medical school with universities, and focused medical education on the basic sciences. From this point forward, it was science that drove medical education, and medical education drove medicine. An implicit contract arose between the medical education establishment and society. This contract was that the medical schools were now committed to community values and focused on the training of high quality physicians. The end result would be the provision of high quality medical care in the community and on research to provide medicine with advances in care over the course of time. Society, in turn, supported the profession of medicine and its leadership in shaping medicine and health care in the United States.[4]

By the second decade of the twentieth century, medicine had gained the trust of society in general and its political leaders in particular. Medicine was now in control of its educational system and of the licensing of its graduates. These training programs were necessary to improve the quality and credibility of medicine, and to assure the public of appropriate medical care. Starr argued that from this favored position there evolved a sovereignty of medicine over everything medical and broadly over health care. Yet the favored status and power of medicine was both new and fragile. It needed to be managed carefully. This led to conservatism in organized medicine with regard to the recognition of new techniques and fields of medicine.

It was in this era of medical authority and conservatism that the first rehabilitation medicine services and programs began. It was not a propitious time for a new discipline or new field of medicine to try to emerge.

THE INITIAL EFFORTS TO RESPOND TO
PHYSICAL DISABILITY BEFORE AND DURING
THE EARLY 20TH CENTURY

The roots of physical medicine can be traced to the ancients. Occupational therapy was practiced in Egypt in ancient times and heliotherapy and hydrotherapy were practiced during the time of the Roman Empire. During the 18th century, work therapy was common in Europe for mental patients; and during the 19th century, the application of electrical current was utilized as a therapeutic method in Europe. In the late 19th century, a Danish physician by the name of Niels Finsen developed the use of ultraviolet light as a tool of medicine. He received the Nobel Prize in 1903 for this achievement. It was also about this time that Duchenne made his contributions to electrotherapy.

About 1890, d'Arsonval introduced the use of high frequency currents from diathermy machines in France for both medical and surgical purposes. These machines produced heat in body tissue from electric current. Unfortunately, the United States was not as advanced at that time as Europe in medicine in general.[5]

In the early 20th century, some American physicians experimented with the use of physical agents in the care of patients. This field of medicine involved the application of physics to health care, an area that moved far more slowly than the application of chemistry to medical care. Simon Baruch was the first well-known practitioner of hydrotherapy in the United States. He applied these techniques in the first years of the twentieth century. By 1907, Baruch was urging the use of public baths in New York City, and by 1917, the city provided baths for its residents. These baths were primarily for hygienic purposes, although Baruch wrote of the therapeutic effects of water used in whirlpools or used for heat.[6]

The period from 1900 until World War I was notable primarily for efforts by physicians in the United States to develop physical agents to treat disease and by the growth of physical and occupational therapy as disciplines in health care. The focus, however, was not on the organization of multidisciplinary team oriented rehabilitation medicine services. Nor was the focus on the person disabled from injury or disease, and the restoration of his or her function. The focus seemed to be more on the traditional disease model on which all of medicine operated. The site of practice was the physician's office. The physicians most involved in the early days of this field were primarily academically based. The best known of these was Dr. John Coulter, who exercised a very positive influence on the field of physical therapy and was a non-surgical physician who worked collegially with physical therapists. When World War I broke out, the physicians interested in physical agents were primarily focused on acute illness and the "specialists who were more experienced with injuries and disability were orthopedists and industrial physicians."[7]

WORLD WAR I AND MEDICAL REHABILITATION

It was the advent of World War I that produced the first rehabilitation medicine services. Orthopedic surgery had taken the initiative as early as 1916 to begin planning for medical care in wartime. Dr. Joel Goldthwait of Massachusetts General Hospital was chair of an American Orthopedic Association (AOA) Committee on this topic, which submitted its recommendations to the Surgeon General of the United States in 1917. Both prior to and during WWI,

Massachusetts General Hospital had programs in massage, hydrotherapy and exercise in its Medico-mechanical Department under the leadership of ortho-pedists Elliot Brackett and Joel Goldthwait. The far-reaching report of the AOA recommended a broad program including not only surgical services, but also services for physical restoration and for vocational training of soldiers who were disabled and about to be discharged from the military. All of these services were to be part of the program of the Reconstruction Hospitals rec-ommended by the AOA. Orthopedist Fred Albee, Dr. Kessler's mentor, was also very much in the forefront of the effort to plan for the Reconstruction Hospitals that were intended to bring the fruits of rehabilitation to the victims of war. Brackett and Goldthwaite were sent to Europe by Surgeon General William Gorgas soon after the Report was submitted. Their job was to inves-tigate the British and French "reconstruction" programs and make recom-mendations to the Army Medical Corps on their application to the Corps. Those programs became models for the development of rehabilitation ser-vices in the Army Medical Corps. Later Brackett and Goldthwait became leaders in the Army Division that was responsible for the U.S. Reconstruction Hospitals.

Dr. Fred Albee was active in providing care in the reconstruction hospital established in New Jersey. The development of this program for medical care and rehabilitation in the Army was the first example of a major, nationally recognized medical rehabilitation system of health care. Its initiation was, however, hindered by bureaucratic battles between federal agencies and be-tween physicians and vocational rehabilitation experts.[8]

Rehabilitation services were also developed during WWI by Colonel Harry Mock, a physician serving under Colonel Billings in the Division of Physical Reconstruction and Rehabilitation in the Surgeon General's Office of the Army. Mock was not a surgeon, but like Coulter, was a medical person com-mitted to the use of various physical therapy services and other rehabilitation techniques to treat the war wounded. Mock emphasized the need to not only rehabilitate the wounded soldier sufficiently to allow a return to military duty, but also to assist those not able to return to military service to be productive contributors to society. "Rehabilitation of the below par soldier and the dis-abled soldier to make the one fit for Army service and the other fit for future economic usefulness were the underlying purposes of these efforts," Colonel Mock said of his programs. Mock also quoted President Wilson: "This nation has no more solemn obligation than healing the hurts of our wounded and restoring our disabled men to civil life and opportunity."[9] President Wilson's statement was the initial clarion call from a national political or medical leader for a rehabilitation program. Mock described the best rehabilitation hospital programs and hospitals of WW1 as involving physical therapy, occupational therapy and vocational training. As with today's medical rehabilitation programs, the services were in inpatient hospital services and were generally under the supervision of physicians.

Dr. John Coulter was also an Army physician in charge of organizing the Army physical therapy programs. Dr. Granger, an orthopedist from Harvard, was the first Chief of the Division on Physical Therapy. Despite the availability of these knowledgeable rehabilitation physicians, Dr. Mock accurately complained that the Army had physical therapy, occupational therapy and vocational training in the hospitals but little or even no well trained physician leadership.[10]

The efforts of the AOA and of physicians like Goldthwait, Brackett, Albee, Mock and Coulter to establish Reconstruction Hospitals and expand rehabilitation medicine services for the military were well intended, but produced a bureaucratic battle which slowed progress in developing rehabilitation medicine services for soldiers remaining in active duty and disabled veterans of World War I. The problems they faced were not unlike the current effort of our government to provide the best in rehabilitation and other medical services for the soldiers returning from Iraq and Afghanistan. The rehabilitation medicine services recommended by the AOA and made available in Reconstruction Hospitals included vocational training and job placement in the civilian sector for the returning wounded war veterans. These services were modeled to some extent on the work of Drs. Goldthwaite and Brackett at Massachusetts General Hospital before the entry of the United States into the war.

Although idealistic in its intent, the AOA Report offended the members of the Federal Board of Vocational Education, which had been set up before our entry into the war to administer the federal vocational education program. The federal vocational education program was one of the very first federal social programs. The Board submitted its own plan, which had the Board controlling the provision of vocational training and job placement services to soldiers who were disabled and who were to be discharged from military duty. The War Department called a major conference in 1918 to resolve the dispute between the Army Medical Corps and the Federal Vocational Education Board and invited the AMA, the American Federation of Labor (AFL), representatives of the manufacturing companies, and the Red Cross, among others.[11]

The solution adopted by the Conference was to support the AOA position, which the Surgeon General of the Army had already adopted. But, as with departmental disputes today, the White House and the Council of National Defense intervened and took the position of the Vocational Education Board that its personnel would be responsible for the vocational training for wounded soldiers who were to be discharged. Military hospitals would remain under medical and military control. Congress also became involved in this discussion. Its involvement marked the beginning of leadership by Congress in the field of rehabilitation and disability. The Board of Vocational Education and the Surgeon General had both submitted plans to Congress for the operation of the military medical programs and the Reconstruction Hospitals (which included vocational training programs). The final legislation of 1918 authorized Reconstruction Hospitals and military health care programs for on duty soldiers and discharged veterans under medical control as recommended by the Surgeon General; it assigned to the Board of Vocational Education the administration of the vocational training and placement programs for on duty and discharged soldiers.

This legislation separated the programs based on the services provided, but not on the basis of on duty or discharged status. Since military policy did not allow civilians in military hospitals, the Congressional solution produced an unintended fragmentation in the administration and delivery of the services that were intended to be integrated and comprehensive in the AOA and Army recommendations. The Congressional accommodation never worked well and may have resulted in a reduced number of Reconstruction Hospitals established in the United States. The split between medical and vocational rehabilitation was to hang over the field of rehabilitation medicine in the civilian sector for many years and limit its growth as a comprehensive rehabilitation program. The later establishment of an agency for veterans complicated the problem regarding the disabled veteran, since medical care was fragmented between the military and veterans agencies though the program of the veterans' agency was comprehensive regarding rehabilitation. The vocational programs now overlapped the veterans and vocational rehabilitation agencies.[12]

The development of the rehabilitation programs of World War I moved forward in 1917 despite the bureaucratic battles, particularly in Europe. The first medical rehabilitation services offered included physical therapy, occupational therapy and vocational training. Nearly a dozen facilities were set up in Europe with physical reconstruction units at Angers, Bordeaux, Brest, Nantes, Savenay and Vichy. Sixteen of the Army's general hospitals in the U.S. had some type of reconstruction program for disabled soldiers. Among the hospitals most notable for their rehabilitation services were Walter Reed Hospital in Maryland, Letterman Hospital in San Francisco, Fort McPherson Hospital in Georgia and Lakewood Hospital in New Jersey. It was the latter in which Dr. Albee practiced. It was also where Albee developed the model for the rehabilitation clinic in Newark at which Dr. Kessler began his practice of rehabilitation under Dr. Albee's tutelage in 1919. Many of these U.S. military hospitals would become training grounds for rehabilitation medicine physicians after World War II.[13]

According to Howard Rusk, while physical therapy services, occupational therapy services and vocational training services continued to develop after World War I, the concept of total rehabilitation died. The civilian sector never developed the facilities to house and support the concept of medical rehabilitation. There was also a dearth of trained and knowledgeable physicians to lead such a civilian effort.[14]

WORKERS COMPENSATION PROGRAMS
AND REHABILITATION

A second stimulus for rehabilitation medicine services in this period was the Workers Compensation programs that a number of states had initiated prior to 1920. Workers compensation programs were one of the Progressive Era's political responses to the abuse of working people as a result of the unrestrained growth of American industry in the late 19th and early 20th centuries. Social reformers of the 20th century were concerned with the effects of industrial injury and disability, and politicians heeded their call. In 1919, Dr. Albert Lambert (representing the AMA), called for an effort to salvage the individuals maimed and crippled by industrialization. This early responsiveness of the AMA leadership to a rehabilitation goal for medicine boded well for the later efforts of Frank Krusen to establish a medical specialty related to rehabilitation. The political movements to provide assistance to persons affected by war or industrialization were closely related.

Governor Lafollette of Wisconsin, considered the major political leader of the Progressive movement in the country, initiated one of the first Workers Compensation programs. Programs typically included medical care, and frequently included vocational rehabilitation as well. Orthopedists were the leaders in developing these programs, just as they had been in the wartime medical programs. These programs served as the precursors of the national Vocational Rehabilitation program of 1921. Between 1918 and 1919, the states of Oregon, California, North Dakota and New Jersey also adopted workers compensation programs. In Wisconsin, the program was supervised by an Industrial Commission. That agency included Tracy Copp and I. S. Falk, two leaders who went on to assist in planning and developing the national Vocational Rehabilitation program and the Social Security Disability program.[15]

The Workers Compensation program in New Jersey was one of the most creative in fostering rehabilitation services. The major reason for this was the presence in New Jersey of the internationally acclaimed orthopedist Dr. Fred Albee. Dr. Albee was a New Englander who had made famous the surgical procedure of bone grafting. His operation became the standard of care for spinal tuberculosis. After World War I broke out, he was invited to speak in Germany, France and England on how his procedure might be used in the recovery of war casualties. He toured through forty hospitals in France and many in Canada, and was dismayed by the lack of care for amputees and other severely disabled soldiers in those countries. There were no programs to provide an artificial limb and training for its use after surgery. There also weren't exercise programs to rehabilitate the wounded and disabled. He wrote to the U.S. Surgeon General to recommend that there be coordinated inpatient rehabilitation programs in the U.S. so no war casualty would leave the hospital without having the range of services necessary. Since there were no civilian vocational rehabilitation agencies at this point, it was not unusual to suggest that the local military hospital provide vocational services. His request was timely, as the American Orthopedic Association had issued a report with similar recommendations. Three civilian hospitals with comprehensive rehabilitation programs were planned for the Army, but only one was actually supported (General Hospital #3 in New Jersey). The hospital was outfitted with all necessary surgical and medical services. It also had physical medicine in all forms including physical therapy, occupational therapy, hydrotherapy, functional re-education and an artificial limb and brace shop. The hospital had 2000 beds and served over 6000 casualties from 1918 to 1919.[16]

The Governor of New Jersey was very proud of the Reconstruction Hospital in his state. Having just signed into law the New Jersey Workers Compensation program, it occurred to him that civilian casualties of industrial accidents should have the same facility available. He brought Albee and Lewis Bryant, who was the New Jersey Commissioner of Labor, together and asked if it was possible to replicate the military rehabilitation hospital program for injured civilian workers. With the help of the legislature, a law was enacted in 1919 establishing a state rehabilitation clinic, the first in the country, and a Commission was established to administer it with Albee as Chairman. While the clinic was not as grandiose a program as the one in the military hospital, it operated on the same basic principles. Dr. Henry Kessler began his long and illustrious career in medical rehabilitation in this clinic in 1919. It was there that he was introduced to Colonel Bryant and Dr. Albee, who described their new state supported rehabilitation program to him. Kessler offered to assist the clinic in return for the assistance he had been given at the medical school by the Labor Department, and the arrangement was begun. The paltry initial appropriation by the state to the clinic, however, limited the scope of the program.

Dr. Albee stressed to Kessler that to mean anything the program had to be based on "three legs of a tripod: Physical restoration services, vocational guidance, and placement."[17] Albee's philosophy foreshadowed that advocated by Mary Switzer for the federal Vocational Rehabilitation program in the 1950s, and represented the clearest commitment at the time to the integration of vocational rehabilitation with medical services. The clinic was housed in a loft at 9 Franklin Street, Newark, New Jersey. Kessler served for a year without pay, assisting Albee in surgery, overseeing the rehabilitation care, and providing routine nursing care for the patients. The clinic was a floor below the New Jersey Worker's Compensation Bureau and was an integral part of the New Jersey Workers Compensation Program. Patients in the New Jersey Workers Compensation Program who were assessed as having vocational potential were referred to the clinic below on 9 Franklin Street, which then provided the rehabilitation.[18]

Albee and Kessler thus began the effort to translate the success of the military programs in rehabilitation medicine to the civilian sector using a workers compensation program as the vehicle for their work.

Across the Hudson River from the New Jersey rehabilitation programs of Albee and Kessler, the first major philanthropic contribution to medical rehabilitation occurred in 1917 during the time of our participation in World War I. Jeremiah Milbank, then only thirty years of age, established the Red Cross Institute for the Crippled and Disabled Men in New York City with a gift of $50,000 to the Red Cross. The concept of the Institute was comprehensive rehabilitation, similar to Albee's concept for the New Jersey clinic, although the program was far more comprehensive and better financed than that of Albee and Kessler. The Institute became the first U.S. civilian rehabilitation hospital for disabled persons. The provision of medical services, prostheses and orthoses, therapy and vocational training and placement were all parts of the program. In 1919, the Institute sponsored a major international conference on rehabilitation. This conference promoted international exchanges of information on rehabilitation, and led to the establishment of the first U.S. international program in rehabilitation.[19]

In the early 1920s, Dr. Albee sent Dr. Kessler to the Institute for training regarding prosthetics and limb construction, which was evidence of the quality of the Institute's program, since Albee was himself an expert in types of prostheses. The Executive Director of the Institute, Douglas McMurtie, was also often sent to Washington with the blessing of Milbank to advocate before Congress for rehabilitation programs for persons with disabilities. These efforts bore fruit in 1921 with the creation of a national rehabilitation program. Later the Institute would become the major training ground for rehabilitation physicians in World War II.[20]

Another rehabilitation facility was established at about this time in Milwaukee on the grounds of Columbia Hospital, the Workshop for Occupational Therapy. It was renamed the Curative Workshop later in the century. Given the emphasis on rehabilitation in the Wisconsin's workers compensation program, it is likely that the Workshop was at least in part stimulated by this state program under the leadership of Governor LaFollette. By the 1970s, the Curative Workshop was affiliated with the University of Wisconsin Medical College and became a national leader in rehabilitation medicine under the direction of Dr. John Melvin, who would become President of both the American Academy of Physical Medicine and Rehabilitation and the American Congress of Rehabilitation.[21]

In Cleveland a service for vocational guidance and placement was initiated by Miss Bell Greve that was affiliated with the Association for Crippled and Disabled. This program also included an innovative kindergarten for children with disabilities. While neither of these programs was a medical rehabilitation program like Albee's and Milbank's, they evidenced the beginnings of facilities for services to persons with disabilities that would mark the growth of the rehabilitation field in the late 1940s and beyond.[22]

By 1920, the first programs in rehabilitation medicine offering physician services, physical and occupational therapy, vocational training and job placement were in place. These programs were the result of responsiveness by leaders in medicine, the government and philanthropy to the needs of injured soldiers and workers during WWI. Future leaders in medicine, the government and philanthropy to the needs of injured soldiers and workers during WWI. Future leaders in medicine, government and philanthropy would build on the foundation created by these programs.

NOTES

1. Bloom, *The Progressive Presidents Roosevelt, Wilson, Franklin D. Roosevelt, Johnson*, WW Norton and Company, 1980, 16–17; Grant, 10, 11.

2. Gabriel, *The Course Of American Democratic Thought*, The Ronald Press Company, 360–62.

3. Gabriel, 352–60; *also see* Menand, *The Metaphysical Club*, for a discussion of the ideas of James, Dewey, Holmes and Pierce and experimentation, empirical thought and pragamatism.

4. Ludmerer, *A Time To Heal, American Medical Education From The Turn Of The Century To The Era Of Managed Care,* Oxford University Press, Inc., 1999, 1–8;Starr, *The Social Transformation of American Medicine*, Basic Books, Inc., 1982, 117–23.

5. DeLisa, Currie and Martin, *Rehabilitation Medicine*, Third Edition, Edited by DeLisa and Gans, Lippincott-Raven, 1998, 14; Gritzer and Arluke, *The Making Of*

Rehabilitation, A Political Economy Of Medical Specialization, University of California Press, 1985, 54; Kottke, Coulter Lecture, Arch Phys Med Rehabil, Vol. 50, 57.

6. Krusen and Keys, Arch Phys Med Rehabil, Vol. 26, 549–57; Krusen, In Memoriam of Bernard Baruch 1870–1965, Arch Phys Med Rehabil, Vol. 46, 549–52.

7. Murphy, *Healing the Generations, A History Of Physical Therapy And The American Physical Therapy Association*, American Physical Therapy Association, Alexandria Va., 1995, 89–91; Krusen, Arch Phys Med Rehabil, Vol. 50, 1; Gritzer and Arluke, 39–40.

8. Gritzer and Arluke, 39–52; Murphy, 34–35.

9. Mock, Arch Phys Med Rehabil, Vol. 50, 474.

10. Rusk, Arch Phys Med Rehabil, Vol. 50, 463; Gritzer and Arluke, 41–44.

11. Gritzer and Arluke, 46–48.

12. Gritzer and Arluke, 49–50.

13. Murphy, 45.

14. Rusk, Arch Phys Med Rehabil, Vol. 50, 463.

15. Gritzer and Arluke, 38–40; Berkowitz, *Rehabilitation: The Federal Government's Response to Disability* 1935–1954, Arno Press, a New York Times Company, 1980, 4.

16. Kessler, *The Knife is Not Enough*, 39–43.

17. Kessler, 43.

18. Kessler, 39–43.

19. *50 Years Of Vocational Rehabilitation In The U.S.A. 1920–1970*, Manuscript published by the U.S. Department of Health Education and Welfare, Social and Rehabilitation Services Administration, 1970, 1; Rehabilitation Record, May and June 1970, edited by Rigdon, U.S. Government Printing Office, 1970, 23.

20. *50 years Of Vocational Rehabilitation In The U.S.A. 1920–1970*, 1; Rehabilitation Record May and June, 1970, 24.

21. Rehabilitation Record May and June 1970, 22–23.

22. Rehabilitation Record May and June 1970, 22–24.

Chapter Four

The 1920s and Small Steps Forward

With the end of World War I a new period began for the United States as the brief peace that followed brought a period of normalcy, compared to the fast pace of the War. Major government involvement in daily economic and social life under President Wilson during the War was succeeded by a period of reduced government involvement. Calvin Coolidge followed Woodrow Wilson as President. Unlike the leaders who came before him such as T. Roosevelt, LaFollette, Brandeis, and Wilson, Coolidge was not a Progressive in his philosophy of government. Coolidge and the two presidents who succeeded him took a more conservative approach than their predecessors to the use of government in peace time as a vehicle for social and economic change. Yet the principles of the Progressive Era of American politics survived well into the twentieth century and were the foundation for much of the social and economic legislation enacted in the period from 1932 through the 1970s. The hallmarks of this foundation included productivity as a goal for our economy and social system, and rights and protections for the individual in a world of large corporate interests.

World War I clearly enhanced the status of America in the world. At home, the war had also enhanced the status of medicine, which had already been viewed positively. The critical factor during this time for the development of a new medical field was the existence of well-trained professionals in medicine and related fields of health care, and the leaders who could enable such development. Some of these leaders included physicians such as Albee, Goldthwait, Brackett, Coulter and Mock. Others were physical therapists (or reconstruction aids as they were called then), such as Mary MacMillan. These leaders made the public aware of the contributions of medical care to the war effort and made people aware of the value of medical rehabilitation. Programs in rehabilitation medicine existed at the Massachusetts General Hospital and the Mayo Clinic. A program in physiotherapy was started at the Mayo Clinic, within its Orthopedics Section and diathermy in its Therapeutic Radiology Department in the mid-1920s.

Scientific advances had been crucial to the war effort, and those advances also affected medicine and medical schools. From about the time of the War onward, the scientific capability and research productivity of a medical school became the chief measures of its worth. Science drove medical education and medical education drove medical care. But the medical schools did not have physical medicine or medical rehabilitation expertise or programs. This failure was to restrain the development of the entire field of rehabilitation medicine for many years.

The first medical school programs in rehabilitation began in the latter part of the 1920s and their initiation was important in the development of rehabilitation medicine. Foremost among the first programs was one begun at Northwestern Medical School by John Coulter, who was recruited by orthopedist Paul Magnuson. It was Magnuson who later developed the Veteran's Administration (VA) medical programs and founded the Rehabilitation Institute of Chicago. Major developments in rehabilitation medicine, however, did not really begin to occur in our medical colleges until the late 1940s under the leadership of Bernard Baruch.[1]

A related weakness in rehabilitation medicine before 1920, which inhibited its growth, was its lack of professional and scientific societies. Such societies typically provide medical education, encourage research among their members and advocate for programs and services in medical care. In many ways, they have a role similar to a department in a medical school. Professional societies in rehabilitation medicine began in the 1920s and made important contributions to the development of rehabilitation medicine.

THE VOCATIONAL REHABILITATION ACT OF 1920

The debate during World War I as to how the military programs for medical care should deal with vocational rehabilitation services set the stage for Congressional consideration of a national rehabilitation program for both disabled veterans returning from World War I and workers injured on the job. Douglas MacMurtie, Director of the Institute for Crippled and Disabled Adults in New York, had urged such a national program during the period immediately preceding 1920. He spoke with the added authority of Jeremiah Milbank, a nationally renowned philanthropist who had established the Institute in 1917. The rehabilitation services program recommended to the military during

World War I by the professional society for orthopedists (and by individual orthopedists such as Goldthwait and Albee) included vocational training and placement as a necessary service. This was subject to the medical model of management in the Reconstruction Hospital program model. While Mac-Murtie's proposal was modified because of the opposition of the Board of Vocational Education concerning the use of the medical model for management of vocational training, it did establish the importance of including both physical restorative services and vocational training as parts of a rehabilitation program for a recently injured individual. The Congressional consideration of this dispute about the role of the medical model for vocational training and placement in 1918 resulted in renewed interest in a civilian vocational rehabilitation program.

The debt acknowledged by Woodrow Wilson on behalf of American society to soldiers who were wounded or disabled in the course of World War I, was a debt that many in the Progressive Era felt was owed to America's injured workers as well. After all, their injuries were incurred in the course of their work to develop America's industrial support for the war effort. This sense of obligation led to enactment of state Workers Compensation programs, as well as to interest in having a separate federal vocational rehabilitation program. The leaders of the state Workers Compensation programs lobbied for such a program at the federal level.[2]

Congress began consideration of Vocational Rehabilitation legislation in 1919 and finished in 1920. The legislative advocates for the program were Senator Hoke Smith of Georgia and Congressman Simeon Fess of Ohio. The proposal would lodge authority for the program in the Federal Vocational Education Board. This Board was probably the only existing federal agency with experience in vocational training issues, but had little experience with persons with disabilities or with actual job placement activity. Opposition came from conservative members of Congress, who feared intrusions by the federal government into what they felt was the domain of state governments. Opposition also came from veterans, who were concerned about the future independence of the veterans' vocational rehabilitation program started in the military during World War I. The first objection was met by provisions to have state agencies administer the program, with states matching federal funds to finance the services. These provisions seemed to satisfy the opponents concerned mainly about state control. This approach was also consistent with the operation of the Workers Compensation programs. The veterans groups were supportive of a civilian rehabilitation program, as long as the program for veterans was kept separate. To resolve this dispute Congress included a provision to remove the veterans' vocational rehabilitation program from the Board of Vocational Education, which had been criticized in the past for its administration of the veterans program. The legislation also included an agreement regarding the Army medical and rehabilitation services program. This agreement placed all medical aspects of rehabilitation services under the control of the Surgeon General of the military, but left the vocational training and placement services under the control of the Board of Education. As a result, the legislation for a new civilian rehabilitation program did not include any specific authority for the use of funds for medical services, including services such as physical therapy and occupational therapy. The bill was signed into law by President Wilson on June 2, 1920, and was entitled the Industrial Rehabilitation Act.[3]

The young program was funded at $750,000 in 1921. It resulted in 523 individuals being rehabilitated in 1921, and 4500 by 1924. The staff included Mary Switzer's friend from Wisconsin Tracy Copp, as well as four others working under the leadership of John Kratz. Soon the program became known for its close partnership between the states and the federal government. Although the statute did not authorize medical services, most of the clients had orthopedic disabilities and needed medical care. The state agency employees were adept, however, at obtaining volunteer services from orthopedic surgeons, who were very supportive of the program, and from hospitals.[4]

In 1926, the state of New Jersey established a state rehabilitation program and placed it under the administration of a Rehabilitation Commission. The first Chair of the Commission was Dr. Albee, marking the beginning of a long relationship between state vocational rehabilitation and medicine. Dr. Kessler became very involved with the state vocational rehabilitation also. About this time, a professional society of those involved in the state vocational rehabilitation program was created. Dr. Kessler was the first physician member, and attended the first annual meeting. He maintained his relationship with the federal and state vocational rehabilitation programs for approximately 40 years.[5]

THE PROFESSIONAL ORGANIZATION IN REHABILITATION MEDICINE

Health care professional societies have traditionally been a major influence on medical education, the quality of medical care, public awareness of medicine's achievements, and legislative advocacy throughout the past century. Professional societies serve some of the same functions as academic programs in that they serve to educate their members and provide credibility with the public for the professions involved. Medicine achieved its newfound public credibility in the early 1900s due to the work of the AMA, particularly its dedication to improving educational programs and requiring certification of skill through licensing. After the Flexner Report on the need for improved medical education and standards for medical professionals, which the AMA sponsored, medical education programs were held to high standards. This resulted in improved quality of physicians, but came at the expense of a decrease in the overall number of trained physicians. An example of a professional society establishing standards for care was demonstrated by the influence of the American Orthopedic Association on the Army in establishing the standards for medical care to injured soldiers.[6]

The 1920s saw the development of a number of physician professional societies whose memberships included physicians with interests in the use of physical agents to diagnose and treat patients. The first of these was the American Electro-therapeutic Association, which was formed in 1891 by Dr. George Betton Massey, a Philadelphia gynecologist. This organization was affiliated with the AMA, and AMA membership was a precondition to membership in the Association. The focus was limited to electricity as a physical agent to treat disease. The Association published the Journal of Advanced Therapeutics, and in the early 1900s articles were presented on forms of therapy other than electricity such as hydrotherapy, exercise and dietetics. The editor of the Journal of Advanced Therapeutics in this period was Dr. William Snow, who was a graduate of Columbia College of Physicians and Surgeons. Snow was the leader of this Association for almost thirty years until his early experimentation with radiology resulted in his death. Radiology was very involved with the use of electricity and related physical agents to diagnose disease.[7]

Radiologists were instrumental in the formation in 1923 of another organization, the American College of Radiology and Physiotherapy (ACRP). This organization was the first to focus fully on the field of physical medicine and its rehabilitative techniques. The first President was Dr. Samuel Childs of Denver. The membership included many of the physicians who had been involved with rehabilitation medicine in World War I, including John Coulter. To some extent this organization was a competitor of the Radiology Society of America. After apparently having healed their rift, the radiologists joined to form the American College of Radiology (ACR) in 1925, which still exists today. The members of the ACRP who were not radiologists remained in the ACRP and renamed it the American College of Physical Therapy (ACPT). They adopted the Archives of Physical Therapy, X-Ray and Radium as the official journal of the ACPT (Archives).[8]

The first President of the American College of Physical Therapy was Dr. Curran Pope, a neurologist and hydrologist from Louisville. The second President was Dr. Coulter, who was probably the first leader of these organizations to be a specialist in rehabilitation medicine much as we know it today.

Interest in this field of medicine was limited in the beginning, but included physicians from many disciplines of medicine (especially neurology, gynecology, radiology and orthopedics). In his Presidential Address, Coulter described the College and the field of medicine it represented as being "composed of physicians who use physical agents in the treatment of disease in combination with medicine and surgery."[9] He went on to add that the members of the College needed to educate medical students, physicians and technicians in the physiological effects of heat, water, light, electricity, massage and exercise. The Archives was owned and managed during the late 1920s by Albert Tyler, a professor of Radiology at Creighton Medical School in Omaha. Disraeli Kobak was named Editor of the Archives in 1928. He had become a rehabilitation medicine specialist and a key figure in the field. He served as Editor until 1940.

In 1930, the word College in the name of the ACPT was changed to Congress. The name of the organization changed again in 1945 to the American Congress of Physical Medicine; and then again to the American Congress of Physical Medicine and Rehabilitation in 1952. The current name, the American Congress of Rehabilitation Medicine (ACRM), was adopted in 1966. Membership has been open over the years to physicians of all specialties and its members have included orthopedists, neurologists, internists, family physicians and dermatologists with interests in physical medicine and rehabilitation. Membership in the ACRM was opened in the late 1960s to non-physician health professionals in rehabilitation medicine.[10]

What distinguished these first physicians in the field of physical medicine from the later generation of physicians who established the field of physical medicine and rehabilitation was the focus of physical medicine on acute conditions and the limitation of the services offered. Vocational and social services were not ordinarily included in their programs and practices. As Gritzer noted in his review of the field, very few articles could be found in the journal of this specialty, which focused on disability and the rehabilitation process during the 20-year period from 1920 to 1940. The focus of the journal was almost entirely on the use of physical agents to diagnose and treat acute conditions. This is understandable, since medicine in general was still in its formative years and trying to establish its credibility in dealing with disease. The entire focus of medicine was on disease and acute conditions. The phenomenon of chronic conditions was quite unknown at that time. The treatment of traumatic injury was still in its infancy, and largely the focus of orthopedic surgeons (who were often the physicians who dealt with traumatic injury when it occurred).[11]

At about the same time the physician organizations concerned with the use of physical agents were organizing in the 1920s, 30 former Reconstruction

Hospital aides during World War 1 and six physicians gathered in New York City and created the American Physiotherapy Association (APA). Dr. Granger of Harvard, Chief of the physical therapy section of the Surgeon General's Office during World War I, was one of the organizing physicians. Dr. Harold Corbusier was also an organizing physician. Membership in the APA was open to all who were graduates of schools of physiotherapy or physical education and who had experience in massage and therapeutic exercise. During World War I and immediately thereafter schools had been created to train physiotherapists. Among them was one at Reed College in Oregon, which was headed by Mary Macmillan, the most prominent physiotherapist in the nation at this time. Like the AMA, the APA focused on setting standards for care and on accrediting schools for physical therapy. The overall goal was to establish professional credibility for the field and to protect the public from unprofessional practitioners. Increased hospital demand for physical therapy providers led to many flawed efforts to educate students in the field. Often these efforts were run by commercial organizations. While very concerned with the possibility of medical domination of the profession, the APA began work in the late 1920s with the AMA on the matters related to education and professional standards.[12]

The history of Occupational Therapy began with the establishment of the National Society for the Promotion of Occupational Therapy in 1917. The founders included Dr. William Dunton, a psychiatrist interested in the use of work as therapy for mental patients. Another important founding member was George Barton, by training an architect and also a tuberculosis patient, who had founded a workshop for convalescents. By the early 1920s this organization had 500 members and was larger than the physical medicine organizations or the APA. The name of the organization was changed in 1923 to the American Occupational Therapy Association (AOTA), and the name has remained the same to this day.

The focus of occupational therapists was primarily on mental patients in the early days of the organization. During World War I, however, occupational therapy was an integral part of the services of the Office of the Surgeon General and the Reconstruction Hospitals. This contrasted with civilian hospitals (general and orthopedic), which did not recognize occupational therapy services. Despite this, Dr. Dunton was successful in getting orthopedists, neurologists and family practitioners to make occupational therapy referrals. The Rehabilitation Act of 1920 covered occupational therapy services, and that helped stimulate demand for these services. By 1923, the AOTA had established standards for occupational therapy services and its own certification program.

Occupational therapy was broader in its scope than physical therapy, treating mental as well as physical illness, and working in schools with children who had emotional or mental problems. But it was less focused on a precise service dealing with disease and physical ailments as required by the medical model of care. As a result, acceptance by the field of medicine was more difficult for occupational therapists to achieve than for physical therapists.[13]

The AMA began taking an active interest in physical medicine and physical therapy in the early nineteen twenties. In 1923, the APA requested that the AMA consider an affiliation arrangement between the organizations. The APA wanted to obtain the benefit of AMA credibility in the establishment of its standards for education and practice. This approach may have been due in part to the urging of physicians who were involved in the creation of the APA. These included Dr. Granger from Harvard. In 1924, Dr. Ray Lyman Wilbur, President of both the AMA and Stanford University, addressed the annual meeting of the APA. He urged the association to study hard in its field and keep its practitioners from making extravagant claims as to its capabilities. He stressed that: "The future of physiotherapy is going to depend on the confidence shown it by the medical profession."[14] The same could probably be said of the field of physical medicine. Wilbur was to play a major role in the creation of rehabilitation medicine and the medical specialty of physical medicine and rehabilitation some 20 years later when he chaired a national committee established by Bernard Baruch, which studied the field and funded its start.

In 1925, the AMA established a Council on Physical Therapy to oversee and set standards for the development and marketing of therapeutic equipment. The Council was chaired by Dr. Harry Mock, a member of the American College of Physical Therapy. The Council expanded its scope to include oversight of the practice of physical therapy, which it claimed was being harmed by the practices of osteopaths and chiropractors. The work of the Council focused on eliminating bad influences on the field of physical therapy. It also reported that some unscrupulous practitioners were unnecessarily treating incurable patients whose care was being paid for by state Industrial Commissions.

A negative view toward government involvement in financing health care was prevalent in the AMA at the time. The AMA feared the adverse effects of government control of medical decision making at a time when the field of medicine was still in the process of establishing its legitimacy. During this same period, however, Henry Kessler and Fred Albee were treating industrial injury cases for the New Jersey Workers Compensation program without negative government involvement. Kessler viewed the New Jersey Workers

Compensation program as supportive of medicine, and in 1923 succeeded Albee as its Medical Director.[15]

Another example of the role of professional societies in shaping rehabilitation medicine and establishing its credibility was a 1928 publication of the American College of Surgeons (ACOS), which undertook to create standards for physical therapy departments in hospitals. John Stanley Coulter led this effort and published a paper on the "Minimum Standard for a Physical Therapy Department in a General Hospital." The ACOS was one of the more active of the voluntary medical organizations. It had been successful in establishing standards for medical records at hospitals in the 1920s. Although he was not a surgeon, Coulter was utilized by the ACOS to assist it in producing standards for the therapy departments of hospitals. He was selected because of his well-known expertise in physical therapy and the use of physical agents.

Coulter stressed in his paper the importance of employing the very best trained physical therapists, and suggested that they were most often members of APA. Coulter was viewed by the APA as one of its strongest physician supporters. He downplayed the relative value of the machines in physical therapy. His standards dealt with massage, muscle training and exercise, ultraviolet radiation, the use of high frequency current, and whirlpool baths. By the 1920s, the hospital was becoming the focus for active treatment of patients. In earlier years, it had mainly been a holding place for incurable cases. Physicians were instrumental in the creation and control of hospitals, which gave them a place to care for the most acutely ill of their patients. Physicians like Coulter were concerned with the quality of care in the hospitals, and physician groups continued to be the policing and regulatory agencies for American healthcare. Counter also served as President of the American College of Physical Therapy Physicians in 1926.[16]

The National Rehabilitation Association (NRA) was formed in 1925 and became one of the most effective national advocacy associations for rehabilitation in the 1940s, 1950s and 1960s. The leading role played by Dr. Kessler in that organization and the federal and state vocational rehabilitation programs were portents of a healthy partnership between rehabilitation medicine and vocational rehabilitation. The NRA had about 28,000 members by the late 1960s. Due to the advocacy of Dr. Kessler, the membership was open to everyone interested in rehabilitation, and was not limited to state vocational rehabilitation personnel. The NRA focused primarily on advocacy for the federal and state vocational rehabilitation program and its funding. The assistance of the NRA was critical to the incorporation of medical rehabilitation into the program, as well as adding research and training authority.[17]

THE INITIAL DEVELOPMENT OF
ACADEMIC PROGRAMS IN PHYSICAL MEDICINE

The academic medical programs of training and research were essentially keys to the kingdom of success for a field of medicine in the early years of the 20th century. Scientifically based education and research were the twin pillars of medical school success, and graduation from a successful medical school led to success in practice. The earliest academic programs related to rehabilitation medicine were at Northwestern, established by Paul Magnuson in 1919 and directed by John Coulter beginning in 1926. A program was established at St. Luke's Hospital in Chicago in the mid-1920s by Harry Mock, MD. Frank Krusen established the first department of physical medicine at Temple University School of Medicine in Philadelphia in 1929.

Krusen came to his role in academic physical medicine as a result of two factors: his exposure to patients with tuberculosis during his stay as a patient and physician in a sanitarium; and his exposure to the influence of his mentors during his surgical residency training. These mentors included the director of his surgical residency program at Jefferson Medical College Dr. J. Chalmers DaCosta; as well as his father. Krusen's father was a professor of gynecology at Temple Medical School, and encouraged Frank to focus on research, medical education and writing. When Krusen returned from his stay in the sanitarium, he began a career in academic medicine.[18]

Krusen returned to Philadelphia and Temple medical school. He became an associate dean of Temple Medical School when he was only 27 years of age, and began his pursuit of achievements in medical education and research in physical medicine. The Dean of the medical school was Frank Hammond, a close friend of Krusen's father and after whom Frank was named. One of his first accomplishments as Associate Dean was to manage Temple's efforts to be accredited as an "A" type medical school. Krusen became deeply involved in mastering the educational standards of the AMA for medical schools. He was successful in obtaining this sought after designation, and in the process began to hone his skills at managing the intricate process of politics and administration of organized medicine. These lessons would pay great dividends in the next 25 years as he managed the process of obtaining specialty status for the field of physical medicine and rehabilitation. He was also assigned the task of planning for the construction of a new medical school. He devoted himself intensely to learning the detail of good school construction, and visited other medical schools in the region.

In 1929, his mastery of educational standards and interest in physical agents led him to begin developing a department of "physical medicine," a term he coined. He employed two physical therapists and they began a program of patient care and medical education. Krusen also served as team physician for the Temple University football team and received fan support for the successful return of the players he treated to the field of play. The new dean of the medical school, Dr. William Parkinson, was much taken with the idea of creating the first such department. Soon afterward the Department of Physical Medicine was begun, the first one in the country, with Krusen as its chair.[19]

PHILANTHROPY AND REHABILITATION MEDICINE IN WARM SPRINGS, GEORGIA

Franklin Delano Roosevelt was stricken with severe paralysis from an infection with the polio virus in 1921 in Campobello, Maine. His obsessive focus on his own rehabilitation led him to try the baths of Warm Springs, Georgia in 1924. Roosevelt loved the Georgia countryside and swimming in the warm waters of the baths. He had become very knowledgeable about polio and the possible treatments for the disease. He was aware in detail of the muscles involved in his own paralysis, and believed the baths and his swimming made a positive impact on his rehabilitation. In 1926, he committed a large part of his fortune to purchase a resort facility at Warm Springs and expand it to include a better pool and more space for roomers. People with polio from throughout the nation came to the facility after reading of Roosevelt's experience. He personally welcomed them and worked with them in their efforts to regain strength and physical function. The facility was soon one of the first rehabilitation centers in the nation, although limited to warm baths, swimming, aquatic and other exercise. He also brought physicians to Warm Springs to serve patients. He even obtained the stamp of approval of the American Orthopedic Association for his program, after it was reviewed by an orthopedist who found that all of the 23 patients he reviewed had some measure of improved function. Roosevelt's commitment to his fellow polio patients and his expertise and dedication to improve medical rehabilitation approaches to this disease from 1923 throughout his life were described well and movingly by Hugh Gallagher, (who also had polio and was treated at Warm Springs), in his book *Splendid Deception*. The following quotation is in relation to the period prior to his visit at Warm Springs, but captures Roosevelt's drive to find rehabilitation techniques and his compassion for fellow polio patients.

In his search for an effective therapy Roosevelt consulted expert medical opinion across America. He developed an extensive correspondence with polio victims and the doctors treating them, which he carried on throughout the rest of his life. At first he was seeking advice and exchanging ideas. In due course, he was providing advice, as he became expert and an innovator in the new field of rehabilitation medicine".[20]

Roosevelt was often referred to as "Dr." Roosevelt by the polio patients at Warm Springs. The principles that he and others applied through active therapy "were later incorporated into a coherent theory of rehabilitation."[21] What Roosevelt had started was also one of the first self help rehabilitation programs for persons with disabilities, although Roosevelt eventually brought in a physician to oversee the medical treatment. The social and recreational environment and the group support provided were all of the self-help type.[22]

Roosevelt, polio, and rehabilitation medicine are discussed in a later chapter on the polio epidemic and its impact on rehabilitation medicine in the 1930s, 1940s and 1950s. The rehabilitation medical facilities and rehabilitation medicine services established by the military in World War I were not established in the civilian sector in the decade of the 1920s. This was a major disappointment of many leaders in medicine. However, the decade did witness the establishment of legislation creating a national vocational rehabilitation program for the civilian sector, which rehabilitated 4500 disabled persons in 1924. The decade of the 1920s also produced many professional societies whose members were largely of those individuals engaged in providing rehabilitation services. Those societies would supply the leadership for the development of rehabilitation medicine over the next 80 years. Academic programs dedicated to training professionals in the field of rehabilitation also began in this decade, and the spread of polio resulted in the development of rehabilitation medicine services to treat its victims. The field of rehabilitation medicine did not flourish in this period, but it did make progress and would be prepared for expansion in the decades to come.

NOTES

1. Kessler, 39–44; Murphy; *Healing the Generations*, 40 *et seq.*; Ludmerer, *A Time to Heal: The History of Medical Education,* 50–55, 79–81.

2. Berkowitz, *Rehabilitation*, 83–87; Switzer, Arch Phys Med Rehabil, Vol. 37, 542.

3. *50 years of Vocational Rehabilitation in the U.S.*, 2–3; *also see* Gritzer for general background, 47–50.

4. *50 Years of Vocational Rehabilitation*, 5; Rehabilitation Record, May/June 1970, Fiftieth Anniversary Edition, 22.

5. Kessler, *The Knife is Not Enough*, 48, 51–54; *50 Years of Vocational Rehabilitation*, 5–6.

6. Starr, 117–123, discussing the role of licensing and regulation of education in medicine; Ludmerer, 6 and 7 discussing the impact of the Flexner Report and medical education in the early 1900s.

7. Gritzer, 61–85; DeLisa, Currie and Martin, 14–16; Kottke, Arch Phys Med Rehabil, Vol. 50, 57, Coulter Lecture.

8. Frederick Kottke and Miland Knapp, Arch Phys Med Rehabil, Vol. 69, 5–6.

9. Coulter Presidential Address, Arch Phys Med Rehabil, 1926, 1.

10. Kottke and Knapp, Arch Phys Med Rehabil, Vol. 69, 6.

11. Gritzer, 62–63.

12. Gritzer, 70–75; Murphy, 71–82.

13. Gritzer, 55–58, 78–80.

14. Murphy, 82.

15. Murphy, 82; Kessler, 39–50.

16. Murphy, 90–91; Starr, 145–150, 177; Paul Magnuson M.D., *Ring the Night Bell*, Mass Market Paperback, 1962, 146, 225.

17. Kessler, 51.

18. Opitz *et al.*, Arch Phys Med Rehabil, Vol. 78, 443.

19. Opitz *et al.*, Arch Phys Med Rehabil, Vol. 78, 443–444.

20. Gallagher, Splendid Deception, Dodd Meads and Company, 1986, 23–24.

21. Gallagher, 53.

22. Gallagher, 34–58.

Chapter Five

The Thirties, Medicine, Social Insurance and Rehabilitation at the Mayo Clinic

American medicine was at the pinnacle of its power during the 1920s and 1930s. It had been successful in establishing licensing authority for physicians, standards for their medical education, and control of the education of other health professionals. It had successfully limited the role and influence of government and the private for profit sector in civilian health care. In the 1930s hospitals were increasingly becoming the locus of care for the very ill, and physicians exercised control over the hospital system. Specialists were in demand, and the thirties saw major growth in specialty boards and certification programs, which were also under the control of the AMA. Nine new boards were created in this decade: obstetrics and gynecology; psychiatry and neurology; pediatrics; dermatology; orthopedic surgery; radiology; internal medicine; pathology and anesthesiology. Prior to 1930, only ophthalmology had a specialty board and certification program.[1]

The Democratic Party and President Franklin Delano Roosevelt (FDR) came to power in 1932. FDR already had made a reputation for strong leadership as Governor of New York. He stressed the need for bold federal action to deal with the nation's economic depression. The President also had a severe physical disability himself, having been stricken with polio in 1921 at age 39. He was paralyzed from the waist down and his mobility was severely impaired. As described in the previous chapter, Roosevelt had developed a very close relationship with others who had polio, and he learned a great deal about rehabilitation techniques during his efforts to rehabilitate himself. He had been under the personal care of Robert Lovett, a renowned orthopedic surgeon at Massachusetts General Hospital, who specialized in polio care and who used exercise as treatment. Lovett was a colleague of Drs. Goldthwait and Brackett, who had developed programs for rehabilitation therapies and the use of medical equipment in treating disabling conditions.

Rehabilitation medicine grew only very little in this period. The inability to emulate the military programs of World War 1 in the civilian sector in the twenties signaled a general slow down in the growth of the field. Despite this, Dr. Kessler maintained his New Jersey program and the Institute for the Crippled and Disabled in New York City was expanded. In 1930, Jeremiah Milbank built the first new building to house a rehabilitation medicine inpatient and outpatient program at the Institute for the Crippled and Disabled, which he had founded in 1917.

Growth did take place in the professional societies of physicians with an interest in the physical medicine modalities; as well as in physical therapy and occupational therapy professional societies. Dr. Krusen realized in this period that to succeed in creating a new field of medicine, the active backing of the American Medical Association was required. He began to apply his enormous energy, organizational talents and academic skill to achieve specialty status for physical medicine. Krusen also moved his practice and teaching to the Mayo Clinic, establishing a program of physical medicine in the model of a medical care practice.

SOCIAL INSURANCE, DISABILITY AND HEALTH INSURANCE

Near the end of the 1920s the AMA created a Committee on the Cost of Medical Care; which was to report not only on the costs of care, but also on its availability to all Americans. This effort represented active leadership by the AMA on problems of health for the nation, and it occurred just prior to the impact of the depression on health care. The Committee on the Cost of Medical Care was chaired by Ray Lyman Wilbur, a former President of the AMA and Chancellor of Stanford University. The Executive Director of the Committee was bacteriologist I.S. Falk, who had been supported together with Harry Hopkins by the Milbank Foundation to study health care in New York City. The report proved to be very controversial, and both majority and minority viewpoints were published when the report was released in 1932. The majority within the AMA, which included academic physicians and public health figures, supported a voluntary health insurance program for those who could afford it, and public appropriations to support care for those who could not. The majority also urged the establishment of community health centers, which would contract with medicine for services to the poor. The majority report was signed by 17 Committee members. The minority report, signed by eight, who were primarily private practitioners, opposed this approach and viewed it as a move in the direction of socialized medicine. The minority also included the leadership of the AMA. The report set off a major debate inside and outside of medicine about the role of government in health care, and the best methods to deal with the provision of care to all Americans. The American College of Surgeons endorsed the majority report regarding health insurance. This debate has not stopped even to this day and still rages.[2]

Mary Switzer became involved in this debate over the role of government in extending health insurance to all Americans in an unexpected way. She was at work in the Treasury Department providing administrative support to the new Secretary of the Treasury, Henry Morgenthau. Upon the release of the AMA report, President Roosevelt believed he needed someone to aggressively handle the issue of health care, particularly in light of the AMA Report and the reaction to it throughout medicine. The Public Health Service was in the Treasury Department and it was the locus for health decision making at the federal level in the 1930s. In late 1934, President Roosevelt named Josephine Roche as Assistant Secretary of the Treasury for Public Health. Roche was a graduate of Vassar and involved in social welfare issues in the private sector. A native of Colorado, she had returned home in the early thirties to take over and successfully run her family's coal mining business. Her most significant success may have been her negotiation of a settlement in 1933 with the mine workers under the leadership of John L. Lewis, which had struck many of the nation's mining companies. Secretary of Labor Perkins asked her to assist in the settlement of the continuing coal mining strikes in 1933. In 1934, she ran for Governor of Colorado on the Democratic ticket and lost, after which FDR named her to the Treasury post. When Roche arrived in Washington, she needed staff to assist her in navigating the ways of the Treasury Department. At this point Mary Switzer had been looking for increased responsibility in the Department and had let that be known. Her network assisted her in connecting with Roche, and she became Roche's assistant at a time when the federal role in health care was just in its infancy.[3]

In 1934 President Roosevelt created a Cabinet Committee on Economic Security chaired by Secretary of Labor Frances Perkins, which included Harry Hopkins, the President's primary assistant and in fact his chief of staff. The committee also included three other Cabinet secretaries, including Secretary of the Treasury Morganthau. Roche often attended the meetings of this Committee in place of Secretary Morganthau. Mary Switzer was frequently there with Roche, and served as a note taker. The focus of the Committee was largely on methods to deal with unemployment, as well as with the aged and their economic security. A Public Advisory Committee was created by the Committee, which included representatives of labor, industry, social work and the public.

The AMA set up its own Advisory Committee in order to be prepared on any issue, which might arise in the Economic Security Committee that could affect health care and medicine. The AMA Advisory Committee, not to be confused with the earlier Wilbur Committee on the Cost of Medical Care, prepared a major report to Perkins and her Committee on healthcare as it might impact economic security. It recommended that the roles the government should play in health care were preventive care and the funding of hospital construction. Some 10 to 20 years later, these two roles and medical research would become the linchpins of major health initiatives of the 1950s. The AMA Report emphasized the need to have an adequate supply of hospital services and preventive services, but did not raise the issue of how health care might be paid for. It asked for more time to submit a report on health insurance, although its position had been fairly well established in its response to the report of the Wilbur Committee on the Cost of Medical Care.[4]

In 1934, I.S. Falk was well at work for the Social Security Board, developing proposals for income support and services for the Economic Security Committee. These proposals included disability insurance. The disability proposals would cover both lost wages and health services. Roche was an advocate for inclusion of these programs in any administration legislation intended to deal with economic security. In the end, the AMA recommendation for no inclusion of health insurance for any category of needy person won out, and the final recommendation from the Committee to the President did not include either health insurance or disability insurance. The social security legislation, which was passed by Congress and signed into law in 1935, included a federal old age retirement program and a federal-state unemployment insurance program. The final legislation also included healthcare in the form of Title 5 of the Social Security Act, which covered Maternal and Child Health via grants to the states. It included a permanent authorization of the Vocational Rehabilitation program with an increased appropriation authority; and it included grants to the states for assistance to families with children and the blind. This state grant in aid program to needy families with children covered medical care for the eligible populations and the AMA did not object. It was a precursor to the Medicaid program that would be enacted some 30 years later.

The Vocational Rehabilitation program still was without authority to fund medical services, but that would change in eight years at the urging of advocates such as Dr. Kessler and state directors of vocational rehabilitation. According to Secretary of Labor Perkins, who chaired the Economic Security Committee of the Administration, which produced the Social Security Act proposed to Congress, FDR took more pleasure in the enactment of the Social Security Act than in any other New Deal program. The Act stressed assistance to persons with disabilities in many of its provisions, including the Crippled Children's program, public assistance, and the related extension of the Vocational Rehabilitation Act.[5]

The AMA was agreeable to the Maternal and Child Health program and the health services to needy families with children, since both were run by state agencies that were funded by annual appropriations from Congress. These programs were controllable and would probably be limited in scope. Neither presented the problems of an insurance program for health care run by the federal government, which would not be limited just to the poor and would cover all Americans. The result of such an insurance program would undoubtedly be, according to the AMA, the incursion of the government in decision making regarding medical services. About 60 years later, the AMA concern became a reality, and not just in government programs for health care.

After the Committee had completed its work, I.S. Falk, (who had served with Roche on the Technical Board advising the Committee), urged Hopkins and Roche to fund a national health survey to look at the incidence of disability and its implications for healthcare. Roche and Falk were strong believers that disability had to be a federal responsibility and that it should include health services for persons with disabilities. Mary Switzer was assigned the task of establishing a national health survey on disability, and from it began her life long interest in health and disability. The survey demonstrated what Falk had assumed, that there was a large population of individuals who were ill or had temporary or permanent disabilities.[6]

After President Roosevelt was informed by the Economic Security Committee of the need to continue at least a study of the issue of health care and disability, he created a Committee to Coordinate Health Resources with Josephine Roche as Chair in 1938. Mary Switzer worked as staff to Roche and the Committee. The Committee recommended a prevention grant in aid program to be administered by the states; a hospital construction grant program; a new grant in aid program for medical care to those on relief; and a disability compensation program that included cash assistance and health care. The Committee decided to convene a National Health Conference to focus primarily on the more controversial issue of a national health insurance program. The Conference heard many calls for a national health program, including national health insurance, and Roche spoke in favor of it. The President was a supporter of the idea as well. The AMA representatives were somewhat split on the issue, but when the AMA House of Delegates met in September it voted to oppose any national health insurance program. That opposition became the AMA's final position. The AMA did support disability insurance, as long as it did not include health insurance, and supported health care grants in aid for the indigent to be administered by the states.

It was about this time that the Congressional elections of 1938 took place and produced a victory for the more conservative Congressmen of both parties. Roosevelt concluded that it was better to await the 1940 elections to see how the public felt about the programs enacted in 1935, before pressing for the passage of national health insurance or for disability insurance (with or without health provisions). The other programs recommended by the Committee were also shelved for at least the time being.

By 1940, World War II had begun in Europe and Roosevelt and his party were preoccupied with the issue of whether to enter the War on behalf of the those in western Europe threatened by the armies of Adolf Hitler. A small lesson to be derived from this experience is that one should not wait to advocate for a major issue if it is necessary since intervening events are always likely. It is possible, however, that national health insurance, or disability insurance with health coverage, would both have failed to pass if put up for a vote. Once a bill fails to be enacted, Congress often will not revisit it for a considerable period of time. A new challenge also appeared for Roosevelt as Robert Lafollette, son of the Governor and Senator from Wisconsin, organized a Progressive Party to challenge the Administration's approach to economic security. The new Progressive Party supported jobs and focused on productivity rather than economic security and cash assistance, which were the end results of the 1935 Social Security Act. The Progressive Party politicians of the first three decades of the twentieth century had been supporters of a national health insurance program of some kind as a method of assuring necessary care and productivity for members of the workforce and their families.[7]

Mary Switzer attributed the demise of national health insurance in 1938 to the power of the AMA. She wrote that medicine has "a well knit trade union . . . and the public is its victim, as well as a large percentage of its members."[8] It is more likely that the conservative attitude of the public in the Congressional elections of 1938 was responsible for Roosevelt's failure to propose national health insurance or disability insurance in 1938 or 1939, although the AMA opposition was undoubtedly a factor. From this point on Mary Switzer was very attentive to the positions of the AMA and other parts of medicine as she dealt with issues in health care. She later became a close liaison to the AMA during World War II. These connections that she developed with medicine would serve her well as the leader of the vocational rehabilitation agency in the 1950s as she sought to expand vocational rehabilitation in the medical field.

In 1939, President Roosevelt created the Federal Security Agency as an independent agency with administrative responsibility for the new social security programs, the employment service, the Public Health Service and the Office of Education. In the Eisenhower Administration, this agency became the Department of Health, Education and Welfare. In 1939, it was the chief agency responsible for domestic social programs. President Roosevelt appointed former Governor of Indiana Paul McNutt as Administrator. McNutt was a Vice Presidential candidate in 1940 and possible Presidential candidate in 1943, as FDR considered not running for another term. McNutt became an interested and creative leader of rehabilitation programs. Mary Switzer was then in the Public Health Service (PHS) as Assistant to Josephine Roche, the Assistant Treasury Secretary for PHS. She was asked by staff working on the reorganization to move to the new Agency to serve as an Assistant to Paul McNutt. This was an important increase in responsibility for Mary, although still a staff position. She would now have general responsibility for Public Health Service, social security, and education programs; including the Vocational Rehabilitation program in which her friend Tracy Copp labored with devotion. The placement of rehabilitation in the same agency with the Public Health Service also was an important factor in the future development of rehabilitation medicine programs in the Office of Vocational Rehabilitation.[9]

Disability received much Congressional attention in 1939, although no disability insurance or health insurance program was enacted. Senator Robert Wagner of New York introduced legislation creating a permanent disability insurance program. He and Senators Murray and Dingell also introduced the first national health insurance program, which would cover all Americans including persons with disabilities. (Senator Dingell was the father of Congressman John Dingell, who has been a staunch advocate for healthcare and rehabilitation medicine for the past 35 years.) The Congressional leadership on disability and rehabilitation, both in 1939 and after World War II, reflected the beginnings of a trend of Congressional influence beneficial to rehabilitation medicine. This influence became critical to the field from the 1970s to the present.[10]

KRUSEN, THE MAYO CLINIC AND THE DEVELOPMENT OF PHYSICAL MEDICINE

"Rehabilitation is to be a key word in medicine," said William Mayo in 1925. He was one of the founders of the Mayo Clinic. Charles Mayo, son and nephew of the founders, said in 1963: "My late uncle made this prediction . . . and ten years later he brought to the Mayo Clinic in Rochester, Minnesota, the physician who, perhaps more than any other individual, has helped make this prediction come true."[11]

William and Charles Mayo were brothers, born in 1861 and 1865 respectively, both of whom had become surgeons by the late 1880s. They were practicing medicine in Minnesota at the same time that Simon Baruch was developing his practice in New York City. The Mayo brothers soon came upon the
idea of integrating surgical and medical practice through a group practice
structure. The group was a corporation and physicians were employed by it.
The group began in 1892 in Rochester, Minnesota. This type of practice was
innovative and very controversial with most of medicine. The AMA was generally opposed to group practice because it interjected a corporate entity between the physician and his or her patient. It also made physicians employees
of the corporate entity, which they felt interfered with a physician's independent medical judgment. At one point, the AMA was sued by a national group
practice association for interfering with its efforts to assist physicians in practicing in group settings. The Mayo Clinic, however, was highly respected in
medicine, since it was an obvious example of quality medical practice. It was
also the predominant medical practice in the mid and far West. Its practitioners were leaders in the AMA and other medical associations. Other well
known groups in the Midwest derived their start from the Mayo experience,
notably the Menninger Clinic in Kansas and the Guthrie Clinic in Wisconsin.
Mayo also strongly stressed education and research. In 1915, the Clinic
established the Mayo Foundation to support medical education and clinical
research.[12]

Mayo brought diagnostic services, such as pathology and radiology, to
practice in the same setting with the surgical services. By 1920, the diagnostic services were considered on a par with the surgical ones. Around
1918 the Section on Orthopedics, under the leadership of Dr. Melvin Henderson and Dr. Henry Meyerding, established a department of physiotherapy. By 1925, that department had 11 physical therapy staff members. In
1924, another Mayo program became involved in physical modalities for
treatment purposes. Radiologist Arthur Desjardins acquired a diathermy
machine for the Department of Therapeutic Radiology and proceeded to
staff the diathermy service with nurses acting as technicians. The service
grew rapidly and Lucille Fitzpatrick, R.N., R.P.T. became supervisor of the
program from 1924 to 1967. The existence of two programs in physical
therapy in separate parts of the Mayo organization was not consistent with
the Mayo focus on integration and efficiency, however, and proposals
arose to consolidate the programs. From 1926 to 1930, the physical therapy services of all types were placed in the Orthopedics Department, but
later on, in 1930, the services were transferred to the Therapeutic Radiology Service under Dr. Desjardins. In 1926, both Dr. Henderson and Dr.
Desjardins advised Mayo to place the physical therapy service under the

direction of a medical man, referring to a physician in one of the medical specialties as opposed to surgical or diagnostic ones. Dr. Desjardins recommended that the service be a separate department under a medical person with experience in the physical medicine modalities.[13]

Mayo physicians were active in national medical societies, particularly the AMA, where they met other physicians from a variety of specialty areas, including physical medicine. Dr. Desjardin was especially active in the AMA, particularly on issues dealing with physical therapy. By the early 1930s, the Radiology Department and the Orthopedics Department were both aware of and encouraged by developments in physical medicine. They saw its potential for integration with the surgical services to provide better patient care. Dr. Desjardin had been seeking a possible leader for the therapy department from 1930 to 1935 and had become acquainted with and impressed by Dr. Frank Krusen at AMA meetings. Krusen had already established himself as an effective Associate Dean of a medical school, as a well-recognized team physician for Temple University athletic teams, and as an accomplished academician. He had also published a curriculum for physical therapy in the Journal of the American Association of Medical Colleges. In the early 1930s, he taught physical medicine and physical therapy to physicians, nurses and therapists at Temple University. He also taught courses to physicians in practice as part of the Philadelphia Medical Society educational programs.[14]

Krusen was very active in medical society matters. He was a member of the Philadelphia Medical Society, (of which he was President in 1932), and active in the AMA. He was appointed in 1934 to the AMA Council on Physical Therapy, Chaired by John Coulter. He worked with Dr. Desjardins on that committee. Dr. Desjardins arranged for Dr. Henderson to meet with Dr. Krusen in Philadelphia. Henderson observed the professionalism and organization of the Physical Medicine Department at Temple and was favorably impressed. The two men recommended Krusen to the Mayo Board to direct the therapy services in a new department. Using Dr. Desjardins as an emissary, Dr. William Mayo offered Dr. Krusen a position at the Mayo Clinic and an opportunity to establish a department of physical therapy there. Dr. Krusen took the position in 1935. With the solid support of the Departments of Radiology, Orthopedics, Internal Medicine and Neurology, Krusen established the new Department of Physical Medicine at the Mayo Clinic, and also at the Graduate School of Medicine of the University of Minnesota (with which Mayo had an academic affiliation). The Department flourished due to referrals from medical and surgical colleagues at Mayo. Physical Medicine fit perfectly as an integrated service within the Mayo group practice model; and Krusen fit perfectly in a structure, which stressed excellence in clinical services, education and clinical research.[15]

From 1935 to 1940 the Physical Medicine Department at Mayo grew and prospered. The number of patients seen increased from about 2600 annually in 1934 to 5,450 in 1935 and 8,489 in 1940. Referrals came from all parts of the Mayo Clinic and involved a variety of conditions from arthritis and back-ache to scoliosis, sciatica, fibrositis and poliomyelitis. The staff during that period included Dr. Krusen, residents rotating through the program on a peri-odic basis (who might at one time number as many as four) and at least one physician in special training from Mayo or another medical school or pro-gram. From 1935 to 1940 there were usually between 10 and 12 physical ther-apists on staff under the supervision of Frank Wiechec, a physical therapist whom Dr. Krusen recruited from Temple University.

Eight education programs were initiated in the department as Krusen sought to spread the knowledge and credibility of the field. In 1936, he es-tablished the first three-year physical medicine residency program in the na-tion, which was a collaboration between the Mayo Graduate School of Med-icine and the University of Minnesota Medical School. The program regularly received 5 residents on rotation from other specialties. By 1936, Krusen had eight residents and he and the residents treated 7,000 patients in the Depart-ment. In 1938, Krusen established a School of Physical Therapy, similar to the school he had established at Temple. He also established advanced courses for physical therapists already in practice; which included 55 hours of instruction in areas such as anatomy, kinesiology, psychology, exercise, massage, electrotherapy and hydrotherapy. A special physician training pro-gram of one month to one year was intended to spread the knowledge of phys-ical therapy and physical medicine throughout the country. Physicians from the military, the Cleveland Clinic and Stanford University attended and re-turned to their institutions, often to create physical medicine programs of their own. Dr. Arthur Watkins became chair of the Department of Physical Ther-apy at Massachusetts General Hospital after completing the special physician program, and Dr. Walter Zeiter returned to the Cleveland Clinic to become chair of its Physical Therapy Department. Zeiter became a leader in the movement to establish a specialty in physical medicine and was the first Ex-ecutive Director of the American Academy of Physical Medicine and Reha-bilitation. The Academy has established an annual Zeiter Lecture in his honor that is given at the Academy's annual meeting.[16]

The research program of the new Department also developed quickly in the period from 1935 to 1940. The topics of research reveal the focus of the field at this early stage in its development. The emphases seemed more on disease treatment than on disabling conditions from injury. The effects of both radi-ant heat and diathermy on skin temperature, and research on other forms of radiation therapy were frequent research topics at this time at the Clinic. Physical therapy techniques such as massage and therapeutic exercise were also investigated. Specific studies were done that examined the impact of exercise on bronchial asthma, scoliosis and osteoporosis. Cervical traction as a treatment modality was evaluated for its efficacy.[17]

Krusen's organizational work within the AMA benefited from his relationships with Mayo colleagues who were also active AMA members. His association with a premier medical program like the Mayo Clinic enhanced the national stature of physical medicine a great deal within the AMA and with other colleagues. But Krusen was still somewhat dispirited by the lack of knowledge, bordering on prejudice, of physical medicine throughout medicine. He felt it was essential to educate other physicians about the field, and other health professionals as well. As he noted in his "History of Physical Medicine and Rehabilitation" published in 1968, the Report of the Council on Physical Therapy of the AMA noted that the field was "still violently condemned by some physicians."[18] He considered the pioneers, (whom he defined as himself, Coulter at Northwestern, Bierman and Kovacs in New York, and Zeiter of the Cleveland Clinic), to have faced great prejudice in their efforts to establish the field. While the use of chemical agents in the form of medicines was a common and accepted practice, physical agents derived from the science of physics were new and viewed as unproven. Proof of the efficacy of chemical agents was far from common at this point, however, since this was before the time of the FDA and its emphasis on clinical trials to establish efficacy.[19]

At this stage in his career, Krusen also viewed the practice of physical medicine as inherently related to rehabilitation. In the early days of seeking recognition for the field, this connection to rehabilitation seemed to have little appeal, but the connection would eventually prove essential to recognition and growth. In 1969, Krusen described physical medicine in the early days of the 1930s and indicated that rehabilitation was the goal of the process: "We were deeply concerned with the rehabilitation of the disabled. The goals are psychological, social and vocational rehabilitation."[20] Krusen and others made these points about rehabilitation and physical medicine in 1944 in the Baruch Committee Report (discussed in the next chapter), and Krusen endorsed the need for vocational training as part of physical medicine services as early as the 1920s when he worked at the Cressen Sanitarium. Krusen's Mayo program and other programs of the 1930s in physical medicine, however, emphasized the use of specific physical medicine techniques. They were focused on acute disease states and a goal of ambulation more than broader, rehabilitation services and goals.[21]

PROFESSIONAL SOCIETIES AND PHYSICAL MEDICINE
IN THE 1930S

Krusen and Coulter continued their efforts within the AMA to achieve recognition for physical medicine in the mid-nineteen thirties. The focus of their effort was on establishing physical medicine as a recognized medical specialty by the AMA and its Council on Medical Specialties. This would require the establishment of a certifying board and examination process. Their focus was also on establishing quality standards for physical therapy services and other services that would be part of the physical restoration of patients.

The AMA Council on Physical Therapy had been established to assist the American Physiotherapy Association (APA) in providing quality standards for therapy services. John Coulter had been active in the Council from its onset. Frank Krusen became a member of the Council in 1934. The APA also was concerned about the quality of education and professional knowledge among those practicing physical therapy and sought to establish a certification process for practitioners to assure their competence. As Krusen noted in his history of the field of physical medicine and rehabilitation in 1968, physicians generally were very skeptical about physical therapy in general, and their skepticism was not limited to those few who were not trained at appropriate schools. The AMA efforts with the APA did not extend to assistance with the certification process. In the late 1920s the APA had asked the American College of Physical Therapy (ACPT), later the American Congress of Physical Therapy, to assist it in establishing a certification process. This effort failed, but in the early 1930s the Congress was again approached by the APA to assist it with a certification program. The Congress formed a committee chaired by William Bierman MD of Sinai Hospital in New York City, which recommended the establishment of a national Registry of Physical Therapy Technicians (ARPTT) to offer and conduct certification exams. The Registry was established in 1935 within the American Congress of Physical Therapy. It was incorporated in Illinois and its first board members included John Coulter, Frank Krusen and William Bierman.[22]

In the excellent history of the APA, (now referred to as the American Physical Therapy Association), *Healing the Generations*, the author described the process as follows: *With APA's good friend John Coulter as its guiding force, the American Registry of Physical Therapy Technicians was created . . . Sponsored and controlled by the American Congress of Physical (sic) Medicine, the ARPTT took as its standard the minimum education requirements on which the APA and AMA had previously agreed.*[23] The ARPTT and its standards were agreeable to the AMA Council of Physical Therapy, on which Dr. Coulter sat. Coulter was a bridge between the professions of medicine and

physical therapy. That bridge was to be more important in the future as rehabilitation medicine and its inpatient team approach to care began to develop.[24]

The Registry proved to be very important to physical therapists as they embraced the new federal program for crippled children, Title 5, Part 2 of the Social Security Act of 1935. An appropriation of $2,850,000, a substantial sum
of money at the time, was available in the first year of implementation of the
program. The Children's Bureau of the Public Health Service administered
the program and established criteria for facilities and agencies receiving the
federal funds. The Registry was invaluable in convincing government that
physical therapy was a credible and recognized health profession. Title V, Part
2 of the Social Security Act was also the first federal civilian health program
to recognize and pay for any of the services of rehabilitation medicine. The
vocational rehabilitation program would also offer payment for services some
eight years later, and by doing so would extend the service to adults with
physical disabilities.[25]

Another example of collaboration between professional societies in the rehabilitation medicine field was the joint meeting between the American Occupational Therapy Association (AOTA) and the American Congress of Physical Therapy in 1938. The AOTA had developed close relationships with
physicians and hospitals for two decades beginning in 1920, and often depended on these organizations for members. However, unlike the APA, the
AOTA set up its own registry and certification system for occupational therapists. It was less committed to the medical model for its services than was
the APTA. Occupational therapy was a field of services, which also dealt with
mental illness and retardation, rather than just physical impairments. It furnished many of its services in non-medical sites such as schools.[26]

Despite the dominant position of medicine in American health care in the
1930s, the physicians in physical medicine, (such as Krusen, Coulter, Zeiter
and Bierman), were not recognized as having a specialty of medicine and did
not have an AMA approved national certifying exam. This began to change
in 1937 as "the AMA Board of Trustees authorized recognition of the American Congress of Physical Therapy as a medical specialty society."[27] The real
test of recognition, however, was the existence of a national board and a certifying exam, which the Congress did not have. At this point, the Mayo Clinic
connections of Dr. Krusen had a major impact on this issue. Drs. Krusen and
Coulter led a delegation of physicians to present the case for a specialty in
physical medicine to the AMA controlled Advisory Council for Medical Specialties. The President of the Council was Dr. Louis Wilson of the Mayo
Clinic, a professor of pathology and Director of the Mayo Graduate School of
Medicine. The Mayo Clinic Departments of Radiology and Orthopedics were
supporters of the request by Coulter and Krusen. Wilson told Krusen: "It is

time for a certifying board in physical medicine."[28] But the procedure to establish a certifying board required the presentation of a petition of at least a hundred physicians in fulltime practice to justify a seat on the Advisory Council of Medical Specialties and eventually a board to certify competence.

Krusen and Coulter, together with eight other physicians, created a new society at the 1938 meeting of the American Congress of Physical Therapy. The sole mission of the new Society of Physical Therapy Physicians was to achieve full specialty status for physical medicine and meet the AMA criteria for specialty recognition. The likely reason that Krusen and Coulter and their colleagues did not use the Congress as the organizing society for achieving specialty status was that the Congress had members who were not full time practitioners of physical medicine for diagnosis, treatment or both. Some of the Congress members were in radiology, others in neurology, internal medicine or surgery.[29]

Only 42 physicians were engaged in the full time practice of physical medicine at the end of the 1920s, and not many more than that were full time at the end of the 1930s. The lack of residency training programs was probably the major reason for the small numbers of full time practicing physical medicine specialists. Most of the full time practitioners were in academic medicine and had university or medical school affiliations. There was a large concentration of them in New York City. Others were in the Midwest at the Mayo Clinic, Northwestern University, Washington University in St. Louis, or the Cleveland Clinic.

An estimated five to ten physical medicine practitioners were practicing in California. Dr. Jay Hibben was in private practice in Pasadena and was a charter member of the American Society of Physical Therapy Physicians in 1938, after having been the president of the American Congress of Physical Therapy in 1935 and 1936. Dr. Fred Moor was at the College of Medical Evangelists in Los Angeles. He was considered one of the early pioneers in the field by Dr. Frederick Kottke, a historian of the field, and served as the Society President in the 1940s. Kottke, a second generation leader of the field, has speculated that a reason for the interest of these men in physical medicine modalities for diagnosis or treatment was their Eastern European, German or Scandinavian backgrounds. In those regions of the world physical therapeutics, hydrology and spa therapy were accepted as important elements of medical practice. But there were also physicians who practiced in other specialties such as surgery who saw rehabilitation services as an adjunct to their practice. This was particularly true of orthopedic surgery, from which the major leadership in rehabilitation medicine had come in WWI and throughout the 1920s and 1930s.[30]

CIVILIAN REHABILITATION FACILITIES IN THE 1930's

The rate of growth for rehabilitation medicine services in civilian hospitals and clinics was very slow during the thirties. The best known comprehensive program was at the Institute for Crippled and Disabled Adults in New York City. By the late 1930s, George Deaver had arrived at the Institute to provide medical leadership and served as its first medical director. In Kottke and Knapp's history of physical medicine before 1950, Deaver was characterized as the progenitor of rehabilitation medicine. He was the "first to initiate programs for rehabilitating the very severely handicapped" such as the spinal cord injured. He was also the earliest physician to establish methods to evaluate abilities in the activities of daily living (ADLs).[31] In her commemorative address on 50 years of vocational rehabilitation in 1970, Mary Switzer cited Deaver as one of the three most important physicians in the development of rehabilitation medicine.

In addition to the inpatient and outpatient programs established by Krusen at the Mayo Clinic, Kessler and Albee had an active rehabilitation program linked to the New Jersey Workers Compensation program and to their surgical practices. The rehabilitation program for polio patients established at Warm Springs, Georgia by FDR grew rapidly and served to educate the nation of the disease and of the need for rehabilitation therapies. FDR expanded the national effort to attack polio in 1937 by establishing the National Infantile Paralysis Foundation, which proceeded to raise substantial funds for treatment, education and research.[32]

During the 1930s a precedent was set for a federal role in providing social insurance. This would ultimately lead to the enactment of Disability Insurance in 1956 and Medicare in 1965. Both programs would include support for rehabilitation medicine services, and Medicare would be the stimulus for the maturity of rehabilitation medicine in the health care system. The vocational rehabilitation program was extended and expanded and a new program was created to support rehabilitation services to crippled children. The most significant events in the development of rehabilitation medicine during this period were the national leadership role of rehabilitation advocate Mary Switzer in the Public health Service; and the development of the physical medicine department at the Mayo Clinic. This department quickly became a national leader in clinical medicine, under the leadership of Frank Krusen. These developments during the 1930s, although not dramatic, would facilitate the major expansion of the field, which occurred in the next decade, principally as a result of World War II.

NOTES

1. Ludmerer, 88.
2. Walker, 52, 53; Starr, 261, 268.
3. Walker, 44–53; Berkowitz, 28.
4. Walker, 53–57 and Berkowitz, 16–35; *also see* Starr, 261–269.
5. Berkowitz, 28; Walker, 54–56; Smith, *FDR*, Random House, 2007, 350, 352–53.
6. Walker, 56–57; Berkowitz, 30–32.
7. Starr, 276; Walker, 58–61; Berkowitz, 35–37.
8. Walker, 61.
9. Walker, 63 *et seq.;* Smith, *FDR*, 461–462.
10. Berkowitz, 58–60.
11. Robison, 9.
12. Starr, 209–220.
13. Opitz and DePompolo, *History of the Mayo Department of Physical Medicine and Rehabilitation*, 1911–2002, Mayo Foundation For Medical Education and Research, 2006, 1–11.
14. Opitz *et al.*, Krusen Diaries, Arch Phys Med Rehabil, vol. 78, 443–44.
15. Opitz *et al.,* Arch Phys Med Rehabil, vol. 78, 443; Opitz and DePompolo, 12.
16. Opitz and DePompoulo, 18–30.
17. Opitz and DePompoulo, 32–35.
18. Krusen, Arch Phys Med Rehabil, vol. 50, 1.
19. *Ibid*, 1–2.
20. *Ibid*, 2.
21. Fowler, *A History of Physical Medicine and Rehabilitation in California*, California Society of Physical Medicine and Rehabilitation, 1998, 9; personal communication with William M. Fowler, Jr., September 10, 2004.
22. Krusen, Arch Phys Med Rehabil, vol. 50, 1–2.
23. Murphy, *Healing the Generations*, 102.
24. Gritzer and Arluke, 74–76; Murphy, *Healing the Generations*, 102.
25. Murphy, *Healing the Generations*, 99–101.
26. Gritzer and Arluke, 80–82.
27. Frederick Kottke and Miland Knapp, Arch Phys Med Rehabil, vol. 69, 2.
28. Opitz *et al.*, Krusen Diaries, Arch Phys Med Rehabil, vol. 78, 444.
29. Ibid; DeLisa, Currie Martin, 15.
30. Fowler, 9; Kottke and Knapp, Arch Phys Med Rehabil, vol. 69, 3.
31. Kottke and Knapp, ibid.
32. Switzer, Rehabilitation Record, The Great Ones, 6; Kessler, *The Knife Is Not Enough*, 56; Gallagher, *Spendid Deception*, 145–151.

Chapter Six

World War II, Howard Rusk, Henry Kessler, and the Baruch Committee

The decade of the 1940s witnessed the occurrence of a number of major events which provided a great impetus for the development of rehabilitation medicine on a large scale. Those events reflected the impact of the three major factors in rehabilitation medicine's development and their interaction: war, politics and philanthropy. The World War II effort included the creation of inpatient rehabilitation programs, and stimulated both the governmental and the philanthropic sectors to plan for the services necessary to rehabilitate the returning veterans. Howard Rusk, Henry Kessler and Frank Krusen were involved in the establishment of these military programs. Mary Switzer and her colleagues at the Federal Security Board undertook a major conference on civilian disability and rehabilitation needs generated by the war that resulted in new legislation passed by Congress. Bernard Baruch, in his early seventies, committed his wealth and time to the establishment of a private commission to plan for programs for veterans and civilians. Jeremiah Millbank and his Institute for the Crippled and Disabled advocated at the national level for a comprehensive medical and vocational rehabilitation program for civilians. Neither the federal nor private actions would have occurred without the war, but each took rehabilitation well beyond military and veterans programs. War, politics and philanthropy and their interaction would continue to play major roles in rehabilitation medicine from the early 1940s onward.

Prior to the 1940s, World War I and the workers compensation programs of the states had provided some impetus for rehabilitation. But the impetus of World War I was very short lived and the impetus of the workers compensation programs was slight and varied depending on the state involved. The 1940s was the period that laid the foundation for the future growth and the eventual acceptance of rehabilitation medicine as a part of the healthcare system.

It was also helpful to the development in rehabilitation medicine that the nation's view of health care had broadened a great deal from earlier in the century, and that health care was beginning to be perceived as a right to which American citizens were entitled. In 1946, the WHO defined health as "a state of complete physical, social and mental well being and not merely the absence of disease."[1] The Commission on Medical Education reported that the greatest need for medical education was getting medical services to people. The geographic maldistribution of physicians, as well as their low number, was one of the causes of this problem. At about the same time the private sector was stimulating the growth of health insurance. Commercial insurers were expanding in competition with Blue Cross and Blue Shield. Unions were using their newly won organizing and collective bargaining rights, created in New Deal legislation, to demand health insurance purchased by employers. With the advent of tax code provisions making employer contributions to the health insurance of employees tax exempt, private health insurance became a private sector approach to the health aspects of social security; which both unions and employers wished. But the aged, disabled, unemployed, and some employees were still left out of health insurance coverage, a situation that would be remedied in part in another 25 years with the Medicare and Medicaid legislation championed by Lyndon B. Johnson.[2]

WORLD WAR II AND ITS IMPACT
ON HEALTHCARE AND REHABILITATION

The success of the United States in World War II was to some extent due to the rapid advances in science and technology the country witnessed in the period prior to the War. These advances were evident in the improved medical care, including rehabilitation medicine, available during the War. Ludmerer, in his history of medical education referred to the fact that a major result of the War was "...that only 3% of wounded soldiers died and new surgical and rehabilitative treatment allowed much speedier recovery and much less permanent dysfunction."[3] It was during World War II that rehabilitation medicine began to develop as a recognized part of modern healthcare.

Although the USA entered World War II on December 7, 1941 after the attack on Pearl Harbor, many in and out of government had been preparing for a possible war as early as the late 1930s. Sometime in 1939 or early 1940, the AMA had established a War Preparedness Committee and had circulated a questionnaire to members to solicit data on physician availability to serve if war broke out. That questionnaire did not include physical therapy. The American Congress of Physical Therapy (ACPT) journal included an article criticizing this omission. In June of 1940, the ACPT wrote a letter to the Surgeon General of the Army offering to assist in establishing a physical therapy division in the army. Not long after that letter was sent, John Coulter (a leader of the ACPT), was asked to prepare a report on the need for physical therapists for the Army in the event of war. Coulter did his usual thorough analysis and eventually reported that, assuming only a European Theatre of War activity, 300 hospitals of 1000 beds each would be needed. That in turn created a need for about 2100 military physical therapists. Coulter then surveyed the civilian sector and concluded that about 1600 physical therapists were needed for civilian hospitals, and about 2400 for crippled children's schools and the Children's Bureau field service for the crippled children's program. The total need was for over 6000 physical therapists, far above the supply existing in 1940. Coulter issued a moving message in the Review, the journal of the APA, calling on all physiotherapists to make the necessary sacrifice for their country. This sacrifice was made more difficult by the lack of a federal law creating a professional status for military physical therapists, which was unlike many other health professionals. But the APA responded and the military had physical therapists available to staff its facilities when the war broke out. There was also a corresponding need for physicians in physical medicine and other disciplines related to rehabilitation medicine to enlist, but it is unclear whether a specific physical medicine request came forward from the military.[4]

Nevertheless, after Pearl Harbor, efforts proceeded to train physicians in physical therapy and physical medicine techniques for application during war. Frank Krusen initiated a training program at the Mayo Clinic in 1942. He was encouraged by the American Congress of Physical Therapy Physicians to do so, and he also received requests from the US Army and Navy to set up a program to train medical officers in physical medicine on an emergency basis. The program trained 10 to 12 physicians per three month period. The program lasted from 1942 through 1947. A total of 171 government physicians were trained in this emergency program, including Veterans Administration physicians.[5]

Krusen also reviewed training programs in physical medicine and physical therapy at N.Y.U., Harvard and Northwestern. He was also involved in research for the military on the impact of frostbite on infantry men and sunburn on aviators. Ten military hospitals, Stanford University, and the DT Watson School of Physiatrics in Pittsburg all had physical therapy training programs in this same time period. The Institute for the Crippled and Disabled in New York established a major program to train therapists and physicians under the leadership of George Deaver.[6]

The so-called "90 day wonders" trained by Mayo under Krusen's direction had a lasting impact on the specialty of physical medicine and rehabilitation. Many of these trainees would go on to make up the necessary 100 physicians required to petition for a board in physical medicine. One of these trainees, Leonard Bender, MD, went on to be President of the American Academy of Physical Medicine and Rehabilitation and to help establish one of the finest academic departments in the field at the University of Michigan.

While training programs for physicians and physical therapists to serve during World War II were ongoing, the rehabilitation medicine service established in World War I had not been maintained. There were no rehabilitation service units in the military facilities. There was no organizational structure in the military health bureaucracy or in military facilities to utilize the personnel being trained. Everything had to start anew, and into this breach stepped Howard Rusk and Henry Kessler.

Howard Rusk was forty years old when the United States entered World War II. He had been in practice in St. Louis Missouri for 15 years. His practice was very successful, and by 1940 he had three associates practicing with him. Their practice was in general internal medicine, and two of his associates focused on cardiology and gastroenterology. Rusk held staff appointments at two of the best hospitals in the city, St. Lukes and Barnes. He taught at Washington University Medical School, one of the nation's finest. He was also a member of the American College of Physicians, the society for physicians who were in medicine and its subspecialties. He had done research and published a number of papers in peer reviewed journals, the best known of which, in his opinion, was one on urticaria (hives) that was published in the Journal of the American Medical Association (JAMA). His practice and teaching did not deal with physical disability, at least as he described it in his autobiography. Despite this successful practice and his age when the United States entered the War, Rusk felt it was his duty to enlist and do his part for his country. From that point on, his career took a major new direction, which he had never before considered.[7]

Howard Rusk possessed a personality that was as large as his tall frame. He also possessed a boundless concern for people. He understood people and the importance of maintaining their optimism with respect to improving their lives. His vision of life was probably best exemplified by the title of his biography, *A World To Care For.* His optimistic view of life and its possibilities fortunately was coupled with great energy, intelligence, and a straight forward commitment to getting the job done. He was also a very dedicated person who saw causes that he believed in as missions to be accomplished. These traits marked his career from his entry into World War II onward.

Of the five founders of rehabilitation medicine described in this book, Rusk was the only one with whom I had significant personal contact. I knew him for a period of about 10 years toward the end of his career and was impressed by his warm and engaging personality, his social and political contacts at the very highest level, (many derived from his experiences in the 1940's), and his charismatic leadership ability.

Rusk joined the medical service of the Army Air Force as a Major in August of 1942 and was assigned to Jefferson Barracks outside of St. Louis. He was one of the medical staff at this 1,000 bed military hospital, who were soon to be faced with the daunting task of caring for 1,000 patients. Initially most of these patients were simply convalescing from some debilitating illness, since the war wounded had not yet arrived. For a practical person like Rusk there was a very apparent need to get these young men active again, once their illness was under control and they were fit for activity. To get them physically active and retrained for either military duty or civilian life seemed very important to him.

Later in 1942, the war wounded began arriving at Jefferson Barracks. Rusk soon realized that the problems he faced in restoring these wounded men for military duty were far more daunting than he had initially surmised when his patients were convalescents from an episodic illness. The returning wounded were often missing limbs, paralyzed, or had head injuries. Rusk recommended that the hospital establish a special convalescent/rehabilitation center to effectively treat these patients. He kept notes on the activities and outcomes of his programs. In November of 1942, on his way to a regional medical meeting in Richmond, Rusk went to the central office of the Army Air Force and presented his program to its medical leadership. This group recommended that their superior, General Hap Arnold, be advised of the program. Arnold was an outgoing and personable leader, and was renowned for his organizational skills in developing the Air Force "virtually from scratch."[8] Arnold immediately saw the possibilities for the Air Force as a whole, and ordered Rusk to Washington to develop and administer the new program. In the short span of about six months, Howard Rusk had recognized a problem, attacked the problem, and was sent to Washington to solve it, and to develop national policy. The remainder of his career in rehabilitation would move with equal speed and achievement.[9]

Rusk became chief of the Army Air Force Reconditioning and Recreation Program in Washington, serving under General Arnold, and pursued his vision of centers for rehabilitation throughout the Air Force. (Keep in mind that the Air Force at this time was part of the Army.) One particular model for his approach was the rheumatic disease special treatment hospital at Davis Monthan Field in Tucson, Arizona. Lowell Thomas, Jr. had been a patient in that program in 1943, and was restored to full pilot status. His father, the famous radio commentator (who was comparable in influence to Walter Cronkite in a later decade) came to Washington to see Dr. Rusk and others and thank them for their efforts. Rusk, exhibiting his acute sense of timing and salesmanship, used the opportunity to advocate for his concept of rehabilitation centers in the Air Force to restore pilots to either flying status or another effective career in the military or in civilian life. Thomas was impressed and mentioned a perfect site for such a program in Pawling, New York where he lived. Rusk and General Arnold, who had demonstrated support for Rusk's programmatic ideas, visited the site and saw its potential. Soon arrangements were made for a major east coast rehabilitation program in Pawling, which was just north of New York City. Rusk took personal charge of the program and soon began making contacts with those medical professionals who could help him develop the program. Under Rusk's direct supervision, it became a broad medical and vocational rehabilitation services program.[10]

It should be noted that Rusk was still only two years out of his active internal medicine practice in St. Louis. He had never had formal training or experience in physical medicine, or the medical management of severely disabled patients like the ones he encountered in 1942 and 1943. The other medical officers of the Army Air Force also had no previous training in physical medicine. The patients Rusk saw in the rheumatic fever hospital in Arizona, as well as the initial convalescent patients at Jefferson Barracks, were well within his sphere of professional expertise as an internist. The severely disabled and war wounded, however, were not. As was frequently the case, Rusk was aware of his limitations, but was not willing to allow them to prevent him from achieving his goals. Like the leaders in orthopedics and radiology at the Mayo Clinic in the 1930s, he recognized the need for a person with specific medical expertise in rehabilitation techniques to oversee the training of the additional physicians who would be needed to oversee the services. He contacted Dr. George Deaver, the Medical Director of the Institute for the Crippled and Disabled in New York City, visited him, and arranged for a crash training program for Army Air Force medical officers on the techniques of rehabilitation medicine. This arrangement began a long and productive relationship between these two talented physicians, which would eventually result in the creation of a model civilian rehabilitation hospital for the world. With some trained medical personnel, the Center at Pawling opened in early 1944 and soon there were twelve Army Air Force rehabilitation centers throughout the nation.[11]

Yet another rehabilitation program was started during 1943 and 1944 with Rusk's involvement. While working at the Pentagon overseeing his Army Air Force rehabilitation programs, Rusk was visited by a man named Henry Viscardi, who was working for the Red Cross and teaching patients with amputations at Walter Reed Army Hospital how to walk. Today the Walter Reed Army Hospital is a world leader in caring for persons with amputations and in the development of advanced technology for their use. Viscardi had a congenital deformity of both legs that left him incapable of ambulation without special braces, so he was well aware of the needs of the amputees. Viscardi arrived to see Rusk with a number of very angry soldiers who were amputees, but who had been fitted with only temporary paper mache artificial legs. Rusk immediately took the group of soldiers to see Commander General Arnold, who was infuriated by the treatment of these men who had given their limbs in battle. He not only obtained limbs for them, but established a prosthetics research program at Walter Reed with a $5 million appropriation in 1944. Sixty years later that program and others, expanded to include recent technology, are currently effectively serving the returning soldiers with amputations from Iraq. Rusk and Viscardi thus began a partnership which lasted for 30 years.[12]

While Rusk was developing his rehabilitation and reconditioning programs in the Army Air Force in 1943, Henry Kessler was in the Pacific Islands serving as a surgeon in Samoa. He had been in the Naval Reserve since 1932, and with the bombing of Pearl Harbor was called up as a Lieutenant Commander in 1942. By October of 1943, he had been assigned to Mare Island Naval Hospital in the San Francisco Bay area. The Hospital was to be transformed into a center for persons with amputations. When Kessler arrived he saw that the efforts of Dr. Albee 25 years earlier during World War I had gone for naught. There were no remnants of the reconstruction hospitals of that period in 1943. Rusk was later to note this same tragic loss. Under Dr. Kessler's leadership, however, the Mare Island facility became the foremost amputee and rehabilitation center in the Navy, serving most of those with amputations from the Pacific theater. The amputee center at Mare Island also served other orthopedic cases and neuropsychiatric cases, displaying the breadth of Kessler's concern for rehabilitation. Kessler was most known for his surgical and rehabilitation care with amputees for which the Mare Center was famous.

One example of the rehabilitation afforded at Mare for amputees was the care of Patricia Ditunno's father. Patricia Ditunno is the wife of Dr. John Ditunno, who was mentored by Dr. Krusen at Temple University in the midnineteen sixties, and went on to become one of rehabilitation medicine's foremost leaders in the 1980s and 1990s. His father-in-law was a Navy pilot in the Pacific who was wounded during Pearl Harbor and lost one of his legs. Sometime after his initial care and prosthesis, he was sent to the amputee Center at Mare Island and fitted with a much improved artificial limb. Despite his amputation, he remained in the Navy until retirement and participated in the testing of the atomic bomb in 1945 as the chief of the drone flights (which measured radioactive fallout from the explosion). The rehabilitation medicine program Kessler established at Mare Island was comprehensive, even more so than the one Rusk was starting at Pawling. The Mare Island program had physical therapy, occupational therapy, psychological services, vocational training and job placement services. It also had a prosthetic device service with the capability of on-site manufacturing of prostheses. Kessler also created an Advisory Board of faculty from the University of California. This group eventually became an advisory body for the National Research Council's major amputee research program.[13]

It is both interesting and ironic that neither Kessler nor Rusk seemed aware at the time of the programs the other was developing. They finally met in 1944 when they were each the recipient of a major award given by Lord and Taylor's Department Store Corporation. They and two other recipients were recognized for their contributions to rehabilitation in the Army, Air Force and Navy. Kessler writes in his biography that Rusk said to him at the event: "Dr. Kessler the surface has just hardly been scratched," referring to the rehabilitation movement the two of them had resurrected during World War II.[14] Kessler reported that from this point on in his career he was dedicated to enlarging the rehabilitation movement worldwide. Rusk joined that effort as well.

In their efforts to build programs in medical care that were focused on rehabilitation during their duty in the military, both Rusk and Kessler demonstrated their skill at enlisting the support of well connected lay people, whether philanthropists or politicians. Both got to know Eleanor Roosevelt and she visited their programs. Kessler had many Hollywood stars visit his facility to assist in getting the publicity he needed to obtain the resources necessary to develop his program. Those celebrities included comedian Jack Benny, who was a frequent supporter of the troops during World War II, and actress Joan Crawford. Rusk made very effective headway with philanthropists such as Bernard Baruch. He also used the press in obtaining necessary support and resources for his Air Force programs. He became acquainted with Helen Reid, whose family owned the New York Herald Tribune; and Arthur Sulzberger, the publisher of the New York Times. Both were of assistance to him in his advocacy for rehabilitation. Kessler and Rusk would use their skills in attracting political, journalistic and philanthropic support to build rehabilitation programs in the USA and abroad for at least 25 years after the War.[15]

As the War drew to a close, Rusk was getting frustrated because the programs he was establishing were not being utilized in the Army outside of the Army Air Force. The effectiveness of the programs had been recognized in the peer reviewed literature and by papers presented at an AMA symposium during its annual session in 1944 on "the Abuse of Rest in the Treatment of

Disease." The Symposium papers were published in the Journal of the American Medical Association (JAMA). Future conferences of the AMA focused on the value of early ambulation as an element in the effort to rehabilitate the disabled person. In 1944, Rusk had an opportunity to get his views on expanding the rehabilitation programs to the highest levels of government. He and Bernard Baruch were both on the program at an event sponsored by Helen Reid of the New York Herald Tribune. Rusk was a member of the Baruch Committee established in 1943 to study physical medicine and rehabilitation programs for war wounded (discussed later in this chapter). Never shy about advocating for his cause, and knowing that Baruch had an interest in disability and physical medicine, Rusk asked Baruch for assistance. Baruch had served as an advisor to President Roosevelt, and knew FDR and Eleanor well. He took Rusk aside and showed him how such matters were most effectively handled. He drafted a brief note to the President asking for his consideration of the issuance of an order to the Army requesting it to establish a rehabilitation medicine service comparable to that of the Army Air Force program. He had Rusk draft a letter that the President could sign and send to the Secretary of War. The two letters were sent for the President's consideration by Baruch, and not long thereafter the Army was ordered to establish the program. Now all branches of the military had established rehabilitation programs. Rusk also learned from this experience some invaluable lessons on how to affect national decision making at the highest levels from one of the nation's most astute practitioners of that art. In very short order, he was to be practicing these skills directly in relationships with Presidents Truman, Eisenhower, Kennedy and Johnson, members of their cabinets, and Congress.[16]

It is now generally accepted in the field of rehabilitation medicine that the establishment of these military inpatient rehabilitation programs was the cornerstone for the development of rehabilitation medicine in general and the specialty of physical medicine & rehabilitation in particular. Without these programs, the development of the specialty of physical medicine and rehabilitation, the inpatient rehabilitation hospital, and the professions of physical and occupational therapy would have progressed much more slowly and likely would have had much less impact on national health care.

MARY SWITZER AND WAR MOBILIZATION, THE NATIONAL REHABILITATION CONFERENCE, AND THE EXPANSION OF VOCATIONAL REHAB

Mary Switzer had visited Mare Island and the rehabilitation clinic Dr. Kessler had created during World War II. She had also met Dr. Rusk during one of the meetings of the War Procurement and Assignment Board with which she worked on behalf of Administrator McNutt of the Federal Security Agency. These were her first encounters with the two physicians with whom she would work for a quarter of a century to further the cause of rehabilitation medicine and other rehabilitation services. In a commemorative issue of the Rehabilitation Record in 1970, Mary Switzer wrote: "World War II brought us to the point of being able to see the long range potentialities of rehabilitation. The work of Dr. Howard Rusk and Dr. Henry Kessler, particularly, in the Air Force and the Navy, are now facts of history." The two of them recognized "...the potentialities of what could be accomplished through the mobilization of all that could be brought to bear for the disabled veteran."[17]

It was also in her role with the Procurement and Assignment Board that Mary Switzer was able to forge strong ties to medicine, which would serve her well later in her career as the head of a federal agency. Despite her differences of opinion with the AMA over the desirability of National Health Insurance, Mary became a close colleague of many AMA leaders in this period. During her work with Josephine Roche, Mary had become a strong advocate for some type of national health program to assure that all Americans obtained needed healthcare. The AMA had created insurmountable obstacles to that program in her opinion. But, progressive and pragmatist that she was, Mary decided to work with the AMA to achieve whatever progress was possible toward improving access to health care for Americans.[18]

The War Procurement and Assignment Board (the Board) was charged by Presidential Executive Order with assessing the military need for health professionals and obtaining their assignment to the necessary branches of the military, as well as assuring a continued adequate supply of health professionals in civilian facilities. The Board "...recognized that active rehabilitation could help relieve the civilian manpower shortage."[19] This was a major victory for rehabilitation, which was only in a formative stage. It was also an early recognition of the value a person with a disability brought to the private sector. This policy of participation by disabled persons in the civilian workforce during wartime would be emphasized by Dr. Arthur Fleming, Chair of the Board during the Korean War. The mission of the Board involved the first program for planning the distribution of health professionals to assure adequate health care for not only the military serving in a war effort, but also for the civilian population (which was essential to support the war effort through its productivity). The Chairman of the Board was the distinguished surgeon Dr. Frank Lahey, a former President of the AMA and the founder of one of the nation's great medical clinics, the Lahey Clinic in Massachusetts. Lahey was also a friend of Dr. Rusk, although he advised Rusk at the end of the war to return to internal medicine where he belonged. Two years later, Lahey admitted his advice was erroneous and personally discovered the value of Rusk's rehabilitation approach to medical problems.[20]

The Board proved very successful at planning and meeting the needs of the military for healthcare personnel. Medicine, nursing, physical therapy and occupational therapy were all cooperative with this effort. Mary Switzer was the key federal bureaucrat responsible for the execution of the program. She developed a close relationship with Morris Fishbein, MD, Editor of JAMA and an AMA leader. The cooperation of the AMA in the war effort convinced Mary that government and AMA cooperation was possible in peacetime planning around a national civilian health program.[21]

Mary Switzer was also involved with another wartime effort that affected rehabilitation in general, and rehabilitation medicine in particular. As Assistant to Administrator McNutt of the Federal Security Agency, she was McNutt's line of ongoing communication with both the Public Health Service, (where she had worked before her assignment to the Administrators Office), and the Office of Vocational Rehabilitation (OVR). Her close friend Tracy Copp, one of the top staff members in the OVR, kept Mary briefed on all issues affecting vocational rehabilitation. One of the key war related issues was the responsibility for the rehabilitation of wounded members of the military. This same issue had arisen during World War I. The Veterans agency (VA) asserted full responsibility for care of these personnel, but the military branches were unwilling to rely on the VA to carry out this role, since the soldiers were still "on duty." The military also believed the VA was unable to deal with the badly war wounded. The military won this battle among bureaucracies during World War II and Drs. Rusk and Kessler proceeded with their excellent rehabilitation programs in the Army Air Force and Navy. It was also true that during the war the VA had far fewer capable physicians and other health professionals than did the military.[22]

Once the wounded were discharged and became civilians, the responsibility for their medical care and rehabilitation was even more unclear. The vocational rehabilitation program had asserted it should have that mission but the VA disagreed. The vocational rehabilitation program was disadvantaged in this dispute because it had no legal authority under the Rehabilitation Act to provide medical services for the rehabilitation of disabled persons. This problem needed to be addressed regardless of the veterans' needs, since vocational rehabilitation for employment clearly involved medical services as well as job training and placement. The ultimate solution to this problem in 1943 would directly affect the development of rehabilitation medicine.

Before the outbreak of World War II, Federal Security Agency Administrator Paul McNutt had been prescient in his interest in better cooperation between the Public Health Service, the OVR, and the Labor Department employment service relative to the rehabilitation and employment of persons with disabilities. In anticipation of the possible outbreak of war, he was concerned with the ability of the government to fully utilize persons with disabilities in the war effort, including employment in civilian industries crucial to that effort. When the USA entered the war after Pearl Harbor, Mary Switzer urged McNutt to request a national conference on civilian rehabilitation and the war effort. No President had ever called for a national conference on rehabilitation or disability, so that alone was noteworthy for the development of the field of rehabilitation. Roosevelt, who was well aware of the value of rehabilitation from his own experience with the Warm Springs rehabilitation program, readily agreed.

The conference was held on December 22, 1941. Those present included representatives of the War, Navy and Labor Departments, the Public Health Service, Veterans Administration, and the Vocational Rehabilitation Office. The conference raised many issues, which were referred to the President for action. Among them was the question of which agency, the VA or the OVR, would be responsible for the vocational rehabilitation of veterans disabled during combat and unable to return to duty. This question involved whether the current vocational rehabilitation program had the authority to provide medical care as a part of a rehabilitation program for discharged war wounded or civilians. In choosing between the VA and OVR, there was also a choice between a program operated directly by a federal agency (the VA program), or a joint federal and state program such as Vocational Rehabilitation. The OVR had already taken the political initiative and drafted a bill, which made it an independent office in the Federal Security agency. The bill also separated the Office of Vocational Rehabilitation from the Education Board, authorized more money for the program, and made the program responsible for war casualties. Mary Switzer and Tracy Copp had produced this draft. Interestingly, the bill did not mention coverage of medical rehabilitation services.[23]

The outcome of the conference was the creation by President Roosevelt of a Committee to recommend legislation authorizing and funding a national rehabilitation program for veterans and civilians with disabilities. The field of rehabilitation medicine could not have asked for more, although it is unclear that its leaders even knew this activity was occurring (based on their own accounts and those of others during this time). On the Committee was Colonel John Smith, the Director of the Institute for Crippled and Disabled (ICD) in New York City, which Jeremiah Milbank had established in 1917. Smith and his predecessor, MacMurtrie, had both been advocating for expanded national rehabilitation services with an emphasis on medical approaches. By 1942, when the Committee started its work, Dr. George Deaver was the Medical Director of the ICD and the Institute was renowned for its medical and vocational rehabilitation services to severely disabled patients. The Committee recommended, and President Roosevelt approved, legislation making the OVR independent within the Federal Security Agency; providing authority for both civilians and veterans with disabilities to be served by the OVR; and authorizing the OVR to deliver rehabilitation medicine and other medical services to veterans and civilians with disabilities. The new program was to be a mix of federal and state responsibilities, with the federal agency having the authority to contract for necessary services; except for vocational training, which state vocational rehabilitation offices would control.[24]

All seemed well at this point for the creation of a program according to the Administration's wishes. But the process required new legislative authority and therefore Congress became involved. The Congress of 1940 was a more conservative one than its immediate predecessors and more independent of the President. The President had responded to the 1938 Congressional elections, which created a more conservative Congress, by deciding not to press for either national health insurance or disability insurance. In this instance, with regard to rehabilitation, he took a more assertive position in another controversial area.

While Congress considered legislation regarding the rehabilitation of both disabled veterans and civilians in 1942, the leadership of the federal vocational rehabilitation program faced demands for service veterans disabled in battle and the need to provide civilian manpower for positions necessary to the war effort. But the agency had been very little noticed and its budget and staffing were limited. In addition, the agency had no authority to provide the medical services necessary for rehabilitation, and it had no authority to serve the blind, mentally ill, or mentally retarded applicants for service. (Please note that these medical terms are being used because they are historically accurate. They are not meant to be politically incorrect or to disagree with the more modern terminology.) The agency had allowed four states to provide medical services in 1942 as a demonstration of the value and need of the services; but there was a need for national authority as the President's Committee had recognized. The President's Committee had focused on some, but not all of these problems in its report submitted to Congress by the President. The National Rehabilitation Association, formed in 1925, joined the Administration in lobbying for the necessary legislation. A bill was soon introduced by Senator LaFollette of Wisconsin, and Congressman Barden of North Carolina to achieve the Administration's program.[25]

The President's Committee had fashioned legislation, which created an independent vocational rehabilitation agency reporting directly to the Administrator of the Federal Security Agency. This was a unified federally controlled program to serve veterans and civilians with the authority to provide medical and surgical services related to the rehabilitation of persons with a disability. The bill provided more extensive authority for the rehabilitation program than the bill drafted by Mary Switzer and Tracy Copp for the OVR, as it included extensive medical services among those the program could provide. It also created an integrated program for veterans and civilians. The OVR draft had not extended coverage of rehabilitation services to medical services, and seemingly left to the VA the authority to provide the medical services to veterans.

Interest group politics began in earnest as Congress considered this bill. The veterans groups opposed the unified program concept and urged a separate program for veterans. They supported the expansion of a civilian program in OVR, but the veterans were intent on having a veterans' agency be responsible for all veterans' needs. They did not want veterans to have to compete within the same agency for resources regarding the needs of the civilian disability population. The state offices of vocational rehabilitation and their staffs objected to the lack of state involvement in managing the new program proposed by the President's Committee, although not objecting to its expansion to cover veterans. The organizations for the blind were persistent in advocating for a separate program for the blind. The end result of this interest group pressure was, as it usually is, an attempt to balance all the political interests. Everyone got some aspect of what they wished. The Administration bill was changed substantially regarding the unified program in OVR for veterans and civilians. The new compromise bills were managed successfully in the House by Congressman Larrabee (Indiana), and Barden (North Carolina); and in the Senate by Senator Robert La Follette (Wisconsin). La Follette was the son of "Fighting Bob" La Follette, Governor and Senator from Wisconsin in the early nineteen hundreds and a leader of the Progressive political movement of 1890 to 1920.[26]

On July 6, 1943, President Roosevelt signed into law the Barden-La Follette Act, Public Law 113. The Act made the OVR separate from the Board of Education and established a direct reporting line for OVR to the Administrator of its parent agency, the Federal Security Agency. The law authorized the furnishing of corrective surgery or therapeutic services to alleviate or reduce a physical disability that constituted an impediment to employment, and it covered 90 days of hospitalization related to the surgery or medical therapeutic service. As Edward Berkowitz has described it: "The law permanently altered rehabilitation. . . . The law permitted a national medical attack on the problem of disability by allowing the federal government to subsidize medical service."[27] The program was, however, controlled largely by the states, although functioning with federal funds and under federal guidelines. It has continued to function this way for the past 60 plus years. The law did not create a uniform program for veterans and civilians who had disabilities. The veterans' groups got their way regarding having a separate program for medical care for veterans. Public Law 16, the companion legislation to P.L.113, was enacted and placed responsibility for the program of medical and rehabilitation services for veterans with the Veterans Administration. Senator Tom Clark of Missouri said on the Senate floor that he had never seen the veterans' organizations so worked up as they were over the proposal to "pitchfork it [veteran's services] into a general scheme for social rehabilitation affecting all the people in the United States."[28] The organizations for the blind were also successful in establishing their own program for rehabilitation of persons with visual impairment in the Barden-LaFollette Act. The Act was also expanded to include coverage of services to the mentally ill and retarded citizens, thus closing a serious eligibility gap in the civilian rehabilitation program.[29]

Mary Switzer and her colleague Tracy Copp had labored hard to create this landmark legislation, which raised the status of rehabilitation in the federal government and expanded the scope of its services and clientele. It established the rehabilitation program of OVR as one of the comprehensive rehabilitation services. Switzer and Copp were convinced that the most important aspect of the legislation was getting the OVR removed from the bureaucratic limitations of the Board of Education and giving it an independent status within the Federal Security Agency. Mary would come to lead this agency some seven years later.

Ironically, Congress reversed this structural change in 1980 and removed the Office of Vocational Rehabilitation (now called the Rehabilitation Services Administration) from the successor to the Federal Security Board, the Department of Health, Education and Welfare. The Rehabilitation Services Administration (RSA) was placed in the new Department of Education. Switzer's view that rehabilitation had to be independent of Education was essentially disregarded in 1980.

The two new laws, P.L.113 and P.L.16, enabled the new programs of inpatient rehabilitation for active duty soldiers established in the military health systems by Rusk and Kessler to be maintained; and new programs in the OVR and VA to be implemented for both disabled veterans and civilians. The powerful new mandate to the VA would result in the nation's first major inpatient hospital system integrating academic medicine and health care for veterans, including a major rehabilitation medicine service. The expansion of funding and services in the Barden-LaFollette Act of 1943 established mechanisms, which a decade later would support the creation of medical rehabilitation facilities, provide medical rehabilitation services to disabled people, and stimulate research and teaching programs. The opposition of medicine to the establishment of federal programs to pay for medical services to civilians had been overcome by the use of states as the administrative agencies. Despite the national commitment to medical rehabilitation that these two new laws represented, no planning had occurred to prepare the rehabilitation medicine community for its enhanced roles. At this point, Bernard Baruch, with an exquisite sense of timing, entered the rehabilitation medicine equation and used his influence and wealth to create a national plan for rehabilitation medicine to meet the needs of veterans and civilians, as well as a national philanthropic agency to assist in its development.

BERNARD BARUCH AND THE BARUCH COMMITTEE

Bernard Baruch had served as Advisor to President Wilson and Chair of Wilson's War Mobilization Board during World War I. He had also served in advisory roles to President Roosevelt on economic matters and maintained an interest in not only the defense of the nation, but also its economy and social structure. His biographer, James Grant, referred to Baruch during the FDR administration as an "eminence grise." He was viewed by many as actually running the administration from without. A dedicated Democrat, he had given FDR $250,000 for his campaign in 1932, an amount that would be the equivalent of many millions of dollars in campaign gifts today. FDR was often Baruch's guest at his famed Hobcaw Barony, a large plantation on the South Carolina shore. The vast estate included sandy beaches, beautiful salt marshes, four rivers and was a perfect place to obtain needed rest. At the height of the War effort and of negotiations with Churchill and Stalin regarding an end to the war in 1944, FDR spent a month at Hobcaw. Roosevelt referred to this vacation in his correspondence to Harry Hopkins: "I really had a grand time at Bernie's." He went on about reminiscing with Baruch of their years working in politics and government during the Wilson administration.[30] Despite these connections and being only 62 years old when FDR's administration began, Baruch never received a cabinet position. Speculation has it that his vast wealth and power was not viewed as an asset for a cabinet position in this Democratic administration, especially during a depression. He was also known as a man of very strong convictions, self-confidence and ego who might be difficult to control if he disagreed with presidential policy. He did serve in many advisory positions for FDR including Chair of the Defense Coordinating Board prior to the War. He was appointed as the Czar to solve the rubber crisis during the war. He was also offered the position of head of the Office of Economic Stabilization and of the War Production Board, but turned down both. He turned down the latter due to health problems. Baruch had also developed close relationships with members of Congress. He had a direct line to many important Senators and Congressmen, including the Chair of the Senate Finance Committee, and Senator James Byrnes of South Carolina (who became Secretary of State in the Truman administration). He often testified before Congress and its Committees on economic and defense matters.[31]

Baruch's closest friends in the President's family and cabinet were Eleanor Roosevelt, whose social causes he gave to liberally and Frances Perkins, the Secretary of Labor with whom he kept in very close touch. Baruch was very conscious of social problems and eager to apply America's resources to solve them, at least if the solutions were consistent with strengthening the nation and its economy. In 1945, he recommended a national health insurance program, and gave substantial sums to the Arthurdale project of Eleanor Roosevelt which provided health care, rehabilitation, and cash support to disabled miners. Mary Switzer was a member of the Arthurdale Committee representing the Social Security Administration and the Public Health Service, although it is not clear whether Baruch knew her. In his later years, Baruch clearly reflected his father's values and commitment to improve the lot of his fellow Americans who were in need.[32]

In 1943, Baruch launched what would be his monument to the memory of his father and his lasting commitment to medical care and rehabilitation medicine. Motivated by a concern for the need to have appropriate care for returning veterans and for the memory of his father (whom he viewed as a pioneer in medical therapy for persons with disabilities), Baruch established a Blue Ribbon Panel to plan for the expansion of physical medicine and rehabilitation services, research and training. The timing of this effort was perfect as the War was demonstrating the importance of rehabilitating wounded soldiers. In discussing this project with Frank Krusen, Baruch said that he wanted "...to make a comprehensive study of the whole subject..." of rehabilitation medicine. "I can't help but feel it will be one of the most useful ways of restoring our wounded soldiers to normal life. I have seen disabled people who never expected to walk again do so after rehabilitation and the sight of their joy is something to behold."[33] Baruch donated over a million dollars to the Committee to implement its well-documented recommendations. He was aware of the progress in rehabilitation in the military and particularly of Rusk's programs in the Army Air Force. In his usual fashion, he wanted a thorough and expeditious report to be finished by early 1944, three months after the first meeting of the Committee. The report was to serve as a guide for the development of a field of medical care to provide rehabilitative services to persons with disabilities (civilians and veterans), and to support the training of professionals to provide quality care and research to enhance it.

The prestige and political power of Baruch and the members of the Committee presaged the effectiveness of its work. Baruch selected Dr. Ray Lyman Wilbur, Past President of the AMA and Chancellor of Stanford, to chair the Committee. Wilbur had chaired the AMA Committee on the Cost of Medical Care in the late 1920s. Wilbur was the most prestigious physician in the country at the time. His willingness to serve was evidence of Baruch's stature and of the growing importance of rehabilitation medicine in the opinion of national leaders.

Baruch selected Frank Krusen as Executive Secretary and primary organizer of the Committee. He was aware of Krusen's work in physical medicine and of his textbook on the subject. The textbook included a chapter on hydrology and hydrotherapy, and Baruch's father was one of the first experts on these two subjects. There is very little in the history of the Committee's formation or work that would explain precisely why Krusen was chosen by Baruch, but the reasons were most likely his vast writing on the topic of physical medicine (especially hydrology), and his activity within the AMA. Probably only John Coulter knew as much about physical medicine and its' potential, and had been involved as long in supporting physical medicine and rehabilitation concepts and programs. It is also likely that Wilbur may have known of Krusen and his expertise from Krusen's AMA activity, and from seeking AMA advice on appointments to the Committee. Krusen took leave from his position at the Mayo Clinic to carry out this assignment with the Committee. He served as a member of the Committee, its Executive Secretary, organizer, and Chair of two its Subcommittees. The mission of the Committee was "...to make a study of the use of physical procedures in care of the sick, identify medical school programs most likely to advance physical medicine through teaching, research and clinical services and to give particular attention to ways in which physical medicine could contribute maximally to the care of injured soldiers and sailors."[34]

The Committee was made up of 40 outstanding teachers, scientists and practitioners of medicine and engineering. Some, but not all, had experience in rehabilitation medicine. The membership of the Committee included Dr. Alan Gregg, Medical Director of the Rockefeller Foundation; Dr. Morris Fishbein from the AMA and Editor of the AMA Journal; Drs. Rusk, Coulter, and Deaver; and faculty from many of the finest medical schools in the country. These included Harvard, Yale, Columbia, Washington University in St. Louis, Northwestern, the University of Texas and Stanford. Engineering was also represented with scientists from MIT participating. The Committee established subcommittees for public relations chaired by Dr. Wilbur, teaching chaired by Dr. Krusen, basic and clinical research chaired by Dr. Coulter, rehabilitation services (which included Dr. Rusk) and other representatives of the military programs, prevention and body mechanics, occupational therapy and hydrology. The Hydrology Subcommittee included representatives of the three large hydrology programs: Saratoga Springs New York, Hot Springs Arkansas, and FDR's Warm Springs Georgia.[35]

The Committee labored hard and Dr. Krusen energetically coordinated its efforts, traveling 40,000 miles between October 1943 and October 1944 to consult with Committee members and to discuss physical medicine and reha-bilitation with academic and clinical experts. The Committee heard testimony from or consulted with more than 400 scientists. By the end of January in 1944, as Bernard Baruch had directed, his Committee presented its report and recommendations to him and to the nation. The report defined physical med-icine as: "The employment of the physical and other effective properties of light, heat, cold, water electricity, massage, manipulation, exercise and me-chanical devices for physical and occupational therapy in the diagnosis or treatment of disease." Rehabilitation was: "The restoration of people handi-capped by disease, injury or malformation as nearly as possible to a normal physical and mental state."[36] Rehabilitation was the goal of a process includ-ing physical medicine and other interventions such as vocational rehabilita-tion, psychological and social services. The report also noted that physical medicine was not just focused on rehabilitation, but was also a preventive medical approach to diseases such as joint and muscle conditions. It was rec-ommended for use in geriatrics and for rheumatic diseases. The report indi-cated that the field of physical medicine and rehabilitation services should be under medical supervision, recognizing, however, that many of the services were furnished by other trained professionals such as physical and occupa-tional therapists.

The report was quite clear that physical medicine was a strictly medical service. While physical medicine included a broad array of physical agents and interventions, it was narrower than rehabilitation, which included many other services and was the goal for all of those services. The Committee did not focus on the other services necessary for rehabilitation of persons with disabilities. There were no Subcommittees on, nor sections in the Report re-garding vocational rehabilitation, psychological or other mental health ser-vices, or social work and its services. This was 1943 and the concepts of re-habilitation medicine and comprehensive rehabilitation had not been developed. Rusk, Kessler and Deaver were working on them, but they were not yet established.

The Report was clear that physical medicine should include all physical agents, physical therapy, occupational therapy, prosthetic and orthotic de-vices, and the use of other medical equipment. All were part of necessary medical care and essential to the goal of rehabilitation. The final report recommended "rehabilitation service centers," which should provide both medical and vocational rehabilitation services. It was clear that the Committee wanted to encompass vocational training and job placement as part of the rehabilitation program it was recommending. It did not, however, refer to psychological or social services as part of rehabilitation. In subsequent discussions with Dr. Rusk, Baruch indicated that he quite clearly viewed the area of mental health services as outside the gambit of his conception of physical medicine and rehabilitation. Rusk disagreed with that perspective and told Baruch so. Debates on the scope and focus of physical medicine and rehabilitation as well as the requirement of medical supervision of all services in medical settings would continue for the next 60 years.[37]

The Baruch Committee Report was primarily focused on persons with disabilities and their needs and secondarily on the need for highly trained professionals in physical medicine to serve disabled people. It began with a statement of the problem with which the report was concerned and noted that in 1940, before the USA entered World War II, about four million people had permanent disabilities and that annually 800,000 people became either partially or totally disabled. It also noted that this number would increase dramatically as a result of the war. The Report observed that there was little research being done in the field of physical medicine, and that a need existed for the integration of basic and clinical research in physical medicine at academic medical centers. The Report cited little teaching of physicians in physical medicine, too few professionals in rehabilitation disciplines generally, and few if any civilian rehabilitation medicine service programs. The Committee specifically recommended the establishment of the following programs to meet these needs:

- Teaching and research centers in physical medicine at academic medical centers, and research in physical medicine and rehabilitation in medical schools.
- Residencies and fellowships in physical medicine and rehabilitation in medical schools.
- Training programs for rehabilitation professionals.
- Wartime and civilian medical rehabilitation service programs.
- Integrated centers of both medical and vocational rehabilitation services to deliver services in all sectors.
- A Board of Physical Medicine to examine and certify members of the specialty under the aegis of the AMA.

- Cooperation between labor, industry and medicine to assure understanding of the need for services to persons with disabilities and the methods to provide them.[38]

Bernard Baruch was a man of action and organization, and he wasted little time in setting in place funds and programs to implement the recommendations. He had directed the successful national effort to mobilize American industry for World War I and the rubber industry for World War II. He made over a million dollars available to the Committee under the leadership of Drs. Wilbur and Krusen to fund academic medical centers; and additional funds to directly support fellowships in medicine for individuals interested in physical medicine and rehabilitation. The following medical centers received large grants for research and training programs in 1944:

- Columbia University under the direction of Dr. Robert Darling received $400,000 to establish model teaching and research programs, which focused on undergraduate teaching programs in physical therapy and occupational therapy; and research on the effects of temperature in metabolic change and the use of radioactive isotopes in treatment.
- New York University under the direction of Dr. Deaver received $250,000 to establish training in physical medicine, physical therapy and occupational therapy; and to undertake research to measure gains in function for persons with spinal injury and cardiac disability.
- The Medical College of Virginia in Richmond, the medical school from which Baruch's father had graduated, received $250,000 to study hydrology, electrical stimulation therapy and the impact of muscle atrophy on protein levels.
- MIT received a grant to study bioengineering.
- Harvard received a grant to assess the chemical and behavioral aspects of fatigue attendant to disability.
- The University of Minnesota received a grant to establish a training program in physical medicine and a lab to study biophysics, both headed by Dr. Miland Knapp.
- The University of Southern California received a grant to study muscular and neuromuscular disability, including the use of x-rays to study muscle movement and regeneration of neuromuscular pathways.

Other grants were made to the State University of Iowa College of Medicine, Marquette University, Washington University in St. Louis, George Washington University in the nation's capital, and the University of Illinois.

Grants were made between 1944 and 1946 to about 40 hospitals to establish residencies or fellowship programs in physical medicine. These hospitals included four military hospitals and ten Veterans Administration hospitals (which is about the total number of hospitals that the VA then operated). The Committee funded at least 57 individual fellowships of established physicians to train them further in physical medicine and rehabilitation. These individuals would in later years be referred to as the "Baruch Fellows."[39]

It is remarkable that many of the academic institutions receiving the initial Baruch research and training grants still have major programs in physical medicine and rehabilitation. It is also remarkable that training programs still exist in the majority of the hospitals that received Baruch grants to establish these training programs. The constancy of the programs in some institutions throughout the past 60 years, despite the myriad of changes those years have wrought in healthcare and in education and research, is quite extraordinary. Major research in rehabilitation medicine has been undertaken since 1943 at Columbia, NYU, Virginia Commonwealth University and M.I.T. Training programs and fellowships were established at many institutions which have been leaders in physical medicine and rehabilitation during the past 60 years including the Mayo Clinic, NYU, Columbia, and Harvard The constancy and continued leadership of these programs is a tribute to the thoughtfulness and skill of the Committee and particularly of Baruch, Wilbur and Krusen.

The impact of the Committee Report can also be seen in the development of the medical rehabilitation service programs of the VA. The VA was a leader in medical care throughout the 1950s and 1960s. Continued assistance to implement the recommendations of the Report for rehabilitation medicine services and facilities was also provided by the philanthropic community for at least 30 years. The Foundation for Infantile Paralysis (March of Dimes), Easter Seal Society and the Kaiser Family were major supporters of rehabilitation medicine during this period. The Committee also sought to define physical medicine and rehabilitation and in doing so, the Committee guided the development of rehabilitation medicine for many years. World War II was generating a demand for this broader field of medical care and creating models for it. Physical medicine was a known medical term in 1943 but rehabilitation medicine was not. The military programs started by Drs. Kessler and Rusk in World War II, and Drs. Monk, Coulter, Albee, and Goldthwaite in World War I were not only physical medicine services. In World War II in particular the programs were broad multidisciplinary services offered by physicians (not necessarily physical medicine specialists only), physical therapists, occupational therapists, nurses, psychologists and vocational rehabilitation training and job placement experts. In many amputee clinics, such as the one Dr. Kessler established on Mare Island, the service included prosthetists developing and then fitting artificial limbs. These services were offered on prescription by a physician and under the general overview of the physician attending the patient.

Bernard Baruch continued to be involved in rehabilitation medicine and physical medicine after the Report was submitted and the grants made. In fact the Committee stayed in existence until 1951 with Frank Krusen as chair. Dr. Krusen succeeded Dr. Wilbur as Chair in 1947 after Wilbur's death. It is likely that Krusen saw the continuation of the Committee as a good way to keep Baruch, the invaluable statesman, involved with the field. Baruch did stay involved and advocated with General Omar Bradley, the administrator of a newly invigorated Veterans Administration, to use his Committee's report as a guide for the development of inpatient medical rehabilitation services in the VA. Later in the 1940s Baruch would intervene to assist Krusen with the AMA leadership in the effort to achieve recognition of Physical Medicine and Rehabilitation as a medical specialty. He would also use his relationship with President Eisenhower to keep the AMA from tearing asunder what it had created as a recognized field of medicine in 1952. With the election of President Truman in 1948, Baruch was assigned his most formidable challenge, Ambassador to the UN for Atomic Energy and its work to preserve peace and prevent nuclear calamity. He was 78 years old at the time and still vigorous. His influence on this topic was recognized in the recent Pulitzer Prize winning biography of J. Robert Oppenheimer, even though Oppenheimer did not agree with Baruch's approach to the issue of control of atomic energy. In the late 1940s and 1950s Baruch assisted Dr. Rusk in the development of his inpatient rehabilitation facilities in New York City.[40]

A small, but highly symbolic memorial to Bernard Baruch exists in Lafayette Park across from the White House in Washington, D.C. It is not one of the statutes which adorn the many parks of the nation's capital. It is appropriately a plaque set in the ground to the north of the immediate center of the Park by the park bench on which Baruch would sit for hours pondering the problems of our government and advising his many friends who were in critical positions in the cabinets of Roosevelt, Truman and Eisenhower. Baruch was likewise always available to use his influence with the nation's leaders for research, education and the provision of services in the field of rehabilitation medicine, as well as for the medical specialty of physical medicine and rehabilitation.

NOTES

1. Ludmerer, 134.

2. Ludmerer, 123–134; Starr, 310–320.

3. Ludmerer, 133.

4. Gritzer and Arluke, 89–90; Murphy, *Healing The Generations,* 105–110.

5. Opitz and DePompolo, 30–31; Robison, 95–98.

6. *Ibid*; Murphy, *Healing the Generations*, 107.

7. Rusk, 49–54.

8. Smith, *FDR*, 546–47.

9. Rusk, 4–23.

10. Rusk, 59–64, 69–82.

11. Rusk, 64–80.

12. Rusk, 60–62.

13. Kessler, 106–124; correspondence John Ditunno to author December 4, 2006.

14. Kessler, *The Knife Is Not Enough*, 127.

15. Kessler, 111–12; Rusk, 104–106.

16. Kottke and Knapp, Arch Phys Med Rehabil, vol. 69, 4; Rusk, 87–90.

17. Switzer, "Some of the Great Ones," Rehabilitation Record, May and June, 1970, 1–7.

18. Walker, 95–98.

19. Kottke and Knapp, Arch Phys Med Rehabil, vol. 69, 4.

20. Walker, 97; Rusk, 156–157.

21. Walker, 95–97.

22. Gritzer and Arluke, 92–94.

23. Berkowitz, 98–101; Walker, 103.

24. Gritzer and Arluke, 92.

25. Gritzer and Arluke, 91–92.

26. Berkowitz, 99–103; *50 Years of Rehabilitation in the U.S.A., 1920 to 1970*, 10–12; Gritzer and Arluke, 92.

27. Berkowitz, 103.

28. Berkowitz, 102.

29. Gritzer and Arluke, 92–93; *50 Years of Rehabilitation in the U.S.A., 1920 to 1970*, 12; Berkowitz, 101–104.

30. Smith, *FDR*, 606–607.

31. Grant, Bernard Baruch, *The Adventures Of A Wall Street Legend,* 247, 261 *et seq.*

32. Grant, ibid ;Walker, 84.

33. Robison, 101–102.

34. Kottke and Knapp, Arch Phys Med Rehabil, vol. 69, 9; Opitz *et al.*, Krusen Diaries, Arch Phys Med Rehabil, vol. 78, 446–47.

35. Opitz *et al.*, Krusen Diaries, Arch Phys Med Rehabil, vol. 78, 447; Kottke and Knapp, ibid.

36. Ibid.

37. Ibid; Kottke and Knapp, Arch Phys Med Rehabil, vol. 69, 9; Gritzer and Ar-luke, 94.

38. Ibid.

39. Opitz *et al.*, Krusen Diaries, ibid; Kottke and Knapp, ibid.

40. Opitz *et al.*, Krusen Diaries, Arch Phys Med Rehabil, vol. 78, 563; Rusk, 141; Kai Bird and Martin Sherwin, *American Prometheus, J. Robert Oppenheimer*, Vintage Books, 2005, 342–347.

Chapter Seven

The Immediate Postwar Years: The VA, Private Rehabilitation Facilities, Unions, and a Medical Specialty in PM&R

Writing of the development of rehabilitation medicine in 1969, Howard Rusk explained: "It is paradoxical that through war, a concerted effort to annihilate man, we have learned more and better ways to preserve him. Rehabilitation medicine in its modern concept was conceived in adversity and born of necessity in World War II."[1] A tremendous amount of knowledge had been gained during World War II about effective medical care and rehabilitation for the wounded soldier. It was common knowledge, however, that the VA medical care system available to veterans after World War II was not equipped to meet their needs.

At the war's end in 1945, there was no rehabilitation service available in the hospitals of the Veterans Administration. This was true despite the major White House sponsored Conference on Rehabilitation in 1940; and Public Law 16 which included new VA authority for medical rehabilitation of veterans. The Act specified that the VA would be responsible for the returning veterans with disabilities and their rehabilitation. President Truman, who succeeded President Roosevelt upon his death in 1945, was to make changes to remedy this problem.

Using the recommendations of the Baruch Committee, with Rusk and Krusen as consultants, and under leadership of Dr. Paul Magnuson of Northwestern University, the Veterans Administration began expanding its healthcare and rehabilitation services in the late 1940s. The VA health care system became the first large scale, national hospital program to include rehabilitation medicine in the United States in peacetime. The system was one that served only veterans, but its existence was a model for the civilian healthcare system. Since all VA hospitals were linked to academic medical centers, the VA program also stimulated research and training. The Baruch Committee recommendations and influence also stimulated the development of civilian centers based on the military and VA models, as well as the creation of a recognized medical specialty in the field of physical medicine and rehabilitation.

THE VETERANS ADMINISTRATION HOSPITALS AND REHABILITATION

President Franklin Delano Roosevelt died on April 12, 1945, at 3:35 PM, in Warm Springs, Georgia, where he was staying for rest and relaxation. He had been ill for more than a year before his death, having been diagnosed during 1944 by his cardiologist, Dr. Howard Bruen, as having serious heart disease and hypertension. He died suddenly, most likely of a cerebral hemorrhage, while his portrait was being painted by Elizabeth Shoumatoff.[2] At the time of his death, the *New York Times* editorialized that: "Men will thank God on their knees a hundred years from now that Franklin D. Roosevelt was in the White House." Former Missouri Senator Harry Truman succeeded him as President, after serving only three months as Vice President. The war was winding down to a close on at least the European Front. Germany surrendered in May 1945 and Truman traveled to Potsdam to discuss the wars end and the peace in Europe with Joseph Stalin and Winston Churchill. With him was General Omar Bradley, whom Truman had also assigned the task of reorganizing the Veterans Administration. Truman invited Howard Rusk to join the group for the Potsdam trip, at least superficially for purpose of being available to render medical care to the Commanding General Hap Arnold of the Air Force who would be in the group. Rusk, then only 44, had been a friend of Truman's for some years as both were from Missouri. Rusk had maintained an interest in politics since the time that as a young man he assisted his father's campaign for local office. As Rusk described it in his autobiography:

> *With Japan's surrender in sight there was already much talk about reorganizing the Veterans Administration. . . . I had known Truman for a good many years and he apparently had confidence in me, because he called me in and told me he would like me to have a hand in whatever was done with the VA. He thought it would be a good idea for me to go to the Potsdam Conference with his entourage and though his real purpose was to get me to talk with General Bradley, who had been chosen to take charge of the VA, he suggested . . . I go as General Arnold's doctor.*[3]

General Arnold was the head of the Army Air Force, and Rusk knew him well as he worked for him in the past. He and Arnold agreed on a signal for the time when either Rusk felt Arnold should leave a meeting for his health, or when Arnold wanted to be called away from a meeting due to boredom. After about 10 days at Potsdam, President Truman called Dr. Rusk to the "Little White House," which had been set up at Potsdam. The purpose was to meet General Bradley and discuss the VA health care system. Rehabilitation medicine had reached its pinnacle of political influence, demonstrated by having a private meeting with the President who was a personal friend, and having a cabinet level leader in health care. Bradley was also from Missouri and he and Rusk hit it off well. Bradley told Rusk that he thought: "Rehabilitation would evidently be one of our biggest jobs." He also told him that he was bringing Dr. Hawley, his military medical officer, to Washington to be chief medical officer of the VA.[4]

Shortly after Dr. Rusk had returned home to Missouri and to civilian life in the Fall of 1945, he received a call from Dr. Hawley, then Medical Director of the VA, asking him to become a consultant to assist in the establishment of the VA rehabilitation program. Hawley also asked Dr. Krusen to be a consultant on rehabilitation. Krusen was at that time back at the Mayo Clinic from his stint in managing the Baruch Committee, but was still Chair of that Committee and its Executive Director. General Bradley, the VA Administrator, was a friend of Bernard Baruch's. He had stayed at Baruch's South Carolina barony, Hobcaw. He knew of the work of the Baruch Committee, which he was prepared to use in the development of the VA medical care system. The stage had certainly been set by President Truman for the development of the nation's first major inpatient rehabilitation service.[5]

Rusk later noted that the positive experience with rehabilitation during the war and the bold recommendations of the Baruch Committee Report for development of comprehensive rehabilitation facilities to serve disabled veterans provided the foundation for comprehensive medical rehabilitation in the VA hospitals. The fact that both Rusk and Krusen were VA consultants for the rehabilitation program also helped. Each VA hospital would have a comprehensive rehabilitation service, and Spinal Cord Injury Centers and major research and training programs in rehabilitation medicine would be developed.[6]

Perhaps even more significant than the consulting roles of Rusk and Krusen in the evolution of the VA to a system of excellent medical rehabilitation care was, in Rusk's words, the "...outstanding leadership of Paul Magnuson."[7] Magnuson was a well known and outspoken orthopedic surgeon who was at Northwestern Medical Center as Chief of Orthopedic Surgery in 1945. Like orthopedists Kessler and Albee, Magnuson had long been convinced by his own practice experience of the value of rehabilitation. He had first recognized the need for services to persons with disabilities as a medical student at the University of Pennsylvania in 1905, when the wife of his surgery professor and mentor, Dr. Willard, introduced him to the Widener Crippled Children's Home. The Widener facility sparked an "...interest in rehabilitation of the handicapped which has been a guiding light to me ever since." Magnuson said in his delightful autobiography *Ring the Night Bell*.[8] His practice in Chicago after medical school was a mix of research on surgical procedures and devices, including bone regeneration, and a workmens compensation practice that was very similar to that of Albee and Kessler in New Jersey.

Magnuson also served in World War I with Drs. Brackett and Goldwaite in the Office of Orthopedic Surgery. Brackett and Goldwaite oversaw the Army physical therapy service related to orthopedics during World War I. Magnuson had visited Canada in 1917 to view its medical care for returning veterans. He wrote a long letter to Brackett about the inadequacies of care in Canada, and the need for improvements by the USA in treating its veterans. This resulted in his call to service by Brackett. Magnuson served at the VA Hospital in Brookline, Massachusetts, but found it wanting. During this period he became aware of Dr. Coulter, who had worked with the physical therapy service in World War I. Sometime after the War, Magnuson brought Coulter to Northwestern to establish a medical service in physical therapy. Together with Dr. Loyal Davis, they wrote a text on fractures, which included sections on injuries to the nervous system and postoperative therapy.[9]

In 1939, as war encompassed parts of Eastern Europe, Dr. Magnuson, by then a prestigious Chair in Surgery at Northwestern, became disturbed by the possibility of returning veterans again failing to receive adequate medical care. He foresaw America's entrance into World War II before most Americans were of that mind, and it was fortuitous that he did. Magnuson was familiar with the Heinz VA General Hospital of 3253 beds in the Chicago area, with its Medical Department ". . . in a sad state of decay." The situation in the VA hospitals "...did not look good to me."[10] In addition, none of the VA hospitals were accredited by the AMA for residencies. Magnuson conceived of a solution and wrote the head of the VA, Brigadier General Hines. He recommended that all VA facilities be placed near, and have contractual arrangements with, good medical schools and teaching hospitals. This would provide them with excellent attending physicians and the necessary medical support in the form of residents. With this arrangement established, the VA hospital would become attractive for returning physicians, nurses and therapists. Magnuson got no response from Hines.[11]

When the war ended in 1945, Magnuson became irate again as he thought of what returning veterans would face in terms of medical care and rehabilitation. During the war he had been preoccupied with working on devices for veterans with amputations, as had Kessler. He now foresaw an ironic situation in which the United States was going to have a large number of returning physicians, nurses and therapists with no jobs and a large number of wounded veterans who badly needed the good medical care they could provide.

One of Magnuson's colleagues was Dr. Lionel Davis, who knew the new VA Medical Director Paul Hawley. They had served together in the Army. Davis thought Hawley a great Medical Administrator and urged Magnuson to talk with him about the VA. Magnuson dug out his 1939 proposal, and the three had dinner. Davis arranged for Magnuson and Hawley to discuss Magnuson's idea for VA hospital and medical school affiliation. Hawley dared Magnuson to come to Washington to put it into effect. Having seen the impact of bureaucracy on the VA healthcare system, Magnuson was skeptical that it could be done. He was persuaded later by General Omar Bradley himself that if he came to head this program, Bradley would back him to the hilt. And so began Paul Magnusson's career as a federal employee, during which time he earned Dr. Rusk's admiration for outstanding leadership in the VA, and for supporting the establishment of the nation's first system of comprehensive rehabilitation in non-military hospitals.[12]

Magnuson eventually became Medical Director of the VA, succeeding Hawley in 1948, but his first task in 1945 and 1946 as a VA employee was to get in place his concept of teaching hospitals being allied with the VA hospitals. He formed what became well known as the Dean's Committee, which was in charge of overseeing the network of medical schools and VA hospitals that was central to Magnuson's idea. He traveled many miles seeking the support of medical schools in selected urban areas for this concept of medical school and VA hospital affiliation. It was fortunate that the Baruch Committee had also recommended the development of rehabilitation medicine programs in all VA hospitals, and the support of academic research and training centers for physical medicine and rehabilitation research and training. In New York, Magnuson met with the Dean of the Columbia University Medical School, who coordinated a New York City VA medical school arrangement involving the many medical schools in the city. In Boston he met with the deans of Harvard, Tufts and Boston University medical schools. In San Francisco, he met with the medical school deans from Stanford, the University of California at Berkley, and the University California at San Francisco. In Chicago, he had the solid support of the city's medical schools, since he knew those deans well and had already discussed the concept with the dean at Northwestern. The idea of affiliation between a medical school and a government hospital was appealing to medical schools and its implementation worked smoothly. The system became a bellwether for the research and training programs of teaching hospitals and the VA hospitals became models for quality medical care.[13]

The specialty of physical medicine and rehabilitation was helped considerably by the increased impact of medical schools on the VA health care system. The VA was very interested in establishing rehabilitation programs in all VA hospitals. This was based on the positive experience of the military programs, the influence of the Baruch Committee recommendations for rehabilitation centers for veterans, and the roles of Rusk and Krusen in advising the VA about the need for rehabilitation medicine services. In a relatively short period of time all VA hospitals had rehabilitation services. The affiliation of medical schools with the VA hospitals permitted the training of physicians in physical medicine to take place in these rehabilitation programs and assured excellent training. By 1949 ten VA hospitals and four military hospitals had Physical Medicine and Rehabilitation residency training or fellowship programs, representing about one-third of the programs in the country. Dr. Ernest W. Johnson, one of the second generations of leaders in Physical Medicine and Rehabilitation and active in VA medical care, has emphasized the very important role of the VA in the development of rehabilitation medicine.[14]

THE DEVELOPMENT OF CIVILIAN REHABILITATION MEDICINE FACILITIES

Rehabilitation medicine is dependent on the availability of facilities to provide for inpatient care. Rehabilitation hospitals or centers arose during both World Wars as a response to the need for major post-surgical care for wounded soldiers and was principally inpatient in focus. The patients were sufficiently impaired and disabled even after surgery that discharge was impossible without a stay on an inpatient rehabilitation medicine service. The patient needed a rehabilitation physician to further attend to his or her post-surgical wounds and other medical problems, as well as to determine when and if the patient could tolerate the rehabilitation therapies which were necessary for physical and vocational rehabilitation. Rehabilitation medicine, as described to me by Dr. William Fowler, (former President of the Academy of Physical Medicine and Rehabilitation and leader of the field in the 1980s), was and still is a service focused on the severely disabled, and provided primarily in an inpatient setting. To quote from Dr. Fowler's history of Physical Medicine and Rehabilitation in California:

> *The 1940's brought the development and utilization of organized physical medicine and rehabilitation services and the expansion of medical practice from its focus on survival and relief from pain to the more comprehensive concept of restoration of the individual to optimum function. . . . During World War II, two groups of physicians developed along individual lines in physical medicine and rehabilitation. One group trained in or attracted to physical medicine comprised the membership of the Society of Physical Therapy Physicians and emphasized*

specific techniques. Physicians in the other group were recruited and trained in rehabilitation medicine in the military and Veterans Administration hospitals and emphasized the comprehensive management of the physically disabled. By 1949 the focus of Physical Medicine and Rehabilitation had changed from the restoration of the physically disabled and ambulation to the comprehensive restoration of these individuals to an optimum level of physical, mental, emotional, vocational and social function.[15]

Dr. Fowler cites for this description of the field the histories by Kottke, Knapp, Martin, Johnson, Gullickson, Granger and Ditunno in the Archives of Physical Medicine and Rehabilitation, 1988, special edition, volume 69.[16]

Rusk and Kessler both saw the need for a specialized inpatient facility, which offered the availability of a variety of health care services and vocational training to achieve the optimal function of the individual. They viewed vocational training not just as a way of making a person economically productive, but also as a therapeutic service which improved health care outcomes for patients. Krusen shared this view of the importance of vocational training and work in the medical care of patients. He had developed that view during his own stay in a sanitarium for treatment of tuberculosis. Organizing a system to effectively provide these many services to severely disabled individuals, who also typically had continuing acute care medical needs, was a challenge. It took physicians with commitment and boldness who were focused on making the various systems of healthcare respond to a need for specialized care facilities. Obviously, a facility that was part of an acute care hospital, or closely connected to one, was important. This usually allowed the patients to be transferred sooner from such facilities, allowing the medical rehabilitation process to start as early as possible. It was also advantageous because the patient might need additional acute medical care, which could better be provided in the acute facility.

Unfortunately, there were few private sector rehabilitation medicine facilities available in the 1940s for the severely disabled person injured on the job or in an automobile, or severely disabled by the effects of a disease such as polio. Rehabilitation medicine was consequently very inaccessible to civilians, and this also constrained the development of the field. Without more civilian facilities in which to provide services and train professionals, the field would forever be linked only to the victims of war. The best known comprehensive rehabilitation inpatient facility in the 1940s was the Institute for the Crippled and Disabled in New York City, whose medical director was George Deaver. The Physical Medicine Section of the Mayo Clinic Chaired by Krusen had an inpatient service at both St. Mary's Hospital and Rochester General Hospital. The inpatient service was headed by Earl Elkins, MD. Elkins was Krusen's first resident at Mayo, when he headed the outpatient service at a clinic on the Mayo campus next to the orthopedic outpatient clinic.[17]

The Baruch Committee focused on the need for more civilian facilities and recommended the creation of comprehensive facilities that would integrate the medical and vocational services. Unfortunately, the Committee did not have the financial wherewithal to fund service facilities in addition to the research and training programs it was funding.

The impetus for the development of private sector rehabilitation facilities came from the initiative of a number of very motivated physicians with the support of a number of philanthropists interested in rehabilitation medicine. Rusk and Kessler were perhaps the foremost, committed to establishing rehabilitation facilities to enable them to carry on their work in the civilian sector, which had been so productive during World War II. Both drew heavily on philanthropy for their successful civilian ventures. The Institute for Crippled and Disabled Adults had been established by Jeremiah Milbank and had drawn support from the Milbank family. Herman Kabat, a neurologist, founded the Kaiser Kabat Institute in Washington, D.C. with the financial and personal assistance of Henry Kaiser. He also established a number of inpatient and outpatient services in California as part of the Kaiser Permanente health care system in the late 1940s and into the 1950s. The facility at Santa Monica was a well known inpatient service which was directed in 1950 by Dr. Rene Cailliet, a physical medicine specialist who would become one of the nation's leaders in rehabilitation medicine and President of the American Congress of Rehabilitation Medicine in the early 1970s. Paul Magnuson followed this with a facility in Chicago in the early 1950s after his stint as Medical Director of the VA had ended.[18]

HOWARD RUSK AND NEW YORK UNIVERSITY

After World War II, Howard Rusk returned to Missouri to sort out his career options. As he described it in his autobiography, the choices were two: "Would I go back to St. Louis where a very comfortable established practice as an internist still awaited me? Or would I follow the uncharted course of rehabilitation in civilian life, where the concept of rehabilitation for the disabled was virtually unknown or unaccepted, even by the medical profession."[19] Luckily for Rusk, the field was not totally unknown in civilian life, in large part due to the work of the Baruch Committee and the recommendations of its prestigious report. Grants had been made by the Baruch Committee to a number of medical schools to develop training and research in rehabilitation medicine or physical medicine. One of those grants, for $250,000, was made to New York University (NYU) and its medical school. That grant would be the equivalent of two or three million dollars today. In March of 1945, Dean Donal Sheehan of NYU Medical School contacted Dr. Rusk and explained that he would like to use the Baruch funds to establish a Department of Physical Medicine and Rehabilitation at NYU medical school. NYU had affiliations with a number of teaching hospitals in New York City. Dean Sheehan, (a PhD) had written a book on the mission of a medical school, which had become the plan used for the NYU medical school. Sheehan knew about the rehabilitation medicine programs in the Army Air Force that were initiated by Rusk. According to Rusk, Dean Sheehan was a visionary and saw rehabilitation medicine as a great new field in healthcare. The Baruch Committee had, during its first years, changed its focus from physical medicine to physical medicine and rehabilitation, and the interest of Sheehan and many others after World War II was on the rehabilitation aspects.[20]

Rusk's own vision was to create an institute of rehabilitation medicine, which would be university-affiliated with patient care facilities and research and training programs. He believed he could have successfully established such an Institute himself in St. Louis. He realized, however, the need to connect such a facility with a large university to attain the needed academic programs. Rusk considered the offer of Dean Sheehan and also approached the faculty at Washington University Medical School about beginning a rehabilitation medicine program at Washington University. The University had also received a Baruch Committee grant, but it was far smaller than the one received by NYU. One of the leading professors on the faculty, Dr. Gregg, a Professor of Surgery, supported Dr. Rusk and his vision. Few others did, however, and in fact they considered his idea "Rusk's Folly."[21]

At this point Rusk went to New York to further consider the NYU position. While in New York, he discussed his career options with a number of prominent New Yorkers with whom he had become acquainted while in the military. During his experience in developing a program in Pawling, New York, Rusk and the military facility had attracted the interest of Arthur Hays Sulzberger, publisher of the New York Times. The two had become friends, and Rusk visited Sulzberger and described his vision for a rehabilitation institute and his options. Sulzberger shared Rusk's views about the value of rehabilitation and saw it as one of the few good things to come from war: An idea developed in wartime and necessary in peacetime for the civilian population. Sulzberger also saw the New York Times as "The greatest University in the United States" and suggested that Rusk come to New York to build his Institute and also to write a column for the Times on medicine and rehabilitation. Sulzberger was a trustee of Columbia University, and he sent Rusk there to present his idea; but the Columbia Medical School faculty was not very interested. Columbia had received a large Baruch Committee grant under the direction of Robert Darling, who became a renowned physical medicine and rehabilitation academic and researcher. Rusk next visited with Dr. Alan Gregg, who had been on the Baruch Committee with Rusk and Krusen and was a Vice President for Medical Affairs at the Rockefeller Foundation. Gregg recommended NYU to Rusk and was very partial to the vision and boldness of Dean Sheehan. At that point, Rusk had made up his mind. He would take the position at NYU, create a Department of Physical Medicine and Rehabilitation at the Medical School, and a rehabilitation institute if possible. He would also take Arthur Sulzberger up on his offer to write a medical column in the *New York Times*.[22]

Upon arriving at NYU in December 1945, Rusk persuaded George Deaver to join him and help build the Department at the medical school and a clinical program wherever they could get the space. Deaver was perhaps the first physician in medicine who had devoted full time to comprehensive rehabilitation medicine. He was viewed by Mary Switzer as one of the three great medical leaders in rehabilitation, together with Rusk and Kessler. He was also viewed by Drs. Kottke and Knapp in their history of PM&R as one of the early rehabilitation medicine pioneers. Deaver had initiated a program for the spinal cord injured, and the first assessment of daily living activity of persons with disabilities. Deaver and Rusk formed a great partnership, with Deaver focusing on the clinical and teaching matters, while Rusk spent much of his time selling the program and raising money for it. As Drs. Kottke and Knapp's wrote in their History of PM&R: "With Deaver's skills, knowledge and experience and Rusk's vision of the potential for comprehensive rehabilitation and his dynamic ability to convey his ideas and inspire people, the Institute of Rehabilitation Medicine at NYU-Bellevue became the bellwether of rehabilitation throughout the world."[23]

Rusk began his search for clinical space for the program by very persistently lobbying Mayor Dwyer of New York City, who was a passionate and liberal politician. Dwyer agreed to provide two wards at one of the municipal hospitals, Bellevue, for the inpatient service. In addition, Samuel Milbank, another member of the Milbank philanthropic family, gave Rusk and NYU an old building near NYU on East 38th Street. Financial assistance for refurbishing the added space, staffing and equipment was provided by Bernard Baruch, Bernard Gimbel of the department store business, and Arthur Hays Sulzberger. Baruch points proudly to this gift in his autobiography as assisting in building the Institute at Bellevue, and a picture of him at the Institute appears in the book. The center at 38th Street had 40 beds. These same benefactors and others, including Samuel Horowitz, a real estate magnate, contributed to the establishment of a facility at NYU. In 1949, the City of New

York also provided space with 100 beds at Goldwater Municipal Hospital. Soon Rusk had beds in every New York City Hospital. He was also effectively raising funds to finance a two million dollar Institute of Rehabilitation Medicine at the NYU Medical Center on 34th Street. The Institute opened in 1951 and was the first facility of the NYU Medical Center. Later it would be renamed the Rusk Institute of Rehabilitation Medicine.[24]

HENRY KESSLER AND THE KESSLER INSTITUTE
IN ORANGE, NEW JERSEY

When he was discharged from the Navy at age 52 in 1946, Henry Kessler returned to Northern New Jersey to reestablish his medical practice. He had appointments at a number of hospitals, including the Hospital for Crippled Children in Newark, before he entered the Navy in World War II. He had also been the Director of the rehabilitation clinic at nine Franklin Street in Newark, which was focused on state workers compensation patients and vocational rehabilitation agency patients. His mentor Dr. Albee had been Chair of the State Rehabilitation Commission prior to World War II, but had passed away by 1946. For Kessler, unlike Rusk, rehabilitation had been a long time passion, preceding his Navy service by 22 years. Like Rusk, however, Kessler did have a vision for his future in rehabilitation and it involved the establishment of his ". . . own rehabilitation center, removed from the red tape and other problems invariably associated with government control of such establishments."[25] Kessler had become disenchanted with the government program for workers compensation, which might explain his lack of enthusiasm for politics and healthcare reflected in the preceding quotation. He was also a surgeon, with the intensity and individualism often seen in surgeons. He was far less involved in government, politics and rehabilitation than Rusk and Krusen.

Kessler began to work on the idea of an independent rehabilitation center after he was approached by a group of women with disabled children at the Crippled Children's Hospital, who requested his assistance in establishing programs for their children after discharge from the Crippled Children's Hospital. The women, however, only wanted a child care facility. Kessler described to them a rehabilitation program he thought would work. "If you go out and raise a little more money which would help us buy the part time services of a physical therapist, an occupational therapist, a speech therapist, and a recreational worker perhaps we can do something for you."[26] His programs also always included prosthetic services for patients who needed them. The women agreed to raise the necessary funds and Kessler began his search for a facility. When Kessler suggested to the Board of Trustees of the Crippled Children's Hospital that a rehabilitation program was needed for the children after their surgery was performed, unfortunately he was met with a derisive response. The Board members thought these children were beyond any help that such a program could bring. They told Kessler to consult the medical staff and get their recommendation. The response of the Board was comparable to those Rusk received from physicians at Washington University Medical School and Dr. Lahey. This response only made Kessler strengthened his resolve to establish a rehabilitation center.[27]

Kessler was a well-trained and highly regarded orthopedic surgeon, whose procedures for shoulder surgery were internationally known. Kessler's characteristics seemed somewhat like those of Paul Magnuson, who was also an excellent orthopedic surgeon. Both were focused, result oriented, and not prone to or tolerant of small talk or inaction when there was a compelling job to be done. Kessler proceeded to disregard the negative responses he had gotten, and set up a cerebral palsy clinic in the orthopedic center of the Crippled Children's Hospital. The service of the center became very popular with the local Board of Education, and they gave Kessler an abandoned school building to expand the clinic program. The patient population of the hospital was mainly adult and orthopedic, and the hospital had undertaken a different mission from its original mission to serve children. At this time the trustees had decided to dispose of a home used prior to the war as a summer camp for disabled children after discharge from the hospital. Kessler had been the largest contributor of such cases to the Hospital and with his departure during the war, the cases decreased and the need for the children's home did as well. Kessler asked the trustees to sell the home to him so he could devote it to the rehabilitation center he had envisioned. The trustees had been convinced of the effectiveness of the rehabilitation service Kessler had started in the cerebral palsy clinic and were now more than willing to sell the home to him. The home had two stories and two wings.

One wing of the home became a 16-bed inpatient facility and the other became the therapy department. The Kessler Institute was up and running in 1948 about the same time Howard Rusk established his 40-bed program at 38th Street in New York City. While the Newark community had physical medicine departments in a number of its hospitals, Kessler did not believe that they were providing the necessary comprehensive services and were: ". . . limited in scope, personnel, equipment and design. . . . Our idea was to treat the whole individual and not just the medical condition."[28]

HENRY KAISER AND HERMAN KABAT, M.D., PHD
IN WASHINGTON, D.C. AND IN CALIFORNIA

Henry Kaiser Sr. was born in 1882 as the son of German immigrants. He dropped out of school, moved west and began a construction company. By the 1920s he had achieved enormous success, having constructed the Hoover Dam. In the 1930s he constructed the Grand Coulee Dam, and during World War II he became a shipbuilder for the war effort. For his businesses he had created a program of prepaid group practice medical services for the employees, headed by Dr. Sidney Garfield. By 1944, this health plan employed 100 physicians, operated three large hospitals, and served 200,000 employees and dependents. During the last year of World War II, Henry Kaiser, Sr. received the daunting news that his youngest son, Henry Kaiser Jr., had been diagnosed with multiple sclerosis. Committed to finding some way to restore his son's health and physical function, Kaiser came upon an article which interested him in Readers Digest magazine by Paul De Kruif about Henry Kabat MD, PhD and his successful treatment of a woman with multiple sclerosis using medication and both passive and active exercise.[29]

Herman Kabat was trained in both neurology and physiology. He was a practicing neurologist at the University of Minnesota Medical School and teaching hospital in the early 1940s. He was among the first neurologists to become known as a leader in rehabilitation medicine. From about 1940 to 1943, his career took a major turn as he became involved in the study of neuromuscular disability through his work with Miland Knapp, a leading physical medicine physician in Minnesota. He also worked with Sister Kenny, about whom more will be told in a succeeding chapter. Sister Kenny came to the University of Minnesota Medical School with a grant from the National Foundation of Infantile Paralysis to pursue her interest in rehabilitation techniques for patients with polio. Knapp and Kabat were believed to have found a basic neurological cause of the effects of polio independent of the impact of damage to the anterior horn motor neurons. It involved damage to the internuncial nerve cells. At this point Kabat decided to devote his work to neuromuscular disability generally and to proceed independent of the Minnesota project and Sister Kenny, whose work he found to be limited by her lack of a fundamental understanding of physiology. He "...came away persuaded that (she) had some good ideas but convinced her limited knowledge of the underlying neurological mechanisms kept her from developing truly effective treatments."[30] Kabat decided to move on and expand his own work.[31]

Kabat began a clinic on neuromuscular disability and rehabilitation in Washington, D.C. in 1943, in conjunction with other appointments he had at local hospitals and with the Federal Crippled Children's Program in the Federal Security Agency. Sidney Garfield talked to Kabat's patients, who were all very positive about their care and treatment. Henry Kaiser contacted Kabat and got Kabat to agree to review his son's case and provide the appropriate treatment. Kabat treated the younger Kaiser and his condition improved dramatically. "What Henry Kaiser, Sr. liked, he organized. Not surprisingly, given his son's progress, he became a devoted advocate for Kabat's rehabilitation program."[32] As a result, in 1946, Henry Kaiser, Sr. funded the Kabat-Kaiser Neuromuscular Rehabilitation Institute in Washington after sending Rene Cailliet, MD, a specialist in Physical Medicine and Rehabilitation, to Washington to learn the program. Kabat had hired Margaret Knott, a physical therapist trained at Walter Reed military hospital, to become his associate in developing a research program and a clinical service. In 1948, a program was established at Vallejo, in a hospital purchased by the Kaiser health care plan. Kabat and Knott moved to California to run the program. Together they developed a therapeutic program referred to as proprioceptive neuromuscular facilitation (PNF), which consisted of using repetitive exercise of muscles in precise patterns of movement. According to Fowler's *History of Physical Medicine and Rehabilitation in California*, PNF facilitated the growth of other neuromuscular facilitation techniques, which became extraordinarily popular in the 1950s and 1960s. At times these facilitation techniques took on an almost "cult like following."[33] PNF also had a major impact on the development of the profession of physical therapy, as it was adopted by leaders in the physical therapy profession such as Dorothy Voss at Northwestern and Signe Brunnstrom at the Kessler Institute and NYU.[34]

In 1948, Kaiser also established a Kabat-Kaiser Institute in Santa Monica, California with Rene Cailliet, MD, as its Medical Director. Cailliet was one of the field's early pioneers nationally and in California. He had been Medical Director of the Institute in Washington, D.C. in the late 1940s. He became President of the American Congress of Rehabilitation Medicine, and was one of the leaders of the field in the 1960's. Both California facilities established by Henry Kaiser Sr. became part of the now famous Kaiser Permanente health care system, which also sponsored one of the first health maintenance organizations. Kaiser thus took his place along with Bernard Baruch, Jeremiah and Samuel Milbank, and FDR as philanthropists who assisted in the early development of the medical rehabilitation facility movement in the private sector. Without their initiative and willingness to back new methods in health care, the eventual growth of rehabilitation medicine might never have occurred.[35]

WOODROW WILSON IN FISHERSVILLE, VIRGINIA AND THE REHABILITATION INSTITUTE OF CHICAGO

In 1947, a visionary State Director of Vocational Rehabilitation in Virginia, aware of the military rehabilitation programs and of the Baruch Committee recommendations for community rehabilitation facilities, decided that the state of Virginia should operate such a facility. Richard Anderson, along with Corbett Reedy (a counselor on his staff), investigated the prospects for a joint vocational and medical facility administered by the state of Virginia. Anderson was referred to by Mary Switzer as one of the great ones in the field of rehabilitation. Reedy remained a national leader in rehabilitation for three decades, and was known for his breadth of view and support for integrated medical and vocational services. Anderson was able to acquire the Army hospital at Fishersville, which had been declared surplus federal property after the war.

It was there that Anderson and Reedy established a comprehensive rehabilitation center named after Woodrow Wilson, who signed into law the original vocational rehabilitation legislation and urged the nation to support rehabilitation for returning veterans of World War I. The state would refer its clients who needed both rehabilitation medicine services and vocational training to the Center. Since the 1943 amendments to the Vocational Rehabilitation Act, the state program had been able to pay for medical as well as vocational services. The Woodrow Wilson Center differed from those of Rusk, Kessler and Kaiser-Kabat in its rural location and its emphasis on education and vocational training. It was a model of the Baruch Committee's recommendations for integrated medical and vocational rehabilitation services. Later in its development, the Center entered into an arrangement with the University of Virginia Medical School to furnish medical services and training, thereby involving another major medical school in the medical rehabilitation movement other than those which had received substantial grants from the Baruch Committee.[36]

Shortly after these developments on the east and west coasts, Paul Magnuson devoted himself to establishing his true dream, a comprehensive rehabilitation center in Chicago. After leaving the VA in 1953, Magnuson embarked on an effort to create the Rehabilitation Institute in Chicago (RIC). As Magnuson describes it in his memoir *Ring the Night Bell*:

Rehabilitation involved a team effort utilizing physicians, physical therapists, psychologists, prosthetists, occupational therapists and vocational counselors. All of this requires a stupendous amount of apparatus-machines for muscle training, special baths, diathermy, electric equipment of various kinds, ma-

chines shops for fitting braces and prosthetic devices, not to mention the para-
phernalia of administration and offices of counseling and job finding services.[37]

This description emphasized in practical terms the difference between rehabilitation medicine and physical medicine as it had developed prior to the
late 1940s. Magnuson approached the many businessmen of Chicago he had
become acquainted with in his 40 years of medical practice in Chicago and
for whom he had worked as a surgeon. He soon had sufficient financial commitments to acquire a building to initiate the project. Like Henderson and
Desjardin at the Mayo Clinic, Magnuson recognized the need for a physician
with a specialty in rehabilitation medicine. He was an admirer of Howard
Rusk, whom he considered to be the father of the field. In 1964, Magnuson
reached out to one of Rusk's fellows for a new leader for RIC, Dr. Henry
Betts. By the 1970s, the Rehabilitation Institute of Chicago, now in its new
building, was one of the nation's largest and foremost rehabilitation facilities.
It became known for its excellence in patient care, teaching programs and
research.[38]

The Baruch Committee had proposed that community rehabilitation centers be established for the civilian population in its 1944 report. The report
recommended that each facility have about 50 beds for inpatient care and an
outpatient program. The staff should include physicians and therapists, vocational counselors; and there would be services for those with mental illness.
The National Easter Seal Society for Crippled Children and Adults used that
plan in developing a design of its own for comprehensive community based
services. Over the next two decades, the Easter Seal Society raised funds and
established a number of rehabilitation centers, although its focus remained
more on outpatient services.

No matter whether the particular focus was medical, educational or outpatient, the rehabilitation facility movement had begun. By 1950, about thirty
comprehensive rehabilitation centers were in existence, seventy percent of
which were established in the decade of the 1940s.[39]

Enactment of the Hill Burton hospital construction program in 1946 assisted in this development of private rehabilitation facilities. Rehabilitation
proponents wanted to include rehabilitation centers in the state hospital plans.
Their wishes received Congressional support when the House Subcommittee
on Aid to the Physically Handicapped recommended ". . . building rehabilitation centers as a vital part of the federal state hospital program."[40] While the
Public Health Service maintained that the law, as enacted, included rehabilitation facilities, the state hospital construction agencies failed to allocate
money to rehabilitation. It was not until 1954 with amendments to the Act,
that were advanced by Mary Switzer and Howard Rusk, that Hill Burton

funds really became available for construction of rehabilitation medicine facilities.[41]

PAYING FOR MEDICAL REHABILITATION
IN THE NEW FACILITIES

As civilian rehabilitation facilities were established, questions remained about the patients who would fill the beds and how they would pay for the care. The VA hospitals were financed by federal appropriations, as were the physician services in VA hospitals. The Woodrow Wilson Center in Virginia had matching federal state vocational rehabilitation funds and possibly additional state appropriations to pay for services to their residents. But a private rehabilitation hospital with medical and vocational services had no such guaranteed source of patients and support. By the late 1940s, about 26 million Americans had some type of hospital insurance, usually a Blue Cross plan, but private insurance at this point in time was of no help to private rehabilitation hospital programs. The hospital insurance plans would not usually cover rehabilitation medicine inpatient care and certainly would not cover the vocational training. A development that assisted in financing rehabilitation medicine services was the interest of unions in health coverage for their members and the use of collective bargaining rights to achieve broad health coverage.[42]

The Wagner Act passed during the New Deal had established a right to collective bargaining between unions and management over wages and conditions of employment. "Collective Bargaining and Social Security were the two institutional legacies of the New Deal in Social Policy."[43] In 1947, the Taft Hartley law had confirmed the right of collective bargaining over conditions of employment, such as health insurance or health coverage. The failure in 1948 of President Truman's national health insurance proposal further stimulated development of the collective bargaining approach to attain privately the security of health coverage that the Social Security Act did not include. The role of unions in pressing employers for health coverage for their members would pay off for rehabilitation medicine.[44]

President Truman used his emergency powers under the Constitution in 1946 to seize the coal mines and bring about a settlement of the strikes in the coal industry. The settlement reached by United Mine Workers President John L. Lewis with the Interior Department, acting for the President, included a retirement and welfare fund for union members. I.S. Falk of the Federal Security Agency (FSA) was put in charge of designing the system. Falk was well acquainted with disability and rehabilitation from his work with Josephine

Roche on the Social Security Act, as well as his work for the FSA planning for disability insurance and health insurance since 1935. The FSA included among its programs and agencies the Office of Vocational Rehabilitation, making Falk well aware of its activity. Falk recommended a two-part fund, with one part for retirement and disability cash payments and the other for health care. This approach was welcomed by the union, which was unhappy with the state of miner medical care under the health benefit program administered by the mine owners. Care had been provided and managed by company physicians whose financial interests were directly linked to the company which was responsible for the cost of care. The union believed that a separate health fund controlled, at least in part, by the union might help matters.[45]

Josephine Roche, who had left the Federal Security Agency in 1937 to return to her private business, was appointed as public director of the two funds providing disability assistance and medical care to UMW workers in 1948. Roche knew rehabilitation well from her days as Assistant Secretary of the Treasury Department for the Public Health Service. She immediately decided she needed a medical director for the health care fund she could trust, and asked Mary Switzer for advice. Switzer was still at the Federal Security Agency as Assistant to the Administrator with responsibilities for the Public Health Service (PHS) and the Office of Vocational Rehabilitation (OVR). She suggested to Roche Dr. Warren Draper, who had recently retired from the PHS. Draper was a Harvard Medical School graduate and Deputy Surgeon General of the PHS before his retirement. He had been a PHS officer for over 30 years. Draper was a member of the AMA House of Delegates and was acceptable to the AMA as the medical manager of the federal health insurance program for mine workers operated by the fund.[46]

Draper surveyed the care being given to miners and was so troubled by what he saw that he asked the AMA to provide some members to visit the sites of care for the miners with him. Draper and others went to see miners disabled by accidents in the mines and found many who had been bed ridden or house bound for years with the attendant bed sores and arthritic joints as well as liver and kidney problems. Draper had decided that the best way to remedy the problem was to direct care to physicians and hospitals known to be capable of delivering the needed service. In 1946, before Roche and Draper were involved with the coal miners' fund, Dr. Sayers (a trustee of the Fund) had sent some cases to Henry Kessler. Sayers knew of Kessler from prior social and professional experience. Kessler cared for the terribly disabled miners at the Hospital for Crippled Children in Newark. By 1948, Kessler, Rusk, Kabat and the state vocational rehabilitation agency of Virginia had specialized inpatient and outpatient rehabilitation centers available to care for the miners. Mary Switzer knew of these programs, and in particular knew of Rusk and Kessler from her liaison position with the personnel procurement board in World War II. She recommended the programs highly to Draper. Care would be paid for by the mine workers health insurance fund, at least as long as the care met the needs of the patients.[47]

1948 was a special year for the union fund because a new agreement had been reached between the unions and companies after another round of strikes. Under that agreement, the union ceased opposition to mechanization in the mines; and the companies agreed to higher wages; a larger royalty contribution to the funds; and to name Josephine Roche as the neutral third trustee of the fund's programs. Labor and industry each named a trustee. Roche's relationship with Lewis assured that the fund programs would be union controlled. Earlier Roche had been named a director of the fund but had less authority in that role than as one of three trustees of both funds. She and Draper and Lewis (with advice from Mary Switzer), redirected the management of care of union members from the company physicians to an approach managed by the trustees and Dr. Draper. Patients were sent to specialized centers and hospitals, including those in rehabilitation medicine. The result for rehabilitation services and facilities was a boom of patients and payment for their care. For the unions, the benefit was the delivery of needed care and the satisfaction of union members with the services they received. Many patients became productive workers and taxpayers once again. Paul Starr described the mine workers' health program and the Interior Department Report about it in *The Social Transformation of American Medicine:*

> *The report estimated there were about fifty thousand miners disabled by mine related injuries who needed rehabilitation. These disabled miners were the U.M.W.A.'s first priority when the fund began operating in 1948. Thousands were sent off to rehabilitation centers in New York and California to be helped to resume more normal lives.*[48]

The fund leaders "trusted Kessler and Rusk because they produced results," as did the other rehabilitation providers.[49] The impact of the fund health program on rehabilitation facilities is demonstrated by the fact that between 1948 and 1950, the majority of the 3340 patients at Kaiser-Kabat programs in California were fund financed patients.[50]

As Rusk was about to refurbish and open his facility on thirty eighth street in New York City, he was visited by Drs. Draper and Sayres from the UMW fund. They told him of the 50,000 disabled and incapacitated miners who needed care, many of whom had broken backs and had been homebound for at least a year after routine, unsuccessful hospital care. When the New York facility opened the UMW sent 27 patients, filling about 70% of the beds that were initially available. Rusk described one of the cases as a miner who had been injured in a mine collapse almost 19 years before admission to Rusk's facility and had lived on a Kentucky mountain side:

His legs were so contracted that it took four surgical procedures to straighten them out. He had eleven bed sores that required twenty six surgical skin flaps to close. And he had a stone in each kidney that had to be removed. It was nine months before we could start training him in ambulation and in a vocation.[51]

The patient eventually learned to walk with crutches and returned home, where he was elected sheriff and served as such for years. Another miner with a broken back and badly infected leg from prior inadequate care required an amputation of the infected leg. The miner also had speech impairment and was uneducated. He learned to walk with his artificial leg, his back became largely healed, and his speech problem was successfully treated by speech therapists. He stayed on with the Institute as a hospital patient attendant and served Dr. Rusk well for many years.[52]

Dr. Kessler had similar patients with broken backs, bedsores, kidney stones and little preparation for any work other than mine work. One in particular required five different surgical specialists. Both legs needed amputation and he was fitted with artificial legs. His bed sores were surgically repaired and his kidney stones removed. After a year, the man was no longer incontinent, had no open sores and could walk with his artificial limbs. He returned to work and married one of Dr. Kessler's nurses.[53]

It is noteworthy that rehabilitation medicine was a beneficiary of one of the first managed care programs in America, the UMW fund, which directed patients to specific rehabilitation centers. The centers had established a reputation for the physical restoration of patients and their return to some form of active and productive life during the war, in treatment of veterans after the war, and in the treatment of injured miners. Eventually some progressive workers compensation insurers, such as Liberty Mutual, would adopt this UMW model and apply effective case management services; which very much benefited rehabilitation medicine in the 1970s and thereafter.

Quite clearly workers' compensation programs had not met the needs of the miners. Dr. Kessler found upon his return from World War II that the New Jersey workers' compensation program had regressed greatly, compelling him to found a center of his own and seek other sources of funding. Private group health insurance was still not extensively used and did not necessarily include coverage for the rehabilitation therapies and vocational training. It would not be for another 20–25 years before a sure source of funding for rehabilitation care was available for persons with disabilities and for the aged in Medicare. In the meantime, public facilities like the VA covered necessary medical rehabilitation care for their special patient population, state vocational rehabilitation agencies

purchased some medical rehabilitation services from medical rehabilitation facilities, and some unions successfully bargained for its inclusion in its contracts
with employers.

ACCEPTANCE BY ORGANIZED MEDICINE
OF PHYSICAL MEDICINE AND REHABILITATION

One of the major recommendations of the Baruch Committee in its initial Report of 1944, was the creation of a Board of Physical Medicine under the aegis
of the AMA's Council of Medical Education and Hospitals and its Advisory
Board for Medical Specialties (ABMS). In the 1940s, the AMA and the self-
policing bodies it had created were still largely sovereign within the world of
medicine and health care. The AMA had been the major force in defeating legislation for national health insurance supported by many within the Roosevelt
Administration and proposed by President Truman in 1948. It had continued
to emphasize the need for the professions to establish policies affecting the delivery of medical care and had encouraged licensing boards at the state level
to control those who practiced medicine and the scope of that practice. The
AMA also sought to establish accrediting bodies to assure standards for and
control over medical education, residency training and specialization.[54]

With respect to specialization, the AMA established standards for specialty
training in residency programs and bodies to provide exams and certification
of qualifications to practice as a specialist. To be recognized as a specialty,
leaders of a field of medicine had to persuade the AMA leadership, which included the leadership of the specialties that already existed, that 1) A field was
a unique field of medicine; 2) It had the necessary interest among physicians
to join it; 3) It had the capability to train and certify qualified practitioners.
Navigating the pathways to achieve Board status was a challenge for the most
astute and persistent of medical leaders, and the task was even harder when the
field was as small as the field of physical medicine. But the obvious need for
rehabilitation medicine services and the lack of trained physicians for the field
demonstrated during World War II prompted the Baruch Committee to take on
this crusade. In the late 1930's, Dr. Krusen had established the Society of
Physical Therapy Physicians to demonstrate that the field had sufficient interest among physicians. The effort had yet to bear fruit in 1943 when the Baruch
Committee was formed. Krusen and his allies, however, had educated many
physicians that the time had come to grant Board status to physical medicine.
The Baruch Committee had defined both physical medicine and rehabilitation,
with the former being a unique area of medical practice and expertise and the
latter the goal of physical medicine and other services for a patient with a dis-

abling condition. Krusen had been focusing his effort on physical medicine for at least 15 years. Rusk, on the other hand, had been involved with care for disabled soldiers for only three. He referred to the field he was assisting to develop as "rehabilitation." The name for the Board was not just a semantic issue. It raised fundamental questions as to the identity of this area of medical practice and the future of its training programs and scope of practice.[55]

While the Baruch Committee had defined both physical medicine and rehabilitation, it seemed to presume that the two were one and the same without actually stating that fact. Krusen had established training programs and curricula based on the premise that physical medicine involved a wide range of therapies to restore physical function, vocational training and job placement, although the latter two services were clearly not within the normal sphere of medical education or medical services. While recognizing that rehabilitation was the goal for the patient with a disability, Krusen had not addressed the inclusion of the psychological and social services that Rusk included in his even broader concept of medical rehabilitation. Kessler included in the scope of his program in the Kessler Institute speech therapy, recreational services and prosthetic services. Krusen had not focused as much as Rusk and Kessler on the need for other physician disciplines, particularly surgery, to deal with the many complexities of injured soldiers and workers. He also hadn't focused as much on the hospital facilities such as those extremely disabled and complicated patients needed. As former American Academy of Physical Medicine and Rehabilitation President Dr. William Fowler pointed out in his *History of Physical Medicine and Rehabilitation in California*, the distinction between physical medicine and rehabilitation medicine involved the focus of the latter on the very severely disabled patient and inpatient hospital care with the concomitant need for teams of professionals to apply medical and other services. Physical medicine, on the other hand, focused on disease and musculoskeletal conditions and the use of physical agents to diagnose and treat them.

During World War II two groups of physicians developed along individual lines. One group trained in or attracted to physical medicine comprised the Society of Physical therapy Physicians, and emphasized specific techniques. Physicians in the other group were recruited and trained in rehabilitation medicine in the military and veterans Administration hospitals, and emphasized the comprehensive management of the physically disabled.[56]

Interestingly, however, Dr. Krusen's physical medicine program at Mayo had both an inpatient service and an outpatient one and served many patients who were paralyzed and had other very disabling conditions. Dr. Elkins took over generally for Dr. Krusen while he was away working for the Baruch

Committee, and Elkins was a specialist in dealing with severely disabled patients and focused primarily on the inpatient service.

The focus of interest in government and the public in the war and post-war years was quite clearly on the rehabilitation of patients severely disabled through injury in war or on the job (such as miners). It was in that area where the training of physicians was found so lacking in World War II. This focus also seemed to shape the approach the Baruch Committee took in making its recommendations on the services and facilities needed, which it characterized as rehabilitation services and facilities, although it used the term physical medicine to refer to the training of physicians and research. To the Baruch Committee, rehabilitation medicine was the comprehensive service needed by persons with severe disabilities. Physical medicine was both a group of clinical services provided or directed by a physician and part of the rehabilitation process; as well as a medical specialty to provide the physician leadership for rehabilitation services.[57]

As the Baruch Committee work began in 1943, Dr. Wilbur, Chairman of the Committee, contacted the AMA to determine the status of physical medicine with regard to the establishment of a certifying Board. His status as a former President of the AMA enhanced his ability to get an honest and timely response. The negative response was disheartening to Dr. Krusen and others in the Society of Physical Therapy Physicians, who had been trying since 1937 to persuade the AMA to support a Board for physical medicine. The Chair of the Advisory Board on Medical Specialties (ABMS) told Dr. Wilbur the ABMS concluded that physical medicine was a legitimate part of every specialty and not sufficiently unique to justify a Board, nor had enough interest been shown by AMA members to support the establishment of a Board. However, the pressure of the Baruch Committee and the continuing need for physicians trained in physical medicine or rehabilitation for the war effort in 1944 and early 1945 began to change minds at the AMA and the ABMS.

Krusen and Coulter stepped up their organizational planning through the Society of Physical Therapy Physicians, and kept insisting to the AMA that a Board was justified. The Secretary of the ABMS and an ABMS Board Member was Dr. Kirklin, Chair of the Department of Radiology at the Mayo Clinic and a supporter of a Board for physical medicine. At the annual meeting of ABMS in February 1947, Krusen was advised that the ABMS would support a Board for physical medicine if it were affiliated with Internal Medicine. Dr. Krusen received a call on June 4, 1947 from the Board of Internal Medicine providing both bad and good news. The bad news was that the Internal Medicine Board did not feel that it could assume the responsibility of affiliation with physical medicine and its board, but the good news was that it suggested it would support an independent board. On June 27, 1947, Dr. Kirklin of the ABMS called Dr. Krusen to say that the ABMS had approved Physical Medicine as a separate Board. Krusen was urged to have exams in August of that year.[58]

Eleven physicians from physical medicine were appointed to the initial Board of Physical Medicine and Krusen served as Chair. On August 31, 1947, physicians were admitted to the first examination of the Board of Physical Medicine and about 54 were asked to take the exam, although they had sufficient experience in physical medicine to qualify. They were asked to take the exam to establish a reference point for the examination scoring. Dr. Kirklin of the ABMS observed the first exam. The initial Board eventually approved 103 physicians for the specialty and Dr. Coulter held certificate number one. Krusen held certificate number two. As Krusen wrote in his diary: "I feel I must record at this point in my diary my extreme gratification concerning the establishment of the American Board of Physical Medicine. After all, this is the culmination of my 18 years of effort in the field of physical medicine."[59] But his work had not ended![60]

The question of the relationship between physical medicine and rehabilitation had not been fully answered. The AMA adopted the term "physical medicine," which was the name that Krusen and his colleagues had been using for 10 years. That question was put directly to the AMA in 1948 by Dr. Rusk, who asked the AMA Council on Medical Education and Hospitals to recognize residencies in rehabilitation medicine. He was not requesting the establishment of a specialty board and certifying exam, but the establishment of residency training programs seemed a precursor to that. There is no discussion in the Opitz analysis of the Krusen diaries or in Dr. Rusk's autobiography of this potential conflict between the two leaders on the question of residency training and board certification. In his autobiography, Rusk lauds Krusen and his efforts to have physical medicine recognized as a specialty, but described why that, in his opinion, he did not do enough to integrate what he (Rusk) envisioned as rehabilitation medicine. "I felt it was not enough because it did not take into account the important nonphysical aspects of rehabilitation—the emotional, social, educational and vocational training which were an integral part of our programs."[61] Rusk made a presentation to the AMA subcommittee of the AMA Council on Medical Education and Hospitals, and all the physicians present except Dr. Krusen were from specialties other than rehabilitation. Rusk's focus from his war experience and miner patients was on severe disability such as spinal cord injury (SCI), other cases of paralysis' and amputations, where the social and emotional needs of patients could be dramatic. While Krusen had included the need for vocational training as part of physical medicine services in his descriptions of the scope of physical medicine, he had not included psychological and social services as part of a physical medicine service.[62]

The AMA Council on Medical Education and Hospitals recommended that Dr. Rusk consult with the AMA Council on Physical Medicine, formerly the Council on Physical Therapy, but renamed since the establishment of a Board in Physical Medicine. Dr. Krusen served on the Council of Physical Medicine. He supported a union of the two fields and described his reasoning in an article in the Archives of Physical Medicine:

> There are phases of physical medicine (as in the definitive treatment of acute diseases by physical agents) which cannot be called rehabilitation. Similarly, there are phases of rehabilitation (as in the psychosocial readjustment of disabled persons) which cannot be called physical medicine. Yet, for the most part, physical medicine and medical rehabilitation are closely interdigitated and it is apparent that it would be illogical for either physical medicine or medical rehabilitation to go its own way.[63]

These words were spoken like the true medical statesman that Krusen was. He seemed very able to put ego aside and work to accomplish a broader sense of good for the medical community of which he was a part. His leadership and statesmanship integrated the two concepts and established one field of medicine. He was also pragmatic enough to realize that the two fields and their leaders would benefit each other much more by working together than by working separately. In 1950, with Dr. Krusen's encouragement, the AMA Council on Physical Medicine approved a motion to rename the residencies it oversaw as Physical Medicine and Rehabilitation (PM&R); the Council as the AMA Council on Physical Medicine and Rehabilitation; and the Board as the American Board of Physical Medicine and Rehabilitation. Dr. Krusen's diaries expressed the view that Dr. Rusk and the Council were both "very happy" and that he was "much pleased."[64]

But all was not well in the house of medicine with this decision. Two major disputes broke out and one was continuous until February of 1955. The least controversial dispute occurred within the physical medicine and rehabilitation family when a number of members of the Society of Physical Medicine and the Congress of Physical Medicine refused to vote to add rehabilitation to the name and mission of the two organizations. The Society was organized in 1938 to create the constituency for a petition to the AMA for Board recognition. The Congress of Physical Medicine had begun in the 1920s as the first organization of physicians with an interest in physical medicine and it included orthopedists, radiologists and others with membership in recognized medical specialties. In 1950 the dissidents defeated a motion supported by Dr. Krusen to so rename the Congress. At that point, Dr. Rusk indicated if the name was not changed that he would establish a separate organization for physicians who were interested in rehabilitation but not certified as physical medicine and rehabilitation specialists by the American Board of Physical Medicine and Rehabilitation. Again, Dr. Krusen acted the statesman and sought to keep the development of two organizations from occurring. He successfully persuaded most of the opponents of the name change to relent and the change occurred in the names of both organizations. The leader of the opposition to the change was Dr. Sidney Licht of Yale. Dr. William Fowler, past Academy President and author of the *History of PM&R in California*, has referred to Dr. Licht as one of the primary leaders involved with the founding of the field. Licht later became the third recipient of the AAPMR prestigious Krusen Award. Licht feared the absorption of physical medicine by rehabilitation medicine and therefore opposed the name change, which implied a change in membership and mission of the Congress. In fact the years 1950 through 1990 demonstrated rehabilitation medicine to be the motivating force for the development of the specialty of PM&R. But it has not resulted in the domination of physical medicine. The integration of the two groups worked well in the Academy and in the Congress (the Congress included many physicians of disparate specialties other than PM&R). Both were focusing on diagnosis and treatment for persons with disabilities, and rehabilitation was the goal of both approaches to medical care. The current Board of the American Academy of PM&R reflects that philosophy well. The settings for services and the range of services delivered today are different than 60 years ago or even 20 years ago, but the goal and focus is on rehabilitation of the person with a disability.[65]

Drs. Kottke and Knapp summarized this period in the development of a medical specialty.

In the period 1946 -1948, there were aroused emotions and competition between physicians championing training in physical procedures and physicians strongly committed to comprehensive rehabilitation. The American Board of Medical Specialties (of the AMA) pointed out that a specialist in the field, to be fully effective, should have all the qualifications advanced by both groups. The diplomatic skills of Krusen and Rusk calmed the more hotheaded advocates of each point of view and in 1949 the American Board of Physical Medicine accepted the advice of the Advisory Board of Medical Specialties and made the necessary changes to become the American Board of Physical Medicine and Rehabilitation. Soon thereafter the Society changed its name to the American Academy of Physical Medicine and Rehabilitation and since then the soundness of the union which resulted in one organization . . . has become increasingly apparent.[66]

The second dispute involved other recognized specialties in medicine. In 1953, somewhat belatedly, the American Academy of Orthopedic Surgery entered an objection with the AMA to the inclusion of rehabilitation in the name and mission of the Board of PM&R, the AMA Section on PM&R and the AMA Council on PM&R. These changes had all been adopted by the AMA following its normal legislative process in 1948, and there had been no overt controversy nor organized efforts to defeat the new Board and its expanded mission. Between 1948 and 1953 the National Foundation for Infantile Paralysis and the American Physical Therapy Association, however, voiced concern over the inclusion of the term rehabilitation in the name of the AAPMR. Krusen's belief was that the APTA had requested support from the orthopedic surgeons and this resulted in its delegates to the AMA indicating they would bring a resolution to the House of Delegates of the AMA to delete the reference to rehabilitation from all three organization's name and scope. The theory of the objections of those three organizations was that rehabilitation was a process of medical care that belonged to all specialties and should not be assigned to only one. To some extent, this objection was similar to the one raised by Dr. Licht. He had feared the inclusion of large numbers of rehabilitation physicians in organizations previously limited to those focused on the use of specific modalities of physical and occupational therapy and the use of heat, light, water and electricity in dealing with physical disability. The AMA established an arbitration committee to consider the matter and the orthopedists and physical medicine and rehabilitation specialists were to present their views to the Committee. The first meeting occurred in 1953 in St Louis at the AMA meeting. According to Dr. Krusen's diary, the orthopedists were adamant in their positions, tendentious and not cordial to Dr. Krusen and his allies. The Committee deferred action on the resolutions suggested by the orthopedists and called for another meeting in 1954.[67]

Dr. Krusen moved expeditiously. He contacted Bernard Baruch, who had actively supported the Board of PM&R and knew of the integral relationship of physical medicine to rehabilitation. According to Krusen, Baruch was incensed at the opposition voiced by the orthopedists and their allies and vowed to make his position known at the highest levels. Although in his eighties at the time, Baruch was very active and had maintained his many contacts in government and politics, including contact with then President Eisenhower. Baruch had served President Truman as his delegate to the United Nations Atomic Committee, was a well known national figure, and was bipartisan, having supported Eisenhower for President in 1952. Dr. Krusen also had Dr. Rusk's support, as Rusk had been elated with the inclusion of rehabilitation with physical medicine in AMA policy. Rusk clearly believed that there should be a special residency training program to train physicians in physical medicine and rehabilitation and that the nation needed physician leaders who were specialists in physical medicine and rehabilitation. To have responsibility spread among all specialties would be a recipe for inaction.[68]

The AMA arbitration committee met again in 1954 and Dr. Krusen negotiated with Dr. Clinton Compere, an orthopedist from Northwestern who had worked with Dr. Magnuson and Dr. Coulter and was well known for his rehabilitation expertise. The two agreed that a solution would be to keep the Board of PM&R as it was, as well as the residency programs it oversaw; but to restructure the AMA Council and create a new Council in Rehabilitation which would have leadership from multiple specialties. PM&R also kept its AMA section. The Council was an AMA Forum for establishing policies about matters on rehabilitation coming up before the AMA. A month later Krusen learned that the AMA Trustees had agreed to keep all references to rehabilitation as they had been. Two further meetings of the arbitration committee were needed to appease the orthopedists who thought the AMA would follow the recommendations of Dr. Krusen and Dr. Compere. In 1955, after almost three years of work by Dr. Krusen, the two specialties met amicably and agreed to the initial recommendations of Krusen and Compere to keep the Board and residency training and the Section on PM&R the same, but to create a Council on Rehabilitation of the AMA. The AMA willingly accepted this compromise.[69]

Krusen learned later that the AMA trustees had met with President Eisenhower shortly before the Trustee's decision of 1954 regarding the inclusion of the term rehabilitation in the name of AMA approved bodies. The meeting was not about rehabilitation. More likely it was about national health insurance and other federal policy issues in health. But at the meeting, the President had indicated how much he supported medical rehabilitation. It is likely that Baruch had communicated with the President before the meeting with the AMA trustees. President Eisenhower knew Dr. Rusk well and had continued him as Chair of the Health Resources Committee, a position to which President Truman had appointed him. Eisenhower had also been directly exposed to the rehabilitation programs in the Army Air Force and Army during his war time service, so it is not hard to believe that he made the AMA visitors aware of his interests in rehabilitation and in PM&R as endorsed by Baruch and Rusk.[70]

The opposition to the field voiced by orthopedists is ironic since many of the leaders in rehabilitation in the early years were orthopedists such as Drs. Kessler, Albee and Magnuson. Dr. Magnuson and Dr. Henderson at the Mayo Clinic, who was involved in bringing Dr. Krusen to Mayo, both believed that rehabilitation medicine needed a medical specialist to oversee the rehabilitation medicine service. They worked with the service but did not believe that orthopedics should run it. They believed that rehabilitation medicine programs should be headed by physicians trained in physical medicine and rehabilitation who were full time PM&R clinicians. Dr. Kessler had chaired a panel on Rehabilitation at the Federal Security Board National Assembly, which was to draw up a health plan for the nation. Kessler recommended that medical schools and hospitals needed physical medicine departments. He believed that Krusen and Rusk were the nation's leading rehabilitation physicians. It is unlikely that any one of these three leaders would have objected to the development of a specialty in rehabilitation medicine.[71]

The existence of the specialty of PM&R has grown to where it is now a specialty of approximately 8,000 physicians. But the union of physical medicine and rehabilitation medicine which occurred between 1948 and 1950 was not an easy one. It has been referred to by leaders of the field as variously a "platypus, which swims, has four legs, possess a duck bill and feathers and is even known to lay an egg;" and as a "shotgun wedding rather than a marriage based on traditional courting and mutual love."[72] But the two fields have become well integrated for reasons related to Krusen's observation that while each has a phase which the other does not, they are interdigitated and practicality calls for their union. Physical therapy has also flourished as a profession, with many fine training programs, leadership in research by its PhD's, and 50,000 members. In retrospect, it has not been limited in its development by the existence of only one specialty which included the term rehabilitation in its name, and physical therapists have developed excellent working relationships with orthopedics despite the nomenclature of PM&R. No medical specialties are limited in their scope of practice by the names or missions of other specialties. Today, as rehabilitation medicine has become prominent, orthopedists, neurologists, internists and family physicians are also involved in aspects of rehabilitation medicine. This is true in both inpatient and outpatient care, and despite the existence of a specialty of 8,000 in PM&R. Medicine has matured!

In 1958, the AMA gave its prestigious Distinguished Service Award to Dr. Krusen for his contributions to medical education, research and medical care, and to the field of Physical Medicine and Rehabilitation. Dr. Krusen was the tenth recipient of the Award, which was initiated in 1948. Rehabilitation medicine had taken a huge step forward.

NOTES

1. Rusk, Arch Phys Med Rehabil, vol. 50, 469.
2. WWW.delanye.org/FDR.

3. Rusk, *A World To Care For*, 91.
4. Rusk, 91–97; Gritzer and Arluke, 109–111.
5. Gritzer and Arluke, 110.
6. Rusk, Arch Phys Med Rehabil, vol. 50, 465.
7. Ibid.
8. Magnuson, *Ring the Night Bell*, 44.
9. Magnuson, 133–147.
10. Magnuson, 227.
11. Ibid, 227–228.
12. Ibid, 235–238.
13. Ibid, 241, 253–258.
14. Email correspondence with Dr. Ernest Johnson, September 16, 2004; Interview Dr. Johnson October 27, 2005; Rusk Arch Phys Med Rehabil, vol. 50, 466.
15. Fowler, *History of Physical Medicine and Rehabilitation in California*, 9.
16. Fowler Interview September 10, 2004.
17. Opitz, DePompolo, History of Mayo Clinic Department Of Physical Medicine And Rehabilitation, 18, 47, 54, 89–94; Berkowitz, 114–117.
18. Fowler, 13–14.
19. Rusk, 98.
20. Rusk, 99.
21. Rusk, 99–107, with quote at 100.
22. Rusk, 105.
23. Kottke, Knapp, Arch Phys Med Rehabil, vol. 50, 9; Switzer, Rehabilitation Record, May, June 1970, Fiftieth Anniversary Edition, 6.
24. Baruch, *My Own Story*, 114–115; Rusk, 115–.120, 141–142, 150–155.
25. Kessler, *The Knife Is Not Enough*, 130.
26. Kessler, 128–129.
27. Kessler, 128–130.
28. Kessler, 131–133, quote at 133.
29. Smillie, *Can Physicians Manage the Quality and Costs of Health Care?*, The McGraw Hill Companies and the Permenente Federation LLC, 2000, 34–36, 49, 79.
30. Murphy, *Healing The Generations,* 165.
31. Kottke and Knapp, Arch Phys Med Rehabil, vol. 50, 9; Murphy, ibid.
32. Smillie, 79.
33. Fowler, 13.
34. Smillie, 49; Fowler, 13–14; Murphy, 167–168.
35. Murphy, 165–168; Fowler, 13–14, 24.
36. *50 Years of Vocational Rehabilitation in the U.S.A., 1920 to 1970*, 18; Walker, 123–124; Switzer, Rehabilitation Record, May /June 1970, 4.
37. Magnuson, 310–11.
38. Magnuson, 309–315.
39. Berkowitz, 117–18.
40. Berkowitz, 130.
41. Berkowitz, 128–131.
42. Starr, *The Social Transformation of American Medicine*, 311.

43. Starr, ibid.

44. Starr, 311–13.

45. Starr, 316–17; Berkowitz, 150–54.

46. Berkowitz, 151–55; Walker, 117–122.

47. Berkowitz, 154–56, 162–63; Walker, 117–19; Kessler, 132.

48. Starr, 317.

49. Berkowitz, 167.

50. Starr, 317; Walker, 117–122; Berkowitz, 162–185; Kessler, 135–36, 138–39; Rusk, 142–46.

51. Rusk, 144–45.

52. Rusk, 145–46.

53. Kessler, 135–36.

54. Starr, 21–29, 331–351.

55. Opitz et al., Krusen Diaries, Arch Phys Med Rehabil, vol. 78, 447–450, 556–58; interviews John Ditunno, MD, October 2005 and email correspondence with John Ditunno, MD, November 24, 2006.

56. Fowler, 9.

57. Opitz et al, Krusen Diaries, Arch Phys Med Rehabil, vol. 78, 556; Interview with Dr. Fowler, 9/10/04; Kottke and Knapp, Arch Phys Med Rehabil, vol. 69, 13; Fowler, 9; Opitz and DePompolo, History of the Mayo Clinic Department of Physical Medicine and Rehabilitation, 47–49.

58. Martin and Opitz, The American Board of Physical Medicine, The First 50 Years, published by the American Board of Physical Medicine and Rehabilitation, 1997, 6; Opitz et al., Arch Phys Med Rehabil, vol. 78, 449.

59. Ibid.

60. Opitz, et al., 448–450.

61. Rusk, 187.

62. Opitz et al., Arch Phys Med Rehabil, vol. 78, 556–57; Rusk, 186–88.

63. Krusen, Arch Phys Med Rehabil, vol. 30, 107–108.

64. Opitz et al., Arch Phys Med Rehabil, vol. 78, 557.

65. Opitz et al., Archives of Physical Medicine and Rehabilitation, volume 78, p. 557–558; Interview Dr. Fowler, September 10, 2004.

66. Kottke and Knapp, Arch Phys Med Rehabil, vol. 69, 13.

67. Opitz et al., Arch Phys Med Rehabil, vol. 78, 563–64.

68. Ibid, 563; Grant, 105.

69. Opitz et al., ibid, 563–64.

70. Ibid.

71. Berkowitz, 132–33.

72. Gordon, Zeiter Lecture, Arch Phys Med Rehabil, vol. 62, 9; and private correspondence, John Ditunno, MD to Richard Verville, January 15, 2005.

Chapter Eight

Polio, FDR, and Rehabilitation Medicine

Poliomyelitis, commonly called polio, is an infectious disease caused by a virus that produces devastating effects through its invasion of the nervous system. It can cause paralysis of the limbs, severe respiratory problems, muscle contraction and atrophy. "The end results of paralytic polio were crippling of extremities and scoliosis, requiring surgical correction and bracing; the obvious residual deformities made it a much-feared disease."[1] Polio had a dramatic impact on the development of rehabilitation over a period of about 25 years, beginning with the election of President Roosevelt in 1932 and lasting into the 1950s. The impact on the development of rehabilitation included the symbolic importance of the disabled President; his support for the rehabilitation programs of the Warm Springs facilities he established and its successor the National Foundation for Infantile Paralysis (NFIP); and the rehabilitation programs of the renowned Australian nurse and missionary Sister Kenny.

When we think of polio today we think of Jonas Salk, Albert Sabin and their discoveries of vaccines in 1955 and 1964 respectively, which prevented the disease. The nation appropriately celebrated the 50th anniversary of Salk's historic discovery in 2005. We can also think of President Roosevelt, his leadership of the free world in World War II, and his monument on the Washington Mall, which includes one portrayal of Roosevelt in his wheelchair. Winston Churchill would often refer to the disability of the President and marvel at his energy and strength. Churchill became quite convinced that much of Roosevelt's capacity to govern effectively derived from his disability, which had created conditions that had strengthened his character and personality. Less known, however, is the role polio played in the earliest development of physical therapy services and rehabilitation medicine.

The first cases of polio were discovered among infants in England in the late eighteenth and early nineteenth centuries. Polio impacted the United States beginning in the early twentieth century. It rose to epidemic proportions in the summer of 1916 when an outbreak occurred in Vermont. Rehabilitation medicine became involved with polio first when orthopedic surgeons adopted what they referred to as "aftercare" rehabilitation programs for the children and adults affected. They enlisted the effort and leadership of physical therapists in these programs. Best known was the program at Boston's Children's Hospital led by the orthopedic surgeon Robert Lovett and physical therapist Wilhelmine Wright. Lovett and Wright were invited by the Vermont public health department to provide acute treatment and follow up rehabilitation to about 235 victims of the epidemic of 1916. This program gained widespread notoriety and was called the "Vermont plan."

Polio had a very significant impact on the development of physical methods of treatment and on the profession of physical therapy. "In the two decades preceding World War II, the search to find better methods of managing patients with acute and chronic poliomyelitis had been the principal engine driving the advancement of physical therapy."[2] In the early days of polio in the United States during the 1920s, the leading medical expert on the treatment of the disease was Robert Lovett. He was using heat, water and limited forms of exercise to improve function of patients. The Warm Springs facility established by FDR also utilized rehabilitation techniques, particularly hydrotherapy.[3]

The impact of polio on the development of rehabilitation was so great that after the vaccines caused the number of new cases in the USA to essentially drop to zero in the late 1950s some feared that rehabilitation would simply disappear from the medical landscape. One physiatrist practicing in this era (whom I will not identify) complained ruefully about having to switch from the treatment of polio victims to those with spinal cord injury patients who were much more difficult to treat. "If you were going to cure a disease, why did it have to be polio? Most of those who got it were highly motivated middle class people with insurance, they still had normal sensation, and we didn't have to mess with the neurogenic bowel and bladder or spasticity."[4]

FRANKLIN DELANO ROOSEVELT, DISABILITY AND REHABILITATION

After graduating from Columbia law School and practicing law in New York, Franklin D. Roosevelt had been an Assistant Secretary in the Navy Department during the second term of the Wilson Administration. Government service and politics were clearly his career paths. Such a career was in line with the family tradition that had been established by his cousin Theodore Roosevelt, who had served as Governor of New York and President. FDR was an unsuccessful Vice Presidential candidate for the Democratic Party in 1920. In 1921, while vacationing on Campobello Island off the coast of New Brunswick, FDR was stricken with polio.[5]

The diagnosis and treatment of FDR's polio has recently been reviewed by two eminent physicians in the field of physical medicine and rehabilitation, Drs. John Ditunno and Gerald Herbison of Jefferson Medical College in Philadelphia. Ditunno is a former President of the American Academy of Physical Medicine and Rehabilitation, and Herbison was a long time Editor of the Archives of Physical Medicine and Rehabilitation. They described in detail the day of activity that preceded the symptoms of polio felt by FDR, who had engaged in swimming, sailing, racing on foot and putting out a forest fire. That evening he had the onset of chills, deep muscle aching and some numbness. The symptoms worsened the following day. He was terribly fatigued, had a fever and dragged his left leg as he walked. The initial diagnosis made three days after onset of the symptoms by Dr. Keen, an eminent surgeon vacationing nearby, was that he had a blood clot in his spinal cord. But polio expert, orthopedist Robert Lovett of Boston, was called in for a second opinion. He arrived on Campobello two weeks after the onset of illness and concluded that the diagnosis was polio.[6]

FDR's polio at first seemed to limit his dreams of a political future as treatments were tried without much success. He was treated by Robert Lovett in Boston and George Draper in New York over the period from September 13, 1921 to February 11, 1923. His treatment included use of hot water baths, physical therapy, gait training, and use of ambulatory aides including crutches. Substantial functional improvement occurred in the muscles above the waist, but there was no improvement in those muscles below the waist. FDR could ambulate with the aid of crutches or a crutch and cane. Ditunno and Herbison concluded that some substantial increase in function occurred, but that the paralysis of the legs remained and prevented FDR from walking independently. The functional improvement during those two and a half years after onset was accomplished as a result of training in balance, coordination, and use of devices and physical assistance. They determined that the functional improvement was not due to actual improvement in the polio-induced paralysis. They noted that FDR's diagnosis and treatment were medically appropriate for the times, although the initial diagnosis by Keen was incorrect. They also noted that the treatment was remarkably good for the time. FDR continued to try all available treatments and to educate himself about the disease he had.

He had seen every specialist, done every exercise, considered every miracle "cure" from electrical stimulation to an oxygen tent that spurred muscle growth, through increased atmospheric pressure. Like other polio patients, Roosevelt was fascinated by hydrotherapy, the use of water to treat disease and disability.[7]

In 1924, three years after the onset of polio, Roosevelt learned about treatment for polio at a Warm Springs, Georgia resort featuring spas similar to those used in Europe and considered by European experts as medically appropriate for the past 50 years. Roosevelt's hopes for a cure for his condition were well described by Doris Kearns Goodwin in her book *No Ordinary Time*:

Still searching for the elusive cure that would restore power to his legs, Roosevelt had first journeyed to the little town (Warm Springs, Georgia) on the side of a mountain in the autumn of 1924 after hearing that the healing waters had made it possible for a fellow polio victim to walk again.[8]

The water temperature of the springs was about 86 degrees. There were health professionals to staff the facility to assure that no one used the springs who might be at risk medically. Roosevelt stayed there for six weeks. According to the administrator of the facility Egbert Curtis, however, Roosevelt's effort to walk across the room of his cottage while leaning against one wall and being guided from the front by the head nurse exhausted him. It took so long that he seemed to become, at that moment, resigned to a life without the use of his legs. The ". . . effort to inch his way forward was so monumental that this was the moment he knew he would never really walk again."[9]

Roosevelt loved the small community and the Warm Springs facility.

It was the one place Roosevelt could truly be himself, surrounded by those who lived and suffered as he did and dreamed the same dreams. There was nothing to hide from the (other) polios, no reason to deceive. To them he was simply Dr. Roosevelt, rolling his wheelchair through the grounds, crawling around on his knees. . . . His correspondence from these years is dotted with remarkable acts of kindness toward fellow patients, from detailed medical advice to notes of encouragement.[10]

With the encouragement of his medical friends, Roosevelt soon bought the resort and all its facilities to devote them to care for those with polio and similar conditions. His law partner Basil O'Connor was persuaded to organize the property and the programs, and to raise other funds for them. In 1926, at O'Connor's insistence, a separate non-profit corporation, the Warm Springs Foundation, was created to hold and manage the real estate and the facilities of the Warm Springs program. Roosevelt planned to build a center for hydrotherapy for persons with paralysis from polio. Soon the facility would be treating about seventy people a day and had a medical and nursing staff. Leroy Hubbard M.D., an expert in polio aftercare, left his position with the New York health department and became the first medical director. Hubbard brought with him Helena Mahoney, a public health nurse, to run the physical therapy department. Mahoney had studied under Lovett in Boston and was an expert in muscle testing. The facility was staffed by graduates from the nearby Peabody School, a leading physical education and physical therapy institution. Alice Plastridge, who was trained by Lovett and Wright in Boston and who had personally treated Roosevelt for muscle reeducation in Hyde Park in 1926, became chief of physical therapy in 1929. Some 25 years later, Robert Bennett, one of the first graduates of residency training in the newly recognized specialty of physical medicine and rehabilitation became the medical director of the Warm Springs program. Bennett had trained with Dr. Krusen at the Mayo Clinic and became a national leader in physical medicine and rehabilitation.[11]

By 1928, Roosevelt had reentered politics and was elected Governor of New York. In 1932, with the nation facing a depression, Roosevelt ran for the Presidency and was elected. Both in 1928 and in 1932 Roosevelt sought to dispel all notions that he was physically unfit to campaign and to hold high office by campaigning "full out." In 1928: "He gave more campaign speeches than any candidate before him." In 1932: "He campaigned across the length and breadth of the country."[12] In his first term as President, Roosevelt proposed reforms of the Social Security Act and signed that landmark legislation into law in 1935. That law was the foundation for the Medicare program that would later be enacted during the term of Lyndon B. Johnson. The Medicare program would ultimately be the engine that would drive the development of rehabilitation medicine to its maturity in the 1980s and 1990s. The 1935 legislation also established the Maternal and Child Health and Crippled Children's programs in Title V of the Social Security Act. The legislation also extended the authority of the Vocational Rehabilitation Act, which had been in an uncertain state prior to that time.

The Crippled Children's program was a direct response to the polio epidemic. The program was administered by the Children's Bureau in the Public Health Service and operated through grants to states, which were required to establish state plans for the operation of the programs. The state administration of the program made it palatable to the AMA and the broad medical community, which feared federal involvement in medical care. The American Physiotherapy Association (APA) became very involved with the Crippled Children's program at its outset and offered its services to the Children's Bureau and to the states in administering the programs. Physical therapy services to children who were the victims of polio had begun in New England in the period between 1910 and 1920, and were prevalent in many parts of the country by 1935. The Crippled Children's program became a means of employment for hundreds of physical therapists, who were otherwise without work in the depression; and enabled the APA to play a leadership role in a field in which it had been active for 20 years. The APA members were among the major providers of care under the program as it grew through the late 1930's.[13]

It was also in the late 1930s that the Georgia Warm Springs Foundation, with O'Connor's leadership, began national fund raising and expansion. The Warm Springs facilities subsequently became a major rehabilitation center for persons with polio. By the late 1930's the facilities included a hospital, rehabilitation center, swimming pool for therapy and recreation, auditorium, and dining hall. The facility also included residential cottages. The President's cottage, which he personally designed, was "unpretentious," but was referred to publicly as the "Little White House." Throughout his life, the Warm Springs rehabilitation center and the patients had a special place in Roosevelt's heart. He tried to spend every Thanksgiving there, sharing the day of thanks with the staff and patients; and he did so over a period of almost two decades. "In late November (1941), as he had done for nearly two decades, the President planned a journey to Warm Springs to celebrate Thanksgiving with the patients and staff of the polio foundation."[14] The President traveled to Warm Springs at least two or three time a year including the Thanksgiving event. It seems that he took great pleasure at being with the other persons who had polio and providing encouragement for them.[15]

During the period when the USA was at war with the Axis powers, Roosevelt became a close friend and partner in political leadership with Winston Churchill. Churchill's opinions of Roosevelt bordered on idolatry at times, and always evidenced great respect for the President's vision and political skills. Churchill knew how very difficult it was for the President to get his country to enter World War II on behalf of the allies, since the American people had just been through World War I (even to this day many feel it was not necessary for the USA to enter World War I). But Churchill had no doubt about FDR's leadership and courage. Churchill attributed much of it to his having overcome a severe physical disability. John Meacham, in his book *Franklin and Winston*, discussed the leadership and courage of Roosevelt in 1942 and quoted Charles Eade about Churchill's view of Roosevelt as compared to Stalin:

His admiration for Roosevelt, however, was clearly of a much greater quality. He spoke of Roosevelt's tremendous triumph over his physical disability ... and he believed that Roosevelt was blessed by the Almighty with a great character shaped in large part by his effort to overcome his disability.[16]

After Roosevelt's death in 1945, Churchill remarked during his eulogy on the floor of the House of Commons:

President Roosevelt's physical affliction lay heavily upon him. It was a marvel that he stood up against it through all the many years of tumult and storm. . . . Not one in ten millions would have tried, not one in a generation would have succeeded, not only in entering this sphere, not only in acting vehemently in it, but in becoming indisputable master of the scene.[17]

Roosevelt symbolized to Churchill an extraordinary effort of spirit to rise above the limitations of life.

In *Splendid Deception*, Hugh Gallagher describes the impact of polio on Roosevelt's life like no other author has. In his last chapter entitled "Apotheosis," Gallagher argued persuasively that to truly understand the man FDR and his capacity for greatness, it is necessary to recognize the impact polio made on his physical and emotional life. It is only then, he argued, that we can also appreciate fully the very human, compassionate and strong person he was.[18]

Roosevelt became perhaps the greatest example of the enormous capacity of the human spirit to overcome the physical and psychological barriers imposed by severe disability. To govern a nation in depression and war took the utmost in human energy, strength and judiciousness. Few, if any, have governed the United States during any period with the skill and good temperament of Roosevelt. He governed for almost 13 years, the longest tenure for any President. Only at the very end did his health become a problem for him. This was true in the case of President Wilson as well, who suffered from a stroke near the end of his second term. FDR's experience with polio and his devotion to improving the ability of society to provide services and support for persons with disabilities had an enduring impact on rehabilitation medicine, and on research into the causes and cures for disease. Gallagher explains clearly that FDR created a necessary "splendid deception" in order to be electable and to lead the country. And lead he did! The times were different during his life with a disability from 1921 to 1945 than they are today. The public knew far less then than it does today about the tremendous vitality and competency of people with disabilities like Max Cleland, Administrator of the Veterans Administration in the Carter Administration and former Senator from Georgia who lost three of his four limbs in battle; scientist Stephen Hawking; or tenor Andrea Boccelli. Being elected to public office if one had a severe disability was far more difficult in the 1930s and 1940s. Suffice it to say many who knew FDR were frustrated by his clear-headed assessment of the possible in politics. Many in the disability movement recognize that very well and give to FDR the recognition he deserves as a great leader and as a compassionate, although eminently practical man.[19]

The story of FDR and his polio is essential to the story of rehabilitation medicine and physical disability, because he remains even today a symbol of creativity and productivity for persons with disabilities. He led efforts to develop rehabilitation medicine programs for polio when such programs were in their gestation period. In his biography *FDR*, Jean Edward Smith refers to the fact that while "Roosevelt had no special training in physiotherapy . . . he became an authentic pioneer in its application."[20] When he was first afflicted with polio, FDR read voraciously on the subject of therapies for polio and communicated with both physicians and patients about the disease and methods of improving the physical function of polio victims. Gallagher noted that FDR even recorded the outcomes of his treatments. His disability led to his spiritual kinship with the less privileged, whether unemployed, physically disabled, or aged. His close friends and Winston Churchill believed that FDR's disability made him the passionate and strong leader he was.[21]

THE NATIONAL FOUNDATION
FOR INFANTILE PARALYSIS AND ITS IMPACT

In the post war years the "National Foundation for Infantile Paralysis (NFIP) was, by a wide margin, the single most popular medical cause."[22] It turned fund raising for medical research and care into an art, and became the prototype for voluntary health organizations such as the National Cancer Society, the American Heart Association, and the American Diabetes Association. It represented another of FDR's contributions to rehabilitation medicine and health care.

During his Governorship and Presidency, FDR continued to support the Warm Springs Foundation. He urged his law partner Basil O'Connor to continue raising funds and investing in rehabilitation programs at the facility. In 1933, O'Connor, then the chief executive of the Warm Springs Foundation, initiated an annual "Birthday Ball" to celebrate the President's birthday and raise funds for the Foundation. These events often took place at fashionable hotels throughout the nation as well as at Warm Springs, where they were styled as wheelchair dances. The events raised enormous amounts of money, more than the Foundation could use for the Warm Springs rehabilitation programs. In 1934 over a million dollars was raised, the largest fund raising event of its time, and O'Connor personally presented the check to the President at the White House. O'Connor announced in 1935 that 70% of the revenues would remain with the local communities that raised them. These funds would go to local chapters to allow them to establish their own treatment programs and rehabilitation centers. But at about that time the controversial policies of the President, such as his court packing scheme and large federal programs, had offended many of the wealthy who might otherwise have given to the Foundation. This resulted in the need for a new strategy regarding fund raising to support polio programs. Roosevelt and O'Connor founded the NFIP as a new strategy to continue national fund raising, and to support national and local rehabilitation and research programs dealing with polio. Roosevelt announced the formation of the NFIP in 1938. "Its major aims," he said, "were to find a cure for polio while providing the best treatment for those already afflicted."[23]

The NFIP would become the model for charitable fund raising to eliminate disease, and for Mary Lasker's disease focused crusade to expand research funding and the programs of the NIH from the 1950s through the 1980s. It also became a leader in shaping the delivery of medical care and in establishing the hospital as the centerpiece in the health care system.

The NFIP under O'Connor's leadership began the "March of Dimes" coin collection program in 1938; for which NFIP became renowned. The NFIP initially used the funds that were raised to make grants to a number of local facilities providing care to children and adults with polio. The money was also used to lend equipment to patients and hospitals, including the iron lungs needed by patients with bulbar polio. In the 1940s and 1950s the NFIP made training grants to numerous departments of physical medicine and rehabilitation and schools of physical therapy.[24]

From the 1930s through the 1950s, the NFIP spent $233 million on polio treatment and rehabilitation. This was a huge amount of money for that time, but it still had not been sufficient to provide for all the needs of polio victims otherwise isolated in homes and without services. The NFIP was aware very early on that a national effort that included the government was needed to make the nation's hospitals adequate to the task of servicing polio patients. The NFIP, the Commonwealth Foundation and the Kellogg Foundation joined the American Hospital Association (AHA) in 1942 to create a National Commission on Hospital Care. The Commission was staffed by the Public Health Service and it recommended a "huge" program of $1.8 billion for construction of hospitals and $375 million annually for their operation. Partly as a result of the recommendations of the Commission and the pressure from NFIP, Congress enacted the Hill Burton program in 1946 to fund hospital planning and construction. The Commission also developed model state survey techniques, which all states eventually adopted and used in their applications for the funds of the Hill Burton program. The Commission effort and the establishment of the Hill Burton program served further to establish the hospital as the major setting for medical care and research. This was good for Physical Medicine and Rehabilitation as it was becoming more of a hospital based specialty due to the growth of inpatient rehabilitation programs in the military, the V.A. and the civilian sector.[25]

The NFIP and the APTA were partners in assisting the Crippled Children's program to meet the demands created by the polio epidemics since the program's inception. When polio epidemics occurred, NFIP and the APTA operated emergency strike teams, which sent therapists to the areas affected by the epidemic. The APTA took over the operation of these strike teams in 1948. NFIP actively supported rehabilitation through funding of professional training and research in physical medicine and in physical therapy and local rehabilitation centers, such as Warm Springs, which would provide services to polio victims.[26]

In the late 1940s, NFIP began turning its attention to finding a cure for polio and to supporting the nation's top virologists including Albert Sabin, Thomas Enders, and Jonas Salk. As Oshinsky described in compelling style, the NFIP started an effort that ended with the nation's largest human experiment in 1954; and the discovery announced in 1955 at the University of Michigan that a polio vaccine using killed viruses was safe and effective. That great effort essentially ended polio in the USA, and was almost single-handedly supported and led by the NFIP. The NFIP relied heavily on physical therapists who participated in large numbers in the administration of the human trials, performing muscle tests on children receiving the vaccine. Prior to the Salk experiment, the NFIP had supported another major clinical trial in which it developed a standardized manual muscle test to determine muscle weakness, improving upon a measurement developed by Lovett in 1917. This test is widely used today in clinical trials and "serves as the gold standard of outcome measures for measuring neurological recovery."[27]

During the 1940s the NFIP also was a supporter of the controversial Sister Kenny who became, like Jonas Salk, a household word, but without the scientific validation of her medical theories.[28]

SISTER KENNY AND REHABILITATION MEDICINE

The arrival of "Sister" Elizabeth Kenny of Australia to the USA in 1940 brought national attention to the use of physical agents in treating disease. Sister Kenny was, in fact, neither a Sister nor a trained physical therapist. She was actually a bush nurse from New South Wales in Australia, who lacked formal training in nursing or physical therapy. In England and Australia in those days it was common to call all nurses "Sister" because most nurses were nuns. Although not a trained nurse, she earned the title of "Sister" when on duty with the Australian Medical Corp in World War I. She exhibited dedication to her work despite being wounded by shrapnel close to the front. After World War I she had dedicated herself to reducing the pain and disability of polio for the thousands of children in Australia who were affected by the disease. Her work in her early career was in the remotest part of the outback called "Never," because travelers vowed to never, never return there. She had a remarkable sense of anatomy (even though she had never studied it formally), and a dedication to remedying the disabling effects of the disease. She erroneously viewed the paralysis from polio as a spasm of the muscles rather than a disease of the nerves. Her treatment regimen was contrary to the general medical view of managing the disease, although not foreign to experts in polio care such as Robert Lovett. She opposed the use of bed rest and bracing and treated patients aggressively with "fomentations" of hot packs applied to the affected areas. She also applied passive exercise and massage. Lovett, on the other hand, recommended complete bed rest until the pain subsided, (which in FDR's case was two to three months), and then active exercise to strengthen the muscles. He used warm baths, but only to sooth pain. It can be said that in general, neither Kenny nor Lovett were right or wrong. Some experts in physical medicine and rehabilitation believe that the long bed rest of FDR may have resulted in his "severely contracted knees which took months to straighten which could have been prevented by (the use of) hotpacks and exercise."[29]

While still in Australia, Sister Kenny proclaimed in 1940 that she had cured six cases of polio and had assisted others in improving their function using her method as opposed to bed rest. The medical establishments in Australia and Great Britain reacted strongly to her claims and a blue ribbon panel in Australia found her work to be sloppy and without scientific merit. Undeterred, she set out for the United States where physicians had an eagerness to learn, according to Kenny.[30]

In her search for support for her work in the United States, Sister Kenny first approached the NFIP and Basil O'Connor, since the NFIP was the foremost supporter of programs for polio care in the United States. Sister Kenny was a person whom you either adored for her work and commitment; or disliked for her aggressiveness, arrogance and disinterest in learning from others. O'Connor spent three painful hours with her, but did not give her funds. He advised her that NFIP supported institutions that provided care and did research, and not to individuals such as herself. She visited the AMA and also offended Morris Fishbein, MD, the well known Editor of the Journal of the American Medical Association. Both Fishbein and Dr. Thomas Rivers (chief medical advisor of the NFIP) were personally offended by her arrogance, and believed that she had little actual knowledge of polio. From the NFIP and the AMA, she went on to the Mayo Clinic where she was better received; (perhaps because Midwesterners are felt by some to have better manners than the often brusque Easterners) but she did not receive the needed support.

Indomitable in defeat, she traveled to Minneapolis and arrived as an outbreak of polio was occurring. In this time of emergency, her services were badly needed and she was given working space and patients by the Minneapolis General Hospital. The NFIP made a six month grant to the hospital to support Sister Kenny's work. She teamed up with orthopedist John Pohl at the Infantile Paralysis Clinic in the hospital. She also teamed up with Miland Knapp, a specialist in physical medicine and rehabilitation at the University of Minnesota, who directed its physical therapy program. The reception from the public, patients and their families in Minneapolis was extremely positive. "One look and we knew we had something good!" extolled the Mayor of Minneapolis.[31] The views of the visiting NFIP reviewers of her program from Northwestern University, Warm Springs and Baltimore Crippled Children's Hospital were, while more varied than the Mayor's, on balance quite positive. She was getting unusually good outcomes that were unlikely to be the result of chance, although one reviewer felt the failure to use bracing was inappropriate. These reviewers submitted reports to the NFIP. In 1942, the Committee on Research for the Prevention and Treatment of Infantile Paralysis of the NFIP endorsed her work at a scientific meeting of the Foundation. The APA, soon to become the APTA, awarded her its prestigious Gold Key Award and the APA Journal gave an article by her a lead position. Physical therapists flocked to Minneapolis to be trained by her and the NFIP continued funding treatment and training there and in similar programs of six satellite centers it established around the USA. Dr. Knapp and Sister Kenny personally led the polio treatment training sessions for therapists and physicians. Frank Krusen became involved with her work along with Dr. Knapp and both wrote articles supporting her treatment methods.[32]

Despite the missionary zeal of Sister Kenny and the many positive results of her work, she had many detractors. Basil O'Connor at the NFIP found her to have a "Jehovah complex." He also felt that she saw him and the NFIP as simply a necessary, but otherwise insignificant, means to her ends. Most of the NFIP polio experts thought she was a quack and saw nothing in the way of scientific evidence to support the claims regarding the effectiveness of her services. They were obviously at odds in their views with the APA and Drs. Krusen, Knapp and Pohl, who observed her work first hand in Minneapolis. Henry and Florence Kendall, physical therapists of the Baltimore Children's Hospital, who later would become well known for their ground breaking work on measures of normal flexibility in trunk and leg muscles, continued to critique the approaches of Kenny (now referred to as the Kenny method).

In 1944, Dr. Pohl supported Kenny in publishing data on the effectiveness of the Kenny method at Minneapolis General Hospital, and the results were mixed. The rate of effectiveness was actually less than proclaimed by Kenny. While the treatment effectiveness was good, an article in Lancet commenting on the data found that it was only as good as ordinary treatment programs; and arguably not as good as the results from specialized polio hospitals. The AMA debunked her claims for the effectiveness of her treatment in 1944, and in 1945 the NFIP ended its major support for her program at what was then called the Kenny Institute in Minneapolis. "Life magazine called her the most publicly controversial figure in the medical world today."[33] She remained in Minneapolis, however, and continued to have the support of Knapp, Krusen and others in the area. Despite the controversy swirling about her, a Gallop Poll regarding the ten most admired people in the United States ranked her ninth. Movie star Rosalind Russell played Sister Kenny in a popular film of her life story. She was an American folk hero from the mid-forties until she left the United States in 1951.[34]

Sister Kenny's contributions to rehabilitation medicine were many. She increased the visibility of rehabilitation medicine methods of treatment for polio. She specifically contributed to the prevention and treatment of contractures with the use of hot packs and passive range of motion. These two treatments remained parts of the accepted treatment approach to polio. Her work, and the support of the NFIP for training and rehabilitation services, made rehabilitation medicine accepted as a treatment for a "disease," and not just for wartime injuries or industrial accidents. It brought notoriety to the field before Howard Rusk and Henry Kessler had developed their highly visible rehabilitation medicine programs in the military.

Sister Kenny added significantly to our knowledge of polio and neuromuscular diseases. She recognized that muscle spasm, which was first shown by Harry Bouman MD to be a hyperexcitable stretch reflex, was the cause of the initial deformities of poliomyelitis. She and Knapp introduced the concept of the cutaneous gamma reflex.[35]

While her specific techniques were not as efficacious as she touted them to be and had mixed results, the use of physical therapies for polio treatment were better known and accepted as a result of her efforts in the United States. Her personality, with its stridency and propensity to overstate, often led to her being criticized by others in the field. Her commitment and willingness to press for rehabilitation treatments for polio were her lasting contributions.[36]

Sister Kenny returned to Australia in 1951, suffering from Parkinson's disease. She died in Australia in 1952 from a brain hemorrhage. But her impact continued in rehabilitation medicine through the Elizabeth Kenny Institute, later renamed the American Rehabilitation Foundation. The Institute was established in 1943 when the City of Minneapolis donated a building to Kenny for her training programs. The Foundation was rocked by a scandal in 1960 when its Executive Director was accused of misappropriating large sums of money (for which he was convicted in 1961). Shortly after the scandal occurred, Frank Krusen was asked by supporters of the Foundation to help restore its credibility. Krusen saw the problems of the Foundation as problems for the field of rehabilitation medicine. He became the medical director of the American Rehabilitation Foundation and its spokesman in assuring the public and sponsors of the integrity of the operation. In 1962, he and Dr. Frederick Kottke, with the essential assistance of Senator Hubert Humphrey and Mary Switzer, were instrumental in obtaining $250,000 in federal funding for the University of Minnesota and the Foundation to operate a research and training center. This funding enabled the Foundation to survive and to continue its mission of education and training in rehabilitation medicine. Krusen resigned as medical director of the Foundation in 1963. As he said to a young John Ditunno whom he was recruiting to join him at Temple University, he had "taken to the stump" and "lived like a monk" for two years in an effort to save the Foundation and the field.[37] This effort was comparable to his efforts as Executive director of the Baruch Committee in the 1940s.[38]

Polio has continued to have an impact on the development of rehabilitation long after the cure for the disease was found. Advocacy for persons with disabilities from the late 1960s to date owes a great debt of gratitude to polio survivors whose lives and leadership will be discussed in later chapters of this book. Three of the best known disability advocates in the period 1960 through 1990 and the ultimate enactment process of the Americans with Disabilities Act (ADA) were Justin Dart, Jr., Ed Roberts, and Judy Heumann, all polio survivors. More will be said of them in later chapters. Dart was Chair of the President's Committee on Employment for the Handicapped in the years of Presidents Reagan and Bush, and was the clear leader of the movement to enact the ADA. He later became a recipient of the Presidential Medal of Freedom. Ed Roberts was the first severely disabled person to hold a major federal or state position in the disability and rehabilitation world, as Director of the California Vocational Rehabilitation Agency in the 1970s. Judith Heumann was Assistant Secretary for Special Education and Rehabilitation under President Clinton. She and Roberts were founders and leaders of the Independent Living movement.

NOTES

1. Kottke and Knapp, Arch Phys Med Rehabil, vol. 69, 8.

2. Murphy, *Healing the Generations*, 123.

3. Murphy, 34–35, 94–95; Oshinsky, *Polio An American Story*, Oxford University Press, 2005, 16.

4. Personal Communication.

5. Oshinsky, 24.

6. Ditunno and Herbison, FDR: Rehabilitation from Poliomyelitis, American Journal of Physical Medicine and Rehabilitation (hereinafter cited as Am. J. of PMR), vol 81, 558–59; Oshinsky, 25–26.

7. Quote Oshinsky, 35; Murphy, *Healing the Generations*, 95–97; Ditunno and Herbison, Am. J. of PMR, vol. 81, 560–65.

8. Goodwin, *No Ordinary Time*, Simon and Schuster, 1994, 116.

9. Goodwin, 117, quoting from Curtis; Murphy, *Healing the Generations*, 95.

10. Oshinsky, 39.

11. Murphy, *Healing the Generations*, 95–96; Oshinsky, 46–47.

12. Gallagher, 72, 86.

13. Murphy, 98–101.

14. Goodwin, 284.

15. Goodwin, 560–64.

16. Meacham, Franklin and Winston, *An Intimate Portrait Of An Epic Friendship*, Random House, 2004, 195.

17. Meacham, 353.

18. Gallagher, 207–216.

19. Oshinsky, 31–35; John Kemp Interview, April 12, 2005; Peter Thomas Interview, April 12–13, 2005.

20. Smith, *FDR*, Random House, 2007, 216.

21. Gallagher, 214–18.

22. Starr, 346.

23. Oshinsky, 53.

24. Oshinsky, 49–53; Murphy, 98–99; Kottke and Knapp, Arch Phys Med Rehabil, vol. 69, 8–9.

25. Oshinsky, 65–68; Starr, 348–51.

26. Murphy, 158–59.

27. Correspondence from John Ditunno, MD, December 11, 2006.

28. Oshinsky, 93–128, 199–216; Murphy, 158.

29. Ditunno correspondence to Verville, December 11, 2006, regarding quote and other material on Kenny and Lovett methods; Oshinsky, 73–74 on Kenny and Lovett methods; Murphy, 125–26.

30. Oshinsky, 73–74; Murphy, 123–24.

31. Oshinsky, 75.

32. Murphy, 125–27; Oshinsky, 75–77; Kottke and Knapp, Arch Phys Med Rehabil, vol. 69, 8–9.

33. Oshinsky, 76–77.
34. Oshinsky, 76–78; Murphy, 128, 155–57.
35. Kottke, Knapp, Arch Phys Med Rehabil, vol. 69, 9.
36. Murphy, 157; Kottke, Knapp, ibid.
37. Correspondence Ditunno to author, April 30, 2005.
38. Walker, 191–92; Opitz, *et al.*, Krusen Diaries, Arch Phys Med Rehabil, vol. 78, 564.

Chapter Nine

The Expansive 1950s:
Rehabilitation Medicine Develops
under the Leadership of
Mary Switzer and Howard Rusk

Health care, biomedical research and medical education were the major domestic priorities of the 1950s. In the immediate postwar period, the public began to demand and expect that health care would be available to them when they needed it. Health care was considered a right by many Americans, despite the failure of President Truman's proposal for national health insurance. Expenditures on health grew from 4.3% of the Gross Domestic Product (GDP) to 7.3% between 1950 and 1970, and the GDP was increasing. "National health care expenditures grew from $12.7 billion to $71.6 billion. . . ." in this period and the nation built up an ". . . immense medical research establishment," and enlarged and equipped the most scientifically advanced hospitals in the world.[1] The hospital became the centerpiece for the development of health care. The VA hospital system, developed under the guidance of Paul Magnuson, had placed the hospital at the hub of the VA medical care and research enterprise. The VA model was one that the private sector could and often did follow. The VA preeminence in hospital care clearly boded well for rehabilitation medicine, as it was well entrenched in the VA hospital system thanks to Dr. Magnuson, Dr. Rusk, and President Truman. Rehabilitation medicine was also becoming a recognized part of civilian hospital care with the advent of private facilities in New York, New Jersey and California.[2]

The 1950s saw the emergence of a political partnership in health between labor, the AMA, the American Hospital Association and other health care interest groups. This alliance focused on the issues in health care on which there was no disagreement: hospital construction, medical research and the VA health care system. The economy was producing sufficient federal funds for substantial investment in these areas and in the establishment of community health centers. These programs focused on the creation of resources for the

131

advancement of medical care, but avoided the question on which the interests disagreed, that being government national health insurance. In this period, the Hill Burton hospital construction program boomed and members of Congress could assist in bringing new or expanded hospitals to their districts and states. But the focus of this growth was on acute care and general hospitals. The VA health care programs expanded greatly and the National Institutes of Health became the world's leader in medical science, although providing no home for rehabilitation medicine research.[3]

In the private sector, health insurance, (the contentious issue for the alliance), began to expand dramatically as union and management collective bargaining agreements included health insurance and employers were enabled to deduct the health insurance costs in their income tax filings. The AMA had no objection to the expansion of private health insurance, since it had some control over it through its sponsorship of Blue Cross and Blue Shield, and the government was not involved. Insurance coverage for health services expanded so fast that demand for services began to outstrip the supply of facilities, personnel and technology. It was not surprising that both medicine and politicians began to press for federal support of hospital construction, research and personnel training.

Science and technology were viewed as America's greatest assets, and had assisted the USA and its allies in winning World War II. They had produced the machinery so necessary to the War effort. They had also produced the atomic bomb, whose distribution the USA and it's UN Delegate for atomic issues, Bernard Baruch, were attempting to control. It had also produced breakthroughs in medical science such as penicillin and the polio vaccine. "Medical science epitomized the postwar vision of progress without conflict. All could agree on the value of medical progress. . . ."[4] This belief in the ability of science and those trained in science, including health professionals, to provide for America's progress was a reiteration of the views of Progressives in the early 20th century.

The National Institutes of Health (NIH) became the leader in the effort to expand the impact of medical science. Its appropriations grew enormously in this period. The effort to develop NIH science was led by Director of the NIH James Shannon and two extraordinary women who were private citizens, Mary Lasker and Florence Mahoney. Both were from families of great wealth, and came from a tradition of philanthropy and social activism. The leader of the private medical research lobbying and public relations effort was Mary Lasker, wife of Albert Lasker, a very successful Chicago advertising executive who was a close friend of Bernard Baruch. Mary Lasker remained a fixture in American politics and philanthropy for nearly 50 years. She and her husband were dedicated to providing both financial support and political leadership to health research and health care. They had been active in the 1930s in support of National Health Insurance, but soon after the war began to emphasize medical research. Mary Lasker's focus was on the public benefit of science in the conquest of disease, and she led battles in the 1940s and beyond for research in mental health, cancer and heart disease. She got to know Howard Rusk in the late 1940's and was aware of his creative work in World War II and at his NYU program in medical rehabilitation.[5]

It was fortuitous that the field of rehabilitation medicine began its development in the late 1940s, since it positioned the field exceedingly well to benefit from the upcoming dramatic expansion of health care facilities, medical research and education. The rise of the hospital as the primary site for the development of health care was also very positive for rehabilitation medicine, since it was mainly a hospital based medical care program.

But the field actually faced a number of serious problems in its search for further development and maturity. It had no national leadership in government to foster it, since the Baruch Committee was coming to an end in 1951 and Paul Magnuson was to leave the VA in the early 1950s. The medical specialty of physical medicine and rehabilitation, the only specialty primarily concerned with rehabilitation medicine, was a fledgling organization which had much less influence than other fields of medicine. The non-physician rehab-related professional societies, while well organized, did not have the same clout in economic and political spheres as medicine. A positive factor in finding new federal leadership, however, was the prominence of Dr. Rusk and the public stature he and others had recently achieved for rehabilitation medicine. Fortuitously, a federal position became available in the health and rehabilitation field and Mary Switzer entered the scene with Rusk's prompting.

MARY SWITZER AND THE OFFICE OF VOCATIONAL REHABILITATION

The seminal event of the 1950s in rehabilitation medicine was the ascendancy of Mary Switzer to leadership of the national vocational rehabilitation agency in 1950, and her aggressive advocacy for rehabilitation medicine and expanded rehabilitation services, research, professional training and facility construction. By 1950, Mary Switzer had 30 years of government service and had become a passionate advocate for health care and the Public Health Service. She was a well connected, astute politician and bureaucrat who recognized opportunities and used them to the fullest to achieve her mission of improving health care for the nation's needy. Dr. Henry Betts, who was trained by Rusk and succeeded Rusk as the foremost advocate for rehabilitation medicine after 1975, described Mary Switzer this way: "She was extraordinary and she and Rusk made the field of rehabilitation medicine. She was indefatigable and a political courtesan with tremendous powers of persuasion. She had great charm, particularly with men, was bright and decisive."[6] Mary Switzer's background in the Public Health Service and its programs, was a special benefit to rehabilitation medicine. She readily took on the cause championed by Krusen, Kessler, Rusk and Baruch.

In the late 1940s Mary Switzer had labored feverishly to create health care legislation for the mentally ill, a disability area which was becoming well organized, and medical research at the NIH. In these efforts she became well acquainted with Mary Lasker, the preeminent citizen advocate for health, who would assist her greatly in her future career in rehabilitation. Mary Lasker and her husband Albert had led the effort for improved care and research for persons with mental illness. In this early legislative work, Mary Switzer also learned the intricate ways of legislation and of methods to achieve consensus in the face of conflicting opinions and opposition. The legislative work on mental illness with Mary Lasker and Dr. Karl Menninger, a specialist in care for the mentally ill from Kansas, also brought Mary Switzer into direct contact with leaders of the Congress on health care. These leaders included Senator Lister Hill of Alabama, Senator Hubert Humphrey of Minnesota, Congressmen John Fogarty of Rhode Island and Melvin Laird of Wisconsin. These contacts would prove invaluable to Mary Switzer in her future role as an agency head and as an advocate for rehabilitation and rehabilitation medicine in the 1950s and 1960s.[7]

Mary Lasker was taken with Mary Switzer's political skill and commitment. In the late 1940's she suggested to Howard Rusk, whom she had come to know in New York where Rusk was building his NYU programs, that he get to know Mary Switzer as a way to further the development of his interests in rehabilitation medicine within the Federal government. Rusk had met Mary Switzer during World War II when he made a presentation to the Procurement and Assignment Board, which Switzer staffed for the Public Health Service. Despite his involvement with a new and unproven field, Rusk may well have been the foremost physician in public life in the late 1940s due to his closeness to President Truman, his Chairmanship of President Truman's Health Resources Planning Board and his column in the New York Times. He was dedicated to the development of rehabilitation medicine as a national program, and he needed civilian government leadership similar to that he had received in the military and at the VA. The Office of Vocational Rehabilitation (OVR) in the Federal Security Agency was a likely place for leadership for the field and Mary Switzer was the main assistant to Administrator Ewing of the Federal Security Agency.[8]

As the legend goes, the Director position for OVR became vacant in 1950 and Mary Switzer and other Federal Security Agency personnel were reviewing names of possible applicants. Dr. Rusk was advising them. One evening Mary Switzer, Dr. Rusk and other Federal Security Agency personnel dined at the Army Navy Club and considered the applicants for the position. They had ruled out all the applicants as failing to meet the leadership requirements for the tasks at OVR. In a joking manner Mary Switzer said that maybe she should take the position. Rusk encouraged her and the effort soon resulted in Mary Switzer having a new position. For the first time, she would be running an agency and not working as staff.

It is unlikely, however, that the position was obtained by Mary Switzer in this relatively offhand way. It is far more likely that her friend of 30 years and an OVR employee of 26, Tracy Copp, had urged Mary to seek the position. It is also likely that after 30 years of staff work, Mary Switzer wanted a line position running an agency. It also seems likely that she would have sounded Rusk out before offering to be a candidate for the position, knowing of Rusk's influence within the Administration. Howard Rusk was a likely supporter from the beginning, since he knew Mary and saw in her the answer to his need for an advocate for rehabilitation medicine at the federal level. Rusk had great political insight and was always looking for methods and people to lead the development of his new field of interest. History seems to support this view as the two very quickly became close colleagues in an almost unparalleled public private political partnership in the health and social service area.[9]

The first task facing Mary Switzer was expanding the financial support for the programs of OVR and she had the savvy and political allies in Congress to do just that. Mary Switzer had a very short learning curve for her new position as she had been a liaison for the Administrator of the Federal Security Agency to the OVR and had managed the 1943 amendments through the Congressional process. She immediately became a strong advocate for increased Congressional appropriations for the vocational rehabilitation program using the skills she had witnessed Mary Lasker using for mental health and NIH research. She was supported in her efforts to expand the program by Administrator Ewing and Howard Rusk (from his position of Chair of the Health Resources Planning Board).

Ewing and the Federal Security Agency hosted a national assembly of experts in 1948 to chart the future goals for the nation's health care. A special panel was established for rehabilitation chaired by Henry Kessler, who had recently finished a report on rehabilitation medicine needs for the Federal Resettlement and Retraining Administration utilized for post-war planning. The final report by Administrator Ewing to the President made rehabilitation one of the goals for the nation's health care and called for the provision of rehabilitation services to at least 250,000 men and women disabled by injury or illness annually. Ewing proposed a form of regional medical care with a medical center supported by a medical school and affiliated community hospitals and clinics. This idea would later be adopted by the Johnson Administration as the essence of its regional medical plan. A rehabilitation center was to be part of the medical center and each community hospital was to have a department of rehabilitation medicine. Ewing's report stressed the need for rehabilitation research and for a major expansion of the vocational rehabilitation program. This recommendation by Administrator Ewing to President Truman was the first time a major document on national health care would highlight rehabilitation medicine in both service delivery and in research. It owed much, in all likelihood, to the influence of Rusk as Chair of the Advisory Board to the President and Kessler in his role as chair of the rehabilitation panel. The document would be extraordinarily useful for Switzer in her new role of leading the OVR.[10]

Howard Rusk and the National Rehabilitation Association, headed by E.B. Whitten, (a skilled advocate and former rehabilitation professional), added their advocacy to the effort by Mary Switzer and the OVR to obtain greater appropriations for rehabilitation programs. The NRA had a meeting with the President, the first such meeting since the 1920s, and urged expansion of the rehabilitation programs of OVR. Rusk used his New York Times columns to tout the vocational rehabilitation program. The result of this team work between Ewing, Switzer, Rusk and Whitten was that between 1951 and 1958 the OVR programs doubled in size. Switzer and her allies stressed two policies as bases for the program's growth. The first policy was support and development of comprehensive rehabilitation centers providing medical and vocational rehabilitation services like Rusk's and Kessler's and the Woodrow Wilson Center in Virginia. The second policy focused on services to the more severely disabled, including the mentally ill. Switzer used expanded special projects funds to support the rehabilitation centers and services to severely disabled persons, and she directed the state rehabilitation agencies to support the centers with their federal and state grant in aid money. The effort was enhanced when President Truman issued a public statement to the effect that only a fraction of those needing vocational rehabilitation services were getting them.[11]

WAR INTERVENES AGAIN

As Mary Switzer assumed her new role at OVR, the Korean War broke out. The period from the end of World War II until the outbreak of the Korean War had been one of war preparedness as our one time ally, Russia, became an enemy. The Truman Administration had established a containment program of the Russians in the year after the end of World War II. Once again, the nation had to respond to a war effort and another government agency was established to assist in the mobilization of national resources for the war against North Korea, which most Americans believed was acting as a surrogate of Russia and possibly China.

The issue before the War Mobilization Board in 1950 affecting rehabilitation medicine, however, was different than in World War I and World War II. This time as the nation prepared for war, Howard Rusk was Chair of the President's Health Resources Planning Board. This Board had the responsibility for the policies and planning related to the need for and use of health facilities and personnel. With regard to a war effort, the Board would normally have an opportunity to assist in planning for use of health personnel in the war effort and in supporting civilian war mobilization. But Rusk and his Board went further, and made a relatively novel recommendation for the use of persons with disabilities. The plan was to employ persons with disabilities to assist at home in the war effort, replacing those who had been called or volunteered for military duty. The War Mobilization Board was chaired by Arthur Fleming, a very progressive President of the University of Minnesota and later Secretary of the Department of Health Education and Welfare. Fleming endorsed Rusk's concept and created a National Task Force on the needs of the disabled and their employment in the war effort. Switzer dedicated staff to the Task Force and led its efforts.[12]

The Task Force led by Mary Switzer issued a major report on the need to expand rehabilitation services and to employ persons with disabilities in the civilian sector war effort. The City of Knoxville and the Tennessee Vocational Rehabilitation Agency developed a model program for employment of persons with disabilities in the Knoxville community. The state agency, using a demonstration grant from Mary Switzer, documented a need for additional labor in a community adjacent to the Atomic Energy Commission operation in Knoxville. Fifteen hundred persons with disabilities receiving welfare assistance were targeted for rehabilitation services. The community leaders were canvassed for jobs that might be available as the war effort took labor from the community. The program became a model of rehabilitation services and employment. Rusk and Switzer had used their positions to create a needed initiative and to raise the visibility of rehabilitation of persons with disabilities in the eyes of the government leaders and the public.[13]

The war in Korea ended in about two years. It had offered Switzer and Rusk a unique opportunity to demonstrate how effective rehabilitation could be and how productive persons with disabilities could be when offered appropriate services and an opportunity to work. The Korean War would also result in Howard Rusk beginning his world rehabilitation mission, as he would travel to Korea to build bridges between Korea and the USA.

THE ELECTION OF 1952 AND A BOLD NEW ADVOCATE FOR REHABILITATION

In 1952, General Dwight D. Eisenhower was elected President and Richard Nixon, formerly a Senator from California, Vice President. They represented the first Republican leadership in the White House in 20 years. The Republican Party also controlled Congress for the first two years of the Eisenhower Administration. The Republican victory was very much an election about the popularity of General Eisenhower, whose coattails assisted Republicans in gaining seats in Congress. Given the strong support of Presidents Roosevelt and Truman for Social Security programs, health care and rehabilitation however, the change in Administrations brought many fears to the rehabilitation movement. The fears of those in the rehabilitation movement included loss of job security, program cuts and redirections. Mary Switzer feared for her position as Director of OVR, since she had been in her new position of leadership for less than two years. Mary and those who worked for her did not know what to expect from a party that had often opposed the federal programs proposed by Presidents Roosevelt and Truman as being too expensive, and involving too strong a role for the federal government.

General Eisenhower was not a partisan Republican, however, and had even considered running as a Democrat when the Democratic Party approached him about it. Vice President Nixon, while known primarily for his strong anti-communist positions, was a member of the Progressive wing of the party. He had served on the committee that oversaw rehabilitation legislation while a member of the House of Representatives, and had co-sponsored national health insurance legislation with Senator Jacob Javits of New York.[14]

In 1953, President Eisenhower proposed cabinet status for the Federal Security Agency, which had long been a desire of those in the Agency. He named Oveta Culp Hobby, former Commander of the Women's Army Corps under Eisenhower in World War II, as the first Secretary of the Department of Health, Education and Welfare. Hobby knew Eisenhower well and enjoyed a close line of communication with the President. The connection between war and the development of rehabilitation medicine was to be advantageous once again as both General Eisenhower and Commander Hobby knew of Howard Rusk and of the contributions that he and rehabilitation medicine had made to the war effort and to the veterans of World War II. Oveta Culp Hobby also knew Mary Switzer and told Howard Rusk that, in her new role as Secretary of HEW, she would depend on Mary. The new Department included all the programs of the Federal Security Agency and was created not to consolidate existing agencies but to give the required visibility to the programs in the new Department. These programs included NIH sponsored research; the maternal and child health and crippled children's programs; education programs; Social Security Act benefits; and programs of the OVR. President Eisenhower also asked Howard Rusk to stay on as Chair of the National Health Resources Planning Board in recognition of his good work in that role and of Eisenhower's knowledge of Rusk's value to the military and the VA.[15]

But all was not well for Mary Switzer and her hold on her new position at OVR. Soon it was rumored that the President had someone else in mind for the position of OVR Director. Despite Secretary Hobby's support for her, she had to tell Mary that she should begin looking for another job. When Howard Rusk heard of this he jumped into action. He had finally found a leader and a federal agency willing to support civilian rehabilitation medicine, and she was about to be replaced. He visited Secretary Hobby immediately and was told that the Secretary wanted Mary Switzer in the position, but that Vice President Nixon had a candidate for the position from California who had worked on his campaign. The position of Director of OVR was a political appointment and Mary could be removed in favor of those who had assisted the new Administration in the campaign. Dr. Rusk visited Sherman Adams, the President's Chief of Staff; and General Snyder, who was both the President's personal physician and the White House physician. Rusk was still highly influential in the Administration, despite not having the personal friendship with President Eisenhower that he had enjoyed with President Truman. He remained in his position at the Health Resources Planning Board with the President's support and he was asked by John Foster Dulles, the Secretary of State, to visit Korea for the Korean Foundation created by the Dulles brothers to assist in postwar assistance. It is a testament to his great skill and diplomacy, as well as his sincere dedication to the country and health care, that he was trusted by a new Administration that had been out of power for 20 years. Rusk pleaded with Adams and General Snyder to keep Mary in the position at OVR. He argued that Mary was excellent in her position at OVR and that her removal would make the disability community furious.[16]

Rusk used his best political skill to enlist support for Mary among others who might have the Administration's ear. He enlisted Dr. Ted Klump, President of Winthrop-Stearns Chemical Company, and George Merck of the pharmaceutical giant bearing his name. Both were members of the Task Force created by Arthur Fleming to advise on the needs of persons with disabilities and their civilian employment in the war effort. They were both friends and supporters of Switzer and Rusk. Klump wrote letters and Merck made calls. At nine in the evening after Rusk's call, "Merck began calling legislators. . . . And by seven the next morning called Rusk back to say he had been on the phone all night." President Eisenhower confirmed Mary Switzer as Director of the OVR and Howard Rusk as Chair of the National Health Resources Planning Board for another five years. The lobbying campaign for Switzer had paid off.[17]

THE 1954 AMENDMENTS TO THE VOCATIONAL REHABILITATION ACT

In 1953, Secretary Hobby and Undersecretary Nelson Rockefeller, soon to be the Governor of New York and a Presidential candidate in 1964, visited President Eisenhower to discuss the rehabilitation program and its need for legislative reform. Undersecretary Rockefeller and Mary Switzer had been charged with developing proposals for improving the rehabilitation program. They established an effective team and created the proposals, which were sent to the President prior to the meeting. In presenting their views to the President, Hobby and Rockefeller stressed the need to reform the Act to provide the resources necessary for the expansion of rehabilitation services, facilities, research and training of professionals. The President asked what number of disabled persons would be rehabilitated under the proposals. The President was dissatisfied with the answer of 100,000 per year and said with enthusiasm the goal should be 200,000 per year. The proposals of the Administration for the Act followed these recommendations. They also reflected the recommendations of the Baruch Committee, whose impact continued to be felt and expressed in national policy.[18]

President Eisenhower then proceeded to speak out publicly about the great benefits of the rehabilitation program in a way that no President had before, although many Presidents had been supporters of the program. On January 4, 1954, the President delivered a message to the nation on his legislative program for 1954; which included the Rehabilitation Act, Hill Burton hospital construction legislation and reforming the Old Age retirement program. In his message he cited the rehabilitation program as the model for approaching social programs, for it enabled people to lead lives of usefulness. The President then indicated that two million persons with disabilities needed rehabilitation services but only 60,000 were rehabilitated annually. In the same year, Vice President Nixon, following the lead of the President, publicized 1954 as Rehabilitation Year.[19]

In selling the Congress on the Administration's proposals for reform of the Rehabilitation Act during 1954, Undersecretary Rockefeller and Mary Switzer relied on the numbers of persons who could be served if amendments they proposed were adopted. They also stressed the savings that could be obtained from rehabilitating persons with disabilities who were public assistance recipients. Placement in employment would decrease public assistance payments and might attract tax revenues not previously paid. Assisted by Congressman Barden, House author of the 1943 amendments, the bill moved easily through the Republican controlled House of Representatives in 1954. The Republican controlled Senate also supported the Administration bill. The President subsequently signed the bill at the White House in a ceremony attended by Under Secretary Rockefeller, Mary Switzer, Howard Rusk and E.B. Whitten (Executive Director of the National Rehabilitation Association). In a telling letter about the ceremony, the importance of the Act and its history, Mary Switzer wrote Bernard Baruch that: "The most important person had not been there" (meaning Baruch).[20]

The new Act removed any limit on appropriations for the state vocational rehabilitation services program, specifying that the federal government would match whatever funds the states appropriated. The wealthiest states would get at least a 60% federal match for the funds they appropriated, and the poorer states would get a higher federal matching rate. Such financing demonstrated the commitment of Congress and the President to expansive funding to rehabilitate at least 200,000 persons annually. A national program to train professionals for the rehabilitation field was established in the Act and at Howard Rusk's behest a special appropriation was created for training of medical students and residents in the field of rehabilitation medicine. Research received a specific authorization for its programs to fund medical and vocational rehabilitation research and a construction authority for rehabilitation facilities was included in the Act. Under the construction program, 200 new facilities were created in the next six years. Howard Rusk, E.B. Whitten, and Mary Switzer also obtained amendments to the Hill Burton Act in 1954 for a special appropriation regarding construction and expansion of rehabilitation facilities. The field therefore had two sources of funding for medical rehabilitation facility expansion, the facility construction authority in the Vocational rehabilitation Act and the authority in the Hill Burton Hospital Construction Act. The new Act notably followed the Baruch Committee recommendations for the creation of civilian rehabilitation facilities, training programs in rehabilitation medicine disciplines and research at academic centers.[21]

Mary Switzer had gotten her comprehensive authority for the Rehabilitation program; and the rehabilitation medicine field had national leadership to pursue the work recommended by the Baruch Committee. Rehabilitation medicine would have its own agency, as well as research, training and facility grants under the Rehabilitation Amendments of 1954. The programs in research and training would benefit all rehabilitation professions. Facilities would support vocational and medical rehabilitation services. Rehabilitation medicine would also be the beneficiary of a program to pay for medical rehabilitation services when private insurance was not available. This would be done through the use of state vocational rehabilitation services funds for medical rehabilitation, authorized first in 1943 but seldom implemented by the states. Under Mary Switzer's stewardship of the OVR, the state rehabilitation agencies would also apply vocational rehabilitation funds to rehabilitation medicine services in substantial amounts for the first time.

SOCIAL SECURITY DISABILITY AND
REHABILITATION POLICY

In the 20 years between the enactment of the Social Security Act (SSA) of 1935 and 1956, the Social Security staff had continued to plan for the expansion of Social Security Act social insurance programs to include disability insurance. The Act focused on the retired population over 65, but not on those individuals who had a substantial work history but were unable to work further due to physical or mental disability. The particular disability topic, which the Federal Security Agency staff, headed by I. S. Falk, continued to focus on was medical services and rehabilitation for persons with disabilities. The policy issue facing the planners was whether persons with disabilities would work if their disability were to receive timely medical care, medical rehabilitation and other rehabilitation services. The issue of disability insurance revisited the disagreement about the federal role in health coverage and medical rehabilitation for Social Security Act beneficiaries with disabling conditions. Workers Compensation programs often provided these services with the goal of workers returning to productive employment, although the programs varied greatly by state. New Jersey, for example, had reduced the level and quality of its rehabilitation services under the Workers Compensation program to such an extent that Dr. Kessler, who was a supporter of industrial medicine, was very discouraged. Return to work was also the goal of the Vocational Rehabilitation Act, renewed in 1954, and it was an existing and proven program to serve recipients of a disability insurance cash support program.[22]

In the late 1940s and early 1950s and prior to the election of 1952, Congress was faced with very controversial issues regarding disability that had a direct bearing on its later consideration of disability insurance. At the request of Paul Strahan, a private citizen with a disability, the Department of Labor began an effort to become the lead agency for all disability programs. Its philosophy was one of providing cash assistance to those who could not work and jobs for those who could. It viewed the health and rehabilitation services of medical professionals such as Dr. Rusk and his colleagues and the vocational rehabilitation services of state vocational rehabilitation agencies as being ineffectual and unnecessary. Strahan and the Labor Department developed a bill to create a Commission on Disability housed in the Labor Department, to be responsible for all programs involving disability, including the vocational rehabilitation program. Not to be outdone, the Federal Security Agency developed its own bill with the support of Dr. Rusk, his medical rehabilitation colleagues, and the National Rehabilitation Association. This bill supported the professionals working in the state vocational rehabilitation agencies. Their bill kept OVR with its vocational rehabilitation programs in the Federal Security Agency, made rehabilitation services more readily available to recipients of Social Security Act programs, and emphasized the need for services and a return to work. Initially President Truman sided with the Federal Security Agency and Dr. Rusk. But as the departmental tensions grew, President Truman urged the two agencies to compromise. When a compromise failed, the President left the decision to the Senate and Senator Paul Douglas of Illinois, who was an economist and expert on social insurance. Douglas sided with Rusk and the rehabilitation professionals and his bill became the administration bill, which passed the Senate, but died in Committee in the House.[23]

Senator Douglas took up the disability issue again in 1954 as the Federal Security Agency, now the Department of HEW, pressed for changes to the Old Age Retirement program to protect persons who became disabled before they reached retirement age. His support for the medical and rehabilitation professionals in the earlier debates paid dividends for the field. The issue had to do with the calculation of benefits for a qualified old age retiree if that person had become disabled and left the work force prior to attaining age 65. In contrast to some who wished to have lower payments and used averaging of wages earned to establish the benefit, the Administration urged that the higher wage at the time of disability be used. This approach also involved the establishment of a process to determine when disability occurred and services to provide for a possible recovery and return to work before the person turned 65. The state vocational rehabilitation agencies were used to make these determinations and furnish the services. The Administration was successful in its approach and amendments were enacted in 1954 with the leadership of Senator Douglas. The enactment was a victory for the rehabilitation medicine services model over the narrower approach of cash and jobs advocated by the

Labor Department. The amendments also laid the ground work for the establishment of a disability insurance program to supplement the old age retirement program. I. S. Falk and colleagues at the Federal Security Agency in 1935 and into the 1940s had developed plans for such an insurance program, but had not persuaded the White House leadership to adopt their view. Their approach had included health care and rehabilitation services for the disabled person as well as cash payments.[24]

In 1956, Congress took up directly the question of disability insurance under the Social Security Act. Senator Douglas again was leader of the effort, since he served on the Senate Finance Committee, which had jurisdiction over all Social Security Act matters. Disability insurance was a Social Security Act proposal. The Department of HEW, Dr. Rusk and Dr. Krusen urged that an insurance program be adopted which provided not only cash assistance through insurance for one unable to work due to disability, but also for medical and vocational services to assist in rehabilitating disabled persons so they could return to work and a productive life. Dr. Krusen had testified for the disability and rehabilitation approach on behalf of the AMA. He and others had convinced the AMA to support a rehabilitation approach to disability so long as the states, through the vocational rehabilitation agencies, administered the rehabilitation services programs. Up to that point, the AMA had opposed all national social insurance programs that might involve medical services because of their fear that the federal government would dictate to medicine. The approach chosen by HEW, Rusk and Krusen avoided this AMA objection by requiring the state vocational rehabilitation agencies, supervised by OVR, to administer the rehabilitation services part of the program. HEW would supply most of the funds needed from the Social Security Act funds. Dr. Krusen's testimony in support of the legislation was buttressed by his personal contact with his friend from Minnesota, Senator Hubert Humphrey, who agreed with Krusen's approach. Humphrey wrote to Krusen in 1956 after his testimony. "I shall indeed urge reconsideration of the disability feature of H.R. 7225. I agree with you, the emphasis should be on rehabilitation. . . . I am going to reiterate your views in a letter to the chairman of the committee."[25]

The subsequent enactment of the Disability Insurance Amendments in 1956 was another milestone in the development of a disability and rehabilitation policy for the nation, and one which recognized the need for rehabilitation medicine services to people with disabilities. In 1965 these same Committees, with many of the same members, would enact a Medicare program for the aged and then, in 1972, extend it to disability recipients. The Amendments of 1956 provided for a disability determination process administered by the state rehabilitation agencies; cash assistance for the beneficiary while unable to work due to the disability; and evaluation and rehabilitation services for beneficiaries with the capability to benefit from the service and return to work. Together with the Vocational Rehabilitation Act as amended in 1954, the Social Security Disability Insurance program provided a major federal commitment to financing services to rehabilitate adults with disabilities so they could achieve through their own efforts a productive life.

REHABILITATION MEDICINE TAKES OFF
WITH OVR SUPPORT

Mary Switzer used her new authorities from the 1954 amendments to the Rehabilitation Act and her strong Presidential support for rehabilitation to build programs throughout the country involving both vocational rehabilitation and rehabilitation medicine services. Her dynamic leadership, supported from the private sector by Dr. Rusk, enabled rehabilitation medicine to flourish through professional training grants, research support, and the establishment of local medical and vocational facilities for the provision of rehabilitation services. Rehabilitation medicine was able to expand, just as Starr indicated that other fields of medicine grew in this period of increased support for medical research, training and facilities construction. These forms of support combined to vastly expand the role of the hospital as the epicenter of American medical and medical rehabilitation care, and the teaching hospital as the home for medical research and training.[26]

"In the first year under the new Act, 124 teaching grants were made to institutions and 1,177 to individuals." These grants included ". . . physicians, social workers, nurses, occupational and physical therapists."[27] Over 20% of the training funds were used to teach undergraduate medical students about comprehensive medical rehabilitation, and to train residents in physical medicine and rehabilitation. The new field of rehabilitation counseling received 35% of the training funds, social work 19%, and the remainder was distributed among nursing, occupational and physical therapy and state agency in-service training. Cecile Hillyer was Mary Switzer's energetic staff person who oversaw the growth of this program. Switzer and Hillyer also created a new profession in rehabilitation counseling, which later became the dominant non-health profession for rehabilitation services. From 1954 to 1960, nearly 200 rehabilitation facilities would receive federal support for either their initial establishment or expansion, and many of these were medical rehabilitation facilities.[28]

Mary Switzer made a point of enlisting the many non-profit charities in the United States to become part of this new and developing field of human services; including the Easter Seal Society for Crippled Children and Adults, United Cerebral Palsy, Goodwill Industries, the Association of Retarded Citizens and the Catholic Charities. These charities were following the pioneering efforts of philanthropists Jeremiah Milbank, Henry Kaiser and Bernard Baruch to support rehabilitation services and research. They used federal facility grants or program innovation and expansion grants to broaden the scope of services that they financed privately. It was during this period that medical rehabilitation facilities developed or expanded to become comprehensive service facilities for severely disabled individuals. The vocational and medical rehabilitation facility construction and staffing program was developed according to the guidelines recommended in the Baruch Committee report. The medical rehabilitation facilities included the programs of: Rusk in New York; Kessler in New Jersey; Rancho Los Amigos in Los Angeles; The Texas Institute for Rehabilitation and Research affiliated with Baylor Medical School in Houston that had been established by Dr. William Spencer; and the Rehabilitation Institute of Chicago established by Dr. Magnuson. Mary Switzer also used the grant funds she controlled to assist physical medicine and rehabilitation specialists to obtain leadership of the rehabilitation medicine facilities and programs supported by OVR. She negotiated with hospitals to enable specialists in physical medicine and rehabilitation to direct the rehabilitation medicine programs in those hospitals, often against the will of the hospital. Her role was even greater than that of Rusk, Kessler or Krusen in this regard as she had the leverage to obtain the results she wanted from the grants she was awarding through her agency.[29]

Of all the programs in Mary Switzer's federal armamentarium, her favorite was research. She had worked hard in the Public Health Service in the late 1940s to build the NIH through new legislation and Congressional appropriations, toiling along side the legendary Mary Lasker. She knew how to build research and training programs in medicine, while avoiding tensions and sometimes opposition from the AMA. With regard to the 1954 Rehabilitation Act's training and research programs, this accommodation of medicine took the form of a National Advisory Council on Vocational Rehabilitation. The Council advised on all policy issues affecting the rehabilitation programs carried out under the Vocational Rehabilitation Act. It also approved priorities and programs for the spending of the discretionary grant programs, such as for research and training. Mary Switzer used the National Advisory Council on Vocational Rehabilitation to convince the AMA that bureaucrats would not define medical research or training. The 12 member National Advisory Council "included two of the rehabilitation medicine pioneers: Dr. Frank Krusen and Dr. Henry Kessler."[30] They represented different specialties, physical medicine and rehabilitation and orthopedics, assuring the AMA that no one field would dominate, although both were missionaries for rehabilitation medicine. Krusen's leadership role within the AMA was especially helpful to Switzer and OVR because the AMA throughout the 1950s remained very worried about the intrusion of the Federal government into health care, medical research, and health professional training. The AMA trusted Krusen. In 1955, 45 research projects were approved for institutions in 17 states. Many of these projects were in rehabilitation medicine. The broad state distribution reflected Mary Switzer's deft hand at politics. Research grants focused on orthopedic, neurological, cardiovascular, visual, psychological and speech disorders. These grants would pave the way for the creation of a major new research and training center program in the 1960s.[31]

Frank Krusen took leave from the Mayo Clinic in 1959 and joined Mary Switzer as her Special Assistant with a portfolio of research and liaison to the Public Health Service. Nothing better represents the significance of the OVR and Mary Switzer to the development of rehabilitation medicine than the decision of Frank Krusen to leave the Mayo Clinic and join the OVR. His total dedication to the field is also evident in this stint of public service. The fact both Baruch and Mary Switzer, two astute judges of character and leadership capacity, chose Krusen to direct efforts to establish policies and programs for training and research in rehabilitation medicine suggests strongly that of all the rehabilitation medicine experts in the period from World War II to 1960, Frank Krusen might have been the most respected with regard to knowledge of rehabilitation medicine, research and training. In his new role Krusen built on the concepts developed by the consensus of the Baruch Committee regarding the needs for the field of rehabilitation medicine. Foremost among those was the concept of an academically based center for both research and training in rehabilitation medicine. Krusen established policies for such programs and later joined with Dr. Frederick Kottke to obtain Congressional support for them.[32]

Another important development to rehabilitation services and rehabilitation medicine in the period of 1955 to 1960 was the implementation of the 1954 and 1956 disability insurance amendments to the Social Security Act. These amendments had been championed by the OVR and the Social Security Agency. OVR led the state vocational rehabilitation agencies in carrying out their new roles of determining disability and providing rehabilitation services. Between 1955 and 1959, 1,300,000 workers were referred to state agencies and 140,000 were accepted for rehabilitation services. The cost benefit ratio of rehabilitation was most obvious in cases of disability insurance beneficiaries, who were returned to work and ceased to obtain Social Security payments. The rehabilitation services for which these individuals were eligible included medical rehabilitation services. The state agencies were encouraged by Mary Switzer to refer these workers to the specialized medical rehabilitation programs operated by Rusk, Kessler, the Woodrow Wilson Center, Rancho Los Amigos and the Kabat-Kaiser Institute, among others. The Program was a start on a Social Security health insurance program and served as a precedent for the later policies of Medicare in rehabilitation.[33]

In all of these efforts to expand programs for medical rehabilitation, Howard Rusk played a major role, although it was frequently behind the scenes. His national visibility and respect were assets to the field and Mary Switzer knew she could draw on those assets when necessary. Rusk's New York Times articles continued to tout the value and necessity of rehabilitation services, and the public was made aware of this area of medicine through his articles. The articles were clearly of benefit to Switzer and her agency. When appropriations were held up in Congress in 1952, Rusk wrote an article commending the program. Switzer subsequently wrote to her friend Tracy Copp that "It is wonderful to have Howard's help."[34] In a memorandum briefing the Federal Security Administrator in 1952, Switzer identified Rusk as: "The inspiration and support of our program as no other individual in the country."[35] Politicians were happy to be associated with a field that was gaining such prominence. Rusk had also continued as a member of the National Health Resources Planning Board that was advising President Eisenhower. Rusk used Congressional testimony and personal contacts to obtain the enactment of the 1954 Rehabilitation Act, rehabilitation facility amendments to the Hill Burton program and the disability provisions of the Social Security Acts of 1954 and 1956. In so doing, he achieved greater influence for rehabilitation medicine in the delivery of health services and placed the field in a good position to be recognized by private health insurance and any future federal health insurance programs.

INTERNATIONAL PROMINENCE FOR
REHABILITATION MEDICINE

Rusk's prominence rose during the 1950s as Presidential advisors and Cabinet members asked him to undertake special missions for them involving health care, rehabilitation, sickness and disability throughout the world. Shortly after the end of the Korean War, John Foster Dulles, Secretary of State Designate, formed an American-Korean Foundation to improve relations between the peoples of these two nations. Milton Eisenhower, brother to the President, became Chairman of the Board. Both knew of Howard Rusk's work at NYU and of his service to both Presidents Truman and Eisenhower. They asked Dr. Rusk to travel to Korea for them and report on the health needs of the Korean people. His trip and tour of health facilities left him appalled at the needs for health care and the lack of resources to meet them. When Rusk returned to the United States he reported to President Eisenhower on his findings. He also accompanied Eisenhower to a meeting of railroad executives, whom Rusk addressed. The executives initiated a major effort to obtain contributions of necessary supplies and food for Korea. This mission began a lifelong interest of Dr. Rusk in Korea, which he returned to visit eight times, often at the request of Washington officials.[36]

Dr. Rusk undertook a mission in Thailand in 1955 at the request of the Ambassador to Thailand, Bill Donovan, who had headed the intelligence network of the United States during World War II. Rusk established a training program for rehabilitation professionals from Thailand, and Donovan arranged for their transportation to the United States. The program was so successful that Donovan and Rusk approached Mary Lasker and the Lasker Foundation to continue it. Mrs. Lasker encouraged them to expand the program beyond Thailand and establish a non-profit organization to take on the effort. The result of this meeting was the establishment of the World Rehabilitation Fund (WRF) under Rusk's direction and located at the Institute for Rehabilitation Medicine at NYU. On the Honorary Board of the WRF sat President Hoover, President Truman, Bernard Baruch and Dr. Albert Schweitzer. Mary Switzer provided funding through the Office of Vocational Rehabilitation and David Sarnoff of RCA provided the assistance of his company. The WRF established programs throughout the world for many years.[37]

The missionary appeal of the rehabilitation movement and its application to foreign countries affected many of the leaders of rehabilitation medicine in the 1950s. Henry Kessler was also attracted to the needs of other countries for rehabilitation after World War II. In 1950, the United Nations passed a resolution supporting rehabilitation services to all disabled people throughout the world and offering advice and technical assistance to all member nations. Dr. Kessler then began a new phase to his career as the UN expert on rehabilitation and its traveling physician. His first mission was to Yugoslavia. Other missions took him to Greece, India, Israel and Indonesia. He provided assistance both for orthopedic medicine and rehabilitation medicine. Dr. Krusen was active in the establishment of the International Society of Physical Medicine and Rehabilitation.[38]

The activities of Rusk and Kessler in international rehabilitation were important to the development of rehabilitation medicine in the United States because the service they performed enhanced the appreciation for rehabilitation among the many American leaders who asked for their assistance. It also gave Rusk and Kessler relatively easy access to those leaders when the field needed their assistance. The commitment of all three men to assisting people in need of health care throughout the world reflected the commitment and humanitarian values, which motivated the leaders of rehabilitation medicine in the first half of the 20th century. Those values have been reflected recently in world rehabilitation efforts by leaders in the rehabilitation and disability movements such as Judith Heumann, Lex Frieden, Justin Dart, Jr., Dr. Henry Betts, Dr. John Ditunno, Dr. Bruce Gans, and Dr. John Melvin.[39]

By 1960, in the space of only 15 years, rehabilitation medicine had gone from being unrecognized in the United States to being a priority for not only the U.S. government but for the United Nations and many of its member states. Bernard Baruch's dream for a new field of medical care described in the Baruch Committee Report was well on its way to fruition.

NOTES

1. Starr, 335.
2. Starr, 335–36.
3. Starr, 337; Ludmerer, 140–48.
4. Starr, 336.
5. Starr, 342–344.
6. Interview with Henry Betts, MD, October 7, 2007.
7. Walker, *Beyond Bureaucracy*, 112–15, 152.
8. Interviews with Henry Betts, MD, October 7 and 9, 2004; Walker, 119; Berkowitz, 137–142.
9. Walker, 126; Interviews with Dr. Betts, October 7 and 9, 2004.
10. Berkowitz, 132–38.
11. Walker, 135–37, 141.
12. Walker, 137–40.
13. Ibid.
14. Starr, 285, 334–50; Irwin Gelman, *The Contender, Richard Nixon and the Congress Years,* The Free Press, Simon & Schuster, 1999, 306–43; Remini, *The House*, Smithsonian Books, 2006, 357–75.
15. Walker, 141–42.
16. Walker, 142–44; Berkowitz, 248; Rusk, 201–04.
17. Walker, 143–44.
18. Walker, 149; Berkowitz, 271–73.
19. Berkowitz, 273; Walker, 149.
20. Walker, 149–53; *50 Years of Vocational Rehabilitation in the U.S.A.*, 17–18; Berkowitz, 279–80.
21. Walker, 156–57.
22. Berkowitz, 123–130.
23. Berkowitz, 186–207.
24. Berkowitz, 186–207; Walker, 153.

25. Opitz, *et al.*, Krusen Diaries, Arch Phys Med Rehabil, vol. 78, 564.

26. Starr, 359–60; Ludmerer, 164–67; Kottke, Knapp, Arch Phys Med Rehabil, vol. 69, 9.

27. Walker, 163.

28. Walker, 166–69.

29. Walker, 162, 166–67.

30. Walker, 160.

31. Walker, 160–61.

32. Opitz *et al.*, Krusen Diaries, Arch Phys Med Rehabil, vol. 78, 564.

33. Walker, 171.

34. Berkowitz, 248.

35. Ibid.

36. Rusk, 200–08.

37. Rusk, 220–26.

38. Kessler, 161–218; Opitz et al., Krusen Diaries, Arch Phys Med Rehabil, vol. 78, 559.

39. Kessler, 161–62.

Naval aviation pilot Dale Lyons sitting atop wing of plane he flew with his artificial leg which was fitted while he was at Mare Island Amputee Center directed by Dr. Henry Kessler. Dale Lyons was the father of Patricia Ditunno, wife of Dr. John Ditunno, one of rehabilitation medicine's second generation leaders. Dale Lyons lost his leg during the attack on Pearl Harbor December 7, 1941 but returned to active duty flight status "carrier qualified," demonstrating the efficacy of rehabilitation medicine, and later received the Purple Heart. He piloted a drone craft during Atomic Bomb tests on Bikini Knoll and is believed to be the only WWII pilot using an artificial leg. Photo courtesy of Patricia Ditunno and the WWII Honoree Registry.

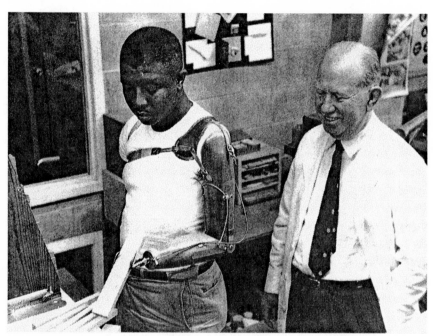

Dr. Henry Kessler, a founder of rehabilitation medicine, seeing a patient at the Kessler Institute for Rehabilitation, Orange, New Jersey sometime during the 1950s. Dr. Kessler established the Institute in 1948 at about the same time Dr. Howard Rusk established the Institute of Rehabilitation Medicine at NYU. The two facilities were the first large scale civilian rehabilitation medicine facilities after WWII. Photo is courtesy of the Kessler Institute for Rehabilitation.

Dr. Kessler at the Kessler Institute for Rehabilitation, displaying the warmth and compassion for which he was well recognized. Kessler was viewed by Dr. Rusk as the true pioneer of rehabilitation medicine. Photo courtesy of the Kessler Institute for Rehabilitation.

President Eisenhower signing the 1954 amendments to the Vocational Rehabilitation Act with the first Secretary of the Department of Health Education and Welfare, Oveta Culp Hobby and the members of the Congressional delegation responsible for its passage. The Act was the first comprehensive law for medical and vocational rehabilitation services, research, and education. Photo courtesy of the Rehabilitation Services Administration and the private collection of the author.

Mary Switzer, another of the five founders of rehabilitation medicine, after appointment as Director of the Office of Vocational Rehabilitation, in 1950. She directed it and later the Social and Rehabilitation Service of the Department of Health Education and Welfare [HEW] from 1950 until her retirement in 1970. In that position, she and Dr. Rusk established a renowned public private partnership to lead development of the entire rehabilitation field. Photo courtesy of Frank Romano and the Rehabilitation Services Administration.

Dr. Paul Magnuson a pioneer in bone and joint surgery as well as rehabilitation medicine who was head of surgery at Northwestern University. Dr. Magnuson recruited Dr. John Coulter to Northwestern to establish a physical medicine program in the 1920's and became chief of medical affairs under General Omar Bradley at the newly organized Veterans Administration post WWII. In 1954 he founded the Rehabilitation Institute of Chicago. Photo courtesy of the Rehabilitation Institute of Chicago, Dr. Henry Betts and Ms. Margaret Gonzalez.

Mary Switzer presenting a Certification of Appreciation to Dr. William Spencer of the Texas Institute of Rehabilitation and Research February 7, 1969 in her last full year as head of the Office of Vocational Rehabilitation and the Social and Rehabilitation Service. Dr. Spencer was one of the second generation leaders of rehabilitation medicine. Photo courtesy of Richard Melia and the author from his private collection.

Dr. Howard Rusk, a founder of rehabilitation medicine and President of the Institute of Rehabilitation Medicine at NYU, second from the left and next to Dr. Henry Betts, President of the Rehabilitation Institute of Chicago, who was mentored by Rusk. Next to Dr. Betts is movie actress Patricia Neal and The Honorable Richard Daley, Mayor of Chicago. The four luminaries were together in the 1960s to present to a Congressional hearing on rehabilitation, for which all were advocates. Photo courtesy of the Rehabilitation Institute of Chicago.

Chapter Ten

Rehabilitation Leadership in the Turbulent 1960s and the End of an Era

The decade of the 1960s represented the height of political expression by Americans since the Revolution of 1776. The 1960s saw Americans express themselves through demonstrations against racial discrimination, poverty, hunger and a war which many failed to see as appropriate for America to have entered. The phrase "The Turbulent Sixties" describes the period well and was used by Dr. Ernest W. Johnson in his History of Physiatry for that decade.[1] The decade was most notable for the assassinations of three American leaders: President Kennedy in 1963, Martin Luther King in 1967, and Senator and Presidential candidate Robert Kennedy in 1968. It was also notable for the enactment of more social legislation than in any period other than in the Depression. New laws provided for health coverage, job training and placement services, the alleviation of poverty, and strengthened civil rights. Organizations of members of under served populations were a formidable force in politics during this decade.

During the 1960s rehabilitation became a federal program that was a model for others seeking legislation. Rehabilitation treated the individual receiving services as a whole person with needs that were medical, educational, psychological and social. This individualized approach to comprehensive services became the prevalent view of policy planners in the 1960s, as they sought to design programs to alleviate poverty and the effects of poverty. The use of the rehabilitation services programs of OVR as a response to the complicated problem of poverty and lack of education that faced many Americans in the 1960s created problems for the professionals in the field. Expectations were high and the capacity to deliver was more limited than optimistic policy planners had assumed.

The most important development for acceptance and maturity of rehabilitation medicine in the 1960s was the creation of a national health insurance program for the elderly. Medicare and Medicaid were enacted in 1965 and both had a role in stimulating the further development of rehabilitation medicine as well as a national policy on disability. The Medicare program of health insurance for the elderly, including the elderly with disabilities, became the major stimulus for rehabilitation medicine programs in the last quarter of the twentieth century. Medicaid provided a source of medical and social services to persons with disabilities who were poor and who had little or no work history. All the work done in the early and mid-century by Baruch, Rusk, Krusen, Switzer, Kessler, Magnuson, Coulter and others, laid the groundwork for the inclusion of rehabilitation medicine in the Medicare and Medicaid programs.

At the end of the 1960s and the beginning of the next decade, the torch of leadership in rehabilitation medicine and disability policy was also passed to a second generation of leaders and their national associations. This leadership came from numerous health disciplines and providers involved in rehabilitation medicine, not from just a few individuals with special influence. More importantly, the torch of leadership was also passed to a newly developing movement of persons with disabilities who wished to lead in their own right and not just rely for leadership on the professionals who provided care to them. The genesis of this movement was rooted in the civil rights movement of the 1950s and 1960s.

REHABILITATION, DISABILITY AND THE KENNEDY FAMILY

The election of President Kennedy in November of 1960 resulted in the issue of disability receiving continued and enhanced national attention. Despite his narrow margin of victory, President Kennedy moved the nation to take action to relieve the burdens of the nation's needy, including persons with disabilities. The President and his family forged a close bond with Dr. Rusk and the rehabilitation medicine field during the next few years, and that bond still exists today and provides a continuous source of support for the field.

The interest of President Kennedy in disability initially involved the field of mental illness and retardation. That interest was the result of the fact that the President had a sister who was a mentally retarded person. Joseph Kennedy, Sr. and his wife Rose Kennedy, moved by the plight of their daughter and others like her, established the Kennedy Foundation to deal with mental retardation. It was similar to the National Foundation of Infantile Paralysis (NFIP) established by

FDR to deal with polio in its focus on research and services dealing with a particular disability. To this day, the Kennedy family has been the nation's leading force for services to persons with mental retardation, and more broadly to all people with disabilities. From the mid 1970s, Senator Ted Kennedy has been a steadfast and effective advocate and lobbyist within Congress for healthcare and for programs and policies to assist persons with disabilities. His sister, Eunice Shriver, has been a constant fund raiser and advocate throughout America for the Special Olympics and for the needs of those with mental retardation.

In 1959 before his son's election to the Presidency, Joseph Kennedy Sr. had come to the Institute of Rehabilitation Medicine (IRM) at NYU to ask Howard Rusk for assistance in a matter of political sensitivity which dealt with health and disability. Some years earlier, the Kennedy family had established its Foundation. Joseph Kennedy, Sr. was a very wealthy businessman who had been active in the Democratic Party for many years and served as Ambassador to Great Britain in the Administration of FDR. Intent on obtaining the Presidency for his son, Senator John Kennedy, the patriarch became concerned about the possible problems the Foundation might pose during an intense election campaign. By 1959, the Foundation was substantial, but the senior Kennedy wanted it revitalized.

I'd like you to help me reorganize the Kennedy Foundation. . . . My son is planning to run for President next year and I don't want anyone to say the foundation made a contribution to a hospital or any other agency for political reasons. Could you take a reading on this and give us your recommendation?

Rusk's prominence in health care and disability and his reputation for political acumen and discretion made him a logical choice for the job.

Rusk proceeded to set up a committee of experts on mental illness and retardation, which advised the family on operating the foundation. Since that time, the Foundation has been noted for its success in fostering independence for persons with mental retardation, including their participation in athletic activity.[2] It did not cause any political problems for the election of John F. Kennedy as President.

In the field of mental retardation great progress has been made in the last 15 years and the Kennedy Foundation has been responsible for much of it. . . . They made funds available that have proven that retarded people can do much more for themselves than they have ever been given a chance to do."[3]

Three years later and after the election of John Kennedy to the Presidency, Joseph Kennedy, Sr. returned to the Institute as a patient after suffering a severe stroke. When the stroke occurred in late 1961, Dr. Rusk was summoned to Palm Beach where the family lived. He made seven trips to Florida and set up rehabilitation services at the local hospital and in the home. In 1962, Rusk and the family decided to have Joseph Sr. admitted to the Institute for Rehabilitation Medicine (IRM) that Rusk had founded at NYU. The family obviously believed that the Institute could provide some assistance and improve the condition of the President's father, even though he was not admitted until five months after the stroke occurred. Today it is common in the best of hospitals to integrate medical rehabilitation services with acute care for treatment of stroke and other disabling conditions, the two services being delivered almost simultaneously and shortly after the stroke's occurrence. Dr. Rusk arranged a special unit for Joseph Kennedy Sr. in Horizon House at IRM so the President could visit his father with privacy. Henry Betts, one of Dr. Rusk's young colleagues, became the senior Kennedy's personal physician. The stroke had paralyzed Joseph Kennedy's right side, resulting in little use of his hand and arm, but 40% use of his leg. He reacted strongly against wearing a leg brace. His greatest disability was his loss of speech, although his mind was clear and active. While some progress was made in walking and ability to exercise, his speech never came back. After two months at IRM Joseph Kennedy, Sr. was discharged and returned to his homes in Hyannisport, Massachusetts and Palm Beach, Florida. Dr. Betts visited him and became a regular within the family. According to Dr. Betts, his closeness to the family resulted in part because he did not try to be a part of it. He was there only to provide necessary care for the President's father. Dr. Betts became a friend of the family in later years and also became one of the field's second generations of leaders.[4]

The responsibility of caring for the President's father brought Dr. Rusk, his institution and rehabilitation medicine, to even greater public prominence. President Kennedy asked him to serve on the Clay Commission on Foreign Aid as his medical representative. Dr. Rusk's World Rehabilitation Fund experience and his travels to the Far East for the Eisenhower Administration had made Rusk a well known international public health personage, and the President trusted him to serve his mission well on this Committee. The importance of third world countries and the developing nations to US foreign policy was a hallmark of the Kennedy Administration, and Rusk's appointment to the Clay Commission was among the highest honors that a physician could receive in the new Administration. This service also assisted in expanding the understanding of rehabilitation medicine within the Administration, and would encourage the development of international rehabilitation programs.[5]

The Kennedy Administration's initial efforts in the disability area involved mental health and retardation and produced a bureaucratic struggle over who would run new programs once they were enacted. Mary Switzer, an alumna of the Public Health Service and a leader of the nation's major disabilities programs, believed that an expanded Office of Vocational Rehabilitation would be the right place for leadership for people with mental disabilities. She had also been involved with Mary Lasker and Psychiatrist Karl Menninger in the passage of the Mental Health Act in the late 1940s, so she knew the fields of mental health and retardation. But the Kennedy Administration had other ideas. Mentally ill and retarded persons were not seen as particularly appropriate for a program and agency, which focused essentially on restoring function to physically disabled adults, training them for jobs and placing them in employment. Many of the persons with retardation were children and not eligible for employment. In addition, the Administration was a devotee of state and local planning to assure coordination among existing federal and state programs and efficient targeting of new resources. This planning emphasis was a common approach to health and social policy in the 1960s, as numerous health programs had been created in the prior 30 years. The Administration wished to bring the benefits of the existing programs, referred to by Walker in her biography of Mary Switzer and by many other writers as a "categorical jungle," to persons who were mentally ill and retarded.[6] The state vocational rehabilitation agencies were viewed as quite insular and not experienced at working with other agencies at the state or local level. The Community Mental Health Center and Mental Retardation Act of the late 1940s, on which Mary Switzer, Mary Lasker and Karl Menninger had labored, was focused on the development of local private agencies to deliver services. Many other federal social programs of the 1960's were focused on establishing private local agencies to run service programs and, as a consequence, bypassed the state and local governments of jurisdiction in the area entirely. This did not seem a particularly efficient way to coordinate resources, but it prevailed in the politics of Washington of that time.

Mary Switzer lost this bureaucratic battle because her program was too focused on working age adults, on physical disability, and was viewed as too insular in the world of government programs. The agencies for the mental health and retardation programs were ultimately placed in the Public Health Service. Losing such battles was uncommon for Mary Switzer. She was, however, soon to win another battle and expand her domain substantially.

MARY SWITZER, OVR, AND REHABILITATION MEDICINE IN THE 1960S

The decade of the 1960s had gotten off to an auspicious start for rehabilitation medicine with the International Congress of Physical Medicine taking place in Washington. Frank Krusen, still an advisor to Mary Switzer, organized and moderated a prestigious panel on rehabilitation for the meeting which included the Surgeon General Leroy Bruney, MD; Congressman John Fogarty of Rhode Island (who chaired the House Appropriations Committee); Senator Hubert Humphrey of Minnesota (who was a leader of the Democrats in the Senate and a friend of Krusen and rehabilitation); Mary Switzer; and AMA President Leonard Larson. The Secretary of the Department of Health Education and Welfare, Arthur Fleming, had spoken to the group earlier. Fleming had been President of the University of Minnesota and, like Humphrey, was well aware of rehabilitation needs and programs from his exposure to the programs of the Mayo Clinic and the University of Minnesota. Fleming had also served as chair of the Mobilization Board during the Korean War, and joined with Mary Switzer and Howard Rusk in establishing an initiative for employment of persons with disabilities.

Surgeon General Bruney opened his remarks by indicating that:

> *Physical medicine has assumed its rightful position among the leading health disciplines. It is now recognized that preventive, curative and restorative medicine form an unmistakable continuum. We believe that every hospital, every nursing home, every medical center is a potential rehabilitation facility.*[7]

The reality, however, was that physical medicine and rehabilitation had only a few hundred practicing physicians that had grown only to a thousand by 1970. Few hospitals, except in the VA system, had rehabilitation programs. But the influence of the field far exceeded its numbers due to leaders like Krusen, Rusk, Switzer and Kessler. John Fogarty, who controlled the purse strings for HEW in the House of Representatives, spoke after Bruney and stressed the needs of the field. He emphasized that research and training must be expanded, that additional facilities were needed, and that all persons in need had to be reached by rehabilitation services. Fogarty also indicated that not only was vocational rehabilitation needed, but some individuals needed services to improve their ability to live independently regardless of vocation. Mary Switzer had educated the Congressman well on her programs. Senator Humphrey then expressed his great support for Physical Medicine and Rehabilitation and referred to Dr. Frederick Kottke (who was sitting in the audience) and lauded his fine program at the University of Minnesota. Humphrey called for a doubling of the number of specialists in physical medicine and rehabilitation and expanding the numbers of physical therapists and occupational therapists. He too spoke of the need for independent living programs for persons with disabilities. As the session ended, Dr. Krusen encouraged Congressman Fogarty and Senator Humphrey to include wording to enable the Rehabilitation Act to support rehabilitation services whose goal was independent living for individuals with disabilities.[8]

The high level of participation in this meeting and the commitments made about needs for rehabilitation attested to the political skill and statesmanship of Dr. Krusen and Mary Switzer. The participants had all been thoroughly briefed on the needs and programs of rehabilitation, and spoke glowingly about physical medicine and rehabilitation. Dr. Frederick Kottke, who had been mentioned by Senator Humphrey in his speech to the International Congress, became another of the second generation of political leaders of rehabilitation medicine in the late 1960s and was a colleague of Dr. Krusen (who was a generation older).

About a year prior to this meeting in Washington, Mary Switzer had created a Task Force on the Future of Rehabilitation to advise the new Administration on rehabilitation in anticipation of possible new initiatives. She chose Corbett Reedy to chair it, who was a national leader in the rehabilitation field and head of the Virginia Vocational Rehabilitation Agency. Reedy had been involved in the late 1940s in the establishment of the Woodrow Wilson Center in Fishersville, Virginia. Reedy was a thoughtful and analytical leader and a perfect choice for the position. His report was ready in December of 1960 when Mary met with new HEW Secretary designate Abraham Ribicoff, then Governor of Connecticut. Reedy's Task Force report made four major recommendations to Mary Switzer, which she presented to the Secretary. The recommendations were timely and targeted, (which are probably the most important characteristics of a successful high level government report). The first recommendation was very prescient. It called for the inclusion of rehabilitation medicine services in any proposal for hospital or nursing home care for the aged. Ribicoff's successor, John Gardner, and his Undersecretary Wilbur Cohen, would later lead the effort of President Johnson in 1965 to enact Medicare and Medicaid. The other three recommendations were related to the Rehabilitation Act, which was to be renewed by 1965. One was to change the financing of the state vocational rehabilitation program in order to expand services and encourage greater state participation consistent with the intention of President Eisenhower and Congressman Fogarty to have the program reach more people. The other two recommendations were for expanded facility construction authority in the Act, and for the establishment of a program of rehabilitation services aimed at independent living goals. The latter recommendation was controversial as it was a major change in policy for a program, which had for 40 years focused solely on services related to employment. Independent living services would expand rehabilitation services to the aged and children who were not of working age and to individuals so severely disabled that they could not necessarily be employed. This Report was to guide Mary Switzer and her agency during the next five years of peripatetic legislative action by the federal government that ultimately resulted in the enactment of the Great Society programs, including Medicare and Medicaid, and a new and expanded Rehabilitation Act.[9]

Mary Switzer's main love was research, for which she had been actively advocating since she and Mary Lasker worked on the mental health research programs in the late 1940s. Switzer saw research as the cutting edge of rehabilitation. She had begun a research program in rehabilitation soon after she took over the Office of Vocational Rehabilitation (OVR). In the 1954 amendments to the Vocational Rehabilitation Act she and Howard Rusk had led a successful effort to authorize a major rehabilitation research program. When Frank Krusen joined Mary's staff as a Special Assistant in 1959, one of his charges was to develop the research programs. Throughout her leadership at OVR Mary was also guided by the Baruch Committee report of 1944, and Frank Krusen had been the Executive Director and was then the Chair of the Committee. The Baruch Report placed a major emphasis on teaching and research and specifically recommended that academic centers in physical medicine teaching and research be established at major medical schools. Grants were made to implement the report, but they were not permanent and had expired by the 1960s. The 1954 amendments had authorized regional Research and Training Centers in academic settings, but none had been funded by 1960. In his role as a Special Assistant to Mary Switzer, Frank Krusen focused primarily on developing the specifications and justification for the regional centers. His work was then used by Mary Switzer to request funding from Congress.

Congress appropriated $723,000 in 1962 for the establishment of the first two regional research and training centers. They were at Rusk's NYU program and at the University of Minnesota under the leadership of Frederick Kottke. The University of Minnesota Center was allied with the American Rehabilitation Foundation, formerly the Kenny Institute. The Mayo Clinic was also affiliated with the University of Minnesota and would be involved in the new program. In 1963, two more medical rehabilitation centers were established at Baylor College of Medicine under the leadership of William Spencer, MD and at the University of Washington in Seattle under the leadership of Justus Lehmann, MD. The first four centers were therefore medical in scope. By 1964, there were ten regional research and training centers, including centers dealing with vocational rehabilitation and rehabilitation of individuals with mental retardation. Additional medical rehabilitation research and training centers were established at the University of Alabama, Northwestern University at the Rehabilitation Institute of Chicago, and Temple University in Philadelphia (where Dr. Krusen had established the first

physical medicine and rehabilitation program). By 1968, there were 19 research and training centers and the budget for the program was $10 million.
The OVR also funded 175 research and demonstration projects. Training
funds were also abundant, and in 1962 alone the OVR funded 240 residents
in Physical Medicine and Rehabilitation.[10]

The regional research and training centers became the academic and patient care leaders for the field of rehabilitation medicine, and to a large extent
that leadership has continued to date. It is not surprising that the second generation of leaders in the field of rehabilitation medicine came primarily from
these centers. The centers became extremely influential in the development of
rehabilitation medicine, since they fostered research and advances in all aspects of rehabilitation medicine, and they stimulated academic leadership in
all disciplines: including medicine, physical therapy, psychology, occupational therapy, speech therapy and rehabilitation engineering. The center at
Emory University was well known for its research involving biofeedback,
and the collaboration of physical therapists Carmella Gonnella, Steven Wolf,
and Ruth Kalish with Dr. J.V. Basmajian. Center grants were large and in today's dollars would equate to between $1.5 million to $2.5 million per center. This was a very attractive addition to the budget of a medical center or
university. PM&R thus became a better respected "commodity" in the world
of academic medicine. The funding also enabled the center to expand patient
care as the research was primarily clinical and involved patients. A not in-
substantial side benefit was the political popularity of such well-funded centers with the Congressmen and Senators in states where the centers were located. Senator Warren Magnuson of the state of Washington and Senator
Lister Hill of Alabama were leaders in funding programs through the appropriations process which they controlled. They stimulated and oversaw the development of their state universities to national leadership positions in medicine. Since the NIH had not been receptive to the efforts by Dr. Rusk and
others to establish rehabilitation medicine research programs or a rehabilitation medicine research institute, the field conceived of the regional centers established by OVR as its analogue to the Institutes at NIH. However, the centers were grant recipients and not grant makers like the NIH Institutes. By the
year 2000, there were about 40 research and training centers, of which 14
were medical rehabilitation in focus.[11]

Another major development in the evolution of rehabilitation medicine involving OVR and Mary Switzer was the 1966 amendments to the Rehabilitation Act. John Gardner had been appointed as the new Secretary of HEW in
1965, and he worked with Mary Switzer and Wilbur Cohen (HEW Assistant
Secretary for Legislation) to press for needed changes in the Act. They were
assisted by Howard Rusk and E.B. Whitten of the National Rehabilitation As-

sociation. President Johnson had succeeded President Kennedy in November of 1963 after Kennedy was tragically assassinated. In 1964 and 1965, Johnson capitalized on the nation's mourning and its desire to fulfill many of President Kennedy's dreams to create momentum for a group of new legislative proposals labeled the Great Society programs. In 1964 and 1965, Johnson prodded the Congress to pass the Civil Rights Act of 1964; the Antipoverty Act of 1964 that created the Office of Economic Opportunity; the Mental Retardation and Mental Health Centers Construction Amendments; the Heart Disease Cancer and Stroke Act that was referred to as the regional medical program (RMP); the Higher Education Act; and perhaps most significantly the Social Security Act Amendments creating Medicare and Medicaid. The Rehabilitation Act Amendments were considered by Congress in this period of major reform and expansion of health, education and social services programs, although enacted a year later.

The Rehabilitation Act had not been reviewed by Congress since 1954 and Mary Switzer and her allies, Howard Rusk and E.B. Whitten, felt changes were due. Switzer testified before the House Education and Labor Subcommittee in support of the Report of the Task Force on the Future of Rehabilitation prepared by Corbett Reedy in 1959. The Subcommittee was chaired by Edith Green of Oregon, a tough minded, tenacious legislator. Also on the full Committee and active on Rehabilitation Act matters were Carl Perkins of Kentucky and Adam Clayton Powell from New York City. The Chair of the Senate Committee that considered the Act was Lister Hill of Alabama, and others on the Committee were Jacob Javits of New York and Jennings Randolph of West Virginia. All three were staunch proponents of rehabilitation. In her testimony to the House Subcommittee and her presentations to the Senate Committee, Mary Switzer requested an expansion of the Act to include support for rehabilitation services. The goals were independent living, new authority for facility construction focused on vocational rehabilitation facilities, and a new financing formula for the program in order to expand the amount of federal support for vocational rehabilitation services. These proposals were all more or less from the Task Force report of Corbett Reedy. The facility focus was only on the vocational facilities, since the medical rehabilitation facilities had finally obtained their share of Hill Burton hospital and clinic construction funding. But the two separate financing sources would result in separate approaches to the support of vocational and medical rehabilitation facilities. The Baruch Committee had recommended constructing facilities, which would integrate the vocational training and job placement services with the rehabilitation medicine services. This separation in the facility support programs and in the facilities themselves was a foreshadowing of the separation of the medical and vocational programs, which the decades after 1980 would evidence.[12]

The proposal for services to enable persons with disabilities to function independently in their communities was very controversial. The services were first characterized by OVR as self-care services. Howard Rusk, however, felt that the focus should be on the ultimate goal and that the services should be called "independent living services."[13] Rusk saw clearly the need to focus on a philosophy of independence and dignity for the person with a disability and not on the more patronizing model of care, even if it was self care. Bureaucratic turf once again affected the OVR. The competing bureaus in HEW were threatened by this new approach to disability, however, and that threatened the legislation's future. Changing the name might have helped, but not enough. The Public Health Service believed such programs for persons with medical conditions, (as they viewed disabilities), belonged to them; although they had no existing service programs for adult disabled persons.

The Welfare Administration, which presided over welfare cash payments and social service funds, believed that support for self-care or independent living services for poor persons with disabilities should be their program. The Welfare Administration had cash support programs for blind and disabled poor persons, but no health care programs. Mary Switzer, Howard Rusk, E. B Whitten and others argued that the OVR should administer all services for persons with disabilities. It had existed since 1920 and had supported medical and vocational services since 1943. It had state agencies in place and professionals able to render the services who were used to dealing with the OVR and state rehabilitation agencies. This interagency battle, like the issue over facility construction, highlighted what was to become an ever present problem throughout the 1970s and 1980s. The problem included political battles between agencies, interest groups and Congress over which programs should focus on which needy populations, exacerbated by the plethora of programs created in the years between the 1930s and the 1960s.[14]

In the end Mary Switzer, Howard Rusk and E. B. Whitten compromised on the independent living issue. By doing so, they obtained not only new facility construction authority, but a revamping of the financing of the state vocational rehabilitation services program. This resulted in a major increase in funding for the programs in all states. The amendments increased the Federal share of financing to 75%. The program had no outer limit on the amount of the federal commitment. The federal dollars matched all the state dollars appropriated. A formula for distributing the largesse was constructed which, to this day, has left most legislators feeling bewildered. The focus of the formula was on not only population but on the poverty of the population.

The compromise on the independent living issue resulted in the creation of a six-month period of extended eligibility for the evaluation of applicants to determine their need for vocational rehabilitation. Applicants with severe disabilities might not necessarily qualify for the vocational rehabilitation services initially, but could receive services during the evaluation period. This might enable them to benefit from the vocational approach after six months. These consumers were generally very disabled and some were older. After six months, the services would end unless the person could then be said to be employable in some fashion. While this was a start for independent living, it was a very limited approach and not really an independent living program. On November 8, 1966, the President signed the Rehabilitation Act Amendments.[15]

By 1966, the appropriations for the federal-state vocational rehabilitation services program had doubled and training programs had expanded to allow more people to obtain services. The funding for the rehabilitation services was over $300 million by 1966, and over 1000 research and demonstration grants were funded and over 526 training programs were supported. The dramatic expansion of programs in OVR reflected the major increase in social program funding generally by 1966. The Department of HEW budget grew almost 50% from 1965 to 1966 when funding reached $10 billion. This was the point of "the rehabilitation program's greatest momentum in history."[16]

By the end of the 1960s, the vocational rehabilitation program began to experience criticism from the disabled persons who were left out of the system. The turbulent sixties had caught up with the program, just as it had with many other government efforts. Citizens and consumers were speaking out. In 1966, Mary Switzer established a National Citizens Advisory Committee to advise Congress and the Executive Branch on the needs of vocational rehabilitation. The nation was in the midst of racial tension and pressure to respond to the needs of the poor and disadvantaged. Both the Congress and Mary Switzer knew that rehabilitation had to be responsive to new demands.

The Committee was called for by the Appropriations bill for the Departments of Labor and HEW that was enacted in 1965. Howard Rusk chaired the Committee, which included Mary Duke Biddle Sedans (Chair of the Duke Foundation), Edgar Frio (Senior Vice President of Coca Cola Bottling Company), and representatives of the labor movement and the state rehabilitation agencies. The Committee issued its Report in 1968. The Report called for expanding the use of the vocational rehabilitation program to meet the needs of individuals handicapped by social, educational, racial and economic factors, as well as by physical handicaps. The primary focus, however, was to remain on persons with physical and mental disabilities. It recommended the decentralization of state vocational rehabilitation offices into local neighborhoods where large populations of the poor and disabled lived. The Report also called for the creation of local one-stop multi-service centers. The Report's focus was in keeping with the political climate of the 1960s, as the nation had turned its attention and focus on the alleviation of poverty and civil rights. The outgrowth of the Committee's work was the National Citizens Conference of the Disabled and Disadvantaged, held in Washington in June 1969.[17]

This Conference marked a turning point for the national rehabilitation program. It brought together consumers of services in active roles in determining policies. Also attending were state vocational rehabilitation agency personnel, rehabilitation professionals and OVR central and regional office personnel. Howard Rusk was General Chair of the Conference and Mary Switzer was a Vice Chair. The final recommendations of the Conference were much like those of the Committee report of 1968, and emphasized the need to broaden the scope of vocational rehabilitation to reach the socially and economically disadvantaged, as well as persons with disabilities. The process was very different, however, as the participants were often unruly and the speeches fiery and angry. The rehabilitation professionals had not faced such anger before. The anger came from disabled people who felt the system patronized them. It also came from the poor and racial minorities who felt the system did not even recognize them. There certainly seemed to be truth to the claim that the program did not reach the poorest of the persons with disabilities and often those persons were persons of color. The professionals, on the other hand, felt they had been doing a good job in rehabilitating those with disabilities with the limited resources available. It was not possible to reach every person with a physical or mental disability given the resource limitations of the programs. There was some truth on both sides. Decentralizing the programs to the neighborhood was not going to solve the resource problem, and neither would creating multi-service centers and new programs unless backed up by major infusions of financing. Rehabilitation had now been projected into a world it had not dealt with before, and for which it had too few budget and human resources. The reactions of those rehabilitation professionals in attendance varied from abhorrence at the unruliness and vulgarity of the participants to recognition that the world had changed and rehabilitation professionals needed to change to meet its demands.[18]

The lasting impact of the Conference was its emphasis on consumer participation in the rehabilitation program and its policies. While the emphasis on rehabilitation of the disadvantaged, as contrasted with the disabled, eventually dissipated during the next decade, consumer participation by persons with disabilities in the rehabilitation programs became a significant element of the programs for the next 35 years. The disability movement was energized and it allied often with the medical rehabilitation community and other rehabilitation professionals and agencies to advocate for new programs in transportation and housing and for civil rights. The need for independent living services and civil rights became a rallying cry for the movement.

The impetus for rehabilitation medicine continued unabated in OVR despite the distractions of reorganizations and new populations making their demands for services known. From 1967 until at least the early to mid-1980s the OVR was the federal agency which supported research, training and service demonstration programs in the rehabilitation medicine field. The OVR budget for the services, training and research programs continued to grow throughout this period and Mary Switzer continued to assist the program, although she was also the Administrator of the parent organization for the OVR, the Social and Rehabilitation Service (SRS). Howard Rusk was the Chair of the National Citizens Advisory Committee on Vocational Rehabilitation and reported to Mary Switzer, John Gardner and Wilbur Cohen on the needs of the program. Rusk and Switzer maintained their effective partnership and Rusk retained his presence as a national leader. He continued to be called upon by Presidents for advice. His role in the years from 1950 to 1970 was comparable to the role Bernard Baruch had played in Washington many years earlier.

It is hard to imagine today that what is now referred to as the Rehabilitation Services Administration (RSA), located in the Department of Education, was the effective lead agency for all rehabilitation services, research and training in the federal government and that the Rehabilitation Act was the basis for most all research, training and services for adult civilians with disabilities. The agency did play that role, however, and it was the main source of leadership for rehabilitation medicine. Having leaders like Mary Switzer, Howard Rusk, Frank Krusen and Henry Kessler made such leadership possible. In 1966, Medicare had just been implemented, and it would be another 15 to 20 years before its impact would be fully felt in rehabilitation medicine. NIH was still not interested in research in rehabilitation medicine or in training support for the field. The aggressive leadership of Mary Switzer made RSA and the Rehabilitation Act a model for all social agencies to follow.

MEDICARE: A NEW FEDERAL ENGINE TO DRIVE THE DEVELOPMENT OF REHABILITATION MEDICINE

Since the Federal Security Agency was first involved in planning for Social Security programs in the early 1930s, a national health insurance program had been one of its major priorities. Initial plans called for social insurance approaches to retirement, disability and health care. Disability and health care were often considered as inseparable. But AMA opposition had deterred President Roosevelt from proposing national health insurance as part of the Social Security Amendments in 1934 and 1935, and stymied President Truman's advocacy for National Health Insurance in 1948 through 1952. While Disability

Insurance, with rehabilitation services provided where necessary, was enacted in 1956, the numbers of disabled persons referred to rehabilitation medicine services were few and the benefit restricted through state administration. In the 1940s and 1950s labor, an ally for advocates of national social insurance programs, focused on achieving health insurance security in the private sector through collective bargaining agreements with business and industry. Health insurance for the employed worker, however, had little value for the retiree, the unemployed or the person with a disability who was unable to work. By the 1960s, the public concern for health insurance had focused on the retiree and poor, for whom private health insurance was not available. Disabled persons under 65 were not a focus in this approach, perhaps because disability insurance had only been enacted in 1956 and it included rehabilitation services.

The health insurance lobbying effort began in earnest in 1958 when Congressman Aime Forand of Rhode Island introduced a modest bill amending the Social Security Act to provide for hospital insurance for the aged who were Social Security retirees. The bill was to be a contributory social insurance program like Social Security cash benefits. Despite the fact that the legislation had no coverage for medical services, the AMA again devoted itself to a major campaign to prevent enactment. The AMA took the position that the bill would involve a threat to the doctor-patient relationship, even though physician services were not covered. Hospitalization coverage might still involve the government in determining when admissions to hospitals were appropriate and when a patient should be discharged. But the focus of the bill on the aged had changed the political terrain and in 1959, the new Senate Subcommittee on Aging held hearings around the country on the needs of the aged. What the Subcommittee heard was an outpouring of support for health insurance. Members of Congress had more mail on this issue than any other. A "ground swell of grassroots support forced the issue onto the national agenda."[19]

Prior to the elections in November of 1960, the Congress passed the Kerr-Mills bill, which was named for its sponsors in the Senate and House. The law was very modest compared to the Forand bill, since its focus was a federal state grant in aid program to cover health care for the aged poor. The federal government matched the state governments' financial contributions, as was the case with the Vocational Rehabilitation Act. The Act met the AMA's objections because it was administered by states and was not based on an insurance model. But the program was limited to the poor, and actually only the poor who were elderly. The public and Congress wanted more than this very modest measure. In addition, the states did little to establish Kerr Mills programs in their states.[20]

President Kennedy supported the establishment of a program of health insurance for the aged retiree without a means test, similar to the Forand bill in its benefits. But the votes were not there yet to support the legislation. When Lyndon Johnson became President after the assassination of President Kennedy in November 1963, he almost immediately began an aggressive effort to enact President Kennedy's stalled legislative program. Medicare was on the top of his list, perhaps second only to civil rights legislation. In 1964, the landslide election of President Johnson and a Democratic Congress provided the momentum for Johnson's entire legislative program. By 1965, the AMA had backed off from total opposition to legislation like the Forand bill and endorsed a voluntary health insurance program for the aged on Social Security called Eldercare, which included both hospitalization and medical services. Polls by the AMA showed that 72% of Americans wanted medical services covered by insurance and the passage of such legislation seemed imminent. It was! Under the pressure of President Johnson and with a strong Democratic majority in Congress in support of health insurance for the elderly, Chairman of the House Ways and Means Committee Wilbur Mills of Arkansas fashioned his creative legislative solution. He proposed a bill with three parts: an involuntary hospital insurance program for the aged retiree financed by a payroll tax; medical insurance for the aged retiree on a voluntary basis with a required premium; and a federal state matching grant program of medical care for the poor who were eligible for state welfare payments. The last category included persons with disabilities who were welfare recipients, but the two other programs did not cover the disabled person receiving Social Security Disability Insurance. They only included the disabled person over 65. The programs were referred to as Medicare Part A for hospitalization, Medicare Part B for medical services on a voluntary basis, and the last program was Medicaid. All three of these programs were enacted in 1965. "Some physicians initially swore they would organize a boycott, but cooler heads prevailed in the AMA, and after it went into effect a year later, the profession not only accepted Medicare but discovered it was a bonanza."[21]

The major impact on rehabilitation medicine came from the hospital insurance program for the aged retiree. As an accommodation to the providers whom the HEW wanted to support the program, the payments for hospital care were on a cost of service basis. Even the capital costs of hospitals and hospital costs incurred in medical education were covered. In addition, rather than have direct federal agency management of the Medicare programs, Parts A and B, the statute allowed for the administration of the program by the private sector. Private insurance companies became fiscal intermediaries or agents of the HEW. These agents were uniformly Blue Cross for Part A and Blue Shield for Part B, companies that the hospitals and physicians had created to provide private health insurance. The cost reimbursement payment system, which included even the capital costs, served to stimulate the development of hospital services and the expansion of facilities. Rehabilitation medicine was a hospital inpatient service and its costs were reimbursed under the hospital insurance program. Physical Medicine and Rehabilitation and other medical residency training programs also received reimbursement for the costs of having a residency training program. Physician services were paid for in all settings, office and hospital. Physical therapy, occupational therapy and speech therapy services were covered if supplied by hospital employed therapists in hospital inpatient or outpatient settings, and such therapy services were covered if furnished by therapists employed by physicians.

At the time of the enactment of Medicare, rehabilitation medicine was a recognized part of the market for hospital and professional services largely because of government programs and the support of public officials. Rehabilitation medicine was still not well recognized by academic medicine nor the medical establishment, but that mattered little when it came to the decisions by public officials about Medicare. High level members of Congress and the Executive Branch who were involved in the decision making appreciated the value of rehabilitation medicine, including Vice President Humphrey, Senator Douglas, Senator Hill, Congressman Fogarty, Secretary of HEW Gardner and Under Secretary Wilbur Cohen. The latter negotiated the legislation with the Congress. Widespread recognition of rehabilitation medicine within the federal government and the Congress existed due to the efforts of Kessler, Baruch, Krusen, Switzer, Rusk and the professional associations over the 20 years prior to Medicare. They had established programs in the well respected Veterans Administration health system; through the OVR rehabilitation service program; the Social Security Disability program; and in the new Regional Medical Program of 1965. Mary Switzer and her Task Force of 1959 and 1960 under Corbett Reedy had urged the inclusion of rehabilitation facilities in any health insurance program. Switzer had presented those findings to Secretaries Ribicoff, Celebreeze and Gardner, and to Wilbur Cohen, an architect of Medicare. The field had eminent lobbyists in Washington for at least 20 years prior to Medicare's enactment, so it is little wonder that rehabilitation medicine was a covered program in the new law.

Given the visibility attained for rehabilitation medicine by 1965, it was not surprising that the language adopted by Congress and the Administration for the hospital benefit in Medicare Part A specified rehabilitation as a hospital program and referred to the disabled and injured in describing the elderly population eligible for rehabilitation and other services under Medicare. The original Medicare statute, Part A, defined hospital for purposes of the hospital benefit as an institution primarily engaged in providing ". . . diagnostic services and therapeutic services . . . for care of injured, disabled or sick persons, or rehabilitation services for the rehabilitation of injured, disabled or sick persons."[22] The program, however, did not include the disabled person who was a Social Security beneficiary due to disability until 1972.

It was also not surprising that the administration of the program by HEW was receptive to the inclusion of rehabilitation as a benefit since Mary Switzer was still a formidable force in the Department in 1965. In 1967, she was the Administrator of the Social and Rehabilitation Service (SRS), which administered Medicaid. Wilbur Cohen, a colleague of hers, was Undersecretary and later on the Secretary of HEW; and Phil Lee was Assistant Secretary of Health (Howard Rusk had been his mentor in policy and politics).[23]

The implementation of Medicare in 1966, with its cost reimbursement, stimulated the expansion of inpatient hospital rehabilitation services and the number of facilities furnishing those services. As the nation aged and chronic disease and disability became more common with those over 65, the program became an even greater stimulus for rehabilitation service expansion. Between 1959 and 1969, the number of rehabilitation medicine services in California hospitals grew from 10 to 26, and most of this growth occurred in the latter half of the 1960s. The number of rehabilitation medicine programs in California doubled in the decade of the 1970s. At the Mayo Clinic the number of new patients grew by 53% in the period of 1965 to 1972, and a new inpatient service was opened at Rochester Methodist Hospital. The APTA leadership determined that the new demand for services generated by Medicare would far exceed what the current supply of physical therapists could accommodate, and it established a new Physical Therapy Assistant profession and training program to assist in meeting the new demand.[24]

In 1964, President Johnson also recommended a heath care program to create regional centers to treat the nation's major diseases. These centers would also address the new demand for services generated by Medicare and Medicaid. This program was enacted in 1965 and called the Heart, Cancer and Stroke Act, and was referred to as the Regional Medical Program (RMP), Public Law 89-239. The program was the recommendation of a Commission on Heart, Cancer and Stroke, appointed by President Johnson in 1964 and chaired by the famous heart surgeon, Dr. Michael DeBakey. Dr. Rusk was appointed by Johnson to the Commission of 25 physician specialists, which allowed rehabilitation medicine to be present at this important table around which decisions were reached upon the elements of an effective health system. These discussions and recommendations were made to the President and Congress just as Medicare was being debated and enacted. The Commission provided guidelines for the operation of Heart, Cancer and Stroke programs under the Act. The Act created regional networks of academic medical centers to focus research, training and services on these three diseases. The delivery of care was left to the discretion of the regional centers.[25]

Debakey asked Rusk to create a Subcommittee to focus on rehabilitation needs and programs for the Act.

The purpose of the group, which included twenty five specialists in various fields, was to work out a master plan of attack against these three number one killers and cripplers. As a member of this group I pointed out that while the basic approach should be prevention and cure, that wouldn't help the persons who were already the victims of one or the other of these afflictions. Here I was arguing for rehabilitation.[26]

Rusk, then 64, brought into the RMP planning process for rehabilitation medicine a number of emerging second generation leaders in the field: Dr. William Spencer of Baylor School of Medicine, Dr. Henry Betts from Northwestern and the Rehabilitation Institute Chicago, Dr. William Erdman of the University of Pennsylvania, Dr. Arthur Abramson of Einstein Medical School New York, and Dr. Paul Ellwood of the Sister Kenny Foundation and a colleague of Dr. Krusen and Dr. Kottke.

DeBakey and his colleagues were very responsive to the Rehabilitation Subcommittee recommendations. Rehabilitation became an essential part of the heart, stroke and cancer programs established in the Commission master plan and later in the RMP enacted in 1965. The RMP gave a place to rehabilitation medicine in the delivery system of services for the treatment of heart, cancer and stroke just like the place it had attained in the early 1950s for the treatment of polio. This recognition of rehabilitation medicine as an essential intervention for major diseases was a dramatic expansion of the scope of the field from its prior focus on injury and polio. It clearly further integrated the field with that of acute medicine. By 1970, there were 70 stroke rehabilitation programs functioning with RMP support and most were in major academic medical centers.[27] Inclusion in the RMP planning by the Commission in 1964 and in the 1965 legislation made it likely that such services would also be recognized in Medicare.

THE END OF AN ERA OF LEADERSHIP

In 1965, Bernard Baruch died at age 95 after more than 50 years as a leader in American finance and politics. His last official role was as President Truman's Representative to the United Nations Atomic Committee, which was the first international organization concerned with the dangers of atomic weapons. He had assisted Frank Krusen in his continuing efforts to establish the medical specialty in physical medicine and rehabilitation into the 1950s. He was an advocate for national health insurance throughout the 1950s and until his death. His role and that of his father in founding physical medicine and rehabilitation was expressed in a tribute by Dr. Krusen in the Archives of Physical Medicine and Rehabilitation after his death. The article, entitled "In Memoriam to Bernard Baruch," read, in part: "The patronage and counsel of Bernard Baruch established firmly and for all time a new and promising field of medical practice which will in the future relieve the suffering of millions of sick and disabled people."[28]

On February 6, 1970, Mary Switzer reached compulsory retirement age in the Federal Civil Service. She had served for one year during the Nixon Administration and hoped to stay in her position, but this time her efforts to retain her position failed. Secretary of HEW Robert Finch, former Lieutenant Governor of California, was not known to Howard Rusk like his predecessors had been and Rusk was unable to assist in retaining Mary Switzer in her position. On the evening of February 6, 1970, a gala dinner was held to honor Mary Switzer's service to the nation. Six secretaries of HEW were at the head table as was Howard Rusk, one of the speakers. Upon resignation, Mary Switzer became Vice President of the World Rehabilitation Fund that had been established by Dr. Rusk, as well as serving on the Board of Gallaudet College and on Secretary Finch's Committee to Study the Public Health Service Commissioned Corps. She had been feeling badly for months before her resignation and Rusk asked her to come to the NYU medical center where he could be involved in her care. The diagnosis was a massive cancer. Mary Switzer died on October 16, 1971, at the age of 71. A memorial service was held in the HEW auditorium. In 1973, the building in which she had worked for so many years as Director of the OVR and then Administrator of SRS was dedicated in her name.[29]

Frank Krusen left the Mayo Clinic in 1963 when he was 67. But he did not retire. True to his academic interests, he returned to Philadelphia and reestablished the Department of Physical Medicine and Rehabilitation at Temple University Medical School, which he had founded in 1929. The field of physical medicine and rehabilitation was still a small and relatively vulnerable specialty and Krusen wished to expand the numbers of academic training programs. He quite clearly wanted to make sure the program he started at Temple was restored. At Temple, he became a mentor to John Ditunno, a future second and third generation leader of the field, who was on the medical staff at Temple from 1967 through 1969. Ditunno would go on to become President of the Academy of Physical Medicine and Rehabilitation in 1981, chair its Legislation Committee later in the 1980s, and become a leader in the American Spinal Injury Association (ASIA). Krusen remained active in politics in these years at Temple. In 1968, having finished his commitment to reestablish the Department at Temple, Krusen moved to Boston where he established a Physical Medicine and Rehabilitation Department at Tufts New England Medical Center. Both the Temple and Tufts programs became successful and in the 1970's received OVR rehabilitation research and training center grants. Lynn Gerber M.D., one of the field's leading researchers and a member of the AAPMR Board in 2005, remembers meeting Dr. Krusen while she was an undergraduate in medical school at Tufts. She remembers receiving his admonition to follow the patient and determine what the patient thinks and needs. Dr. Krusen retired in 1969 and moved to Cape Cod Massachusetts where he died on September 16, 1973. The field had lost its leading academic and medical statesman, whose tenacity and diplomacy resulted in the establishment of a medical specialty in Physical Medicine and Rehabilitation.[30]

Henry Kessler retired as Medical Director of the Kessler Institute of Rehabilitation in 1969. He continued his association with the Institute through work with its education and research programs. He was no longer a national leader in the field after his retirement. He died in 1979 at age 83. He had founded the Institute in 1947 and it had been one of the three major rehabilitation centers in the country at that time. His facility grew and is now much enlarged with facilities at numerous sites both in New Jersey and other states. It is recognized annually as one of the finest rehabilitation hospitals in the nation by US News and World Report. In an article in the Rehabilitation Record in June 1970 on the fiftieth anniversary of the Rehabilitation Act and its federal programs, Mary Switzer wrote of "Some of the Great Ones." She identified three physicians: Howard Rusk, Henry Kessler and George Deaver. Of Kessler she would comment that he was one of the first physicians to establish a rehabilitation program, long before World War II, and that on return from the war she knew he would return to his clinic to help the rehabilitation field and to carry the message around the world. Rusk referred to Kessler in his book "A World to Care for" as the true pioneer of rehabilitation medicine. Of all the leaders in the field of rehabilitation medicine in its early years, he may have been the greatest humanitarian. His interests were always for the patient and the development of programs for them. Henry Betts spoke of Kessler, whom he had met first while a physician in training at the Institute for Rehabilitation Medicine at NYU, as a very intelligent, urbane and cultured man. According to Betts, Kessler and Rusk both shared a special relationship with their patients.[31]

The deaths and retirements of these four founders left only Howard Rusk among the five founders to assist in leading the rehabilitation medicine movement during the difficult time of the 1970s. But Howard Rusk was seventy years old in 1970, and while still active, was delegating to others much of his authority, particularly in the area of political leadership. In 1969, Rusk wrote his last New York Times article, and that vehicle for national advocacy and education was no longer available. He remained President of the World Rehabilitation Fund and Chief Executive of the Institute for Rehabilitation Medicine, but delegated much of his national advocacy activity for rehabilitation to his Clinical Director, Edward Lowman who was an active member and President of the American Congress of Rehabilitation Medicine. Lowman was a worthy successor, as his commitment to disabled persons was extraordinary and his elegance of speech and writing was unexcelled. But no one could replace the individual who had advised Presidents, wrote regular medical columns in the New York Times and was looked to by Congress as a guru of rehabilitation medicine.[32]

During the remaining years of active life, Howard Rusk would focus most on his energy on international programs. Rusk served President Johnson personally on a variety of international missions in the late 1960s, including two trips to Vietnam to report on the health needs of the Vietnamese people. He reported his findings directly to the President. One finding in particular involved a number of paralyzed Vietnamese who were being warehoused in a center, which had no professional staff and essentially offered only attendant services. President Johnson immediately accepted Dr. Rusk's advice and brought the patients by plane to a Veteran's Hospital in Castle Point New York, where they received comprehensive rehabilitation services and numerous surgical procedures. Within 18 months, 52 of the 56 patients returned to their local communities in Vietnam with their function much enhanced. In 1971, Rusk and the World Rehabilitation Fund would host the first event at which U Thant, Secretary General of the U.N., would speak in the U.S. other than at the U.N. During the 1970s Dr. Rusk would on occasion make himself available to meet with Senators and Congressmen at the request of Dr. Lowman or one of the professional associations to which he belonged. He maintained a close relationship with Senator Tom Eagleton of Missouri, Rusk's native state. But, as the decade of the 1970's began, new leadership for rehabilitation medicine was needed.[33]

NOTES

1. Johnson, Arch Phys Med Rehabil, Special Edition 50th Anniversary, vol. 69, 20.

2. Rusk, 248.

·3. Rusk, 252.

4. Rusk, 249–51; Interviews with Henry Betts, July 29, October 7, and October 9, 2004.

5. Rusk, 251.

6. Walker, 175.

7. Proceedings of International Congress of Physical Medicine, Arch Phys Med Rehabil, vol. 42, 661–63.

8. Ibid, 661–774.

9. Walker, 176–77.

10. Walker, 191–93, p.196; Johnson, Arch Phys Med Rehabil vol. 69, 21.

11. Murphy, *Healing the Generations*, 187–88.

12. Walker, 211–13.

13. Walker, 213.

14. Walker, 212–15.

15. Walker, 211–16.

16. Walker, 213–17; quote at 217.

17. *50 Years of Vocational Rehabilitation in the U.S.A., 1920 to 1970*, 25–26.

18. Walker, 245–48; *50 Years of Vocational Rehabilitation in the U.S.A., 1920 to 1970*, 26.

19. Starr, 368.

20. Starr, 368–69.

21. Starr, 369–70.

22. U.S. Code Annotated Title 42, Section 1395x(e).

23. HCFA Oral History, http://www.ssa.gov/history/LEEhtml.

24. Fowler, *History of Physical Medicine and Rehabilitation in California*, 33–39; Opitz and DePompolo, 129–131; Murphy, 192–97.

25. Rusk, 256.

26. Ibid.

27. Starr, 368; Rusk, 256–57; Kliger, Arch Phys Med Rehabil, vol. 52, 47 ; Gullickson, Arch Phys Med Rehabil, vol. 69, 27.

28. Krusen, Arch Phys Med Rehabil, vol. 46, 549.

29. Walker, 253–63, 266; personal correspondence, John Ditunno, MD, who was at the dinner with Dr. Krusen, his mentor, December 2006.

30. Opitz et al., Krusen Diaries, Arch Phys Med Rehabil, vol. 78, 565; Interview with Dr. Ditunno, October 28, 2005; Interview with Dr. Gerber, October 9, 2004.

31. Dr. Betts interviews of October 7 and 9, 2004; Rehabilitation Record May/June 1970, 5–6; Henry Kessler Story, Henry Kessler Foundation Website www.hhfdn.org; Kessler, 287–90.

32. Walker, 291.

33. Rusk, 263–71, 291–95.

Chapter Eleven

The 1970s:
Vulnerability, New Leadership,
and the Disability Movement

Despite enormous progress in the period from 1945 to 1970, rehabilitation medicine was still in its early stages of development and very much in jeopardy as national political leadership of the nation changed. At the same time, the leadership for rehabilitation medicine of the past 25 years was coming to an end with either retirement or death claiming four of the five founders. The fifth, Dr. Rusk, was playing a reduced leadership role. As Leon Reinstein, MD, former President and long time Board member of the AAPMR, said of the field: "In the 1970s there was a good chance the field would disappear. We had only 500 residency positions in PM&R and only half were filled." This same fear was voiced by other rehabilitation medicine professionals. Rehabilitation medicine was still in need of the federal support and protection supplied by Mary Switzer and OVR and the VA.[1]

The new Republican leadership in the Executive Branch resulting from the victory of Richard Nixon in the 1968 Presidential election viewed with some suspicion the rehabilitation programs of the OVR with their state agencies operating independent of the state governors, and their entrenched power with Congress. The White House seemed bent on an agenda of reform aimed at the programs of the past, including Medicare with its unlimited reimbursement for the costs and charges of the nation's hospitals and physicians. Reform could mean losses for the fields that were politically weak, and by 1970 the political leadership of rehabilitation medicine seemed vulnerable.

The 1970s also witnessed a Republican President (Nixon) who, contrary to expectations, would undertake unprecedented regulatory leadership with the imposition of wage and price controls on all sectors of the economy, the creation of a federal Environmental Protection Agency, and experimental programs to control inflation and healthcare costs such as HMOs. A quote from the loquacious and politically astute Undersecretary of HEW, Jack Veneman, summed up the approach of the Nixon Administration to health care and the realities of politics and economics in the decade of the 1970s: "In the past decisions on health care delivery were largely professional ones. Now the decisions will be largely political."[2] The age of medical sovereignty over the health care system was approaching its end, brought on by Medicare and the new responsibilities and power the federal government would achieve through it. The government now had a major investment in healthcare financing and therefore in its delivery, unlike the prior periods when investment was largely in facility creation and medical research.

The federal government had also moved in the direction of assuring the availability of health care to all through the enactment of Medicare and Medicaid. In his Coulter Lecture at the meeting of the American Congress of Rehabilitation Medicine in 1971, Surgeon General Jesse Steinfeld called for the reform of the healthcare system and indicated that money had been thrown at problems but was not meeting them. Programs were not there to cover many needing health insurance and the programs that were there were focused on high cost, hospital based acute care. Reform was the order of the day, but difficult questions remained as to its shape and substance. Steinfeld asked: "How do we give meaning and fruition to the concept that adequate healthcare is a birthright of every citizen."[3] He raised the issue of both rights to healthcare and the capacity to deliver quality care to all. The emphasis on a right to health care was common in 1970, and those who emphasized the right to health care agreed with Veneman that major policy decisions on health care were now political ones rather than professional ones.[4]

Health care policies affecting rehabilitation medicine had always been driven by politics in that it had taken action by politicians, philanthropists and government officials to establish rehabilitation medicine programs in military hospitals, the VA and the polio clinics. Even the continued recognition of the specialty of Physical Medicine and Rehabilitation, espoused by Krusen, came about only with Bernard Baruch's lobbying of President Eisenhower. Rehabilitation medicine did not rebel at the advent of Medicare, but attempted to influence it to assure rehabilitation coverage for the elderly and inclusion in the program of persons with disabilities. It did not shy away from advocacy with politicians for the coverage of rehabilitation services, training or research; it embraced it and was the beneficiary of the work done in prior years by the founders. In this respect, rehabilitation medicine was in a good position to use politics and politicians for its protection, since doing so was not an alien method for the field.

As the rehabilitation field sought new leadership to protect its well-earned programmatic victories, Congress became the focal point of its lobbying more than the Executive Branch. Congress remained strongly Democratic in the 1970s. Many of the leaders in efforts to enact Medicare, the Rehabilitation Act amendments, and the Regional Medical Program (RMP) were still in positions of influence. Notable among the rehabilitation leaders were Senators Magnuson (D-Washington), Kennedy (D-Massachusetts), Williams (D-New Jersey), Randolph (D-West Virginia), Javits (R-New York) and Stafford (R-Vermont).

The field was also aided by the progeny of the civil rights movement of the 1960s. New rights advocacy movements involving rights of migrant labor, women, and persons with disabilities were developing in the late 1960s and 1970s. As Starr noted: "Medical care figured prominently in this generalization of rights, particularly as a concern of the women's movement and in the new movements specifically for patient's rights and the right of the handicapped, the mentally ill, the retarded, and the subjects of medical research."[5] The disability rights movement, while concerned with health care, was more broadly interested in discrimination and segregation affecting persons with disabilities. It began in the late 1960s and early 1970s under the leadership of Ed Roberts of California; and the academic Howard Hahn, a political scientist who articulated the minority group approach to politics for persons with disabilities.[6]

It was an anxious few years for rehabilitation in the early 1970s however. Edward Lowman, colleague of Howard Rusk at NYU, expressed this sentiment well in his Coulter Lecture to the American Congress of Rehabilitation Medicine in 1972. "We are in a new era of medicine which is evolving at frightening speed. We must plan for the future and be aggressive. No longer do we have federal leaders who understand and advocate for our cause."[7] Lowman concluded with an impassioned plea to his colleagues for the preservation of the Rehabilitation Act and its appropriations, and for the creation of comprehensive guidelines for rehabilitation benefits under the Medicare program. He thus initiated an effort among all professionals acting through their associations to become the guardians of the rehabilitation programs Baruch, Krusen, Kessler, Switzer, Deaver, Coulter and Magnuson labored to create but were not present to protect.

A NEW LEADERSHIP ARISES THROUGH NATIONAL ASSOCIATIONS

The 1970s saw the rise of associations of professionals, facilities and consumers as the national leaders for rehabilitation. While professional associations had existed since the 1920s in rehabilitation medicine, they were not particularly forceful in national politics until the 1970s. Leadership had come mainly from prominent individuals such as Baruch, Rusk, Krusen and Kessler; as well as from federal agencies such as the OVR and VA led by Mary Switzer and Paul Magnuson respectively. The leadership of specific individuals ceased to be the norm in the period after 1970. The ways of Washington became even more political and more complex. Political leaders wanted to know how many individuals supported an idea, how many people would be impacted and at what cost before they acted. Political leaders wanted to know if the ideas being proposed were supported by the majority of people affected by the change. The best way to demonstrate that was by showing interest group support.

The American Congress of Rehabilitation Medicine (ACRM), long an association of only physicians, became multidisciplinary in 1967. It had 2,000 or so members in the 1970s and its membership peaked in 1987 at 3,200. The ACRM had been the major association of physicians interested in physical medicine and rehabilitation since the 1920s. By the 1960s and 1970s it had become an association of leaders from various medical and other professional fields in rehabilitation. In 1938, the Society of Physical Medicine was created to organize efforts to achieve specialty status within the AMA for physical medicine. It became the American Academy of Physical Medicine and Rehabilitation after specialty status was obtained in 1948. The ACRM changed its name to the American Congress of Physical Medicine and Rehabilitation in 1952 and then to the ACRM in 1966 and continued to represent all physicians interested in the field.

By the early 1970s the ACRM leadership was multidisciplinary as rehabilitation nurses, psychologists, physical therapists, speech pathologists and occupational therapists served on its Board or as Committee chairs and leaders. The membership requirement established in 1967 was for at least a Masters Degree and specialization in rehabilitation. Most of the members were from academic medical centers or hospitals with large rehabilitation programs. At the height of its membership in 1986, the Congress had more than twice as many physician members as nonphysician ones, so the political power within the organization was still with medicine. The Congress and Academy were also jointly administered, had joint meetings and shared the field's journal with its ownership becoming joint in 1986. The focus of much of the activity of the Congress was on national policy and research. The philosophy of the ACRM related to the value of comprehensive rehabilitation and consumer involvement in the process of rehabilitation. The issues of specialty specific practice matters were handled by the various professional societies representing the various disciplines within rehabilitation medicine. President of the ACRM William Spencer MD focused on comprehensiveness in his 1969

Presidential Address: "Rehabilitation for us health professionals must be viewed as a process of comprehensive and individualized treatment and assistance to a handicapped person. . . . It extends to and includes solution of life adjustment problems."[8] The focus of President Henry Betts MD in his Congress Presidential Address in 1976 was on the consumer and the consumer movement. The entire meeting of the ACRM in 1976, Betts' Presidential year, was on consumerism and participation by persons with disabilities in planning and executing services. Spencer and Betts would be successors to Rusk in advocacy for comprehensive rehabilitation medicine. Harold Wilke, a man with a disability, who was an internationally known minister and member of ACRM, focused his Coulter Lecture on the needs of persons with disabilities and the need for a "Caring Community."[9]

The American Academy of Physical Medicine and Rehabilitation (AAPMR or Academy) was a much smaller organization than the ACRM that focused on establishing appropriate medical education programs and assisting the small field of PMR to achieve credibility within medicine. The number of board certified physicians (referred to as physiatrists) in the field was only 773 in 1969 and 1608 by 1979. This represented a doubling in the number of physiatrists as the expansion of hospital programs driven by Medicare gave rise to a need for more PMR physicians. As compared to other specialties of medicine, however, the field of PMR was still a small one. The AAPMR focus was primarily on education of its members, and it established leading programs in Continuing Medical Education during the 1970s and 1980s. The ACRM and AAPMR acted collaboratively on national advocacy and their leadership was often overlapping. At that time, most members of the AAPMR were also members of the ACRM. The ACRM was the larger and more broadly representative organization, which made it the better of the two for political advocacy. The advocacy spirit of the Academy was ecumenical and far reaching as epitomized in the Presidential Addresses of Arthur Abramson in 1972 and of Justus Lehmann in 1973. Their respective presentations emphasized the role of consumers in allying with physicians to achieve national impact and the importance of comprehensive, interdisciplinary rehabilitation in federal legislation. Abramson was both a physician and a consumer, having been injured in World War II.[10]

The American Physical Therapy Association (APTA) was by far the largest of the professional societies in rehabilitation medicine with a membership of nearly 30,000 by the end of the 1970s. The APTA had developed a very strong national organization by the 1970s, with particular influence on Washington politics in general and the Medicare program in particular. It had active chapters in many states, which it had begun using to affect national legislation. Like most large professional organizations in medicine, it established a

Political Action Committee (PAC) to enable it to be involved in political campaigns. As early as the 1930s, the predecessor to the APTA had allied itself closely to the federal Crippled Children's program and assisted in its implementation. The focus of the APTA in the 1970s was on establishing the legitimacy of physical therapy and physical therapists through national Medicare coverage of therapy services and through state licensing laws recognizing physical therapy and its scope of practice. The APTA also focused on the right of physical therapists to govern their professional future and to be free from "Professional Bondage."[11] It opposed the continuation of the American Physical Therapy Registry controlled by the American Congress of Physical Therapy, renamed as the ACRM in 1967. It also opposed efforts by the Joint Commission on Accreditation of Hospitals (now called the JCAHO) to change the standards for hospitals by renaming the hospital physical therapy service as the physical medicine service. It was successful in both efforts. The APTA pursued new markets and attempted to respond to a vast increase in demand for services generated by Medicare by establishing the physical therapy assistant as an extender of the physical therapist. Helen Hislop, one of its leaders and the Editor of the Physical Therapy Journal, urged the association to focus on research, technology development and specialization as methods to establish a scientific base for the field. Despite tensions with medicine resulting from efforts to achieve more independence, the APTA was a visible and effective lobbyist for the expansion of rehabilitation programs for persons with disabilities, as well as for the rights of physical therapists. The APTA allied itself with other rehabilitation groups whenever possible.[12]

The American Occupational Therapy Association (AOTA) established a Washington office in 1968 and followed the lead of the APTA in establishing a Political Action Committee in 1976. Gritzer pointed out, however, that the APTA had more success in achieving market share for its services because it focused on state licensing authority for its professionals and more autonomy from the physicians. The AOTA had a less combative relationship with the physician community. AOTA had a broader, partially nonmedical, definition of service than the APTA; and was therefore less understood and less utilized than physical therapy in the health system. The AOTA definition of its members' services was consistent with the ACRM focus on comprehensiveness of service and treatment of the whole person. The AOTA developed an effective national advocacy program during the 1970s despite the breadth of its definition of service, and established itself effectively in the Medicare program. It was hard for Congress to argue with the relevance of occupational therapy when the AOTA had 20,000 members already providing services in the health care system in the 1970s. While its membership was smaller than the APTA, it was still a large association with a capacity to use its members for grassroots advocacy for rehabilitation. It also hired professional staff that had substantial experience in government and Washington politics.[13]

The oldest of the professional associations in the rehabilitation field with a focus on national advocacy was the National Rehabilitation Association (NRA). The NRA was established in the 1920s to support the Vocational Rehabilitation Act (VRA) and its programs. Its membership was primarily the professionals who worked for the state vocational rehabilitation agencies and its focus was largely on the VRA, but its membership also included other professionals who worked with the vocational rehabilitation programs. Henry Kessler was one of its first members and Howard Rusk was active with the NRA throughout the 1950s and 1960s as it labored to expand the programs and funding of the VRA. William Spencer, President of ACRM in 1969, was also active with the NRA and the Council of State Administrators of Vocational Rehabilitation (CSAVR). The NRA's Executive Director, E.B. Whitten, exerted major influence on rehabilitation legislation throughout the 1950s, 1960s and 1970s. In many respects the NRA was a model for the medical rehabilitation associations as they sought to continue and expand the programs established in federal legislation by Switzer, Rusk and others.[14]

Associations of facilities and provider agencies also exerted influence as well. The National Association of Rehabilitation Facilities (NARF) represented many medical and vocational facilities. The Goodwill Association represented their vocational facilities. The National Easter Seal Society was both a voluntary association supporting programs for people with disabilities, and an association of medical and vocational facilities.

These organizations and their leadership replaced the Founders as the protectors of the rehabilitation programs in the 1970s. They turned to Congress for action as the Executive Branch seemed intent on cutting OVR programs and other disability programs. The Administration proposed consolidating programs focused on specific constituencies and producing general health and human service programs for all needy persons. What most unnerved the professional and consumer groups about this consolidation approach was that it lodged the decision making power regarding who received what services with the state political leaders. The advocates for these federal programs were comfortable with the federal agencies and Congress to protect their specific interests and were much less comfortable with state politicians.

By the early 1970s, the Democratic Congress had become skeptical of the use of power by the Republican Executive, particularly its efforts to impound funds appropriated by Congress and to eliminate agencies without Congressional approval. By the mid 1970s, Congress had responded by asserting itself in domestic programs and had begun micromanaging the Executive Branch through legislation. The Budget and Impoundment Act was passed to restrict the ability of the Executive to withhold appropriated funds. Congressional leadership for rehabilitation medicine and disability policies was bipartisan however, as it had been since 1945, and Republican Congressional leaders were active in assisting the field in protecting the rehabilitation programs. Chief among the advocates for people with disabilities and rehabilitation programs in the 1970s were Senators Kennedy of Massachusetts, Magnuson of Washington, Randolph of West Virginia, Stafford of Vermont, Javits of New York, Williams of New Jersey and Eagleton of Missouri. In the House of Representatives the leaders were Brademas of Indiana (who would become President of NYU), Simon of Illinois, Quie of Minnesota, Jeffords of Vermont, and Conte and Early of Massachusetts. They succeeded Mary Switzer and her Congressional allies Senators Lister Hill of Alabama, Hubert Humphrey of Minnesota and Paul Douglas of Illinois; as well as Congressmen John Fogarty of Rhode Island, and Melvin Laird of Wisconsin. Javits, Stafford, Quie, Jeffords and Conte were Republicans who assisted in lobbying the Administration on behalf of persons with disabilities.

Despite the admonition of Under Secretary Veneman of HEW that decisions in health care would be made by politicians not professionals, the professionals still had influence. This was especially true for medicine. The AMA had a large and active membership with very active state medical societies. Physicians continued to be recognized legally as the decision makers regarding the provision of medical care and Medicare was evidence of that. Admissions to hospitals were made by physicians and services had to be prescribed and certified as medically necessary by physicians to be paid for by Medicare. Politicians looked to physicians for their opinions as to the efficacy of treatments and necessary research. It was important that rehabilitation physicians have strong medical leadership, whether within the AMA or directly with politicians making decisions about coverage of services or funding of programs and benefits.

Rehabilitation medicine needed more than just political leadership and advocacy, however. Rehabilitation medicine also needed strong leadership for the development of clinical services, training and research programs. The field was small, still new, and subject to takeover by other medical specialties unless it had strong professional leadership to replace the leadership of the Founders.[15]

A second generation of physician leaders in rehabilitation medicine had begun to arise in the 1960s through the efforts of the Founders and took leadership of rehabilitation medicine in the 1970s. These leaders had often been mentored by Krusen or Rusk and received financial support from the Baruch Committee or from OVR grants. Among those physician leaders of the second generation, the most prominent for their long period of effective leadership and lasting impact (as noted by their colleagues and successors), were Frederick Kottke, MD, PhD of the University of Minnesota, Justus Lehmann, MD of the University of Washington, Ernest Johnson, MD of The Ohio State University, William Spencer, MD of Baylor University and the Texas Institute of Rehabilitation and Research (TIRR), and Henry Betts of Northwestern University and the Rehabilitation Institute of Chicago (RIC). All but Spencer were specialists in Physical Medicine and Rehabilitation. Spencer was, however, the first non-specialist in Physical Medicine and Rehabilitation to be awarded an honorary membership in the AAPMR. All developed clinical services, research and training programs in the 1960s. They were leaders of either or both the ACRM and the AAPMR. None were active AMA members like Krusen and Coulter had been, and they focused their national leadership activities on the rehabilitation medicine organizations such as the AAPMR and the ACRM. Each made a special contribution to the legacy of the founders Baruch, Kessler, Krusen, Rusk and Switzer.

THE LEADERSHIP OF KOTTKE, LEHMANN, JOHNSON, SPENCER AND BETTS

If any one state were to be identified as the home of Physical Medicine and Rehabilitation, it would be Minnesota. The Mayo Clinic with Krusen's leadership in the 1930s was the hub for the field. The Mayo Clinic was originally affiliated with the University of Minnesota Medical School to establish its academic credentials for purposes of recognition of its teaching and training programs. Frederick Kottke was at the University of Minnesota Medical School, while Krusen was at the Mayo Clinic.

Kottke was the Chair of the Department of Physical Medicine and Rehabilitation at the University of Minnesota and directed one of the first Rehabilitation Research and Training Centers. He was active in and strongly supported both the American Academy of Physical Medicine and Rehabilitation, of which he became President in 1978, and the American Congress of Rehabilitation Medicine. His colleague and close friend Glenn Gullickson was also a leader of the PM&R programs at the University of Minnesota and in the two professional organizations. Gullickson was President of the American Academy of Physical Medicine and Rehabilitation in 1970 and also served as a Board member of the American Congress of Rehabilitation Medicine. Kottke collaborated with Frank Krusen to rescue the Kenny Foundation and establish a national research and training center in Minnesota in the early 1960s, with the assistance of Hubert Humphrey and Mary Switzer. He was a friend and political colleague of Hubert Humphrey, as was Krusen. He had become involved with Humphrey's first major campaign for government office as Mayor of Minneapolis. Kottke was also well known for his rehabilitation expertise throughout Minnesota. He was also a source of advice for other politicians in Minnesota such as Republican Congressman Albert Quie, the ranking Republican on the Education and Labor Committee, which had jurisdiction over the Vocational Rehabilitation Act.

Like Rusk, Kottke knew politics very well and fully appreciated the positive impact national policy could have on rehabilitation medicine. Although he was not as politically prominent and well known nationally as Rusk, he had an uncanny ability to develop ideas for policy and translate them into political action through the involvement of others. He established a mechanism, supported by the American Rehabilitation Foundation, for the ACRM, AAPMR and related organizations to develop and advocate for national policy in rehabilitation at a time when such coordination of efforts was essential and the organizations had very limited budgets. Through this mechanism the field brought its expertise to bear on issues and programs of the Rehabilitation Act, Workers Compensation and Medicare. Dr. Kottke chaired and hosted at least annual meetings of the Presidents of involved organizations and experts in the field. His respect among his peers enabled him to create such a mechanism despite the fact that it apparently gave him special authority on the politics of rehabilitation medicine.[16]

Through both his published writings and his political leadership, Dr. Kottke provided the intellectual foundation for rehabilitation medicine in the era beginning with the decade of the 1970s. He conceptualized the delivery of rehabilitation medicine services to fit the demands of the era of expanded coverage and cost containment. In his Coulter lecture of 1968, Kottke described the evolution of physiatry and rehabilitation medicine and charted a course for the future. Four phases in the evolution of the field were described by Kottke beginning with exploration, followed by pioneering, development and finally the phase of the future involving the participation of rehabilitation medicine in the emerging health care delivery system. He saw Duchenne and Finsen, the latter a Nobel Laureate, as the explorers in the 19th century; Krusen, Coulter, Bierman, Knapp and Deaver as pioneers in the period of the 1920s and 1930s; and Rusk as the developer in the 1940s.

Kottke himself would be a transmuter, to use his term: one who transmuted the values accepted from a prior generation and applied them to new circumstances. His future phase, to be shaped by a new generation of leaders, was referred to as the phase of organizing health services. Kottke saw well the impact Medicare and health insurance would have on the expansion of services. He admonished the field to establish measures of quality for rehabilitation medicine services, which would assure appropriate patient care and productivity. He also was a proponent of expanded outpatient care to assure continuity of the rehabilitation process and of independent living programs to assure community reintegration for the person with a disability. The field was alerted to the demands the payors of care would make on its providers and forewarned of the confusion, which might occur regarding the relative roles of inpatient rehabilitation programs, skilled nursing facilities, and other forms of post acute care. The organizations followed his advice and research began in the 1970s on measuring outcomes and developing approaches to obtain greater productivity in rehabilitation. Kottke and Douglas Fenderson, PhD, also at the University of Minnesota, were involved in the establishment of one of the first independent living centers for persons with disabilities during the early 1970s.[17]

One of Kottke's close associates and colleagues was Justus Lehmann MD, who had been mentored by Krusen at the Mayo Clinic. Lehmann was born in Konigsberg, Germany, and studied medicine at the Goethe University in Frankfurt and the University of Leipzig .He trained in internal medicine and became interested in physical modalities such as diathermy. As a result, he studied biophysics at the Max Planck Institute of Biophysics. He came to the United States in 1951 to study physical medicine and rehabilitation (PMR) under Frank Krusen at the Mayo Clinic, where he had a Baruch fellowship. In the mid-1950s Lehmann was on the faculty at The Ohio State University in the PM&R Department then Chaired by Ralph Warden, who was a graduate of the PM&R program at the Mayo Clinic under Dr. Krusen. Dr. Lehmann became Chair of the Department of Physical Medicine and Rehabilitation at the University of Washington in 1957, where he established one of the nation's top research and education programs. His interests were in biomechanics and in gait and he remained an active researcher until the end of his career. In the 1960s his program was awarded one of the first four Rehabilitation Research and Training Centers. Dr. Lehmann became President of the AAPMR in 1972 and later served as Chair of its Legislation Committee in the 1970s, and the Research Committee in the 1980s. He influenced the field of rehabilitation medicine for more than 35 years.[18]

Lehmann was very much a follower of the Krusen approach. He was a fine researcher, a demanding but loved teacher and mentor, and a leader in efforts to obtain academic excellence He was committed to academic excellence in all aspects of rehabilitation medicine; emphasizing exceptional training programs in psychology, physical therapy, occupational therapy and other disciplines in the rehabilitation medicine team. He was known to be eminently fair in his recognition of the talents of others of all disciplines. Lehmann's greatest impact was on research and on training and mentoring the future physicians and other professionals who made up the field of rehabilitation medicine. He was, like his mentor Krusen, the academic leader of PM&R during the 1970s and 1980s. His trainees and faculty at the University of Washington went on to chair departments and programs at other academic centers throughout the nation and became leaders of the field. These included Walter Stolov, MD, who succeeded Lehmann as chair at the University of Washington; Barbara deLateur, MD, who became the first chair of Physical Medicine and Rehabilitation at Johns Hopkins University Medical School and the first female President of AAPMR; Joel DeLisa, MD, became Chair of the Department of Physical Medicine and Rehabilitation at the University of New Jersey Medical School and the Kessler Institute, and at the time of this writing is Chair of the prestigious American Board of Medical Specialties (ABMS). Bruce Gans, MD, became chair of Wayne State University Department of Physical Medicine and Rehabilitation, the Tufts University Research and Training Center, and President of the AAPMR in 2004–2005.

William (Bill) Fordyce, PhD, psychologist and faculty member in Dr. Lehmann's department, was one of the nation's foremost academics in the area of pain medicine; and became President of the American Congress of Rehabilitation Medicine. Dr. DeLisa was a third generation leader in PM&R, and successor to Krusen and Lehmann as an academic leader. He remembers Dr. Lehmann as:

> *A strong proponent of comprehensive rehabilitation and multi-disciplinary training of the rehabilitation team. He was a champion for research and formed much of the scientific basis for the specialty, especially therapeutic modalities such as the use of heat and cold. He was very interested in biomechanics, especially as it applied to abnormal gait, and the use of various orthotic and prosthetic devices.*

Dr. deLateur remembers Dr. Lehmann as a man who befit his name, as Lehmann in German meant farmer. Dr. Lehmann, in her opinion, productively plowed the fields of rehabilitation medicine science and education and worked from dawn til' dusk to learn more to benefit the field.[19]

Dr. Lehmann became a well respected envoy of rehabilitation medicine to Senator Warren Magnuson, Democrat of Washington State who was Chair of the Senate Subcommittee for Appropriations for the Departments of Labor and HEW; and to others in Congress. Lehmann spoke for the field as a whole when advising the Senator and his Subcommittee Chief Clerk Harley Dirks. He was extremely effective in advocating for research and education programs for the field as he was learned, humble and his word could always be trusted. He applied his enormous energy and talent, often upon consultation with Dr. Kottke, to advocate for rehabilitation medicine services, at the national level. He was an advocate for expanded rehabilitation coverage in all insurance programs, from workers compensation and no fault auto insurance to standard health insurance. His research advocacy continued through 1990 when he and others successfully established a research program in rehabilitation at the NIH. His enthusiasm and effort were infectious. His leadership produced a future generation of fine academic leaders for the field.

Ernest W. (Ernie) Johnson and Justus Lehmann are the two specialists in PMR who are uniformly cited by the leaders of the current generation as the successors to Krusen and Rusk. The two were colleagues briefly at The Ohio State University where Johnson did his training in Physical Medicine and Rehabilitation between 1954 and 1957. Johnson was mentored by Ralph Warden, one of the first residents trained by Dr. Krusen at the Mayo Clinic. He was also affected by the skill and enthusiasm of Dr. Lehmann, who remained a close colleague and supporter throughout his life. Dr. Johnson became a resident at The Ohio State University PMR program after being in general practice in Findlay, Ohio for a brief period. He was closely connected to FDR and the polio field as he was a Fellow of the National Foundation for Infantile Paralysis during his residency and has served on the Board of the Roosevelt Foundation, a position he continues to hold.[20]

Dr. Johnson's lasting impact on rehabilitation medicine has been in his training of leaders in the field, his development of strong national organizations to lead the field, and his development of electromyography as a clinical tool for PMR. Johnson's residency program at The Ohio State University produced more Presidents of the Academy of Physical Medicine and Rehabilitation during the 1980s and 1990s than any other program. Like Lehmann, Johnson is always viewed as not just a teacher but a mentor and friend by his students. The following residents and/or faculty members became Presidents of the AAPMR: Laban, Kraft, Materson, McLean, Braddom, Weber, Melvin and Wolfe. John Melvin was also President of the ACRM, a leader of the Association of Rehabilitation Facilities, and President of the Council of Medical Specialty Societies. Braddom was also President of the Association of Academic Physiatrists (AAP), and the American Association of Neuromuscular and Electrodiagnostic Medicine (AANEM).

Johnson was very successful in recruiting top notch medical students to go into PM&R at a time when it seemed that very few American medical graduates were interested in the field. His personality and intellect and teaching skills combined to make him what one of his graduates, Randall Braddom, MD, has called "the pied piper of PM&R." Johnson also applied his tremendous energy and enthusiasm to the establishment and development of national professional organizations to assure quality and leadership for rehabilitation medicine. He was a board member and President of the American Academy of Physical Medicine and Rehabilitation; a founder and President of the

Association of Academic Physiatrists (AAP); and a leader and President of the American Association of Neuromuscular and Electrodiagnostic Medicine (AANEM). He constantly encouraged his students and colleagues to be active in and leaders of these organizations and was, as usual, successful in so doing. These national organizations and the Department of PM&R at Ohio State remain leaders for the field of rehabilitation medicine and will likely remain so for years to come.[21]

Johnson is known within PMR as the father of electrodiagnosis (which includes electromyography (EMG) and nerve conduction velocity studies (NCVs)). With these procedures, physicians could diagnosis muscle and nerve pathology. Johnson learned his electrodiagnosis directly from our nation's leading pioneer in electrodiagnosis, Dr. Edward Lambert of the Mayo Clinic. Dr. Lambert trained many neurologists in electrodiagnosis as well, and currently Neurology and PM&R share the nation's electrodiagnostic procedures approximately equally. Johnson and his students became prolific researchers in electrodiagnosis. Johnson also proselytized and helped educate his colleagues in PM&R across the country to learn electrodiagnostic techniques. He was joined in this effort by such leading physiatrists as Dr. Joseph Goodgold, who succeeded Howard Rusk at NYU. Physical Medicine and Rehabilitation had no particular diagnostic tool that it created or was expert in until the evolution of EMG with the work of Johnson. EMG added legitimacy to PM&R in the practice of medicine and justified the specialty domain of the field. Johnson had an impact similar to Krusen's on clinical practice and, like Krusen, wrote articles and texts and did clinical research focused on EMG.

Ernie Johnson also was a leader in the controversial area of disability rights at a time when it was not mainstream or even politically correct. He was an outspoken advocate for persons with disabilities, for which he received the prestigious Betts Award (funded by the Prince Foundation), which is given for outstanding achievement for persons with disabilities. Johnson's contributions to improving life for persons with disabilities included establishing accessibility on The Ohio State University campus and founding the Miss Wheelchair USA contest. He was a team physician for The Ohio State University football team, as Krusen had been a team physician at Temple early in his career.[22]

William (Bill) Spencer was trained as a pediatrician at Johns Hopkins Medical School. In the 1950s he became very involved in care of polio victims, and from that experience his interest in rehabilitation medicine evolved. Spencer arrived at his interest in rehabilitation much like Kessler and Rusk, out of a sense of compassion for patients on whose lives he wished to make an effective and meaningful impact. The careers of both Bill Spencer and

Ernie Johnson were deeply affected by polio during the 1950s. No one better articulated the philosophy of comprehensive rehabilitation than Bill Spencer, not even Rusk or Switzer. He also had a unique relationship with his patients, as Rusk had enjoyed. Lex Frieden was a patient of Dr. Spencer after an injury that left him with paralysis of all four limbs (tetraplegia). Spencer's tutelage resulted in a brilliant career for Frieden as an Administrator at TIRR, and one of the leaders in the disability movement and a leader in rehabilitation medicine. In 2002, Frieden delivered the Coulter Lecture at the American Congress of Rehabilitation Medicine, and true to his mentor's approach he passionately urged advocacy for community based services for persons with disabilities.

In 1956, Spencer, like Kessler and Rusk before him, established a rehabilitation hospital, The Institute for Rehabilitation and Research (TIRR) in Houston, affiliated with Baylor University School of Medicine. TIRR became, like IRM in New York and the Kessler Institute in New Jersey, a national center for patient care and research and training in rehabilitation. In the mid-1960s Dr. Spencer and TIRR received a rehabilitation research and training center grant, joining the University of Minnesota, the University of Washington, and NYU as the first regional centers in the nation. Spencer and Lehmann were dedicated leaders in research and involved directly in it themselves. Spencer had great vision in general, and specifically regarding the possibilities of technology for use by persons with disabilities, and emphasized research in this area. Under his leadership, the Harrington rod to stabilize the scoliotic spine was created and early work on functional electrical stimulation began. Dr. Spencer eventually became the first Director of the field's first research institute in 1979 when he became Acting Director of the National Institute of Disability and Rehabilitation Research (NIDRR) created in 1978.[23]

TIRR is still one of the nation's leading rehabilitation hospitals, and its research and related training programs are likewise distinguished. Martin Grabois was Chair of the Department of Physical Medicine and Rehabilitation at Baylor Medical School while Spencer was Chair of the department of Rehabilitation Medicine at TIRR and at Baylor. (Baylor was perhaps unique in having both a Department of Physical Medicine and a separate Department of Rehabilitation; which have recently merged under the leadership of Dr. Grabois). Grabois was trained in the Temple program under Dorothea Glass, and was then mentored by Spencer. Grabois went on to become President of the American Academy of Physical Medicine and Rehabilitation and of the American Congress of Rehabilitation Medicine. Grabois became a leader of the generation of rehabilitation medicine physicians which followed Spencer, Kottke, Lehmann and Betts. David Cifu, President of the American Academy of Physical Medicine and Rehabilitation 2007–2008 was trained at Baylor under Dr. Grabois. Cifu has become a leader within the VA system in establishing Polytrauma Rehabilitation Centers to treat the nations wounded from the wars in Iraq and Afghanistan, to assure their return to productive lives. The leadership of the field continues without interruption from the founders through the generations.

Spencer was President of ACRM in the late 1960s and was Chair of its all important Legislative Committee throughout most of the 1970's when advocacy was so necessary. He tirelessly devoted his time and energy to advocating with Congress in Washington for programs for persons with disabilities. Spencer, Lehmann and Ditunno became the legislative voices for the ACRM and the AAPMR in the 1970s and 1980s, with Spencer assuming the primary role. Spencer had a close relationship with the Texas Congressional delegation, including Senator Lloyd Bentsen, who at that time was on the Medicare Committee. He also had a close relationship with Congressman Olin Teague, who chaired the House Committee on Science and Technology; and Congressman Bill Archer of Houston, who became the senior Republican on the all powerful House Ways and Means Committee. Spencer would urge upon Bentsen and Archer the cost beneficial aspects of expanding rehabilitation medicine services to persons with disabilities. This was particularly true for those receiving Disability Insurance or Supplemental Security Income disability payments; since enabling such persons to work would reduce cash payments by the federal government and add tax revenue. He was successful in these efforts during debates on Medicare in the 1970s and 1980s.

Under Spencer's and Friedens's leadership, TIRR was "at the cutting edge" of the independent living and disability rights movement. TIRR established one of the nation's first independent living programs in the 1970s. By the 1990s Frieden and TIRR were recipients of a Robert Wood Johnson Foundation grant to review the movement and make recommendations for its expansion. In the 1980s and 1990s TIRR expanded its own independent living program, and Frieden and others in Texas became leaders in the disability rights movement. This leadership is discussed in the next section of this chapter.

Henry Betts is referred to by Lex Frieden, disability and rehabilitation medicine leader, in his Coulter Lecture along with Rusk, Kessler, and Spencer as the leaders of the rehabilitation medicine field and comprehensive rehabilitation. Spencer and Betts were progeny of Kessler and Rusk in their commitment to comprehensive rehabilitation and rights for persons with disabilities. Betts graduated from Princeton and the University of Virginia Medical School. While in medical school, he became interested in rehabilitation medicine during a summer fellowship at Columbia, which had received one of the large Baruch Committee grants in the late 1940's. Betts trained as a resident, post-graduate fellow and faculty member with Dr. Rusk at NYU from 1957 to 1963. Rusk's influence was to make Betts patient centered in his focus and secure in his chosen field of rehabilitation medicine. He also learned well from Rusk the art of politics, both with politicians and with philanthropists, without whom, Betts maintains, rehabilitation medicine would have never been fully effective. He was brought to Northwestern and the Rehabilitation Institute of Chicago in 1963 by Paul Magnuson, who had affiliated again with Northwestern and RIC after his tour of duty at the VA had ended. Betts undertook a major fund raising campaign to build a new facility at RIC in the mid 1960s. The facility was begun in about 1970 and dedicated in 1974. RIC was also a recipient of an OVR regional research and training center in the 1970s. RIC has been recognized for many years as the premier rehabilitation hospital in the world by U.S. News and World Report.

RIC has consistently maintained a rare balance of excellent clinical services, research and training. The research program has been one of the three or four finest in the country year in and year out since the late 1980s. It has received several center grants from the OVR and its successors, and has been the recipient of many NIH research grants. Dr. Betts, like his mentor, has had the ability to attract top academics, researchers and clinicians to RIC during his 40 years of leadership. Zev Rhymer, MD is the Director of Research at RIC and has been so for 20 years. He is a neurologist by training and recognized as the finest of rehabilitation medicine researchers and research managers. Elliot Roth, MD is Chair of the Department of Physical Medicine and Rehabilitation, a specialist in PM&R and a nationally recognized expert on stroke care. The impact of RIC on rehabilitation care throughout the nation is one of Dr. Betts' most important legacies to the field.

Betts' commitment to his patients and the national movement of persons with disabilities is unparalleled in the medical community. He became a leader with Bill Spencer during the 1970s in advocating for rights for persons with disabilities and for independent living programs to assist the severely disabled in community integration. He has become best known for his ability, comparable to Rusk's, to enlist the support of philanthropists and politicians on behalf of rehabilitation and programs and rights for persons with disabilities. His close relationship with Mary Lasker and with Ann Landers, the newspaper columnist, assisted in obtaining public visibility for rehabilitation medicine and rights for persons with disabilities. This was similar to the effect of Dr. Rusk's column in the New York Times and his many political relationships. Betts was a leader in advocating for the creation of the National Institute on Disability and Rehabilitation Research and independent living programs in the 1978 Rehabilitation Act Amendments. He worked tirelessly for the enactment of the Americans with Disabilities Act in 1990 and the creation of a National Center for Medical Rehabilitation Research at the NIH in that same year. More recently he has been a part of efforts to eliminate restrictive provisions in Medicare which have resulted in less comprehensiveness in the rehabilitation medicine benefit. Like his peers and the Founders, he has maintained close relationships with politicians. This is especially true for Senator Kennedy, leaders of Illinois politics including Mayor Daly, Minority leader Bob Michel, and Congressman John Porter. Kottke and Spencer were active leaders in rehabilitation medicine for 30 years and Lehmann, Johnson and Betts for almost 40, matching the duration of contributions from the founders.[24]

By the 1970s, the field of rehabilitation medicine was far more developed than it had been when Krusen, Kessler and Rusk were advocating for rehabilitation programs between 1945 and 1965. Leadership now came from many more sources than in the earlier period, and not all the leadership was medical. The APTA and its leaders were a formidable force in rehabilitation medicine. Occupational therapy and speech pathology were developing more national influence. The American Congress of Rehabilitation Medicine had opened its membership to non-physician leaders in rehabilitation medicine and through it, non-physician leadership for the field developed as well. Notable leaders in rehabilitation medicine of the ACRM were PhD physical therapists Helen Hislop and Carmella Gonnella; Donald Olson in speech pathology; June Rothberg and Dorothy Gordon in rehabilitation nursing; Bill Fordyce, Marcus Fuhrer and Nancy Crewe in rehabilitation psychology; Jean Cole in Occupational therapy; and Irving Zola and Saad Nagy in sociology and disability. Together with a new generation of dedicated physician leaders mentored by Rusk and Krusen, rehabilitation medicine was prepared to continue the leadership of its founders.

THE DISABILITY MOVEMENT

Ed Roberts, who is often referred to as the "father of the independent living movement," described poignantly what the disability movement was about in the proceedings of the Disabled Persons International in Melbourne in 1983:

When I was fourteen, I got polio. When the doctor took my parents aside, my mother asked: "Will he live?" The doctor looked at her and said, "You should probably wish that he dies, because if he lives he will be nothing more than a vegetable for the rest of his life." Well. I am here today as an artichoke. You know, they are a little prickly on the outside with a big heart, and I'd like to call on all the vegetables of the world to unite.[25]

Later in the same proceedings, speaking of the civil rights movement of the 1960s, he advised his colleagues: "If there is one thing we have learned from the civil rights movement in the United States it is that when others speak for you, you lose."[26]

The disability movement began in the late 1960s and developed fully during the 1970s and early 1980s. Its purpose was to organize persons with disabilities on a national and international basis to speak for themselves in politics and act for themselves to achieve their goals. The independent living movement, a related political advocacy effort, had as its purpose attaining support for programs that would enable persons with disabilities to live independently in the community. It is no coincidence that the disability movement began in the late sixties and early seventies. Its leaders were motivated by and learned from the racial civil rights movement of the 1960s. Martin Luther King and the Southern Christian Leadership Conference were models for Ed Roberts and Justin Dart Jr., both of whom led the disability movement in its early years.

Justin Dart Jr., the foremost leader of the movement for civil rights for persons with disabilities, first became involved in protest movements and politics in the civil rights movement of the 1960s. He often referred to the marvelous rhetoric of Dr. King. His funeral was held in the same church where the services in D.C. had been held for Dr. King. The disability movement has been somewhat different in focus from the civil rights movement for black Americans in that civil rights for persons with disabilities involved more than legal protection against discrimination. It involved efforts to achieve independent living arrangements for severely disabled persons through local programs of self-help, comparable to the community action programs sponsored by the Office of Economic Opportunity during the 1960s. The elimination of discrimination against persons with disabilities often involved physical or programmatic changes by the discriminating agency, such as lifts for public transportation or special interpretive services for the deaf in health facilities. Independence and empowerment for persons with disabilities meant a broad array of programs to enable persons with severe disabilities to function independently and assert their rights to education, transportation, housing and employment.[27]

Self-help programs for persons with disabilities, or chronic health conditions which resulted in disability, had existed for many years prior to 1970. Few of these programs, however, had political advocacy as their goal or were organizations of persons with disabilities. FDR's rehabilitation center at Warm Springs had elements of self-help in its programs during the late 1920s and 1930s. It was unique, however, and political advocacy was not on its agenda, since it was difficult in those days just getting services of any kind for persons with disabilities. After World War II soldiers who were disabled organized to argue for medical care, job training and other programs. They formed the Disabled American Veterans Association and the Paralyzed Veterans Association. Individuals with disabilities, like Henry Viscardi and Harold Wilke, had been leaders in rehabilitation as early as the 1940s and 1950s. Leaders like them were few, however, and they tended not to attempt to organize disabled persons politically so that they could speak more vocally and visibly for themselves. The leaders with disabilities of the 1940s and 1950s did not engage in protests and direct political action like the disability movement of the 1970s, in part because the climate was not right for such an effort. That would all change after the 1960s.[28]

The first major organizing effort for persons with disabilities to speak for themselves occurred in 1940 when Jacobus tenBroek organized the National Federation of the Blind. Jacobus tenBroek became totally sightless at age 14. He received his A.B., Masters in Political Science, and Doctorate in Law from the University of California at Berkeley. He taught political science and law at Berkeley and was nationally renowned for his books on constitutional law, politics, and individual rights. He was President of the National Federation of the Blind from its founding in 1940 until his death in 1968. One of the first initiatives of the Federation under tenBroek's leadership was legislation for Civil Rights for those with visual impairment. One of his protégés was Tom Joe, a political scientist, who was a researcher for the California Assembly in the 1960s and Special Assistant to Under Secretary Veneman of HEW until 1973. Joe delivered the Coulter Lecture to the American Congress of Rehabilitation Medicine in 1980 and stressed the need for rehabilitation professionals to ally with persons with disabilities to achieve improved rehabilitation services. He worked very closely with Drs. Kottke, Lehmann and Spencer during the late 1970s on the development of programs to provide medical and vocational rehabilitation services to disabled persons receiving disability insurance benefits.[29]

Shortly after the organization of the National Federation of the Blind, other advocacy organizations for persons with disabilities developed. The Paralyzed Veterans of America founded a civilian organization, the National Paraplegia Foundation in the late 1940s. In 1949 and 1950, the Association of Retarded Citizens (ARC) and the National Foundation of Cerebral Palsy were formed by concerned parents of children with cerebral palsy or retardation. Elizabeth Boggs of New Jersey, a brilliant mathematician and passionate parent of a disabled child, was one of the founders of the ARC and became a leader of the disability movement. She was President of the ARC in 1958, served on President Kennedy's Panel on Mental Retardation (which wrote the Mental Retardation and Mental Health Act of 1963), and was Co-Chair of the

National Task Force on Rights and Empowerment (which led the effort to enact the Americans with Disabilities Act in 1990).

In the late 1940s, Tim Nugent created a program for college students with disabilities at the University of Illinois, urged the elimination of architectural barriers and established national wheelchair athletics. His efforts did involve political action and led the way for Roberts and his colleagues in the late 1960s and 1970s. Nugent and his programs were models for Dr. Ernest Johnson in his efforts to make the campus of The Ohio State University accessible.[30]

In 1969, the National Citizens Conference on Rehabilitation and Disability was held in Washington, sponsored by the OVR and HEW. Persons with disabilities from all walks of life attended. These were not just the few well known persons with disabilities such as Henry Viscardi and the Reverend Harold Wilke. Also in attendance were many persons with disabilities who had not made it and needed an opportunity for work or further education. The Conference was impassioned and even offensive to many of the older rehabilitation professionals who were not used to consumers of their services being demanding, or even rude. But it served to involve the consumer and presaged the efforts in the 1970s to establish rights for the consumer of rehabilitation and special education services to participate in the planning of their services.

By the late 1960s the stage was set for the disability community to become more assertive in advocating for its rights. Leaders had developed, organizations had been created, and opportunities arose. There had been a history of advocacy focused on particular disabilities. There had also been a national civil rights movement in the 1960s, which had successfully achieved legislation for racial civil rights and economic opportunities through protest, demonstrations, and political action. The disability community now needed rights and community action. Ed Roberts, Judy Heumann, Fred Fay, Justin Dart Jr., Lex Frieden and Eunice Fiorito would successfully undertake this effort.

The essence of the disability movement in the early days was the independent living program started in university settings associated often with medical rehabilitation programs. It was begun by Ed Roberts, who was enrolled at the University of California in Berkeley in 1962. He had contracted polio when he was 14 and became a ventilator dependent person with quadriplegia. He was unable to use his arms or legs, required a wheelchair for ambulation, and breathed with the frequent aide of a ventilator. He continued to believe in his enormous ability to function intellectually, spiritually and as a leader; if the world around him would accommodate his abilities. At Berkeley he was confined to a wing in the university hospital where he lived with the assistance of his brother, also a Berkeley student. He, like tenBroek, attained his Masters in Political Science and PhD (except for his thesis) at Berkeley. While there, he and John Hessler organized advocacy for disabled students and formed the Rolling Quads in 1963, dedicated to making the campus barrier free much as Tim Nugent had done earlier at the University of Illinois. With University endorsement, Roberts and Hessler established the Physically Disabled Students Advocacy Program (PDSP), which emphasized the concept of "speaking for themselves." The program included community advocacy and action, community living, and personal assistance services such as those Ed Robert's brother provided for him. PDSP became a model of independent living services and received federal demonstration grant support from the OVR. Roberts remained at Berkeley to complete all his work on his PhD except his thesis.[31]

Judith Heumann was born in 1947 and was eight years younger than Ed Roberts. She contracted polio at age 18, some six and one half years before Roberts contracted the same disease. She was unable to walk and used a wheelchair to move about. As a result of using the wheelchair, she was considered a fire hazard, and was denied a place in the neighborhood public elementary school. Being considered a fire hazard was somewhat analogous to being considered a chattel if one were an African American before the Civil War. Heumann eventually attended Long Island University, where she and others founded a Disabled Students Program in the late 1960s. This was about the same time Roberts and Hessler were establishing their program at Berkeley. After graduation she became a teacher in the New York Public Schools, but only after she used the courts to attain her right to the position. In 1970, the indomitable Heumann established Disabled In Action, an organization representing all persons with disabilities, which used political action to achieve rights. Disabled in Action organized demonstrations and sit-ins against President Nixon and his veto of the Rehabilitation Act in 1972. In 1973, she left New York City and joined Roberts in a partnership that would shape American disability politics.[32]

Fred Fay brought the independent living and disability rights movement to New England in the early 1970s. He was born in 1944, and in 1961 became quadriplegic. He attended the University of Illinois at Urbana in Illinois, where Tim Nugent had established a revolutionary program for disabled students. He received his B.A. in 1967, and inspired by Nugent's program, he and his mother established the Washington, D.C. Architectural Barriers Project. This group negotiated with the DC government on accessibility for disabled persons in transportation programs. After receiving his doctorate, he worked on the Comprehensive Needs Study of Individuals with the Most Severe Disabilities, which was mandated by Congress in 1973. That study established the basis for the federal Independent Living program in 1978. Fay then went to Boston, where he became the Director of Research at the Rehabilitation Research and Training Center (RTC) of Tufts New England Medical Center. There he joined with physician (physiatrist) Paul Corcoran to advocate for rights for persons with disabilities in the Boston area. A spinal tumor exacerbated Fay's quadriplegia in the late 1980s, but from his home he has remained a leader in the rights movement for people with disabilities. The Tufts Independent Living program is considered one of the four national IL centers, which led the IL and disability rights movement during the last 30 plus years.[33]

Lex Frieden and Justin Dart, Jr. were founders of the independent living and disability rights movements in Houston, Texas. Frieden was born in 1949 in Oklahoma and attended Oklahoma State University. Early in his education he was injured in an automobile accident resulting in paralysis of all four limbs. He was treated at The Institute for Rehabilitation and Research (TIRR), that had been founded by Dr. William Spencer in 1956. Spencer became a mentor for Frieden, who went on to get his B.S. in psychology in 1971 at the University of Tulsa. While in Tulsa, he founded Wheel Chair Independence in 1971. He returned to TIRR shortly thereafter and established an independent living program in conjunction with TIRR and Dr. Spencer. In 1975, he established the Houston Coalition for Barrier Free Living. Spencer's Presidential Address to the American Congress of Rehabilitation Medicine in 1969 had urged a broad vision of comprehensive rehabilitation and community integration for persons with disabilities. Spencer in Houston, Corcoran in Boston, Kottke in Minnesota, and Johnson in Columbus were leading efforts to achieve that vision by allying rehabilitation medicine with the growing disability movement and its advocacy for independence and rights.[34]

Justin Dart Jr. was born in 1930 in Chicago and contracted polio in 1948. His father was a renowned businessman who was very active in Republican politics on a national and local basis. Polio required that Dart use a wheelchair for ambulation for the remainder of his life. He received his undergraduate degree in history and education from the University of Houston in 1953, but was denied his certificate to teach because he had a disability. He became a successful businessman in Japan, forming Japan Tupperware in 1963. He also formed an independent living program for persons with disabilities in Japan. Justin Dart Jr.'s involvement in the disability movement and disability rights in the United States began only when he returned from the Far East to Texas in 1974. There he was a supporter of Friedens's independent living program and advocacy efforts and became Chair of the Texas Governor's Committee for Persons with Disabilities. In the 1980s he would become a leader in the Reagan Administration and a consummate advocate for civil rights for persons with disabilities.[35]

In 1974, Fay and Frieden joined with another disability leader, Eunice Fior-ito to establish the American Coalition of Citizens with Disabilities (ACCD), which was officially incorporated in 1975. Fiorito was head of the New York City Mayor's Office of the Handicapped under reformer Mayor John Lindsay from 1971 to 1978. She was blind and cut in the mold of tenBroek, a passionate and persuasive advocate for civil rights. Fiorito was born in 1930 and became totally blind at the age of 16. Despite being discouraged from attending college by her rehabilitation counselor, she graduated from Loyola University in Chicago with a B.S. in science, and received a Masters in Social Work from Columbia University in 1960. After having difficulty finding employment, she worked for the Jewish Guild for the Blind in New York City and founded the nation's first outpatient psychiatric clinic for the blind.

The ACCD was the first national disability advocacy organization to focus on persons with all types of disabilities, also referred to as a "cross disability" organization. It was modeled on Fiorito's New York City program. The ACCD would join with voluntary organizations, professional societies and facility associations in the rehabilitation field to help shape the nation's laws and policies for disability for the next decade. The ACCD initially received funding from the OVR, which had been renamed the Rehabilitation Services Administration in 1973. The ACCD was active from 1974 through 1983, when it dissolved for lack of adequate financial support to maintain an effective national advocacy presence.

The ACCD would be succeeded by the Consortium for Citizens with Disabilities (CCD) in the 1980's as the organizer of the disability movements' agenda. The CCD was initially formed at about the same time as the ACCD, and is an informal coalition of more than 100 organizations; including disability, facility and professional organizations. It has remained active and successful to this day as leader of the disability movement. It has had no paid staff; and has relied on the contributions of staff advocates from the member organizations, led by the Association of Retarded Citizen and its tenacious and persuasive Washington Director, Paul Marchand. Most all of the professional societies in rehabilitation medicine were active members of the ACCD and the CCD.[36]

THE IMPACT AND INFLUENCE OF THE DISABILITY MOVEMENT ON REHABILITATION MEDICINE

The disability movement was founded to enable persons with disabilities to speak for themselves, and to take control of their own lives. It was an independence movement and a protest against paternalism, second class citizenship, and segregation. The movement's focus was on integration of persons with disabilities into life's mainstream. The rehabilitation medicine movement, as envisioned by its leaders, was to advocate for its patients' rights, and to provide the necessary services to enable a person with a disability to achieve optimal independence and be fully integrated into the community. In the early 1920s Kessler had stressed the need for vocational training and job placement, so that a person with a disability could become an active participant in the community once again. Krusen had emphasized the need for vocational training and job placement as part of the physical medicine program, and he readily adapted his visions to accommodate the Rusk concept of comprehensive medical rehabilitation that was developed in the late 1940s and 1950s. Rusk, Spencer, Betts, Kottke, Johnson, Abramson and Corcoran stressed the need for social services, architectural barrier removal, assistance to enable a person with a disability to live independently in the community, and civil rights for persons with disabilities throughout the late 1960s, 1970s, and 1980s. These leaders did more than talk! They created community programs of independent living and advocated actively at state and federal levels of government for integration and independence for persons with disabilities.

A broad alliance of the disability movement with the medical rehabilitation movement should have been natural. However, the disability movement rejected the medical model of care. To the leaders of that movement the medical model of the physician dictating the future for "patients" usually meant both pessimism and lack of participation for the person with the disability. That approach was the very paternalism the disability movement railed against, and with reason. But rehabilitation medicine was different from most other forms of medicine. Rehabilitation medicine was concerned not only about the physical health and function of the patient, but also with his or her ability to obtain employment and live independently in the community. Its connections to vocational training and job placement programs as well as social service agencies and personnel enabled rehabilitation medicine to be a comprehensive rehabilitation approach to the whole person and not just the anatomical being. That difference was what had made rehabilitation's acceptance by organized medicine so grudging. Even by the early 1970s, rehabilitation medicine was not fully accepted by organized medicine and was often thought of as a form of medical social work which had no basis in the physical sciences. But this difference from medicine generally is what made rehabilitation medicine an effective service system and a natural ally for the disability movement. The field was patient oriented and saw medical care as extending into the domain of the community. The question still remained, however, as to whether it would support the political activism, including protests and demonstrations, of the disability movement bent on achieving legal rights for persons with disabilities.[37]

The answer was clear as early as 1972. In that year Arthur Abramson, President of the American Academy of Physical Medicine and Rehabilitation from 1972 through 1973 and Bernard Kutner, PhD, wrote an editorial setting forth the view for the field of: "A Bill of Rights for the Disabled Person." Abramson suffered a spinal cord injury in World War II and was a wheelchair user. He chaired the Department of Physical Medicine and Rehabilitation at Albert Einstein Medical School in New York City, and is often listed as one of the second generation of leaders of rehabilitation medicine. He and Henry Kessler were instrumental in the establishment of the VA rehabilitation service and residency training at the VA Hospital in East Orange, NJ. Dr. John Melvin, a President of both the ACRM and AAPMR, remembers Abramson as one of the new generation of leaders in the 1960s and 1970s. Abramson was a passionate and principled physician who joined with fellow persons with disabilities in their vision of rights. He was also a respected academic at one of the nation's finest medical schools. The Bill of Rights described in the editorial he wrote with Kutner included rights to comprehensive medical care, adaptive devices, equal educational opportunity, equal employment opportunity, a barrier free physical environment, equal opportunity to utilize public transportation and the right to be free from discrimination in all aspects of life. The Bill of Rights was essentially an expansion of the Civil Rights Acts of 1964 and 1965 to apply to persons with disabilities. In his Presidential Address, Abramson called for the members of the Academy and their colleagues in rehabilitation medicine to join with the consumers of their services to advocate for improved medical and other services to persons with disabilities. There could have been no clearer commitment to disability rights than the position of Abramson and Kutner. It preceded the National Council On Disability Report to the President and Congress, which called for a civil rights bill for persons with disabilities by about 16 years, but it cited most of the areas that would be in that seminal document of 1988.[38]

Later in the decade Henry Betts, then President of ACRM, established the theme of the American Congress of Rehabilitation Medicine's annual meeting as the: "Consumer of rehabilitation medicine services, the person with a disability." In his Presidential Address that year, Betts urged the rehabilitation professionals of the ACRM to become involved in issues of barrier removal in the community and of employment opportunities for persons with disabilities. He noted that the person with a disability enters a "hostile world" upon leaving the protected confines of the rehabilitation medicine facility; and that the rehabilitation medicine professional had to become involved in that world and know it in order to change it.[39]

The community action and independent living advocacy by persons with disabilities also found allies in local rehabilitation hospitals. At Tufts New England Medical Center physicians Paul Corcoran, Carl Granger, Glenn Gresham and Bruce Gans worked with the Boston disability leadership. The Tufts program had been led by Krusen from 1968 to 1970 after his re-creation of the Temple program in Philadelphia and after his many years at the Mayo Clinic. Corcoran and Fred Faye, who had come to Tufts to do research on disability and medical rehabilitation, worked very closely to lead an effort to create an independent living center at Tufts. Research on independent living was begun at the Tufts Rehabilitation Research and Training Center (R&T) by Faye with the support and leadership of Gans and Corcoran. In Houston, Bill Spencer assisted Lex Frieden in establishing the Houston independent living center. In Chicago Henry Betts was a sponsor and ally of Marca Bristo as she founded Chicago's first independent living center in 1979. In Minnesota, Fritz Kottke and Douglas Fenderson, PhD were active in assisting the establishment of a center for independent living.[40]

The rehabilitation medicine community welcomed the rise of the disability movement. Rehabilitation medicine expanded its focus to become involved in rights of persons with disabilities and programs to enable community integration and independence. The alliance of rehabilitation medicine with the disability movement enhanced the credibility of both, and the capacity of each to achieve its primary political goals and to create a national policy for disability and comprehensive rehabilitation.

For disability rights and policy, the 1970s became what the 1960s had been for poverty programs and racial civil rights: a Golden Era!

NOTES

1. Gritzer and Arluke, 123–135, 145–58; Interview, Leon Reinstein, MD, October 7, 2004.
2. Starr, 393.
3. Steinfeld, Arch Phys Med Rehabil, vol. 53, 4.
4. Starr, 388–93.
5. Starr, 388–89.
6. Interview by Danovitch with Richard Melia, September 25, 1992, History of the EEOC, Oral History, Archives EEOC, 3–7; interview by author with Melia, April 21, 2004.
7. Lowman, Arch Phys Med Rehabil, vol. 52, 449.

8. Spencer, Presidential Address, Arch Phys Med Rehabil, vol. 51, 189.

9. DeLisa, Currie, and Martin. *Rehabilitation Medicine Principles and Practice*, 1998, 15; Betts, Presidential Address, Arch Phys Med Rehabil, vol. 58, 191; Wilke, Coulter Lecture, Arch Phys Med Rehabil, vol. 58, 260.

10. Fowler, *History of PMR in California*, p.42–p.43; Granger, Arch Phys Med Rehabil, vol. 69, 30–31; Abramson, Arch Phys Med Rehabil, vol. 54, 1; Lehmann, Arch Phys Med Rehabil, vol. 55, 2–3.

11. Hislop, Coulter Lecture, Arch Phys Med Rehabil, vol. 59, 104.

12. DeLisa, Currie and Martin, 16; Gritzer and Arluke, 131–134, 136; Murphy, *Healing the Generations*, 198–99, 210–11.

13. Gritzer and Arluke, 135–45.

14. Walker, 158, 212–13.

15. Interview Reinstein, October 7, 2004.

16. Interviews William Fowler, September 9, 2004; John Ditunno, MD, October 28, 2005; and Dennis Mathews, October 28, 2005.

17. Kottke, Coulter Lecture, Arch Phys Med Rehabil, vol. 50, 57; Kottke, Presidential Address, Arch Phys Med Rehabil, vol. 61, 1; Interview with Melia, April 21, 2004.

18. Interview Barbara deLateur, November 27, 2007.

19. Quote from DeLisa email correspondence to Verville, August 21, 2007; Interviews William Fowler September 9, 2004; Joachim Opitz, September 15, 2004; Leon Reinstein, October 7, 2004; and Barbara deLateur, November 27, 2007.

20. Interview with William Pease, December 18, 2007.

21. Randall Braddom email correspondence, December 17, 2007; interview with William Pease, December 18, 2007.

22. Interviews Opitz, September 15, 2004; Fowler, September 10, 2004; Reinstein, October 10, 2004; Melvin, October 27, 2005; Pease, December 17, 2007.

23. Frieden, Coulter Lecture, Arch Phys Med Rehabil, vol. 83, 150; Interview Fowler, September 9, 2004; Interview Johnson, October 27, 2005; Correspondence from Arthur Sherwood of TIRR, April 29, 2007.

24. Frieden, Coulter Lecture 2002, Arch Phys Med Rehabil, vol. 83, 150; interviews with Henry Betts, July 29, 2004, October 7, 2004; interview with Johnson, October 27, 2005.

25. Driedger, *The Last Civil Rights Movement*, St. Martin's Press, 1989, 7.

26. Driedger, 28.

27. Pelka, *The Disability Rights Movement*, ABC-CLIO Inc., 1997, 85–87.

28. Zola, Arch Phys Med Rehabil, vol. 60, 452; Pelka, 344–46.

29. Pelka, 303.

30. Pelka, 343–48.

31. Interview Melia, April 21, 2004; EEOC Oral History, Interview with Melia, Sylvia Danovitch, September 25, 1992; Pelka, 266–67.

32. Pelka, 152–53, 267.

33. Interview Melia, April 21, 2004; EEOC Oral History Project, Interview with Melia, Sylvia Danovitch, September 25, 1992; Pelka, 120–22.

34. Pelka, 129.

35. Interview Melia, April 21, 2004; Pelka, 85–87.

36. Pelka, 8–10, 123–25.

37. Gritzer and Arluke, 145–48; Abramson, Presidential Address, 1973, Arch Phys Med Rehabil, vol. 54, 7; Betts ACRM Presidential Address, 1977, Arch Phys Med Rehabil, vol. 58, 191.

38. Abramson and Kutner, Arch Phys Med Rehabil, vol. 53, 94–100; Abramson, Arch Phys Med Rehabil, vol. 54, 7; Melvin Interview, October 27, 2007.

39. Betts, Arch Phys Med Rehabil, vol. 58, 191.

40. EEOC Oral History Project, interview with Melia, September 25, 1992; interview with Melia by author, April 21, 2004.

Chapter Twelve

The 1970s: Congressional Leadership and the Golden Era for Comprehensive Rehabilitation and Disability Policy

THE REHABILITATION ACT OF 1973
AND THE 1978 AMENDMENTS

By 1965 Mary Switzer, Howard Rusk and E. B. Whitten of the National Rehabilitation Association had labored hard to enact an independent living program in the Vocational Rehabilitation Act, but had failed. The emphasis of the Vocational Rehabilitation Act (the Act) during the late 1960s was on expanding eligibility to individuals disadvantaged by poverty and assisting them in obtaining employment. Switzer, Rusk and Whitten believed that the Act should focus on persons with disabilities only; but enable all of them, regardless of income and education, to have access to services whether they were employable upon assessment or not. The Department of HEW and the Administration opposed this approach and wanted the program to be limited to individuals with vocational goals; although socially and economically disadvantaged persons would be eligible in spite of not having a recognized physical or mental disability. The Congress sided with the Administration and kept the focus of the Act targeted to vocational outcomes. The Act was amended, however, to allow a six-month evaluation period for severely disabled persons to determine if they might become employable. In 1971 and 1972 when Congress met to consider the renewal of the Rehabilitation Act, the issue of independent living goals for the Act was resurrected.[1]

Other issues faced the vocational rehabilitation program, which complicated the effort to obtain independent living services and goals in the program. Many persons with disabilities felt they were not getting vocational rehabilitation services that they need, and many agencies providing the services felt the demand for services far exceeded the resources available to serve all in need. Funding had been doubled by the 1965 amendments, as well as the appropriations which followed; but the numbers of persons in need was great. The aroused consumer movement felt that the money was not being targeted on those most needing the services. They argued not only for the program to have an independent living goal to assist those with no vocational potential, but also for rehabilitation services to be provided to the most severely disabled who believed they had a vocational goal. The case of Ed Roberts would be "a case in point." After being turned away from the California vocational rehabilitation program as being too disabled to be employable, he later became the Director of that program in 1975 after getting an education and leading a self-help rehabilitation agency.

In 1972, Congress created legislation that established a new program for comprehensive rehabilitation services for those who did not have employment goals. At the urging of the disability movement, Congress also added requirements for consumer participation in the planning of vocational rehabilitation services. The rehabilitation plan would be developed jointly by the rehabilitation counselor and the consumer. The legislation included provisions assuring that priority for services would be for the most severely disabled persons who could benefit from vocational rehabilitation services. The Act focused on special groups of severely disabled individuals through the establishment of a "model spinal cord injury" program of direct grants to rehabilitation medicine facilities to provide comprehensive services to the spinal cord injured patient from early medical rehabilitation to vocational and social services. Most importantly, at the urging of the disability movement led by Fred Fay, Title V of the legislation included civil rights provisions modeled on Title VI of the Civil Rights Law of 1965. Title V prohibited discrimination in all programs receiving federal assistance, created an affirmative action program for the federal government and its contractors, and established an Architectural Barriers Commission to enforce requirements that federal buildings be accessible for persons with disabilities. The Act also required that the President hold a White House Conference on the Handicapped by 1977 to establish recommendations for amendments to the Act and to other programs in 1978 when the Rehabilitation Act of 1973 expired.

The champions of this comprehensive legislation in the House were Congressman Brademas of Indiana and Congressman Quie of Minnesota. In the Senate, the leaders were Senator Randolph of West Virginia and Senator Cranston of California. The civil rights provision was the result of efforts of Congressman Charles Vanik of Ohio, who added the provision to the bill when it was pending business on the House floor. Vanik served in the House for 26 years and was known for his commitments to Social Security and Medicare as well as the right of emigration from Russia and other soviet bloc countries. (He died at age 94 in August of 2007.) Vanik's provision had no difficulty passing in the Senate. Unlike the battles over the Civil Rights Act of 1964 and the prolonged and contentious deliberations over other civil rights provisions, Title V of the Rehabilitation Act was not a problem for members of Congress. It was also not a problem for the Nixon Administration.[2]

The Administration opposed the new Comprehensive Rehabilitation Services program because it shifted the goals of the Act from its historic, successful employment goal to a less measurable one, and one the Administration felt the rehabilitation agencies were not equipped to handle. In late 1973, President Nixon unexpectedly vetoed the legislation, along with a number of other bills, on the grounds the bills were too costly and that the Rehabilitation Bill also included the new independent living program. Although the Congress was unable to override the veto, it served as a rallying call to persons with disabilities and protests took place in New York led by Judy Heumann.

In 1973, the new Congress revived the legislation and passed it again, but this time without the Comprehensive Services Title, and with some reduction in the authorized budgets for the other programs. Most all other changes in the original bill survived, however, and had lasting effects. The role of consumer participation was recognized in the vocational rehabilitation program, so that the consumer with a disability could speak for himself during the rehabilitation process. The Act also required an order of selection for clients. Individuals with the most severe disabilities were to be served first. The model program for the spinal cord injured, often the most severely disabled of clients, was established. The model spinal cord injury program became a vehicle for great progress in the medical care and rehabilitation of persons with spinal cord injury as the program integrated medical rehabilitation care with acute medicine. The Title V civil rights provisions were enacted without amendment from the original legislation passed by Congress, and the Administration was supportive. The 1978 White House Conference was included in the final law, as was a requirement for a Comprehensive Needs Study regarding the rehabilitation needs of persons with disabilities. Instrumental in passage of this legislation was Ed Lowman, Rusk's protégé in politics, as he applied his personal persuasion wherever possible and urged colleagues throughout the country to join the effort and to contact their members of Congress. Lowman realized how essential it was to create strong legislative provisions to protect the program during times when there was a lack of leadership from the rehabilitation agency and White House.

Implementation of the far reaching provisions of the 1973 amendments became another hurdle to be cleared. The rehabilitation medicine community was intimately involved with this process of implementation. The provision in the federal-state vocational rehabilitation program requiring service to the most severely disabled and the spinal cord injury model systems grant program demanded more involvement of the medical rehabilitation community with the vocational counselors (who were the managers of rehabilitation services under the state rehabilitation program). Walter Stolov, MD, who was in the Rehabilitation Medicine Department of the University of Washington in Seattle with Dr. Lehmann, created a medical textbook for use by the vocational rehabilitation counselors, as they sought to expand their roles to deal with more complex disabilities. The model spinal cord injury program was extremely innovative, and was not limited to a focus on vocational goals. It also became the model for similar programs caring for burn victims and those with brain injury. Dr. John Ditunno, who became President of the Academy in 1981, was a leader in the model systems program development in the late 1970s (and made it one of the premier rehabilitation programs under the Act of 1973).

While the Rehabilitation Act of 1973 did not have an independent living program, it did include a Comprehensive Needs Study of Individuals with the Most Severe Handicaps; and this study became the basis for future legislation for persons with disabilities. Fred Fay at Tufts New England Medical Center was the senior research associate on that project. The civil rights provisions were not as broad as those found in the Civil Rights Act of 1964, but they opened the door to the development of case law regarding education for children with disabilities and accessible transportation. Perhaps most important, the civil rights provisions generated detailed regulations which established clear rights in all areas covered by the Act; and educated the disability movement as to the exact nature of their rights. But the regulations proved contentious and the Nixon and Ford Administrations delayed the development and approval of them because they were too regulatory. The regulations were finally issued in 1977 by the Carter Administration after protests took place throughout the nation, including sit-ins at the office of HEW Secretary Joseph Califano. The sit-ins were led by Judy Heumann and Eunice Fiorito.[3]

By 1977, the Rehabilitation Act would soon need to be reauthorized. Democrat and former Governor of Georgia, Jimmie Carter, had been elected President in 1976 and this improved the chances of enacting a comprehensive bill. Carter was a moderate Democrat and had a strongly Democratic Congress with which to work. He was also assisted by a Washington savvy and experienced Secretary of HEW in Joseph Califano, who had worked for President Johnson on domestic program policies including Medicare, Medicaid and rehabilitation. While inflation and federal deficits remained problems, President Carter and Secretary Califano did not espouse the cuts of social programs urged by the Nixon Administration, and this pleased rehabilitation advocates.

Carter was also aware of issues involving disability from the perspectives of persons with disabilities. Among his colleagues and supporters were Max Cleland, who had suffered the loss of three limbs during the Viet Nam conflict, whom he appointed to head the Veterans Administration, and Tom Joe, an ally of rehabilitation medicine who had been mentored by the blind civil rights scholar tenBroek. President Carter had been briefed on HEW programs during the transition period between his Administration and that of President Ford by Joe who was a blind social policy expert, who later would receive one of the coveted MacArthur Foundation's "Genius Awards." Joe had worked closely with Drs. Kottke, Lehmann, and Spencer on projects to integrate medical and vocational services more effectively, particularly for persons receiving disability benefits. In 1981, Joe delivered the Coulter Lecture to the American Congress of Rehabilitation Medicine. President Carter also appointed Bob Humphreys as Commissioner of the Rehabilitation Services Administration. Humphreys was a legislative assistant to Senator Jennings Randolph, who was one of the leading Congressional advocates for rehabilitation. While no one could probably ever provide the same dynamic leadership as Mary Switzer, Bob Humphreys knew rehabilitation and was supported by members of Congress. Howard Rusk spoke highly of him and advised the rehabilitation community that programs would be safe under Humphreys' leadership.[4]

A White House Conference on Handicapped Individuals was held in 1977, with over 3,000 persons with disabilities in attendance. The Conference was the first White House Conference for disabled persons and was required by the 1973 Rehabilitation Act. Henry Viscardi chaired the Conference. The Conference report became the focus of efforts by the rehabilitation and disability communities for the next 20 years to enhance health coverage, encourage work for persons with disabilities, and expand civil rights for persons with disabilities. The Act's intent was to have recommendations from this Conference available to Congress when it reviewed and reauthorized the Rehabilitation Act in 1978.

The recommendations of the Conference were for comprehensive health insurance that included rehabilitation services for persons with disabilities, independent living programs, and elimination of Social Security Act work disincentives for persons with disabilities. The recommendations of the Conference also included an expansion of civil rights for persons with disabilities, to be accomplished by amending both the Civil Rights Act of 1964 and the Voting Rights Act of 1965 to include persons with disabilities. The 1973 Amendments dealt only with civil rights protections for persons with disabilities in programs receiving federal aid. By the end of the decade of the 1980s most of these recommendations had been enacted.[5]

The Rehabilitation Act of 1973 was reconsidered by the Democratic Congress in 1978. Once again independent living advocates joined forces with the medical rehabilitation community to urge enactment of a new program for comprehensive rehabilitation services with independent living as the goal. The rehabilitation medicine field also urged the establishment of a comprehensive research program for rehabilitation services to persons with disabilities, and the creation of community based comprehensive rehabilitation facilities. The House Education and Labor Committee under the leadership of Democrat John Brademas of Indiana held extensive hearings. Testimony was heard from many leaders in the rehabilitation medicine field. A formidable array of talent joined Howard Rusk in proposing a major expansion of the scope of the Act and its funding. Witnesses included Dr. Spencer of TIRR and Baylor, Dr. Betts of RIC and Northwestern, June Rothberg Ph.D. who was President of the ACRM, and Dr. Joseph Goodgold, who was President of the AAPMR and a colleague of Dr. Rusk's at NYU. The leadership of the APTA and AOTA also testified on behalf of a major expansion of the Act. The witnesses all supported the creation of a new rehabilitation program for comprehensive services. The Comprehensive Needs Study mandated by Congress in 1973 had documented the need for comprehensive services available to all persons with disabilities who could benefit, whether employment was a goal or not. Such services would also be provided to children and to those who were beyond employment age.

The advocates for comprehensive rehabilitation services were successful and the 1978 Amendments to the Rehabilitation Act of 1973 created two independent living programs. One supported grants to state agencies to administer a program of independent living services. The other provided grants from the RSA to support the establishment of local independent living centers. The programs had an appropriation authorization of $400 million in 1983, which would represent about $1 billion in today's dollars.[6]

At about the time the Education and Labor Committee was having hearings on the Rehabilitation Act, hearings on the research needs of persons with disabilities were also being held. These occurred after Congressman Olin Teague of Texas, who chaired the Science and Technology Committee, was convinced by Dr. Spencer of TIRR and Baylor that the hearings needed to be held. Teague was an amputee and had a close relationship with Dr. Spencer and TIRR, as did many other members of the Texas Congressional delegation. Teagues' Committee hearings involved medical, social, vocational and technology research to benefit persons with disabilities. Rehabilitation medicine again supplied many expert witnesses, including Dr. Spencer, who was speaking for the ACRM and the AAPMR. The Committee recommended a major national effort on research for persons with disabilities. Teague agreed, however, that the Education and Labor Committee should deal with this issue because it was responsible for the Rehabilitation Act under House of Representatives rules. The Education and Labor Committee would act as Teague recommended.

Howard Rusk continued to be an active advocate for the field of rehabilitation medicine in the 1970s, although he was no longer in Washington as an adviser and confidant of government leaders as he had been earlier in his life. He had testified on the Rehabilitation Act before Congressman Brademas and had emphasized expanded services and research. He had never been able to interest the NIH in rehabilitation medicine research, so he had helped create a vibrant research program with Mary Switzer through the OVR (renamed the Rehabilitation Services Administration or RSA in 1973).

In 1978, with the urging of his colleague Ed Lowman, Rusk contacted philanthropist and citizen lobbyist Mary Lasker to get her advice about how to handle the need for expanded rehabilitation research. A meeting was arranged in New York that included Rusk, Mrs. Lasker, Lowman, Betts (who was also a friend of Mrs. Lasker), Jack Duncan (staff director of the Brademas House Subcommittee), and three members of Congress who were interested in rehabilitation. The Congressmen were John Brademas, Chair of the Subcommittee considering the Rehabilitation Act; George Miller of California, who was on the Subcommittee; and Fred Richman of New York City (and a friend of Mrs. Lasker). The matter of research needs was raised and the idea of an Institute on Rehabilitation Research was discussed. Mrs. Lasker was viewed by many in the world of Washington politics as the ever active mother and protector of NIH research. She favored a Rehabilitation Institute in the NIH, but the Brademas Subcommittee had no jurisdiction over the Public Health Service Act and programs, which included the NIH. The result was an agreement to use the Rehabilitation Act as the vehicle for the creation of an Institute on Research and to establish it as a parallel agency to the RSA with a Presidential Appointee as Director and a National Council to oversee it that was comparable to those used at NIH. The legislation that emerged from the House Committee had just such an entity, and it became law in 1978. The new law established a budget authorization of $100 million for the Institute, which was triple the existing funding. It also created programs for research and training centers, model systems of care, and engineering centers. In 1979, Dr. William Spencer of Baylor and The Institute for Rehabilitation and Research was appointed by HEW Secretary Califano as the first Director of the Institute. Spencer was following in the footsteps of

Frank Krusen, who had left the Mayo Clinic in 1959 to become Special Assistant to Mary Switzer for research and public health.[7]

The 1978 Amendments also created The National Council on Handicapped Individuals to advise the President and Congress of the needs of persons with disabilities, as well as to oversee the Research Institute. The Council has played a very effective role for the past 25 years in advocating for services and rights for persons with disabilities, including the monumental civil rights legislation: the Americans with Disabilities Act. The Amendments created a facility construction loan program and a grant program to support community based Comprehensive Rehabilitation Centers, whose services were not to be limited to persons with an employment goal. The rehabilitation medicine organizations had uniformly supported the new programs of the Act and were especially effective in advocating for independent living services and research. The Research Institute was a particular interest and success for Drs. Rusk, Spencer and Lowman.[8]

The 1978 Amendments to the Rehabilitation Act of 1973 represented the culmination of 25 years of effort by Mary Switzer and her staff, Howard Rusk, Frank Krusen, Frederick (Fritz) Kottke, Justus Lehman, and Bill Spencer to establish comprehensive rehabilitation service programs; a major agency dedicated to rehabilitation research; and Presidential level leadership for rehabilitation and disability. The funding estimated for the new programs of independent living, community service employment and research would total about $800 million in 1982. The total estimated funding for the Act in 1982 would be nearly $2.5 billion. Together with the spending generated by Medicare and Medicaid in medical rehabilitation, the federal commitment to rehabilitation services would be very significant by 1982. The Congressional leadership for the Amendments was bipartisan and included: Congressmen Perkins, Brademas, and Quie; and Senators Williams, Randolph, Cranston, Kennedy, Javits and Stafford. [9]

THE EDUCATION FOR ALL
HANDICAPPED CHILDREN ACT: P.L. 94-142

Two years after the enactment of the Rehabilitation Act of 1973, Congress addressed the issue of services to children with disabilities; and passed landmark legislation that was comparable, in retrospect, to the ADA in impact. P.L. 94-142, the Education for All Handicapped Children Act, was modeled on civil rights legislation and particularly on the rights of Title 5 of the Rehabilitation Act. It called for equal educational treatment for children with disabilities and for education in a setting that was the least restrictive for the child. Unlike Title V of the Rehabilitation Act of 1973, however, P.L. 94-142 provided federal funding to carry out the equal treatment mandate. P.L. 94-142 provided that all children age 3 to 21 with a health impairment affecting educational performance would receive a free and appropriate public education furnished in the least restrictive setting. The purpose of the Act was to mainstream children with disabilities and to integrate them with their peers. The Act required an individualized education plan to be jointly developed by the teachers, the student, and parents. This provision was modeled on the individualized written rehabilitation plan for each vocational rehabilitation client that was included in the Rehabilitation Act of 1973. Consumer participation called for by rehabilitation leaders was becoming a fait accompli. The services that were required included special education, and related services such as medical rehabilitation. The ACRM, AAPMR and other rehabilitation professional societies supported P.L. 94-142, since it was another federal law expanding the rights of persons with disabilities and supporting their full community integration. The Congressional sponsors were essentially the same group that had led the effort on the Rehabilitation Act of 1973 and the 1978 Amendments.[10]

By 1990, the funding of P.L. 94-142 had reached about $2 billion, and had grown to $12 billion by 2005. This program grew much faster than the Rehabilitation Act programs, which were about $1.8 billion in 1990 but only about $2.5 billion in 2005. The legal rights to a free and appropriate public education established in P.L. 94-142 were instrumental in achieving the increased funding. Since rehabilitation medicine services for children with disabilities were funded by Medicare if a parent of a disabled child were eligible for Medicare, Medicaid and private insurance, P.L. 94-142 was not necessary for the health needs of children with disabilities and was better used for education. P.L. 94-142 and the Rehabilitation Act of 1973 (as amended in 1978), vastly expanded the programs and funding available for comprehensive rehabilitation services to disabled persons of all ages.

COVERAGE OF PERSONS WITH DISABILITIES AND COMPREHENSIVE REHABILITATION MEDICINE SERVICES UNDER MEDICARE

The original Medicare statute did not extend coverage to persons eligible for Social Security benefits on the basis of disability. Coverage was provided only to persons who qualified for Social Security benefits on the basis of age. Many individuals over 65 had disabilities and required Medicare coverage of rehabilitation medicine services. However, those under age 65 who were unable to work because of a disability and who qualified for Social Security Disability payments were not eligible for any services under Medicare. The original Forand bill endorsed by President Kennedy, and Medicare as proposed by President Johnson, only applied to seniors. The recommendations for hospital rehabilitation coverage which Mary Switzer and her Task Force on Rehabilitation recommended to the Administration in 1964 and 1965 had also focused only on the aged retiree.

Disability Insurance and coverage of health care for disability beneficiaries had been key elements in the Social Security recommendations to President Roosevelt and his staff as early as 1935. When Disability Insurance cash benefits were enacted in 1956, a basis was finally laid for the extension of health care benefits to this population. But the focus of public pressure was on the larger population of aged retirees in 1965, and the first step in this national health insurance would be limited to the aged retiree. The Medicare expansion to cover Disability Insurance beneficiaries, like most Social Security Act expansion, would come incrementally. In the first major Medicare Amendments in 1972 Congress brought up this needed expansion of coverage. The Congress, however, was concerned about the potential cost to a Medicare program that was already expanding beyond expectations. Consequently the bill required that those receiving Social Security disability benefits have a 24–month waiting period from the time of Social Security Disability Insurance eligibility to obtain Medicare coverage. The Social Security Disability process already included a five-month waiting period from the time of initial application for benefits so the total waiting period for Medicare coverage for a disabled person was 29 months. This waiting period still exists, despite legislation proposed in almost all Congresses to eliminate it.

The expansion of Medicare to include persons with disabilities who received Social Security benefits was a signal achievement for persons with disabilities and the rehabilitation medicine field, despite the addition of the waiting period. The major problem that remained, however, was that the many persons with disabilities who had insufficient work experience to qualify for Social Security Disability Insurance were not helped by this expansion of Medicare coverage.

Another major provision of the 1972 Social Security Amendments, however, did provide assistance to disabled persons not eligible for Social Security Disability Insurance due to an inadequate work history and contributions to the Social Security trust fund. The 1972 Social Security Amendments created a new federal income assistance program for poor persons who were aged, blind or disabled. This was the Supplemental Security Income (SSI) program. This program was the remnant of the effort by President Nixon and his Domestic Policy Advisor, Daniel Patrick Moynihan, (later a Democratic

Senator from New York), to enact a Guaranteed National Income program and replace the state based welfare programs of the original Social Security Act. Because SSI was a federal program with federal criteria for eligibility and payment, a national framework was created for assistance to aged, blind and disabled persons. With the enactment of SSI came automatic Medicaid eligibility for all SSI recipients. The Medicare program for disabled persons receiving Disability Insurance and the Medicaid coverage for disabled persons whose income and assets met the SSI requirements put in place two distinct national health insurance programs for persons with disabilities who were unable to work. As a result of these changes, the rehabilitation medicine programs now had the funding streams needed to broaden the coverage for their services.

Also included in the Medicare provisions of the 1972 Social Security Amendments was the addition of a new benefit under Medicare Part B to cover the services of private practicing physical therapists. The provision was later expanded to cover private practicing occupational therapists. It required that a physician develop a plan of care and refer the patient to physical or occupational therapy. The existence of this provision expanded the availability of outpatient rehabilitation therapy services through payment of private practicing therapy professionals. This was in addition to the existing payment available to physicians and hospital outpatients.

The stimulus of Medicare financing of capital costs and services in hospitals, together with expanded coverage to persons with disabilities under 65, produced rapid growth in hospital inpatient rehabilitation medicine programs. "During the 1970s the increase in community acute care hospitals with PM&R programs was the largest of any decade; twice that of the 1960s."[11] Thirty new rehabilitation medicine services programs arose in California alone during the 1970s, more than doubling the programs in that state and bringing the total programs to 56 facilities; ten of which were in the Kaiser Permanente health system. PM&R growth in California occurred in all major metropolitan areas from the Bay area in the north to the central valley, Los Angeles, Orange County and San Diego.[12]

While rehabilitation medicine programs in hospitals expanded greatly as a result of Medicare, they were also subject to the same regulatory provisions as the rest of medicine. Ed Lowman's Coulter Lecture in 1971 raised the reality of cuts in payment to rehabilitation hospital programs due to the lack of clear Medicare guidelines defining the scope and level of hospital care in rehabilitation. His clarion call for political action from rehabilitation medicine professionals to deal with this issue got its response and the situation was turned around to the benefit of the field. The Medicare statute had included rehabilitation programs as a hospital benefit, but had not defined the term.

Retroactive denials of payment occurred for many hospitals with rehabilitation programs and large sums of money were often required to be paid back to the federal government. In addition, the Congress had required Utilization Review Committees in each hospital to review hospital admissions and local Professional Standards Review Organizations (PSRO's) to develop and review standards for admission and services in hospitals. The policies governing these organizations would have a major impact on the scope and intensity of care delivered in hospital rehabilitation programs.[13]

The field of medical rehabilitation responded through Committees on Peer Review and Quality Assurance of the AAPMR and the ACRM. Under the Chairmanship of John Melvin, then Chair of the Department of PM&R at the University of Wisconsin Medical School in Milwaukee, (which was affiliated with the historic Curative Workshop of Milwaukee), the Committee established screening criteria for admission to hospital rehabilitation programs. Melvin was one of many graduates of The Ohio State University residency program Chaired by Ernest W. (Ernie) Johnson who ultimately became leaders of the field. The Quality Assurance Committee of the American Academy of Physical Medicine and Rehabilitation was later chaired by Leon Reinstein of the University of Maryland Department of PM&R, who had been trained by John Ditunno at Jefferson Medical College. Both Melvin and Reinstein became part of a third generation of leaders in rehabilitation medicine who would succeed Kottke, Lehman, Johnson, and Spencer. Betts and Ditunno spanned the second and third generations. The criteria they and their Committee created have survived largely intact, and have served to define inpatient rehabilitation medicine since their inception. They have created the foundation of comprehensive inpatient medical rehabilitation services. The guidelines involve comprehensive therapy services provided by an interdisciplinary team, a goal driven scope of services with a focus on restoration of function; and a requirement that the level of care be one requiring at least three hours each day of therapy services, close medical supervision, and regular skilled rehabilitation nursing services. The Quality Assurance Committee was requested by the national PSRO program to identify the most likely cases to be admitted to the facility for purposes of developing standards of care. Those conditions became the basis for the ten conditions used in the 1980s by Medicare to define a qualified rehabilitation hospital and unit. Their redefinition in recent years has become the bane of the rehabilitation facility movement's existence, as it has resulted in reduced admissions.

In defining inpatient rehabilitation the leadership of the professional associations provided a great contribution to the growth of the field from the late 1970s until today. The standards resulted in the dramatic reduction of payment denials by the late 1970s.[14]

By the decade of the 1970s the hospital had become such a dominant force in American medical care, and Medicare Part A, the hospitalization benefit, had solidified that position sufficient that outpatient care and preventive services had been neglected. In the early 1970s Lewis Butler, an influential Assistant Secretary in HEW, saw the need to expand the number of physicians who would serve in the community and expand the incentives for preventive care. He and a consultant, Dr. Paul Ellwood, who had been involved with rehabilitation medicine in Minnesota with Drs. Kottke and Krusen and had served on the RMP Rehabilitation Subcommittee chaired by Rusk, developed a proposal to create federal support for Health Maintenance Organizations to respond to the need for a focus on prevention and wellness. In his Presidential address to the AAPMR in the late 1970s, Dr. Kottke stressed the need to emphasize programs in rehabilitation medicine which were community based and had independent living and community integration as their goals. His view was that the objective of rehabilitation medicine was to restore each individual to a participating member of society; and this required community based rehabilitation. Kottke, Betts and Spencer shared this view and stressed it in their leadership roles with the AAPMR and ACRM. Community service providers were a logical approach to the patient care goal of community integration for the disabled person.[15]

The establishment of community based centers of care to manage patients with chronic problems and to ease transitions from inpatient care was a cause that Kottke and leaders in the field frequently advocated. The Rehabilitation Act of 1973 as amended in 1978 established a facility construction and staffing program to enhance comprehensive outpatient rehabilitation services at the community level, but the program was not adequately funded to stimulate such outpatient care.

Without adequate financial support under the Rehabilitation Act to finance the establishment of new comprehensive outpatient facilities, the field turned to the Medicare Act. In the late 1970s the ACRM, AAPMR, the National Association of Rehabilitation Facilities, and the National Easter Seal Society joined forces to propose the creation of a Comprehensive Outpatient Rehabilitation Facilities (CORF) benefit under Medicare. The purpose of the proposal was to enable the financing of comprehensive outpatient rehabilitation services through community facilities. Hospital outpatient departments already were reimbursed for outpatient care by Medicare, but it was not a priority in hospital operations and the link to the community was often lost after discharge from the outpatient department. Hospitals also were not always near and accessible to patients, while community facilities could be smaller and more easily accommodated in local neighborhoods than hospitals. Prior to 1980, nonprofit facilities, such as those operated by the National Easter

Seal Society, offered physical therapy, occupational therapy, speech, and psychological services under medical direction. They were unable, however, to recover their costs from Medicare for those services. Private practicing physicians and therapists furnished services in their offices, but the services were limited in scope to physician services and physical and occupational therapy services.

The rehabilitation medicine interest groups were eventually successful in their lobbying efforts for comprehensive outpatient rehabilitation facility (CORF) programs. In the Omnibus Budget Reconciliation Act (OBRA) of 1980, Congress passed Medicare amendments, which included the CORF benefit. Covered services were as comprehensive as they were in inpatient settings; and included physician services, physical therapy, occupational therapy, speech pathology services, respiratory therapy, prosthetic and orthotic services, social and psychological services, nursing care, medical equipment, and home evaluation for accessibility and accommodation. The reference to home evaluation for accessibility emphasized the community reintegration goal of the CORFs.

Facilities were required to meet a number of conditions to participate in the program, including having a medical director and furnishing at least physical therapy and psychological services. The services covered were more extensive than outpatient hospital services, and far more comprehensive than would be provided by an independent physician or physical therapy practice. Payment for the services was on a cost basis comparable to the then payment methods for hospitals. Costs included the costs of services provided as well as the capital costs of establishing the facility amortized over a period of years, with a return on equity for profit making entities. The impact of the amendments was the same as the impact on hospitals of the original Medicare law; to stimulate expansion of services on an outpatient basis. Throughout the 1980s, CORFs developed not only in the non-profit sector (with organizations like the Easter Seal facilities), but in the for profit world as well. HealthSouth Inc. of Birmingham, Alabama was the first for profit organization to speed development of CORFs, and from those origins sprang what is now one of the nation's largest health care providers. With the enactment of the CORF provisions Medicare now offered coverage of inpatient comprehensive rehabilitation services and outpatient comprehensive rehabilitation services.[16]

In the late 1970s rehabilitation medicine professional associations, the National Easter Seal Society, and disability organizations joined forces to correct another problem in the Social Security Act affecting access to rehabilitation medicine services for persons with disabilities. The issue was one involving provisions of the Social Security Act that conditioned receipt of

Disability Insurance (DI) and SSI benefit payments, and therefore eligibility for Medicare or Medicaid, on the earning power of the person with a disability. If you had substantial earning power, you would not qualify for the cash payments and would also be ineligible for health coverage under Medicare or Medicaid. The overall result of this was good coverage of benefits, but a strong disincentive to work. The 1977 White House Conference on the Handicapped had identified this problem of work disincentives in the Social Security Act as a priority area for government corrective action.

The definition of disability to determine eligibility for DI and SSI was based on whether the person with a disability could engage in substantial, gainful employment activity. That term was, in turn, defined as earning above a fixed amount per month. The impact on rehabilitation of such provisions was dramatic, since a person with a disability risked losing DI or SSI cash payments and health coverage if he or she worked full time (the dollar limit of the earnings provision was very low and would easily be exceeded). After lengthy hearings and discussions with Congressional Committees, legislation was produced which established a number of incentives for return to work and to job training while benefits were maintained. Leaders in the enactment of this legislation were Senators Daniel Patrick Moynihan of New York, Lloyd Bentsen of Texas, Bob Dole of Kansas, Congresswoman Martha Keys of Kansas, Congressman Pete Stark of California, and Congressman Andy Jacobs of Indiana. A number of disability leaders from California led the consumer movements lobbying for these changes. The Disability Amendments of 1980 became law in the summer of 1980 and provided Disability Insurance and Medicare coverage during work training and trial work periods. The Disability Amendments of 1980 also provided for SSI benefits and Medicaid coverage when recipients had earnings, with the benefit partially reduced commensurate with the level of earnings. The Amendments also made rehabilitation medicine services available to an expanded class of recipients; and persons with disabilities were encouraged to obtain employment while having their health coverage maintained.

Despite the loss through death or retirement of the leadership of the founders of rehabilitation medicine, the field flourished during the 1970s through aggressive advocacy with the bipartisan leadership of the Congress. The torch of leadership passed from the founders to a broader and more varied group of rehabilitation professionals, the professional associations they led, and the newly formed disability movement. New professional leadership included physicians Kottke, Lehman, Johnson, Spencer, and Betts of generation two; and Ditunno, Melvin, Fowler and Reinstein who, with Betts, established a bridge to a third generation of medical rehabilitation leadership for the 1980s and 1990s. Leaders in other rehabilitation medicine professions also became prominent in this decade including June Rothberg (Dean of the Adelphi School of Nursing), William (Bill) Fordyce (an eminent psychologist and colleague of Justus Lehmann), Helen Hislop (leader in academics and editor of the Journal of the APTA), Carmella Gonnella (a leading researcher in physical therapy from Emory University Research and Training Center), and Donald Olson (a speech pathologist who was Director of the Education programs at the Rehabilitation Institute of Chicago). The lessons of Baruch, Switzer, Rusk, Krusen and Kessler about advocacy and political involvement had been well learned by the professionals who followed them. Their aggressive leadership in Washington and that of the newly emergent disability movement resulted in a remarkable list of legislative achievements. The major question that would arise in the 1980s was how to finance the new programs enacted in the 1970s.

NOTES

1. Walker, 214–16.

2. *New York Times*, September 1, 2007, A11.

3. Verville, Arch Phys Med Rehabil, vol. 60, 447; vol. 69, 64; Melia Interview April 21, 2004; Pelka, 124, 152–55.

4. Rusk, Zeiter Lecture, Arch Phys Med Rehabil, vol. 59, 156.

5. Pelka, 322–23, 352.

6. Public Law (PL) 95-602.

7. Betts Interviews October 7 and 9, 2004; Verville, Arch Phys Med Rehabil, vol. 60, 141.

8. PL 95-602; ibid.

9. Verville, ibid.

10. *Physical Medicine and Rehabilitation Secrets*, Hanley and Belfus Inc., Chan *et al.*, Legislative Issues, 94; Verville, 17th Spencer Lecture TIRR, unpublished manuscript, October 31, 2003.

11. Fowler, A., *History of Physical Medicine and Rehabilitation Programs in California*, 42, quote on 47.

12. Fowler, 42–54.

13. Lowman, Coulter Lecture, Arch Phys Med Rehabil, vol. 53, 49.

14. Granger, Arch Phys Med Rehabil, vol. 69, 33–34; Gonzalez, Arch Phys Med Rehabil, vol. 69, 48–49; Interview with Reinstein, October 7, 2004.

15. Starr, 394–95; Kottke, Arch Phys Med Rehabil, vol. 61, 283.

16. Verville, Chan, PM and R Clinics of North America, "Medicolegal Issues", May 2002, 1999–2000.

President Nixon signing the Rehabilitation Act of 1973, the foundation for modern vocational rehabilitation services, research and education and disability rights, at the White House with Dr. Rusk on the far right. Rusk is the only member of the group who is not either a member of the Congress or the Executive Branch. Senator Robert Dole of Kansas is second from the left and on the far left next to Senator Dole is the Secretary of HEW Caspar Weinberger. Photo courtesy of Frank Romano and the Rehabilitation Services Administration.

Henry Viscardi, Chair of the first White House Conference on the Handicapped, presenting the final report of the Conference to Congressional leaders from left to right, Senator Jennings Randolph of West Virginia, Senator Ted Kennedy of Massachusetts, Viscardi, Senator Robert Stafford of Vermont, and Congressman John Brademas of Indiana on March 2, 1978. The Conference recommended and Congress enacted legislation calling for independent living programs for persons with disabilities, expanded civil rights for people with disabilities and research. Photo courtesy of Frank Romano and the Rehabilitation Services Administration.

Dr. Frederick Kottke on the far right, a member of the second generation of leaders who succeeded the founders beginning in the late 1960's and early 1970's, with then-President of the American Academy of Physical Medicine and Rehabilitation, Dr. Randall Braddom, center, and former President of the Academy Dr. Richard Materson, both among leaders of a third generation succeeding to leadership in the late 1980's. Photo credit to and courtesy of Dr. Randall Braddom and his private collection.

Dr. Justus Lehmann, a second generation leader of rehabilitation medicine, who mentored and trained many of the third generation leaders at his renowned research and training program at the University of Washington. Lehmann was a pioneer in research regarding biomechanincs and gait and the leading researcher of his generation. Photo courtesy of Joel DeLisa and his private collection.

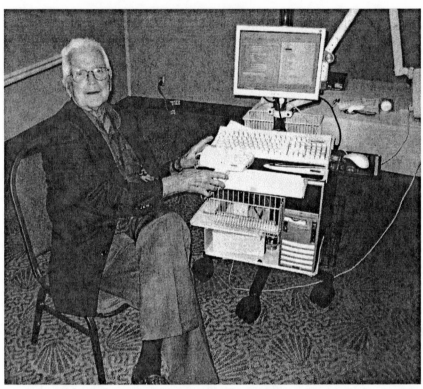

Dr. Ernest Johnson in his electromyography lab, The Ohio State University School of Medicine. Dr. Johnson was another of the second generation leaders arising in the 1960's and is renowned as the father of electromyography and for having established one of the elite training programs for specialists in physical medicine and rehabilitation. He was also among the earliest advocates for disability rights and accessible facilities. Photo credit to and courtesy of Dr. Randall Braddom and his private collection.

Dr. William Spencer, second row third from left, a second generation successor to the founders whose leadership began in 1956 when he established the Texas Institute for Rehabilitation and Research in Houston. He is with a group of distinguished leaders in rehabilitation medicine, including Dr. Krusen, first on the left in the front row, and Dr. William Erdman, Chair of Physical Medicine and Rehabilitation at the University of Pennsylvania, in the center front row. Photo courtesy of the John P. McGovern Historical Collections and Research Center Houston Academy of Medicine-Texas Medical Center Library and Pamela R. Cornell MEd, Archivist.

A third generation of leaders is born with the mentoring of the second. Dr. William Spencer, on the left, with Dr. Martin Grabois, Chair of the Department of Physical Medicine and Rehabilitation at Baylor University, at a meeting of the American Academy of Physical Medicine and Rehabilitation and the American Congress of Rehabilitation Medicine. Photo courtesy of the John P. McGovern Historical Collections and Research Center Houston Academy of Medicine-Texas Medical Center Library and Pamela Cornell MEd.

Dr. Henry Betts, left, and Dr. Kristjan Ragnarsson representing the second and third generation of leaders in rehabilitation medicine, both mentored by Dr. Rusk. Dr. Ragnarsson, Chair of Physical Medicine and Rehabilitation at Mount Sinai School of Medicine, New York City, remembers Dr. Rusk as a role model "who infected me with his missionary spirit" and his moral commitment "to the cause that you work for," rehabilitation. Photo credit to and courtesy of Dr. Randall Braddom and his private collection.

At a recent American Academy of Physical Medicine and Rehabilitation Past Presidents Luncheon, Dr. John Ditunno, left, a second and third generation leader, and Dr. Gail Gamble of the Mayo Clinic Department of Physical Medicine and Rehabilitation, a third generation leader, reminisce about the field. Photo credit to and courtesy of Dr. Randall Braddom and his private collection.

Steny Hoyer, Congressman from Maryland and currently House Majority Leader, and the author in 1985 at the beginning of the effort to enact the Americans with Disabilities Act [ADA], which Hoyer stewarded through the House of Representatives in 1989 and 1990. The ADA was the culmination of efforts to establish rights and a comprehensive approach to disability. Photo credit to Martin LaVor and courtesy of the author and his private collection.

Dr. Henry Betts, right, with his friends and colleagues in advocacy for disabled persons Philanthropist Fred Prince, left, and Judith Heumann, disability leader and U.S. Assistant Secretary for Special Education and Rehabilitation, U.S. Department of Education in the Administrations of President Clinton, at the Capitol during advocacy for the ADA. Photo courtesy of Frank Romano and his private collection.

Chapter Thirteen

The 1980s: Medicare Expansion; Rehabilitation Research at NIH and the Maturation of Rehabilitation Medicine

The 1980s brought a new approach to the control of escalating costs in health care: the market place. Ronald Reagan was elected President in 1980, served two terms, and was succeeded by his Vice President, George H.W. Bush. Those 12 years of Republican Executive Branch rule resulted in much less federal regulation and federal agency leadership in establishing programs. The era of a Mary Switzer working with allies in the private sector to build programs was over. Having lost the influence of the Founders in the 1960s, the field of rehabilitation medicine lost the leadership of the federal agencies that had nurtured it in the 1970s and 1980s. The Rehabilitation Services Administration and the VA both ceased to play major leadership roles in rehabilitation during the 1980s and thereafter. Efforts by Congress to assert that leadership ran into a White House that would veto legislation that it interpreted as asserting too much federal intervention.

The cost of federal programs grew as did the deficit. The major growth in federal programs was in the entitlement programs of the Social Security Act, particularly in Medicare and Medicaid. That cost was to be contained using competition as a model rather than regulation. To quote William Fowler, M.D., a leader in the field of physical medicine and rehabilitation in the late 1970s and 1980s: "The visible hand of regulation was replaced in part with the invisible hand of competition as a method of cost containment."[1] The most important factor affecting medicine in the 1980s, according to medical sociologist and historian Paul Starr, was the economic market place and the rise of corporate medical care from the stimulus of the marketplace. Medicare, the principal payer of health care and certainly for rehabilitation medicine, adopted national prices for both hospital and medical services between 1983 and 1995. The price setting system for hospitals had the unintended consequence of setting off a boom in inpatient rehabilitation care, which resulted in expansion and maturity for rehabilitation medicine.[2]

THE DEMISE IN INFLUENCE OF THE REHABILITATION SERVICES ADMINISTRATION AND THE VA

The Rehabilitation Act of 1973 as amended in 1978 expanded rehabilitation services, provided for civil rights protections for persons with disabilities, and created a National Institute of Handicapped Research (renamed the National Institute of Disability and Rehabilitation Research or NIDRR in the 1980s). The first Director of the NIDRR in 1979 was Dr. William Spencer of Baylor Medical School and The Institute of Rehabilitation and Research (TIRR). Spencer was the first physician in rehabilitation medicine to lead one of the federal rehabilitation agencies. Spencer took the position on an interim basis and commuted from Houston each week. He had the respect of the entire research community (being a leading researcher), and of the consumer organizations (having established one of the first independent living programs at TIRR). Spencer laid out an ambitious agenda for research and actively engaged the research community in its formation. Spencer's leadership and his relationship to the Secretary of HEW, Joseph Califano, boded well for the field of rehabilitation medicine.

But in 1980, the last year of the Carter Administration, the President proposed and Congress passed legislation to create a Department of Education. This was done to provide greater federal leadership for education, and to satisfy the nation's teachers and their unions. In the legislation, the Rehabilitation Services Administration and the NIDRR were transferred to the new Department of Education despite the protestations of Secretary Califano of HEW, the rehabilitation medicine organizations and most consumer organizations. Supporters of the move were Congressional leadership, the state rehabilitation agencies, the NRA (representing the many employees of the state agencies), and some consumer groups. The bill to create the new Department was considered by the House Education and Labor Committee, which also had jurisdiction over the Rehabilitation Act, but not health or social service programs. The Administration proposal survived a failed effort to amend the Department of Education bill to keep the RSA and NIDRR in the Department of Health and Human Services (HHS). This amendment was offered by George Miller of California (now Chairman of the Education and Labor Committee, but then only a young member of Congress with little seniority). Miller was opposed by Chairman Perkins of the Committee and John Brademas (Chairman of the Subcommittee considering the bill), as well as by the

White House. The Department of Education was subsequently created with the RSA, NIDRR and the Office of Special Education included in a division of Special Education and Rehabilitation Services overseen by an Assistant Secretary of Special Education and Rehabilitation Services.

The new Department resulted in the administrative separation of rehabilitation programs under the Rehabilitation Act from the other programs that greatly impacted persons with disabilities, including: Disability Insurance, SSI, Medicare, Medicaid, the programs of the Public Health Services Act for children with disabilities and persons with developmental disabilities, and the research programs of the NIH. The culture of the new Department was also not one generally conducive to health care services or research. There were no health service programs in the Department of Education except for those still supported under the Rehabilitation Act, and they would not be supported much longer. While most rehabilitation medicine research programs still resided in the NIDRR, they did not receive the attention from the department's leadership that such programs had enjoyed under Mary Switzer. More significantly, the high level leadership which the Democratic Administration of President Johnson and his HEW leadership (John Gardner and Wilbur Cohen) had assigned to Mary Switzer and rehabilitation only 12 years before had been significantly downgraded by President Carter in 1980.

The expansive funding envisioned by the Rehabilitation Act of 1973 and the 1978 Amendments for independent living services, community based comprehensive rehabilitation facilities, and research was not provided by the Democratic Congress and the Republican Executives during the ensuing 12 years. In the 25 years after 1980, the special education programs grew almost eight fold, while the rehabilitation programs only doubled. This rate of increase of only about 3% per year for rehabilitation programs was less than inflation in this period and, as a result, the budgets of rehabilitation programs were not increased in real dollars during that 25–year period. The independent living programs never reached their anticipated level of funding of $400 million for 1990, and are now supported at about $100 million annually. In today's dollars, the intended funding levels for the independent living program created in 1978 would be about $1.2 billion. The 1978 amendments authorized NIDRR research funding at about $100 million by the early 1980s. NIDRR funding never reached that level until the 21st century, twenty years beyond the target date. Projecting similar growth between 1985 and 2005, the NIDRR budget should have reached about $400 million.

The failure of Washington to provide the anticipated funding for the rehabilitation programs in the 1980s and 1990s can be attributed in part to the lack of high level leadership for these programs from the Department of Education. But an equally significant factor was the growth in funding for rehabilitation services from both Medicare and Medicaid in this period; support of the graduate medical education program of Medicare for residency training; and the Public health Service Act training programs for physical therapy, occupational therapy, speech pathology and audiology. The professional and facility interest groups focused far more on these programs during the 1980s than on the Rehabilitation Act programs, since Medicare and Medicaid was "where the money was." Medicaid also supported heath services and rehabilitation medicine programs, and unlike Medicare, provided support in many inventive states to health related services such as assisted living, recreational therapy and social services that enabled many persons with disabilities to live in the community rather than in institutions. These programs have surpassed the independent living programs of the Rehabilitation Act as the major supporters of services for assistance in community reintegration for persons with disabilities. The isolation of RSA in the Department of Education and the dramatic growth in entitlement funding for Medicare and Medicaid rehabilitation services and medical education left NIDRR as the sole Rehabilitation Act agency, which had a leadership role for rehabilitation medicine by the early 1980s.

The VA health care system that Dr. Magnuson had so carefully and boldly developed was no longer a leading health care system by the 1980s. Joel DeLisa, MD, one of the third generation of leaders in rehabilitation medicine, reported in 1984 that the VA Rehabilitation Medicine service, which had been a world leader for years after World War II, was declining and was no longer a comprehensive rehabilitation service. A report of an AAPMR VA Task Force on Rehabilitation in 1980 reported that the rehabilitation medicine service was fragmented and that the research program had produced minimal research.

Medicare and private health insurance were now the major supporters of rehabilitation medicine care. The Medicare and the Public Health Act professional education grant programs were the primary financiers of medical education in the rehabilitation field by the 1980s and beyond. VA hospitals continued to provide rehabilitation medicine services and residency training experience, but they were no longer shaping the rehabilitation field as they had in the preceding four decades. By the 1990s the VA health care system had reengineered itself to become more of a primary care provider for veterans of World War II, Korea and Viet Nam. Rehabilitation medicine became a lesser concern, although it is reengaging with the VA in 2007 to assist with care for the wounded veterans of the wars in Afghanistan and Iraq. Joel DeLisa served on the VA Secretary's Medical Advisory Group from 1992 until 2005, and in that role urged a strengthening of the rehabilitation service. More recently, he lamented the focus of the VA on primary care for veterans of World War II, Korea and Viet Nam; to the disadvantage of the rehabilitation service that was now badly needed to meet the needs of those injured in the wars in Iraq and Afghanistan.[3]

REHABILITATION MEDICINE, SPECIALIZATION AND HEALTH WORKFORCE POLICIES

The 1980s saw tremendous growth in medical technology and the specialization of physicians. The economic market place, whose competitive model the Administrations of the 1980s espoused, fostered both of these related developments. Technological developments in medicine resulted in new diagnostic tools, drug therapies, surgical and medical interventions and prostheses. These developments stimulated a demand for physicians who specialized in the use of such technologies.

Rehabilitation medicine benefited from the growth in medical technology during the 1970s and 1980s, just as many other fields of medicine did. Specialization did not affect the relationship of the rehabilitation physician to his or her patient in that period, although financial restraints in the 21st century would inhibit and erode that relationship.

Technology on a large scale first arrived in physical medicine and rehabilitation with the development of electrodiagnosis as a diagnostic tool. Electrodiagnosis involved electromyography, which used electronic equipment to measure the pathology of nerve and muscle through insertion of needle electrodes into muscles. Electrodiagnosis also involved nerve conduction studies, done by stimulation of nerves to determine nerve conduction velocity. The physician who popularized electrodiagnosis in this country was chiefly Dr. Edward Lambert of the Mayo Clinic, who was a neurophysiologist. Electrodiagnosis then went on to be further developed and popularized both in the fields of neurology and in rehabilitation. Ernest Johnson of The Ohio State University is viewed by many experts as the physiatric father of this development over the latter half of the twentieth century. In the 1980s a medical organization was founded to focus specifically on education and standards for this new technology and its application. It was first known as the American Association of Electromyography and Electrodiagnosis (AAEE), then as the American Association of Electrodiagnostic Medicine (AAEM), and currently as the American Association of Neuromuscular and Electrodiagnostic Medicine (AANEM). The membership was originally mainly rehabilitation physicians, but more recently has been both neurologists and physiatrists, in approximately equal numbers.

Another technology developed by the field of rehabilitation medicine was measurement of patient function involving tools to precisely measure progress of patients receiving rehabilitation medicine services. Carl Granger of Tufts New England Medical Center (who was President of the AAPMR in 1975), and Byron Hamilton of the Rehabilitation Institute of Chicago, were among the first to develop a functional measurement tool for use in the field. They began their work in the late 1970s, and by the end of the 20th century their functional measure (FIM™) was being used in rehabilitation facilities across the country and in many other parts of the world.

Dr. John Ditunno reflected recently that the era of the 1970s and 1980s was one in which specialization within physical medicine and rehabilitation occurred, in part driven by the new technology such as electromyography.[4]

In this period, the medical school and the teaching hospital became very clinical in focus, and those departments and residencies which produced the most revenue were the most likely to gain the favor of medical school and teaching hospital leadership. Hospital based specialties had much to gain from this development. Physical Medicine and Rehabilitation fared well, since it was a hospital based specialty at this point in its history and its services were in demand. It would become even more in demand as the 1980s progressed. Primary care specialties such as internal medicine and family medicine did not fare as well, however.[5]

By the late 1970s health policy leaders in the Administration and in Congress had become concerned about both a perceived oversupply of physicians and the growth of specialization and sub-specialization, with a focus on acute care medicine. Congress created the Graduate Medical Education National Advisory Committee (GMENAC) to analyze the issue of physician specialization and its impact on the supply of physicians and access to health care. The GMENAC was a prestigious panel, Chaired by Alvin Tarlov, MD of the University of Chicago Medical School. It was well funded to conduct original research and to do data analysis.

The medical school funding under the Public Health Service Act had rewarded medical schools for the number of students trained, and the unlimited cost reimbursement of Medicare for graduate medical education had incentivized the system to train physicians in large numbers. Congress and the public had both demanded that; but by 1980, Congress and the public were concerned about the cost of medical care and believed that an oversupply of physicians and greater specialization within medicine might have produced higher costs. Many felt that having an oversupply of physicians would not necessarily make the nation any healthier, but would certainly increase medical costs.

Congress and health policy experts were also concerned that the focus of medical training on increased specialization had diminished consumers' access to primary and preventive care. This issue had been raised by the HEW leadership in the Nixon Administration, led by Assistant Secretary Lewis Butler. GMENAC's mission was to analyze these issues and create a framework for Congress and the Executive Branch to decide if something should be done to reform residency training programs and their impact on the geographic and specialty distribution of physicians. The GMENAC effort would have implications for the delivery of health care generally, since the GMENAC methodology involved assessments of demand and need for medical services generally. The findings of GMENAC suggested needs for more than just primary care or internal medicine. Findings for the specialty of Physical Medicine and Rehabilitation involved forecasting of the health service needs in rehabilitation medicine generally; and therefore had implications for all professions and facilities in the rehabilitation field.

The GMENAC began its deliberations in 1978, but did not initially focus on the smaller specialties such as PM&R. In 1980, the AAPMR board reestablished the Commission on Rehabilitation Medicine to supply data to the GMENAC on PM&R needs. Drs. Kottke and Honet (Presidents of the Academy in 1979 and 1980 respectively), testified before the GMENAC in 1980 about the increasing demand for rehabilitation medicine services and the future impact of the aging of the population on rehabilitation medicine. Kottke and Honet testified that there was a growing demand for medical services to persons with disabilities, and a shortage of PM&R specialists to meet the demand. The GMENAC entered into a contract with the Battel Group, a research organization based in Seattle, to develop data on the need, demand and supply for specialties not analyzed in their first round of studies. Dr. Lehmann, Chair of the Department of Rehabilitation Medicine at the University of Washington in Seattle, assisted the Battel Group in regard to data for rehabilitation medicine.

GMENAC's final report, issued in 1980 and revised in 1982, forecasted an oversupply of 70,000 physicians by 1990 and 140,000 by 2000. The only specialties forecasted for a shortage by 1990 were PM&R, child psychiatry, psychiatry, anesthesiology and pathology. The final GMENAC Report forecasted a need for 4000 PM&R physicians in 1990, but there were only 1608 board-certified physiatrists in 1979. Their initial report had forecasted a 1990 need in PM&R for only 2,000 physicians, but this was not based on specific data regarding the specialty of PM&R. The initial projection came out before the Battel Institute assessed the remaining specialties with assistance from the Commission on Rehabilitation. The data supplied to Battel by Dr. Lehmann and the work of the Rehabilitation Commission under the leadership of Drs.

Kottke and Honet made a major difference in the outcome of the GMENAC's work.[6]

"No single factor has played a greater role in publicizing the field to medical students, nor had such a positive impact on recruitment as the publication of the GMENAC findings."[7] By 1989, 97% of residency positions in PM&R were filled, compared to less than 70% before 1970. The percentage of U.S. medical school graduates in PM&R residency training increased from 58% in 1983 to 91% in 1993. By 1994, there were 4774 board-certified PMR physicians. "By the late 1980s and early 1990s the resident quality was way up and we had great students."[8]

Beginning in 1980, Physical Medicine and Rehabilitation grew progressively at a rate that doubled the number of physicians practicing rehabilitation in each subsequent decade. The fields of physical therapy and occupational therapy were also growing, and the APTA had about 45,000 physical therapists and the AOTA about 30,000 in the mid 1980s. Not all of the growth in PM&R was attributable to the GMENAC report, as some was attributable to the increased demand created by the exemption of rehabilitation from the Medicare prospective payment system for hospitals under the amendments adopted in 1983 to Medicare Part A (see section below). The GMENAC assessment of need and demand in rehabilitation medicine was, however, a major factor in growth and a validation of the field as a significant and well accepted part of health care.[9]

IMPACT OF THE MEDICARE DRG PROSPECTIVE PAYMENT PROGRAM ON REHABILITATION MEDICINE

By1983 Medicare had been in effect for 17 years and its costs had escalated at rates unforeseen by its creators. It also contributed heavily to the growing budget deficits with which both the Executive Branch and Congress were very concerned. To limit escalating costs the Nixon and Carter Administrations, with Congressional endorsement, had established regulatory programs such as price controls, utilization review in hospitals, and state and local health planning to decrease the expansion of facilities and technology. But these measures had not really been successful. Inpatient hospital care was believed by many experts and politicians to be the major cause of rising health care costs under Medicare, and it became the focus of efforts to constrain costs.[10]

The Reagan Administration proposed a major reform of hospital payments for inpatient care in 1982 to bring hospital inpatient operating costs under control. This major reform was known as a prospective payment system

(PPS). The proposal was based on the market principle that a prospectively fixed price for services would more likely encourage the necessary efficiency. It was felt that PPS would rein in costs better than continuing the cost reimbursement system that was accompanied by regulatory programs such as utilization review, professional standards review, and retrospective denials of cost reimbursement (with the resultant litigation it spawned). Congress acted expeditiously during 1983. The hospital associations reacted strongly against the proposal, claiming it would result in reduced payments and an inability to provide quality care. Images of patients being put out on the street because appropriate care could not be supplied were displayed. The PPS proposed by the Reagan Administration had been the focus of a Yale University Study involving payment per case based on the estimated costs of cases characterized by their diagnosis upon admission. These cases were organized into 467 groupings referred to as diagnosis related groupings (DRGs). The price to be paid for care for each case was a fixed amount; with hospitals losing money if costs exceeded the amount of the price and making money when costs were less than the price. Winning at the new payment system meant reducing costs by reducing hospital stays or cutting hospital staff and equipment. This approach was a radical departure from the original cost reimbursement method of paying hospitals, which encouraged hospitals to increase their costs. It was not at all clear that this approach would fit rehabilitation medicine, however, since rehabilitation cases were managed on the basis of functional limitations rather than just on the diagnosis. There was also little experience and data in the Yale Study regarding Medicare costs and length of stay for inpatient rehabilitation.

The inpatient rehabilitation programs were very concerned for their future under such a prospective pricing program, since they were a small and somewhat insignificant economic part of the hospital care system. Little attention was being paid to the impact on the rehabilitation field of this radical departure in the method of paying for hospital inpatient care. Because rehabilitation was only a small part of the hospital inpatient world, the Yale study had very few rehabilitation cases in its database. One of the DRG categories developed by the Yale study was rehabilitation DRG 462. The estimated payment for this DRG was based on very few cases and assumed a length of stay for inpatient rehabilitation cases at about 15 to 17 days. While that might be adequate for some rehabilitation cases, such as mild stroke or arthritis, it was not sufficient to cover the care needed for a severe stroke, multiple trauma, brain injury or spinal injury with the complications that often accompany those conditions. In addition, by organizing payment according to patient diagnosis, the proposal would not take into account the most significant factor involved with care and its cost in rehabilitation medicine, that being the functional status of the patient. While based on a very few cases, and clearly arbitrary regarding the care needed for the vast array of inpatient rehabilitation cases, the DRG proposal with DRG 462 for rehabilitation was in the proposal the Department of Health and Human Services (HHS) transmitted to Congress.

The threat to rehabilitation medicine from the DRG PPS approach was major, requiring proactive response. It was very possible that the PPS DRG would be adopted for all hospital services; but that rehabilitation would either be overlooked entirely or be underpaid if DRG 462 were adopted. In either case, the field would suffer. As noted earlier in this chapter, the field of rehabilitation medicine had been working on a new approach to measuring quality that would affect payment for rehabilitation hospital inpatient care for the next few years. Carl Granger, President of the AAPMR, in his 1976 Presidential Address, stressed the need for the field of rehabilitation medicine to define the patient population served, the magnitude of the need for services and outcome measures to document progress, and ultimately cost effectiveness. He chided medicine for failing to deal with tough questions of resource allocation. "The time has passed for physicians to deny that allocating resources has anything to do with how they practice medicine." He urged rehabilitation medicine to find "...ethical means to affect allocation decisions." He suggested that rehabilitation medicine define disability and measures for functional restoration and rehabilitation.[11]

Granger and Byron Hamilton, MD (from the Rehabilitation Institute of Chicago) began in the mid 1970s a long and productive research project on the development of a measurement tool based on patient function and of a data system derived from hospitals using the tool. The AAPMR and the ACRM became joint applicants with the State University of New York in Buffalo, where Granger and Hamilton had worked, for a grant to undertake the creation of such a functional measurement tool. The National Institute of Handicapped Research, now the National Institute of Disability and Rehabilitation Research (NIDRR), funded the grant. The work on this grant was well underway by 1982 when the DRG debate took place. In 1982, the NIDRR funded Granger and Hamilton to develop a specific data collection system, the Uniform Data Set (UDS), containing hospital data on patient function and cost. Function was measured using the functional independence measure (FIM) developed by Granger and Hamilton and supported by the federal grant to the AAPMR, ACRM and the State University of New York in Buffalo. In the 1990s the work from these two grants and related projects on functional measurement provided the foundation for the seminal work of Stineman, with the collaboration of Granger, which established the framework for a prospective payment system for inpatient rehabilitation care. In all of these research endeavors the National Association of Rehabilitation Facilities (NARF) was a principal actor and displayed foresight in developing needed ideas and proposals before they were imposed on the field by government.

The various associations of rehabilitation health professionals and rehabilitation facilities were ready to engage in debate over the DRG proposal and inpatient rehabilitation with the Administration and Congress in 1983. The National Association of Rehabilitation Facilities was led by its Executive Director James Cox and lawyers Pat Fleming and Carolyn Zollar. The AAPMR and ACRM had worked closely with NARF on matters of admissions policy and payment approaches, and all three relied on the research being undertaken on functional measures and cost. The facilities had the available data and did an analysis of it. Physicians and other health professionals assisted NARF in designing the policies it would advocate, and also supplied the clinical expertise. Two physicians were leaders on these issues of payment in both the ACRM and NARF, John Melvin (then Chair of the Department of PM&R at the University Of Wisconsin in Milwaukee), and Bud Mackey of Casa Colina Rehabilitation Hospital in California. Melvin was also an active member and later President of the AAPMR.[12]

The work on measurements and patient classification based on function enabled national associations in rehabilitation to collaborate effectively in a lobbying campaign to protect rehabilitation medicine from the impact of the new PPS DRG payment system. The AAPMR, ACRM, NARF and APTA joined forces to convince the Congress that inpatient rehabilitation programs and hospitals should not be part of this PPS DRG system. The case made for such exemption was that there was no data to establish such a system for rehabilitation programs in 1983, and that any payment system organized by patient characteristics should be based on functional characteristics (not diagnosis as the Yale study had been). The advocates also explained that the average length of stay for a rehabilitation patient was in the 20 to 30 day range, unlike the shorter stays for acute patients and the 15 to 17 day stay assumed in DRG 462. They also maintained that the field had functional measures in development and proposed the exemption of inpatient rehabilitation from the DRG system while a study of rehabilitation inpatient admissions similar to the Yale study on acute care payment was conducted.[13]

The Senate leadership at this point included Senator Robert Dole (Republican of Kansas), who had suffered a major disabling injury during World War II. It also included Senator Lloyd Bentsen of Texas, who was very familiar with Dr. Bill Spencer and the rehabilitation programs at TIRR in Houston. In the House, the chair of the committee with jurisdiction of the Medicare program was Congressman Rostenkowski of Chicago, who was very aware of the Rehabilitation Institute of Chicago and its CEO, Dr. Henry Betts. Another senior member of the committee was Congressman Bill Archer of Houston, who also knew about TIRR and Dr. Spencer. Congressman Archer appeared at the retirement of Dr. Spencer in 1986 and made one of the addresses in his honor. The field was blessed with active and well informed associations and leaders such as Spencer and Betts who had carried on the advocacy traditions of Rusk, Krusen and Switzer. Their efforts were rewarded in 1983 when PL 98-21 establishing the Prospective Payment System for acute hospital payment was adopted, but contained an exclusion from the application of the PPS DRG for rehabilitation hospitals and rehabilitation units within acute hospitals. Rehabilitation hospitals and units were defined and a separate cost reimbursement based program was continued for the payment of rehabilitation inpatient services. This triumph marked the beginning of what many leaders in rehabilitation have referred to as the "golden age" or "halcyon days" of rehabilitation medicine. Many felt the sun really rose on the field of rehabilitation with the advent of the new Medicare prospective payment system for inpatient care.[14]

The new prospective payment system also had a dramatic impact on the behavior of acute care hospitals, which benefited rehabilitation very directly. As internist Kenneth Ludmerer said in his history of medical education, *Time To Heal*: "Hospitals made money under the DRG system not by maintaining a high occupancy per se but by attracting a large volume of patients who were admitted and discharged quickly. The new goal of hospitals became a rapid 'throughput' of patients."[15] The beneficiary of the "rapid throughput" of acute inpatients was post acute care. This was particularly true for inpatient rehabilitation as it supplied ready physician availability. The new system was a great incentive for acute hospitals to establish rehabilitation units, since the rehabilitation unit would be available to treat those patients the hospital would likely be discharging from acute care earlier than they had before the new payment system for acute care began. The PPS DRG fixed price per case served as an incentive for acute hospitals to reduce the length of stay for patients and correspondingly the cost per case. If the patient could be transferred to a rehabilitation unit in the hospital, additional payments for rehabilitation would flow to the hospital; which would also retain control of the patient for quality and safety purposes rather than sending the patient home or to another facility. New units or hospitals would also be funded by Medicare with the old cost reimbursement system, which stimulated the growth of new facilities and programs. Combining acute inpatient care with post-acute inpatient rehab care was a classic win/win arrangement for hospitals, and the effects of this new system of payment for hospital care were dramatic. From 1986 when the PPS DRG was fully implemented until 1994, the number of Medicare certified rehabilitation hospitals and units increased from 554 to 1019, an 87%

increase in eight years. Between 1980 and 1990, the number of rehabilitation beds similarly almost doubled from 18,000 to 33,000. That Medicare payment changes were probably responsible for this growth in hospital rehabilitation services and beds is suggested by the fact that between 1985 and 1989 the annual percentage of all patients discharged from rehabilitation hospitals and units whose care was paid for by Medicare increased from 39% to 65%.[16] Hospital administrators quickly learned how to maximize the revenue streams from Medicare, including separate payments for an ER visit, then an inpatient admission, then admission to a rehabilitation unit or center, and then outpatient therapies. The economics of the Medicare program served to stimulate the growth of the inpatient rehabilitation programs well into the 1990s.

The critical point here is that rehabilitation medicine rallied to prevent its possible elimination, and in the course of so doing created a defined program with patient care focused on patient function rather than diagnosis. The defined program also set standards for the staffing and direction of rehabilitation programs to assure quality. Under PL 98-21 and its implementing regulations, hospitals had to staff their defined rehabilitation units with medical directors trained or experienced in rehabilitation medicine, full time rehabilitation nursing, and comprehensive, interdisciplinary services. These clear definitions served to protect the field's growth for the next 20 years. The leadership of Bentsen of Texas, Dole of Kansas, Rostenkowski of Chicago and Archer of Houston, as well as the well informed advocacy by Betts and Spencer and the professional and hospital associations resulted in the dramatic expansion and resulting rise to maturity of rehabilitation medicine.

Perhaps an even more important positive long term effect of PL 98-21 on rehabilitation medicine than the dramatic expansion of inpatient rehabilitation programs, was the integration of those programs with the acute care medical system. As the data on patient discharges from inpatient rehabilitation in the immediate post PPS DRG era indicate, rehabilitation hospitals and units were the beneficiaries of the changed behavior of acute hospitals and the "rapid throughput" of patients. Rehabilitation hospitals and units were locations to which the discharged acute patient could be transferred, knowing that the acute medical condition would be looked after by rehabilitation physicians and rehabilitation nurses, while rehabilitation would simultaneously enhance the patient's ability to function. The impact of this early discharge from acute care and immediate readmission to an inpatient rehabilitation unit or hospital was that patients were seen 'quicker and sicker" in the rehabilitation program. The rehabilitation medicine process also began much earlier in the episode of care, resulting in prevention of complications and in better rehabilitation outcomes. Rehabilitation physicians interacted closely with the attending acute care physicians; and the other professionals on the rehabilitation team were integrated with the other professional hospital staff. Thus, the new approach to payment of acute hospitals and rehabilitation programs encouraged more timely and effective care for patients and greater integration of the professionals in rehabilitation medicine with other professionals and programs in medicine. The overall result essentially was that a revolution in rehabilitation medicine had occurred.

The Rusk vision of a freestanding rehabilitation hospital offering a broad range of services to disabled patients, including social and vocational ones, was fading. "Freestanding rehabilitation facilities became a thing of the past," in the 1980s.[17] The Rusk vision often had the effect of isolating the rehabilitation facility from the rest of medicine and from the health care delivery system. This isolation had been increased to some extent by the separate home for rehabilitation medicine in the Office of Vocational Rehabilitation under Mary Switzer. Transfer of the OVR to the new Department of Education furthered the chasm between rehabilitation medicine and the rest of health care. The 1980s spelled the end of isolation and the beginning of the integration of rehabilitation medicine, whether practiced in units or freestanding hospitals, with acute medical care.[18]

To some extent, the stage had been set for this integration of rehabilitation medicine with acute medicine beginning in the mid-1970s when certain models of care were developed, largely by academic rehabilitation medicine, that focused on early intervention in the acute episode of care. The program at Jefferson Medical College, long known for its clinical focus under the Chairmanship of John Ditunno, was distinguished for its clinical integration of rehabilitation medicine with the other relevant parts of the Jefferson medical system. Ditunno, a late second and third generation leader in rehabilitation medicine, was mentored by Dr. Krusen while working with him at Temple. Ditunno, who was trained in both internal medicine and physical medicine and rehabilitation, developed spinal cord injury as a specialty field. It was a model of integration, with rehabilitation medicine intervening early in the process of surgical and acute care. Physiatrists worked closely with neurosurgeons and orthopedic surgeons in the acute care phase and this cooperation continued in the rehabilitation phase of care. The Rehabilitation Services Administration's Model Spinal Cord Injury Systems program (which Ditunno and his colleagues helped design with Dr. Paul Thomas of RSA) accentuated early intervention and continuity of care. Model System programs in traumatic brain injury and burn injury followed, expressing the same principles of integrated care.[19]

Dick Melia served in the regional and central office of the Rehabilitation Services Administration and the National Institute on Disability and Rehabilitation Research between 1970 and 2005, and brought an insightful perspective to the changes in rehabilitation medicine wrought by PL 98-21 and Medicare. Melia was actively involved with rehabilitation medicine and with the independent living and disability rights movements. He recalled the passion with which rehabilitation physicians were involved in independent living in the early years. This included the instance when Paul Corcoran, M.D., one of the physicians most respected and trusted by persons with disabilities, took the initiative in establishing the Independent Living Center at Boston University by applying a sledge hammer to the walls of an inaccessible toilet. But Melia also acknowledged the "sea change" moving rehabilitation medicine closer to the traditional medical model, which occurred in the 1980s after the advent of the PPS DRG. Melia accurately saw those years and the impact of Medicare on the delivery of rehabilitation medicine services and the training of physicians ". . . as overwhelming the Switzer Rusk partnership."[20] He viewed this development of rehabilitation medicine, however, as a very positive thing for the nation. He believes that medical care has improved and that rehabilitation medicine from the 1980s onward has benefited patients and the professions by emphasizing early intervention, integration with acute medical care, and continuity of care. Most leaders in rehabilitation medicine, professional and lay, would now agree with that assessment (although rehabilitation medicine had become more separated from the comprehensive rehabilitation programs envisioned in the 1960s and 1970s).[21]

Rehabilitation medicine at the end of the 1980's had become an integral part of health care, and Medicare had been the primary driver in that development. By 1996, Medicare was spending $4.6 billion for inpatient rehabilitation services in rehabilitation hospitals and units and there were 1097 such facilities. Most remarkable was that Medicare patients represented 70% of discharges from these rehabilitation hospitals and units. By way of comparison, psychiatric hospitals and units had a 42% Medicare patient case load and cancer hospitals 25%. Post acute care programs including rehabilitation facilities, skilled nursing facilities and home health agencies represented 24% of Medicare Part A payments in 1994, compared to about 8% in 1988. The PPS DRG payment had achieved its objective. It had resulted in earlier discharges and shorter lengths of stay in acute hospitals, which cost Medicare less per case. The need for care, however, was simply provided in other settings that were capable of dealing with patients with continuing medical and rehabilitation needs.[22]

Rehabilitation medicine faced a dilemma, however, since patients were sicker when they were in rehabilitation and required more medical attention. The focus of the rehabilitation physician now was on stabilizing acute medical conditions, as well as on planning and closely supervising the intensive rehabilitation program. The rehabilitation program carried out by the therapeutic team was more complicated to manage and implement due to the continuing presence of an acute condition. In addition, by the late 1980s and early 1990s the pressure of a cap on inpatient rehabilitation payments resulted in lowered lengths of stay for patients in rehabilitation units and centers. Rehabilitation medicine professionals and rehabilitation administrators had less time and resources available in the late 1980s and thereafter for the non-medical aspects of comprehensive rehabilitation; such as vocational training, job placement, and social services to enable independent living arrangements for persons with disabilities.

THE NIH AND RESEARCH NEEDS IN THE FIELD OF REHABILITATION MEDICINE

In the late 1980s as rehabilitation medicine became more integrated with acute medicine and more accepted by it, those interested in research in rehabilitation medicine sought similar acceptance and support for their medical research. The field of Physical Medicine and Rehabilitation was far better accepted in the clinical community, however, than in academic circles. In 1980, Dr. William Fowler startled his academic colleagues when he asserted that this problem was largely due to the lack of research productivity in the field. He argued then and thereafter that the viability of a specialty would turn in a major way on its ability to do or support research to enhance the value of rehab services. Fowler referred to Krusen's recollections, while a resident, of the lecture he received on the need for pursuit of academic scholarship and research from one of his mentors. In his program at the Mayo clinic Krusen pursued research interests and later served as Mary Switzer's Assistant with a focus on developing research programs. John Ditunno, MD, who followed Fowler as President of the Academy, continued the emphasis on research productivity in his Presidential Address.[23]

Ditunno, who was President of the AAPMR in 1981, appointed Fowler as chair of a joint committee of the Association of Academic Physiatrists (AAP) and AAPMR, whose focus was the research mission and strategy for the field. The Committee produced a number of papers on research strategy, including one on research fellowships, which became the source of a new research program at the NIDRR. The Committee also focused on the lack of support by NIH for any research in the field of rehabilitation medicine. Fowler began an effort to influence the NIH and met with the Deputy Director of NIH William Raub, Ph.D. to discuss the NIH peer review system and its lack of any PM&R or other rehabilitation medicine focus. Fowler and his Committee developed a list of qualified reviewers and supplied it to the NIH, but little seemed to change. As a result, the Academy, AAP, and American Congress of Rehabilitation Medicine (ACRM) jointly began a frontal assault on the NIH system by addressing Congress with their requests for support from NIH. Justus Lehmann, John Ditunno and Marcus Fuhrer led this collaborative effort of the three organizations.

In 1985, the NIH reauthorization legislation included rehabilitation research in the mission statement of the NIH. The NIH reported that in 1985 it would spend approximately $46 million on research in rehabilitation medicine. Almost 90% of this money was in the Aging Institute ($13 million), the arthritis and musculoskeletal programs ($9 million), and the National Institute on Neurological Diseases and Stroke ($20 million). In 1988, the NIDRR in the Department of Education had a $40 million rehabilitation research budget, of which about $17 million was medical in content. The remainder of the NIDRR grants were for employment, community integration, independent living research and engineering research unrelated to medical rehabilitation. Drs. Lehmann and deLateur noted in their history of research in the field of rehabilitation medicine that while the NIH spent more research money on rehabilitation medicine than NIDRR, there was no focal point in NIH for program development and leadership. They also noted the lack of any peer review study sections of relevance to rehabilitation medicine. The NIDRR had coincidentally shifted its research priorities to nonmedical research in the 1980s. The 1978 amendments establishing the NIDRR had created a broad mission and mandate but neither Congress nor the Executive Branch sought to sufficiently fund it. As a result, increased interest in new areas such as independent living and technology were initiated at the expense of growth in programs in rehabilitation medicine.[24]

The rehabilitation medicine field concluded that it needed to establish by statute an agency in the NIH responsible for rehabilitation medicine research, in order to improve the focus of science on rehabilitation medicine. NIH was not sufficiently responsive in this regard, so as they had done in all other areas of need since 1970, the associations looked to Congressional leaders for assistance. Senators Wiecker of Connecticut and Kennedy of Massachusetts initially led this effort. They introduced legislation to create an independent Center for Medical Rehabilitation Research in the NIH. Senator Wiecker was Chair of the Senate Subcommittee on Disability, and the Subcommittee on Appropriations for the Departments of Labor, Education and HHS. Senator Kennedy was ranking member on the Senate Committee with jurisdiction of the NIH legislation. Both were the champions in the Senate for the NIH and for rehabilitation; a happy coincidence. In August of 1988, this legislation passed the Senate as Title V of the NIH reauthorization bill, but other issues with the NIH bill prevented its enactment in the 1987–1988 session of Congress. In the House of Representatives, Congressman Douglas Walgren of Pittsburgh had become the leader of the effort to establish a rehabilitation research agency in the NIH. Walgren had a legislative assistant who was a paraplegic individual, and who had interested him in the project. Pennsylvania had a number of fine academic programs in rehabilitation at Jefferson Medical School, Temple, the University of Pennsylvania, and others. Movement of a bill in the House was slow, however.

In 1989 the Deputy Director and then Acting Director of the NIH, Dr. William Raub, established a Blue Ribbon Panel to advise the Director of NIH (himself at the time), on the status and needs of Physical Medicine and Rehabilitation research in NIH. A prestigious 18 person Panel was formed and chaired by Edward Brandt, MD, Executive Dean of the University of Oklahoma Medical School and former Assistant Secretary for Health in the Department of HHS. Six active members of the AAPMR and ACRM sat on the Panel: Henry Betts (former President of ACRM), John Ditunno (former President of the AAPMR), Dorothy Gordon, D.N.Sc. (Board member of the ACRM), Carmella Gonnella, Ph.D. (a leader in the APTA research community and President of the ACRM), Lauro Halstead, MD (a clinician at TIRR for many years and Director of the Post Polio program at the newly established National Rehabilitation Hospital in D.C.), and Douglas Fenderson, Ph.D., (colleague of Dr. Kottke at the University of Minnesota Medical School and former Director of the NIDRR). Other Panel members included Robert Waters, MD (orthopedist who was Medical Director of the Rancho Los Amigos Rehabilitation Center in Los Angeles), Edmund Chao, Ph.D. (Professor of Bioengineering at the Mayo Clinic), and Marilyn Spivack, (President and Founder of the National Head Injury Foundation). The Panel was provided with reports by the various Institutes of NIH on the status of rehabilitation medicine research in their agency. The reports indicated that about $119 million had been spent by the NIH in 1989 on rehabilitation related research. The Panel held hearings at which many professional and scientific societies testified on the needs for the field in rehabilitation related research. The Panel's final report recommended unanimously that the NIH take the initiative to establish a planning and coordination effort involving all aspects of medical rehabilitation research in the NIH. It voted 12 to 6 to establish a Center for Medical Rehabilitation research in NIH to plan, coordinate and fund research and research training with the Center to be either in an Institute or independent. Dr. Raub took this report under advisement.[25]

In 1990, the Congress returned to the NIH authorization bill but failed to move it from Committees due to controversial issues unrelated to rehabilitation research. The AAPMR, AAP and ACRM stepped up their efforts. Mary

Lasker became involved in advocating for the NCMRR at the urging of Dr. Betts, who organized a national effort of interested persons in rehabilitation research. Betts was omnipresent in this legislative effort and was successful in attracting former Hollywood movie star Jennifer Jones to contact members of Congress whom she knew well, including Chairman Waxman of the House Health Subcommittee. In July of 1990, President Bush signed into law the Americans with Disabilities Act assuring the civil rights of persons with disabilities. It was the most significant legislation affecting persons with disabilities ever enacted and it passed Congress with strong bipartisan support. The ADA was an impetus for action on the NIH rehabilitation research legislation.[26]

At the close of the 1990 Congressional Session, Senator Kennedy, (then Chair of the Senate committee with jurisdiction of the NIH bill), Chairman Waxman and Congressman Walgren in the House brought the National Center for Medical Rehabilitation Research provision up before the House and Senate as part of a minor NIH bill including only three amendments to the NIH statute. That bill provided for the establishment of the NCMRR with a defined mission and authorization to make grants to support research and training centers, research training grants and clinical trials. It created a National Advisory Board on Medical Rehabilitation Research and required the Center and Board to create a national research plan to be submitted to the Congress and NIH. The NCMRR was located within the National Institute of Child Health and Human Development (NICHD) at the urging of the NIH leadership.[27]

The leaders of the medical rehabilitation research field had met with leaders of the NIH, including Dr. Raub, and concluded that being located in an Institute was preferable to independence in the beginning, since the NCMRR had no budget and no staff. The organizations concluded that it was not wise to attempt to move the medical research funds and staff managing them from NIDRR to NIH. The location of the new Center in the NICHD was viewed as an interim step toward ultimate independent status. The NICHD was a sensible initial home as it supported clinical research and policy related studies. It was focused on neither the musculoskeletal nor neurological systems, both of which rehabilitation medicine dealt with, but all bodily systems which affected human development of a disabled person of any age. At a conceptual level rehabilitation was a developmental process, which fit well with the concept of human development included in the NICHD title. The person with a disability was intended to progress in functional capacity during the course of the rehabilitation services and ultimately return to community living and independence.[28]

After more than 40 years, the vision of Drs. Rusk and Kessler of a research agency and program at the NIH was accomplished. For the academic rehabilitation medicine community, having an NIH program from which to receive research grants was the "stuff of which" academic status in medical schools was achieved. The Center was the most likely source of funding for basic and clinical medical science in rehabilitation medicine. In the late 1940s and early 1950s Rusk and Kessler had approached NIH for support of medical rehabilitation research, but had no success. In 1978, Mary Lasker had advised Rusk and members of Congress interested in an institute for rehabilitation research to establish one in the NIH, but Congressional leaders were more interested in establishing an Institute of Research under the Rehabilitation Act. Two years later the RSA and the new research Institute were transferred to the new Department of Education, separating them from the health programs that remained in the Department of Health and Human Services. A program of research in the NIH had become an imperative for rehabilitation medicine by the 1980s. Leaders Betts, Lehmann, Fowler, Ditunno and Fuhrer were aware of that and pressed the case hard with the NIH and Congress. By 1990, Fowler and Ditunno (who had emphasized the need for academic rigor back in 1980) could feel that they had accomplished a great deal in achieving greater opportunities for rehabilitation medicine research and enhancing the research productivity of the rehabilitation medicine academic community.

Rehabilitation medicine flourished even more in the 1980s than it had in the prior decades. The loss of the influence and protection of the Founders and the federal agencies that had served to foster the field until 1970 did not impair its growth. The market based competitive approach to medical care of the 1980s greatly stimulated demand for rehabilitation medicine services in the hospital setting. Medicare was the driving force in the growth of the 1980s and thereafter, as it dominated the market for inpatient rehabilitation medicine services. The required coverage of rehabilitation in Part A and the professionally developed comprehensive guidelines defining rehabilitation services for purposes of Medicare coverage in the 1970s greatly facilitated this growth. The field of rehabilitation medicine had also matured sufficiently by 1980 to grow with the expanding economy. By the 1990s, rehabilitation medicine was a major, well accepted part of the health care system and the rehabilitation medicine disciplines became accepted by and were leaders among the health professions. Physical Medicine and Rehabilitation was a popular and growing medical specialty; and physical therapy, occupational therapy and speech therapy had become very large and respected health professions as well. Research in the field was finally recognized by the NIH leadership as worthy of significant attention and investment.

Some would say, however, that the field might have made a Faustian bargain with Medicare and had sold its soul in return for expanded patient revenue and growth. By the late 1990s and the 21st century the growth of rehabilitation medicine in the Medicare program had provoked political leaders to target it for cost controls and regulation just as other fields of care had been targeted earlier. Inpatient care was a particular focus of controls. As a result, outpatient care in rehabilitation medicine became a growth field. The professions in rehabilitation medicine responded to these changes well and PM&R and physical therapy developed substantial and viable outpatient private practice programs. However, comprehensiveness of care for persons with disabilities was no longer a governing principle of rehabilitation medicine, as it sought to survive well under the new constraints of Medicare. The question is whether the loss of comprehensiveness within the rehabilitation medicine system was outweighed by the tremendous growth in access to rehabilitation medicine inpatient and outpatient care for persons with disabilities that has taken place consistently since 1980.

NOTES

1. Fowler, *A History of Physical Medicine and Rehabilitation in California*, 55.
2. Starr, 444–48.
3. DeLisa, Arch Phys Med Rehabil, vol. 65, 388; DeLisa correspondence with author, April 2007; Fowler, Presidential Address, Arch Phys Med Rehabil, vol. 63, 1.
4. Ditunno, Interview October 28, 2005; Granger, Interview October 27, 2005; Johnson, Interview October 27, 2005.
5. Ludmerer, 327, 335.
6. Ditunno, Arch Phys Med Rehabil, vol. 69, 36.
7. Ditunno ibid.
8. Reinstein, Interview October 7, 2004; Ditunno ibid.
9. Fowler, 55, 67, 69; Colachis, Arch Phys Med Rehabil, vol. 65, 291; Granger, Interview, October 27, 2005.
10. Starr, 384–87.
11. Granger, Arch Phys Med Rehabil, vol. 58, 1–3.
12. Interview with Carolyn Zollar, December 22, 2006.
13. Interviews with Melvin, October 27, 2005 and Reinstein, October 7, 2004.
14. Braddom, Zeiter Lecture, Arch Phys Med Rehabil, vol. 86, 1287–88; Reinstein, Zeiter Lecture, Arch Phys Med Rehabil, vol. 77, 219; Interviews with Melvin and Reinstein, ibid.
15. Ludmerer, 352.
16. Chan et al., *New England Journal of Medicine,* vol. 337, 978; Reinstein, ibid.
17. Fowler, *A History of Physical Medicine and Rehabilitation in California*, 55.
18. Reinstein interview, October 7, 2004; Melvin interview, October 27, 2005.

19. Reinstein interview, ibid.

20. Interview with Melia, April 21, 2004.

21. Ibid.

22. Prospective Payment Assessment Commission, Report and Recommendations to the Congress, March 1, 1997, Chapter 2, Post acute Care Providers, 49; Medicare Payment Advisory Commission, Report to the Congress, March, 1999, 73, 81–96.

23. Fowler, Arch of Phys Med Rehabil, vol. 63, 1–5; Ditunno, Arch Phys Med Rehabil, vol. 69, 38–39.

24. Lehmann and deLateur, Arch Phys Med and Rehabil, vol. 69, 59; Verville, Arch Phys Med Rehabil, October 1988, vol. 69, 67.

25. A Report of the Panel on Physical Medicine and Rehabilitation Research NIH, published by the NIH, December 21, 1989.

26. Betts interviews July 29, 2004, October 7 and 9, 2004.

27. P.L. 101-613.

28. Betts interviews July 29, 2004, October 7 and 9,2004; P.L. 101-163.

Chapter Fourteen

The Americans with Disabilities Act (ADA) and Comprehensive Rehabilitation Medicine

Howard Rusk's vision of rehabilitation medicine from 1945 until his retirement in about 1980 extended from the hospital to the community and focused on employment and independent living for persons with disabilities. In his Zeiter Lecture in 1978, Rusk explained: "Our responsibility is not over when the fever is down and the stitches are out. We have a responsibility to restore severely disabled people to the best lives they can live . . . to the hilt of their ability."[1] In 1972, Arthur Abramson, President of the AAPMR, wrote an editorial in the Archives of Physical Medicine and Rehabilitation with Bernard Kutner, Ph.D., calling for a Bill of Rights for Persons with Disabilities. The proposed bill of rights called for rights to comprehensive health care, equal educational and employment opportunities, removal of all architectural barriers, and civil rights laws "to include disability as one of the categories against which discrimination is unlawful."[2] By the 1980s, rehabilitation medicine professionals recognized that the goal of their services included advocacy for and with their patients for legal rights to assure equality of opportunity for jobs and independent living in the community.

The physician leadership of rehabilitation medicine which succeeded Kessler, Krusen and Rusk in the 1970s and 1980s emphasized even more the need to join persons with disabilities in advocating for their rights and opportunities. Perhaps no two people did more to lead this joint effort between 1970 and 1990 than Henry Betts and Bill Spencer, each of whom had been President of the American Congress of Rehabilitation Medicine. In his Presidential Address in 1969, Spencer had asserted that rehabilitation medicine should be viewed as a comprehensive process of treatment and assistance that "...extends to and includes solution of life adjustment problems."[3] Betts in his Presidential Address urged rehabilitation professionals to become involved in the community, beyond the confines of the hospital; and postulated that among the goals of rehabilitation medicine were the removal of architectural barriers, employment, and community living arrangements for persons with disabilities.

In 1979, Frederick (Fritz) Kottke characterized the goal of rehabilitation medicine as involving the fullest possible participation by persons with disabilities in their communities. His close friend and colleague Justus Lehmann, like Kottke a successor to Krusen in academic leadership for rehabilitation medicine, explained in his Zeiter Lecture that: "Unique for the specialty is that adaptations of the environment may have to be included in the management program to allow the patient to functionally progress."[4]

Ernie Johnson, another of the second generation of leaders in rehabilitation medicine, was actively involved in making the campus of the Ohio State accessible to disabled students and in establishing the Miss Wheelchair America competition. Johnson received the prestigious Betts Award for contributions to persons with disabilities in large part for his remarkable contributions to access and other rights for persons with disabilities.[5]

The political leaders for rehabilitation in general, rehabilitation medicine, and disability were also strong advocates for civil rights for persons with disabilities. Among such leaders were Senator Hubert Humphrey, Senator Ted Kennedy, Senator Paul Douglas, Senator Lowell Weicker, Senator Jacob Javits, Senator Tom Harkin, Congressman John Brademas, Congressman Paul Simon (later Senator from Illinois), Congressman Henry Waxman, and Congressman James Jeffords (later Senator from Vermont). Kennedy, Harkin, Weicker and Waxman would lead the efforts for civil rights for persons with disabilities in the late 1980s and 1990.

The national disability movement had begun in the 1960s with the National Conference on Rehabilitation and Disability sponsored by Mary Switzer and chaired by Howard Rusk. It was clear from the meeting that civil rights for persons with disabilities were a crucial element in the agenda of the disability movement. In 1973, the disability movement and rehabilitation professionals achieved the first civil rights protections for persons with disabilities: Title V of the Rehabilitation Act of 1973. Title V requirements, however, were limited to institutions that received federal financial assistance. Private employers and facilities offering services to the public such as restaurants, hotels and theatres, were not subject to the provisions of Title V. The White House Conference on Disability in 1977–1978 called for expanded civil rights for persons with disabilities.

During the 1970s and the early 1980s the disability movement had begun to use many of the successful tactics of the civil rights movement of the 1960s led by Dr. King to achieve civil rights in employment and public accommodations.

In September of 1984, a group of very frustrated individuals in wheelchairs rolled in front of a bus in Chicago to protest the failure of the Chicago Transit Authority to equip its 363 new buses with lifts for persons in wheelchairs or using walkers. Appropriately, the demonstrators wore name tags proclaiming: "My name is Rosa Parks." This was done in honor of the civil rights leader who had refused to give up her seat in a racially segregated bus in Montgomery, Alabama in 1955. They could have added: "And we cannot even get on the bus." Similar protests occurred in other cities throughout the 1980s. Justin Dart, an official in the Reagan and Bush Administrations and leader of the disability civil rights effort, was very aware of the apt analogy to the racial civil rights movement since he had been a racial civil rights advocate in the 1960s.[6]

The disability movement also used the same litigation tactics the civil rights movement had used in the 1950s and 1960s under the leadership of the NAACP Legal Defense Fund, Thurgood Marshall, and Jack Greenberg. In 1975 the Federal District Court of the Eastern Circuit ruled, after a proceeding of almost two years, that the Willowbrook Institution in New York violated the rights of retarded residents by providing them with no services, allowing unsafe and unsanitary conditions to exist, and treating residents as if they were criminals residing in prison. Shortly thereafter, in *Wyatt v. Stickney*, (503 Fed 2nd 1305), the Fifth Circuit Court of Appeals held that residents of the Partlow State Hospital and School had a constitutional right ". . . to receive such individualized treatment as to give them a realistic opportunity to improve his or her mental condition." A similar decision was reached in *Halderman v. Pennhurst*, 44 F. Supp. 1295 (1978), which applied both the Constitution and the Rehabilitation Act Title V to the facts in a similar case of residents in state hospitals.

Transportation accessibility became a focus for litigation as well. In *Lloyd v. Regional Transportation Authority of Northeast Illinois*, 548 F.2d 1277 (1977), the U.S. Circuit Court for the Seventh Circuit held that Title V of the Rehabilitation Act provided a right to a person with a disability to sue for access to mass transit. In *ADAPT v. Skinner*, 881 F.2d 1184 (1989), the Third Circuit Court of Appeals decided a case dealing with the accessibility of mass transit, and held that the Rehabilitation Act and Transportation Department Regulations required minimum standards of accessibility for persons with disability. Independent living accommodations in the community were upheld against a city zoning code, which forbade such facilities in residential neighborhoods in a Supreme Court decision in 1985 in *City of Cleburne v. Cleburne Living Center*, 105 U.S. 3249.[7]

Despite victories in these individual cases, the recognition that limitations in current law remained impediments to achievement of equal rights for persons with disabilities stimulated the development of comprehensive disability rights legislation by the late 1980s. The National Council on Disability would undertake the task of defining the need for rights and fashioning a comprehensive legislative approach to improve civil rights law for persons with disabilities that would both solve legal problems and raise public awareness of the injustices in the economic and social systems.

In the 1978 Rehabilitation Amendments, Congress created the National Council on the Handicapped, renamed as the National Council on Disability (NCD), which was to report periodically to the President and Congress on the state of persons with disabilities and the programs that were to serve them. In 1982, the NCD under the leadership of Vice Chairman and member Justin Dart, Executive Director Lex Frieden and staff attorney Bob Bergdorf, began to focus on the lack of legal protections for persons with disabilities, notwithstanding Title V of the Rehabilitation Act of 1973 and some positive case law in the 1980s. Chair of the NCD, Joseph Dusenbury, a Director of the South Carolina state vocational rehabilitation agency, appointed Dart to document the legal issues faced by persons with disabilities in their quest for independence. Sandra Parrino, who succeeded Dusenbury as NCD Chair, continued the delegation of authority to Dart. Dart's father was a member of President Reagan's so-called Kitchen Cabinet, a term first used to describe an informal group of influential advisers to President Andrew Jackson. Both Justin Dart Jr. and Lex Frieden were Texans with relationships to those around Vice President George Bush and many in the Texas Congressional delegation.[8]

With the backdrop of protests and litigation involving rights for persons with disabilities, the NCD moved forward. In 1983, the NCD issued a report authored by Dart, which called on the Congress to include persons with disabilities in the Civil Rights Act of 1964 and the Voting Rights Act of 1965. Such inclusion would have assured access to public accommodations and equal treatment in employment as well as improved access to voting facilities. Three years later, NCD issued its final and landmark report on legal rights of persons with disabilities entitled "Toward Independence," recommending passage of a comprehensive law requiring equal opportunity for persons with disabilities. It included detailed specifications for such legislation as an appendix. The NCD began consultation with interest groups and lawyers in Washington, the author included. The bill was ready for introduction by 1988.[9]

The Senate was led by Republicans for part of the decade of the 1980s. It also had a large number of members who were leaders on issues for persons with disabilities in both parties. The Senate had established a Subcommittee on Disability of the Senate Committee on Labor and Human Resources, which was a perfect place for comprehensive legislation on disability rights to be considered. That Subcommittee would play a leadership role in all programs for persons with disabilities for the next 20 years. The Subcommittee was chaired by Senator Lowell Weicker (Republican of Connecticut) and later, by Tom Harkin (Democrat of Iowa). Weicker and Harkin were both dedicated advocates for persons with disabilities. Like many public officials who assisted in the effort to expand programs and rights for persons with disabilities, they both had family members with disabilities. Weicker was the parent of a child with mental retardation and Harkin's brother was deaf. Both knew well the discrimination and disadvantages which persons with disabilities faced. Senator Kennedy was also a leader on the bill and had long been a leader for disability issues. Senator Orin Hatch of Utah, the ranking Republican on the Senate Committee with jurisdiction of disability programs, had a brother with a severe disability. Senator Robert Dole, the Senate leader of the Republicans throughout the 1980s and who had been severely injured in World War II, was a stalwart on all disability issues. Senator John McCain was also a sponsor and had faced his own challenges as a prisoner of war during the Viet Nam War and later as a cancer victim.

In 1988, Weicker became the chief Senate sponsor of the comprehensive civil rights legislation entitled the "Americans with Disabilities Act." Similar legislation was introduced in the House by Congressman Tony Coelho, a Democrat of California who had progressed rapidly up the leadership ranks within the Democratic Party. Coelho had epilepsy and, like Weicker, had personal experience with discrimination faced by persons with disabilities. The legislation was introduced on April 29, 1988. Unfortunately, Weicker was defeated for re-election in 1988, although he later became Governor of Connecticut. Coelho resigned his seat that year. Despite those two serious losses in Congressional leadership for disability rights, the ADA effort continued.[10]

1988 was a Presidential election year. The disability community pressed both candidates to take positions on the Americans with Disabilities Act legislation. Both Republican candidate George Herbert Walker Bush and Democratic candidate Michael Dukakis, Governor of Massachusetts, supported the legislation in principle. Bush directed himself to the issue more frequently, not the least reason for which was the role that Dart and Frieden played in developing the legislation and in assisting his campaign. A Harris poll indicated that this attention by Bush may have been responsible for the fact that disabled people were shifting their support to him. In May of 1988, Major Owens, Chair of the House Subcommittee on Select Education, which had jurisdiction of the Rehabilitation Act, created a Task Force on the Rights and Empowerment of Americans with Disabilities. Its charge was to gather information and educate the Congress, the Executive Branch, state and local governments and the private sector on the extent of and nature of discrimination against people with disabilities. Owens was an African American Democratic

Congressman from New York City and a very credible leader for a new civil rights bill. Justin Dart Jr. was asked to Chair the Task Force and he appointed a group of distinguished individuals to make up the Task Force, including Dr. William Spencer, with whom Frieden worked at the TIRR in Houston. The theme of the Task Force was "Equal Access to the American Dream." The Task Force held 63 public forums in all 50 states, D.C. and the U.S. territories. The Task Force not only accumulated facts on discrimination, but served to mobilize the public and disabled people in support of the ADA.[11]

In leading the mobilization of support for the ADA, the NCD and Task Force stressed the "cross disability" nature of the effort. The legislation as introduced would affect rights and opportunities to "access the American dream" for persons with disabling conditions of all types; including sensory, mobility, mental, and physiological conditions such as heart conditions, diabetes, cancer and AIDS. The addition of the AIDS constituency was controversial because it raised the issue of an infectious condition, which might pose added problems to enactment. But it was morally important and also added a well organized and persuasive element to the political alliance forming to advocate for the legislation. In Washington, the legislation brought together a Coalition of many organizations representing persons with disabilities, such as the Disability Rights and Education Defense Fund (modeled after the NAACP Legal Defense Fund), the National Council on Independent Living, the Association of Retarded Citizens, the Epilepsy Foundation, the AIDS community and the National Easter Seal Society. The Consortium for Citizens with Disabilities (CCD) served as the umbrella group for all of the disparate organizations and coordinated grass roots lobbying. It was chaired by Paul Marchand, who was Director of the Association of Retarded Citizens Washington Office. Marchand was respected by all disability organizations for his passionate dedication to the cause of disability and his total honesty.

The American Congress of Rehabilitation Medicine, the American Academy of Physical Medicine and Rehabilitation, the American Physical Therapy Association, the American Occupational Therapy Association, and the American Speech and Hearing Association were actively involved in the legislative effort as part of the CCD. The most active of all the physician organizations was the Resident Physicians Council of the American Academy of PMR. Throughout 1989 and 1990, the American Academy of PMR and ACRM had members contact members of Congress to support the ADA, which was on the top of both organizations' priority lists for legislative action. Support from physicians for rights of individuals who might be their patients, as well as friends and colleagues, had a significant impact on members of Congress who might not otherwise have been likely to support a civil rights bill. Physicians were often viewed by members of Congress as leaders in local communities and had special expertise regarding the capacity of a person with a disability to work or recreate. A critical addition to the coalition effort was the Leadership Conference on Civil Rights; which coordinated the work of all major civil rights groups including the NAACP, women's groups, and groups representing the Latino community. The Conference Executive Director was Ralph Nease who had worked in Congress for Senator Ed Brooke of Massachusetts, a Republican Senator and the first African American Senator since reconstruction. Nease had impairments from Guillain-Barre Syndrome.

THE LEGISLATIVE PROCESS WORKS ITS WILL: 1989–1990

The effort to pass the ADA began in earnest in 1989. The bill was redrafted and reintroduced. Initiative was taken in the Senate, although bills more often were initiated in the House. The Senate was the right choice to initiate the ADA because it had only one committee through which the ADA had to pass, the Labor and Human Resources Committee. The House had five committees through which the bill would have to pass. All Committees would have to hold hearings, deliberate, and vote on the bill. The strategy was to obtain a fairly quick, bipartisan victory in the Senate to make the laborious process in the House move more quickly. The House was also believed to be more conservative on civil rights issues than the Senate and having the bill passed in a bipartisan way by the Senate was thought to be likely to assist in moving the House toward passage of the legislation. The Senate Committee considered the bill in the late spring and summer of 1989. Senator Hatch (Republican of Utah) involved the Administration in the negotiations. Jim Swenson, MD chaired the Department of Physical Medicine and Rehabilitation at the University of Utah Medical School. His family members were long time residents of Utah and Dr. Swenson knew Senator Hatch well and urged him to support the ADA. Hatch appeared at the Committee's final meeting in the Mansfield Room of the Capitol to announce that Administration support was forthcoming. In the fall, the bill reached the Senate floor and passed easily with the leadership of Senators Kennedy, Harkin, Dole and Hatch. Harkin and Hatch were elated and spoke with emotion about what the bill meant to them personally, having family members with disabilities.

It was no surprise that the Bush Administration supported the bill considered by the Senate. The NCD, led by Dart, had recommended enactment to the Bush Administration. The Administration also included a number of persons very familiar with disability issues who had also been deeply involved in the movement of the ADA legislation throughout 1989. Legal Counsel to both Vice President and President Bush, C. Boyden Gray, was both a fine lawyer and was also well versed in issues of disability. He advised the President on the ADA and was a valued ear at the White House. Gray's close friend, Evan Kemp, was a significant voice of the disability community within the Administration. He had been appointed as Chairman of the Equal Employment Opportunities Commission (EEOC), which had led an Administration effort to prosecute employment discrimination against persons with disabilities under Title V of the Rehabilitation Act of 1973. His impairment was the result of muscular dystrophy. Kemp was an aggressive enforcer of laws prohibiting workplace discrimination during his tenure as EEOC Chair. Attorney General Richard Thornburgh and his wife Ginny were parents of a severely brain injured son, Peter, and Ginny had been an organizer of programs for people with disabilities at Harvard in 1988 and 1989. The Attorney General was a stalwart supporter of the ADA. Madelaine Will, the Assistant Secretary for Special Education and Rehabilitation in the Department of Education, was the parent of child with Downs Syndrome and was a passionate advocate for persons with disabilities. David Gray, Ph.D., who had suffered an accident while a young man age 33 resulting in quadriplegia, was appointed Director of the National Institute on Disability and Rehabilitation Research under Reagan. Gray later became Deputy Director of the National Center for Medical Rehabilitation Research in the NIH under President Bush. He had been treated at the Mayo Clinic in the Physical Medicine and Rehabilitation Department and to this day attends its events celebrating the contributions of the Clinic and department to health care and patients. These people and the NCD were formidable advocates within the Administration for the ADA. They would also take steps to assure it was supported by Republicans in the House.[12]

Leadership in the House was assumed by Coelho's friend and colleague in the House Democratic leadership, Steny Hoyer, Democrat of Maryland and current House Majority Leader of the House Democrats. Hamilton Fish, Republican of New York and a leader on the Judiciary Committee, was also among the first cosponsors of the bill. The bill had to wend its way through five House Committees, including the Rules Committee, and Hoyer was on none of them. He was in the House leadership, however, and his presence advocating for the bill was evidence that the Democratic leadership of the House was behind it. Hoyer attended all Committee sessions in which the bill was considered. His knowledge of the provisions of the bill and his acute sense of strategy were instrumental in the successful negotiation of the bill through its many House Committees and Subcommittees. The House Education and Labor Committee had House jurisdiction over the employment discrimination sections of the bill, and Hoyer and Major Owens moved the bill through that Committee with relative ease.

The Judiciary Committee, chaired by Jack Brooks of Texas, was the next stop for the ADA in the House. It had authority over the public accommodations provisions and the bill as a whole. Fish and Brooks worked together to assure favorable Committee action. The restaurant association had raised questions about the dangers of infections from food handlers who might have AIDS, but the bill survived without serious amendments. The Public Works and Transportation Committee had jurisdiction over the very critical but controversial provisions for mass transportation accessibility. It was costly to buy new buses with lifts and this provoked some opposition from bus operators, but again the bill prevailed. Congressman Norman Mineta, Secretary of the Department of Transportation under George W Bush, was Chair of the Transportation Committee and an active ADA supporter.

The Energy and Commerce Committee had jurisdiction over the provisions dealing with the communications industry and issues affecting health services. Chairman John Dingell of Michigan was one of the first members to sign on to the legislation and Henry Waxman of California, Chair of the Health Subcommittee, was known for his knowledgeable and strong leadership in all areas of civil rights. Ed Markey of Massachusetts, a communications expert in the House and colleague of Senator Kennedy, was likewise an impassioned advocate for the bill.

The Administration, led by Attorney General Thornburgh and Boyden Gray, were active in providing assistance for the bill during House consideration. They frequently met with disability leaders to share information and negotiate possible changes that might be necessary. The Administration's endorsement of the bill assured that Republican opposition would be minimal and Democrats, led by Hoyer, were solidly behind the bill.

Deliberately and steadfastly, Hoyer brought the bill to the floor of the House of Representatives. The bill, which was amended somewhat from the Senate bill, passed the House on May 22, 1990. By July 12, 1990, the conference between the Senate and House to resolve differences between the two bills had finished its work and a final bill was ready for passage. That day the House passed the final bill 377 to 28 and the Senate passed the bill 91 to 6, a positive vote of about 94% in each body. A celebration would shortly ensue. For the first time since the leadership of Mary Switzer and her Congressional supporters (Fogarty, Laird, Hill and Humphrey), there was successful collaboration between the Executive Branch, Congress, and the disability and rehabilitation movements on significant legislation.[13]

On a beautiful sunny day, July 26, 1990, in the Rose Garden of the White House, the President and First Lady hosted leaders of Congress and some 3,000 invited guests to celebrate the signing of the Americans with Disabilities Act. With the President and Vice President Quayle on the dais to witness the signing were Justin Dart, Evan Kemp, Sandra Parrino (Chair of the NCD), and the Reverend Harold Wilkie. Reverend Wilkie gave the invocation. His Coulter Lecture to the ACRM on the community and disability had moved all who heard it to action. Wilkie, who was born without arms and unable to use artificial ones, passed the signing pen to the President with his left foot. The President said movingly as he signed the bill into law. "Let the shameful wall of exclusion come tumbling down."[14]

Leaders of the rehabilitation medicine professional and facility organizations were also in attendance, including Presidents Erwin Gonzalez, MD of the AAPMR and Dorothy Gordon, R.N., Ph.D. of the ACRM. In a joint editorial printed in the Archives of Physical Medicine and Rehabilitation in November 1990, they captured the spirit and significance of what they had witnessed:

> *It was most gratifying to witness that day when America moved to include disabled persons in that doctrine of "all are created equal." Henceforth Americans cannot be excluded from society on the basis of how tall one stands, or the timbre of ones voice, or ones clarity of hearing, acuity of vision or brilliance of mind.*[15]

They also noted that the AAPMR and ACRM had made the enactment of the ADA a high priority for the field of rehabilitation medicine and the advocacy efforts of members in both organizations gave testimony to this fact. Arthur Abramson would have been pleased to see that the Bill of Rights for Persons with Disabilities that he and Dr. Kutner had described in their editorial in 1972 had finally become law.[16]

IMPACT OF ADA ON REHABILITATION MEDICINE

Henry Betts recently said: "There is no better therapy for a person with a disability than a job."[17] That view also applies to other activities such as recreation, cultural programs, and travel. It reflects perfectly the relevance of the ADA to rehabilitation medicine.

The ADA was important to rehabilitation medicine on many levels. Its declaration of rights and equality for persons with disabilities affected public attitudes about disability, and also reflected the deep humanism which was the underpinning for rehabilitation medicine from its inception. The field developed out of the concern of health care professionals like Kessler, Krusen and Rusk for the totality of life of those to whom they provided service. Kessler, the surgeon, had poignantly suggested this in the title of his autobiography: *The Knife is Not Enough*. Krusen, as a patient with tuberculosis himself, saw the need for tuberculosis patients to not only be cured of their disease; but also to work again and receive vocational training. Rusk defined rehabilitation medicine as including those vocational, social and psychological services which are necessary to enable a person with a disability, no matter how severe, to become an active member of his or her community. Spencer and Betts expressed the need for change in laws and policies to enable persons with disabilities to advocate for themselves and to become fully integrated in society. Leaders in rehabilitation medicine had attempted to realize this vision, in one form or another, from the 1920s to the enactment of the ADA. The ADA, with its strong provisions on employment discrimination and discrimination in all public accommodations including transportation, would assure at least an equal opportunity for employment and for community participation for persons with disabilities.

The ADA also provided new, practical opportunities for rehabilitation for the clients of rehabilitation professionals. It created opportunities for employment, socialization and community reintegration. It therefore added new tools with which the professionals could work. The extent of the opportunities would depend on the responsiveness of the employers, transit agencies and companies, restaurants, hotels and recreational organizations to the spirit and letter of the new law. Rusk, Kessler, Krusen, Betts and others have noted that the most traditional and often important aspect of rehabilitation for a person with a disability is a job and the ability to live independently! In 1999, the Supreme Court of the United States emphasized the importance of the ADA to community reintegration for persons with disabilities. It also cited the relevance of professional opinion on the efficacy of programs that encouraged community living for disabled persons. In its opinion in the Olmstead case, the Court upheld the choice of two patients, when supported by the recommendations of treating health professionals, for community reintegration as opposed to continued institutionalization.[18]

A question fundamental to the success of the ADA is whether society can deliver on the promises of the ADA. The ADA is difficult to fully implement because it involves not only the elimination of traditional non-discriminatory behavior, but also the integration of persons with disabilities in their communities. The latter involves accommodations and outreach by employers with regard to employment opportunities; and by governments and private agencies with regard to health, transportation, housing and social programs. These accommodations also often involve expenditures by government, employers, transit agencies and all facilities of public accommodation. Such expenditures are not likely in times of a stalled economy or one in recession and the nation frequently faces those periods. In reality, it would take not only non-discriminatory behavior, but a major commitment by public and private sectors alike to affirmative action and accommodation for persons with disabilities. If society does not deliver on the promises of the ADA, the opportunities for persons with disabilities generated by the ADA and the visions of rehabilitation medicine leaders for a comprehensive approach to disability would languish. The promises of the ADA were not ones rehabilitation medicine could implement itself. These obligations were for all of society and governments (federal, state and local).

The 1980s came to an end and the 1990s began with rehabilitation medicine being an integral part of American healthcare. Medicare supported inpatient and outpatient rehabilitation medicine, and Medicaid supported those services as well as community-based services to facilitate independent living. Social Security and SSI provided for disability insurance and cash assistance with work incentives. The Rehabilitation Services Administration continued to lead in the provision of vocational training and job placement services. A remarkable law had been enacted to assure that persons with disabilities had rights to an equal opportunity for all that America offered to its other citizens. The vision of rehabilitation promoted by Kessler, Krusen, Rusk, Baruch, Switzer and succeeding generations of leaders, which began with vocational rehabilitation and VA health and rehabilitation services, had evolved to a comprehensive rehabilitation approach with the enactment of the ADA and expansion of Medicare and Medicaid. New leadership encouraged by the founders existed to protect and expand these programs. That leadership included a number of vibrant professional societies, disability organizations, and associations of hospitals and other facilities. Some second generation leaders from the 1970s and 1980s, Henry Betts, John Ditunno, Ernest W. Johnson, John Melvin and Leon Reinstein, remained active into the 1990's and into the 21st century. Whenever the Executive Branch lagged in leading efforts to improve rehabilitation services for disabled persons, the Congress was there to assert leadership, which it did with regularity from 1970 through the 1990s.

Future decades will determine whether the federal, state and local governments will continue to meet the needs of Americans with disabilities for comprehensive services; and whether the private sector will respond to the spirit and requirements of the ADA regarding employment, transportation and other services. If the ADA is effectively implemented and programs such as Medicaid, which supports independent living services, are funded adequately, comprehensive rehabilitation might be achieved despite the growing constraints of Medicare in the 21st century.

Would the founders and their colleagues be pleased with what they would see if they were active today? Quite likely they would all be pleased that rehabilitation medicine has become a well accepted part of health care and that rehabilitation training and research are supported reasonably well. They would be even happier that rehabilitation medicine services are available to more persons with disabilities than ever before, due to the expansion of Medicare coverage to these individuals. But it is also likely that they would be pressing for improvements and progress; particularly in research, and in comprehensive rehabilitation services including vocational training, job placement, and independent living services for persons with disabilities. They would also be urging America to do a better job of providing high quality rehabilitation medicine and other medical care to our nation's veterans of the wars in Afghanistan and Iraq, especially since rehabilitation first arose in response to the needs of our military injured on the battlefield. They would be heartened by the technology now available to many disabled veterans and others, but troubled by the lack of access of many to such technology and to long term community based care. They would probably be urging Bernard Baruch to establish a Commission to review rehabilitation medicine and related care for veterans of the two wars our nation is now fighting and to chart a course for the future of rehabilitation medicine under Medicare and Medicaid.

NOTES

1. Rusk, Arch Phys Med Rehabil, vol. 59, 156.
2. Abramson and Kutner, Arch Phys Med Rehabil, vol. 53, 99.
3. Spencer, Arch Phys Med Rehabil, vol. 51, 189.
4. Lehmann, Arch Phys Med Rehabil, vol. 63, 291.
5. Betts, Arch Phys Med Rehabil, vol. 58, 191; Kottke, Arch Phys Med Rehabil, vol. 60, 1; John Ditunno and Dennis Matthews interviews October 29, 2005.
6. Charles Wilson, "The Other Movement Rosa Parks Inspired," *The Washington Post*, Outlook Section, October 30, 2005, 1, 5.
7. Pelka, 66–67, 111–13, 145–46, 193–94, 326–29, 335.
8. Pelka, 18–22.
9. Pelka, 214–15.
10. Pelka, 18–19; *From ADA to Empowerment*, Report of the Task Force on the Rights and Empowerment of Americans with Disabilities, The Paralyzed Veterans of America and Jill Tarbel, October 12, 1990.
11. *From ADA to Empowerment*, 5, 12.
12. Pelka, 142–43, 181–82, 304–05.
13. Pelka, 18–22; *From ADA to Empowerment,* 5–14.
14. *From ADA to Empowerment*, 13.
15. Gordon and Gonzalez, Arch Phys Med Rehabil, vol. 71, 951.
16. Pelka, 323–24.
17. Betts, Personal Conversation December 7, 2005.
18. *Olmstead v. Zimring*, 119 U.S. 176 (1999).

Chapter 15

A Brief Epilogue

It seemed that rehabilitation medicine might have come full circle by the year 2007. War was again an important factor in American politics and in the delivery of health care. News reports covered in depth the travails of injured soldiers returning from battle from either Afghanistan or Iraq. Many suffered from Traumatic Brain Injury (TBI), amputation or severe burns. More of them had survived because they had better armored protection than in prior wars and medical care for traumatic injury had improved materially. The needs of the 21st century wounded soldiers were for rehabilitation services and assistance in community reintegration. Individuals with severe disabilities such as TBI, paralysis or amputation would be in need of service for 50 years or more. It had been more than 30 years since the military health care system and the Veterans Administration had faced an influx of victims of traumatic battle injuries. In the meantime, the VA had shifted its emphasis to caring for the older veterans of World War II, Korea and Viet Nam, who had mainly primary care and chronic disease needs. It had relatively deemphasized rehabilitation medicine services and hospital rehabilitation beds.

The VA began responding to the new demands of war shortly after the war in Iraq began. In 2005, it created four polytrauma rehabilitation centers to serve the needs of TBI victims in particular, but also of other victims of trauma. The centers that provided comprehensive rehabilitation services on an inpatient and outpatient basis were led by specialists in rehabilitation medicine, including David Cifu, the 2007 President of the AAPMR. Dr. Cifu serves as the Chair of Physical Medicine and Rehabilitation at the Medical College of Virginia where Simon Baruch had trained and to which the Baruch Committee gave one of its first and largest grants, in part to honor one of the first practitioners of rehabilitation medicine. In 2006, the VA established 21 polytrauma networks to afford another component of care at lesser intensity than the polytrauma centers. In addition, there were 75 rehabilitation medicine clinical teams established at VA Medical Centers to provide diagnosis and outpatient care for polytrauma victims. Dr. Barbara Sigford of the Minneapolis VA was the chief of the national PM&R VA service, one which Dr. Krusen had assisted in establishing while he was in Minnesota. Often however, the various VA resources would not be close enough to the communities where the disabled veterans lived with their families. This prompted the AAPMR to initiate collaboration with the VA to make available local rehabilitation medicine specialists to provide the necessary rehabilitation services.

Both the AAPMR and the rehabilitation hospital associations began advocacy efforts to raise the level of resources available for rehabilitation medicine services within the VA and for private sector collaboration with the VA. The Academy established a Task Force on DOD and VA Rehabilitation at its 2005 annual meeting, chaired by Dr. Stuart Glassman of Concord, New Hampshire. He had seen disabled veterans in his practice with undiagnosed TBI and had approached the local VA Medical Center to offer assistance. Meetings with the VA and Congressional leaders took place with a focus on these twin goals.

The rehabilitation medicine field also had leadership positions in the VA at this point, which heightened the visibility of the field and assured that expansion of VA rehabilitation medicine resources would get adequate attention in the agency. It had been two decades since the rehabilitation medicine field had led a strong federal agency.

The AAPMR focused its advocacy on increasing the financial resources for the VA rehabilitation service and its research program. In the 2007 supplemental appropriation bill for the war efforts in Iraq and Afghanistan, resources for both the military health care services and the VA were substantially increased for rehabilitation of victims of TBI, amputations and burns. Bills were introduced and supported by AAPMR regarding the extension of rehabilitation outpatient services to assist in community reintegration and for related research. These bills also emphasized the use of private sector resources for outpatient care whenever the VA care system was unable to meet the demands placed on it by returning wounded soldiers.

It was very apparent that the spirit of Bernard Baruch, Howard Rusk, Frank Krusen, Henry Kessler and Mary Switzer had not died. The field was responding to another societal need created by war, and hopefully would be able to aid the VA and DOD in dealing with its difficult challenges.

A FITTING TRIBUTE TO THE FOUNDERS

On Henry Kessler's 70th birthday in 1966, the Henry Kessler Human Dignity Award was presented by Dr. Kessler and the Board of the Kessler Institute to Dr. Frank Krusen, Dr. Howard Rusk and Miss Mary Switzer. On the stage together were these four great leaders. Dr. Kessler spoke at the presentation of his three colleagues. These words of Kessler express better than I ever could what these four people, and Bernard Baruch, who had died the year before, stood for and accomplished:

> The rehabilitation idea has taught me that there is a miraculous biological safety factor in every human being. Resources that lie dormant can be called upon to remold a personality physically and mentally. I have learned also that there is a safety factor for civilization. It is that powerful fraternity of men and women who believe that the object of all help is to make help superfluous.
>
> So finally this is a story of cooperation-between nations, between the Federal government and the states, between public and private agencies, between the medical and non-medical health professionals, and between the professions and the community.
>
> On my seventieth birthday . . . the board of trustees of the Kessler Institute presented the Dignity of Man Award to Dr. Frank Krusen, Dr. Howard Rusk and Miss Mary Switzer. These three master builders epitomized the great progress that had been made in rehabilitation over the past decades. Dr. Krusen has made rehabilitation a key word in medicine. Dr. Howard Rusk, physician, journalist, educator and crusader, has dramatized the cause. When Mary Switzer came on stage in 1950, the joint program of the Federal government and the states listed 60,000 cases as rehabilitated. By 1967, due to her role as director of the OVR in Washington, this number had reached 175,000.[1]

NOTE

1. Kessler, 11–12.

Bibliography

BOOKS

Albrecht, Gary. *The Disability Business, Rehabilitation in America*. California: Sage Publications Inc., 1992.

Baruch, Bernard. *My Own Story*. New York: Buccaneer Books Inc., 1957.

Berkowitz, Edward. *Rehabilitation: The Federal Governments Response To Disability, 1935–1954*. New York: Arno Press Inc., 1980.

Bird, Kai, and Martin Sherwin. *American Prometheus J. Robert Oppenheimer*. New York: Vintage Books, 2005.

Bloom, John Morton. *The Progressive Presidents, Roosevelt, Wilson, Franklin D. Roosevelt, Johnson*. New York: W.W. Norton & Company, 1980.

Brandt, Edward N. Jr., M.D., and Andrew N. Pope. *Enabling America, Assessing the Role of Rehabilitation Science and Engineering*. Washington, DC: National Academy Press, 1997.

Driedger, Diane. *The Last Civil Rights Movement, Disabled People's International*. New York: St Martin's Press, 1989.

Fowler, William M. Jr., M.D. *A History of Physical Medicine and Rehabilitation in California*. Published by California Society of Physical Medicine and Rehabilitation, 1998.

Fowler, William M. Jr., M.D., Lieberman, James M.D., Johnson, Ralph M.D. and Kilmer, David M.D. *Coming of Age, The History of the Department of Physical Medicine and Rehabilitation, School of Medicine University of California Davis, 1968–2000*. Published by the Department of PMand R, Davis, California, 2002.

Gabriel, Ralph Henry. *The Course of American Democratic Thought*. New York: The Ronald Press Company, 1956.

Gallagher, Hugh Gregory. *FDR's Splendid Deception*. New York: Dodd Meade and Company, 1985.

Gelman, Irwin. *The Contender, Richard Nixon and the Congress Years*. New York: The Free Press, Simon & Schuster, 1999.

259

Goodwin, Doris Kearns. *No Ordinary Time, Franklin and Eleanor Roosevelt: The Home Front in World War Two.* New York: Simon & Schuster, 1994.

Grant, James. *Bernard Baruch, The Adventures Of A Wall Street Legend.* New York: John Wiley & Sons Inc., 1997.

Gritzer, Glenn, and Arnold Arluke. *The Making Of Medical Rehabilitation, A Political Economy Of Medical Specialization.* California: The University of California Press, 1985.

Johnson, Ernest, M.D. *Ernie's Editorials 1962–1987, College of Medicine Journal.* Published by The Ohio State University College of Medicine, Columbus, 1987.

Kessler, Henry M.D. *The Knife Is Not Enough.* New York: W.W. Norton & Company Inc., 1968.

Ludmerer, Kenneth M., M.D. *Time to Heal, American Medical Education from the Turn of the Century to the Era of Managed Care.* New York: Oxford University Press, 1999.

Magnuson, Paul M.D. *Ring The Night Bell.* Mass Market Paperback, 1962.

Martin, Gordon M.D. and Joachim Opitz, M.D. Editors. *The First Fifty Years, The American Board Of Physical Medicine and Rehabilitation (ABPMR).* Published by ABPMR, Rochester, Minnesota, 1997.

Meacham, Jon. Franklin and Winston. *An Intimate Portrait Of An Epic Friendship.* New York: Random House Inc. and Random Trade Paperback Inc., 2004.

Menand, Louis. *The Metaphysical Club, A History of Ideas in America.* New York: Farrar, Straus and Giroux, 2001.

Mullan, Fitzhugh, M.D. *Plagues and Politics, The Story of the United States Public Health Service.* New York: Basics Books, Inc., 1989.

Murphy, Wendy. *Healing The Generations: A History Of Physical Therapy And The American Physical Therapy Association.* Connecticut: Greenwich Publishing Group, 1995.

Opitz, Joachim L. M.D., and Robert W. DePompolo, M.D. *History Of The Mayo Clinic Department Of Physical Medicine And Rehabilitation, 1911–2002.* Published by Mayo Foundation for Medical Education and Research, Rochester, Minnesota, 2005.

Oshinsky, David M. *Polio, An American Story.* England: Oxford University Press, 2005.

Pelka, Fred. *The Disability Rights Movement.* Santa Barbara: ABC-CLIO Press Inc., California, 1997.

Pope, Andrew N., and Alvin R. Tarlov, Editors. *Disability In America.* Washington, DC: National Academy Press, 1991.

Remini, Robert V. *The House, The History of the House of Representatives.* New York: Smithsonian Books and Harper Collins Publishers Inc., 2006.

Robison, Mabel Otis. *Frank Krusen, M.D., Pioneer in Physical Medicine.* Minneapolis: T.S. Denison and Company Inc., 1963.

Rowland, Louis P., M.D. *NINDS At 50.* New York: Demos Medical Publishing, 2003.

Rusk, Howard A., M.D. *A World To Care For, The Autobiography Of Howard A. Rusk M.D.,* New York: Readers Digest Press Book, Random House, 1972.

Smillie, John G., M.D. *Can Physicians Manage the Quality and Costs of Health Care? The Story of The Permanente Medical Group.* California: The McGraw Hill Companies and The Permenente Federation, LLC, 2000.

Smith, Jean Edward. *FDR.* New York: Random House, 2007.

Starr, Paul. *The Social Transformation of American Medicine.* New York: Basic Books Inc., 1982.

U.S. Department of Health Education and Welfare. *50 Years Of Vocational Rehabilitation In The U.S.A. 1920–1970.* Published by The Department of Health Education and Welfare, 1970.

Walker, Martha Lentz. *Beyond Bureaucracy, Mary Elizabeth Switzer and Rehabilitation.* Lanham, MD: University Press of America Inc., 1985.

ARTICLES AND BOOK CHAPTERS

Abramson, Arthur M.D., and Bernard Kutner, Ph.D. "A Bill of Rights for the Disabled Person," Archives of Physical Medicine and Rehabilitation (Arch Phys Med Rehabil), Vol. 53, 94.

Abramson, Arthur M.D. "Consumerism and Rehabilitation Medicine," Presidential Address American Academy of Physical Medicine and Rehabilitation (AAPMR), Arch Phys Med Rehabil, Vol. 54, 1.

Baruch, Bernard, "Summary of First Annual Report of the Baruch Committee," Arch Phys Med Rehabil, Vol. 27, 97.

Betts, Henry M.D., "Community Involvement," Presidential Address American Congress of Rehabilitation Medicine, Arch Phys Med Rehabil, Vol. 58, 104.

Braddom, Randall M.D., M.S., "Medicare Funding for Inpatient Rehabilitation, How Did We Get to this Point and What Do We Do Now?," Arch Phys Med Rehabil, Vol. 86, 1287.

Chan, Leighton M.D., M.P.H., Thomas Kopsell, M.D., Peter Esselman, M.D., M.P.H., Jodie Haskelhorn, M.D., M.P.H., Joseph Lowery, Ph.D. and Walter Stolov, M.D., "The Effects of Medicare Payment System for Rehabilitation Hospitals on Length of Stay, Charges and Total Payments," *New England Journal of Medicine*, Vol. 337, 978 .

Chan, Leighton M.D., M.P.H., Richard Verville, J.D., and Mary Richardson, Ph.D., M.P.H., "Legislative Issues in the Field of Physical Medicine and Rehabilitation," PM and R Secrets, Hanley and Belfus Inc., 2002, Chapter 13, 90.

Colachis, Samuel M.D., "Presidential Address American Congress of Rehabilitation Medicine," Arch Phys Med Rehabil, Vol. 65, 241.

Coulter, John M.D., "Future of Physical Therapy," Presidential Address American College of Physical Therapy, Arch Phys Med Rehabil, Vol. 27, 86.

DeLisa, Joel M.D., M.S., Donald Currie, M.D., and Gordon Martin, M.D., "Rehabilitation Medicine Past Present and Future," Rehabilitation Medicine Principles and Practice, Third Edition, edited by Joel DeLisa, M.D. and Bruce Gans, M.D. Lippincott and Raven Publishers, Philadelphia, 1998, Chapter 1.

Bibliography

DeLisa, Joel M.D., M.S., "Rehabilitation Medicine in the Veterans Administration," Arch Phys Med Rehabil, Vol. 65, 388.

Ditunno, John F. Jr., M.D., "Maturation of a Specialty, The Early 1980's," Arch Phys Med Rehabil, Special Edition October 1988, 35.

Ditunno, John F. Jr., M.D., and Gerald Herbison, M.D., "Franklin D. Roosevelt, Diagnosis, Clinical Course and Rehabilitation from Poliomyelitis," *American Journal of Physical Medicine and Rehabilitation*, Vol. 81, No. 8, 557.

Ditunno, John M.D., Presidential Address AAPMR, Arch Phys Med Rehabil, Vol. 64, 191.

Fowler, William, M.D., Presidential Address AAPMR, Arch Phys Med Rehabil, Vol. 63, 1.

Frieden, Lex M.S., "Listening for Footsteps," Coulter Lecture, Arch Phys Med Rehabil, Vol. 83, 150.

Gonzalez, Erwin M.D., and Dorothy Gordon, R.N. Ph.D., "The Americans with Disabilities Act, The Crumbling of Another Wall," Arch Phys Med Rehabil, Vol. 71, 951.

Gonzalez, Erwin, M.D., "The Medical Practice Committee of the AAPMR, Evolution and Growth," Arch Phys Med Rehabil, Special Edition October 1988, 47.

Gordon, Edward M.D., "Of Species and Specialties", Zeiter Lecture, Arch Phys Med Rehabil, Volume 62, 9.

Granger, Carl M.D., "Breaking New Ground-Academy Growth 1975–1979," Arch Phys Med Rehabil, Special Edition October 1988, 30.

Granger, Carl M.D., "Epidemiology, Disability and Physiatric Practice," Presidential Address AAPMR, Arch Phys Med Rehabil, Vol. 58, 1.

Gullickson, Glenn Jr., M.D.," The 1970's – The First Half," Arch Phys Med Rehabil, Special Edition October 1988, 26.

Hislop, Helen Ph.D., "Of Professional Bondage," Coulter Lecture, Arch Phys Med Rehabil, Vol. 59, 104.

Honet, Joseph M.D., "Manpower Planning," Arch Phys Med Rehabil, Vol. 59, 104.

Johnson, Ernest M.D., "Struggle for Identity: The Turbulent 1960's," Arch Phys Med Rehabil, Special Edition October 1988, 20.

Keys, Thomas M.D. and Frank Krusen, M.D., "Dr. Simon Baruch and His Fight for Free Public Baths," Arch Phys Med Rehabil, Vol. 26, 549.

Kliger, Edward M.D., "Rehabilitation in the Regional Medical Program," Arch Phys Med Rehabil, Vol. 52, 47.

Kottke, Frederick M.D., Ph.D., "History of Physiatry," Coulter Lecture, Arch Phys Med Rehabil, Vol. 50, 57.

Kottke, Frederick M.D., Ph.D., "The Future Focus of Rehabilitation Medicine," Presidential Address AAPMR, Arch Phys Med Rehabil, Vol. 61, 1.

Kottke, Frederick M.D., Ph.D. and Miland Knapp, M.D., "The Development of Physiatry Before 1950," Arch Phys Med Rehabil, Special Edition October 1988, 8.

Krusen , Frank M.D., " The American Rehabilitation Foundation and the New Regional Research and Training Centers," Arch Phys Med Rehabil, Vol. 44, 79.

Krusen, Frank M.D., "In Memoriam to Bernard Baruch 1870–1965," Arch Phys Med Rehabil, Vol. 46, 549.

Krusen Frank M.D., "The Historical Development of Physical Medicine and Rehabilitation During the Last Forty Years," Zeiter Lecture, Arch Phys Med and Rehabil, Vol. 50, 1.

Krusen, Frank M.D., Moderator Panel Discussion at International Congress of Rehabilitation Medicine, "Role of Government in Rehabilitation," Arch Phys Med Rehabil, Vol. 42, 661.

LaBan, Myron M.D., "Alice In Wonderland," Presidential Address AAPMR, Vol. 68, 1.

Lehmann, Justus M.D., "Physical Medicine Reflections," Presidential Address AAPMR, Arch Phys Med Rehabil, Vol. 55, 2.

Lehmann, Justus M.D., Zeiter Lecture, Arch Phys Med Rehabil, Vol. 63, 291.

Lehmann, Justus M.D., and Barbara deLatour, M.D., "Research and the American Academy of Physical Medicine and Rehabilitation," Arch Phys Med Rehabil, Special Edition October 1988, 59.

Licht, Sidney M.D., "Origins of Rehabilitation Medicine," Coulter Lecture, Arch Phys Med Rehabil, Vol. 51, 619.

Lowman, Edward M.D., Coulter Lecture, Arch Phys Med Rehabil, Vol. 53, 449.

Martin, Gordon M.D., "Building on the Framework, the Academy in the 1950's," Arch Phys Med Rehabil, Special Edition October 1988, 15.

Materson, Richard S. M.D., "The Academy in the Space Age: Preparing for the 21st Century," Arch Phys Med Rehabil, Special Edition October 1988, 41.

Materson, Richard M.D., "The Citizen Physiatrist," Presidential Address, Arch Phys Med Rehabil, Vol. 69, 1.

Melvin, John M.D., "Funding of Post Acute Care," Zeiter Lecture, Arch Phys Med Rehabil, Vol. 69, 163.

Mock, Harold M.D., "Rehabilitation," Arch Phys Med Rehabil, Vol. 50, 474, reprinted from vol. 24.

Olson, Donald Ph.D., Presidential Address American Congress of Rehabilitation Medicine, Arch Phys Med Rehabil, Vol. 68, 201.

Opitz, Joachim M.D., "Forging the Chain," Arch Phys Med Rehabil, Special Edition October 1988, 1.

Opitz, Joachim M.D., Thomas J. Foley, M.D., Russell Gelfman, M.D. and Jesse Peters, M.D., "Krusen Diaries," Arch Phys Med Rehabil, Vol. 78, four articles at 442–449 and 556–565.

Reinstein, Leon M.D., "Facing New Realities, Back to the Future," Zeiter Lecture, Arch Phys Med Rehabil, Vol. 77, 219.

Rusk, Howard M.D., "The Broadening Horizons of Physical Medicine and Rehabilitation," Arch Phys Med Rehabil, Vol. 30, 26.

Rusk, Howard M.D., "Growth and Development of Rehabilitation Medicine," Arch Phys Med Rehabil, Vol. 50, 463.

Rusk, Howard M.D., Zeiter Lecture, Arch Phys Med Rehabil, Vol. 59, 156.

Spencer, William M.D., "Rehabilitation Benefits No Longer a Matter of Doubt?," Presidential Address ACRM, Arch Phys Med Rehabil, Vol. 51, 189.

Spencer, William M.D., "Is Anybody Listening?," Coulter Lecture, Arch Phys Med Rehabil, Vol. 60, 191.

Steinfeld, Jesse M.D., Coulter Lecture, Arch Phys Med Rehabil, Vol. 53, 6.

Switzer, Mary E., "Role of Federal Government in Vocational Rehabilitation," Arch Phys Med Rehabil, Vol. 37, 542.

Switzer, Mary E., "A Coordinated Approach to Rehabilitation," Arch Phys Med Rehabil, Vol. 50, 355.

Vash, Carolyn Ph.D., "Post Modern World, New Venues, New Allies, New Ways," Coulter Lecture, Arch Phys Med Rehabil, Vol. 71, 643.

Verville, Richard J.D., "The Rehabilitation Amendments of 1978," Arch Phys Med Rehabil, Vol. 60, 141.

Verville, Richard J.D., "Legislative History of Independent Living," Arch Phys Med Rehabil, Vol. 60, 447.

Verville, Richard J.D., "Fifty Years of Federal Legislation and Programs Affecting Physical Medicine and Rehabilitation," Special Edition October 1988, 64.

Verville, Richard J.D. and Leighton Chan, M.D., M.P.H., "The Federal Financing and Regulation of Physical Medicine and Rehabilitation Services," Physical Medicine and Rehabilitation Clinics, Medico Legal Issues Edition, edited by La Certe and Kirst, W.B. Saunders and Co., May 2002, 196.

Wilkie, Harold D.D., "The Caring Community," Coulter Lecture, Arch Phys Med Rehabil, Vol. 58, 260.

Williams, T. Franklin M.D., "Future of Aging," Coulter Lecture, Arch Phys Med Rehabil, Vol. 68, 335.

Wilson, Charles, "The Other Movement Rosa Parks Inspired," *The Washington Post*, Sunday Outlook Section, October 30, 2005, 1.

Zola, Irving, Ph D., "A Speculative History of the Self Help Movement," Arch Phys Med Rehabil, Vol. 60, 452.

Zola, Irving Ph.D., "Aging, Disability and the Home Care Revolution," Coulter Lecture, Arch Phys Med Rehabil, Vol. 71, 93.

OTHER MANUSCRIPTS AND RESOURCES

Corning Peter, A History of Medicare, "The Evolution of Medicare . . . from idea to law", Social Security Administration Publisher, 1969; republished http://www.ssa.gov/history/corning.html,2004.

Danovitch, Sylvia, "History of the EEOC", Interview with Richard Melia, September 25,1992, Transcript of EEOC Oral History, published by EEOC, 1992.

DeLisa, Joel M.D. M.S., Luba Stefaniwsky, M.D. and Richard Sullivan, M.D., History of the Department of Physical Medicine and Rehabilitation and the Residency Training Program, New Jersey Medical School (NJMS), published by Department of Physical Medicine and Rehabilitation, NJMS, 2007.

From ADA To Empowerment, Report of the Task Force on the Rights and Empowerment of Americans with Disabilities. Published with Support of the Paralyzed Veterans of America and Jill Tarbel, October 12, 1990.

HCFA Oral History Interview, Interview of Dr. Phillip Lee by Edward Berkowitz, November 27, 1995, published at http://www.ssa.gov/history/LEE.html.

Henry Kessler Story, Henry Kessler Foundation Website, http://www.hhkfdn.org.

Medicare Payment Advisory Commission Report to the Congress, March 1999, published by the Medicare Payment Advisory Commission, Washington D.C., March 1999.

Mullan, Fitzhugh M.D., "History of the Health Services", Interview with Phillip Lee M.D., October 5, 1988, published at http://www.nlm.nih.gov/hmd/nichsr/lee.html.

Rehabilitation Record, Special Anniversary Edition, May/June 1970, edited by Dorothy Rigdon, published by the U.S. Government Printing Office, Division of Public Documents, Washington D.C., 1970.

Report of the Panel on Physical Medicine and Rehabilitation Research, National Institutes of Health (NIH), published by NIH, Bethesda, Maryland, December 21, 1989.

The Institute for Rehabilitation and Research (TIRR) 1959–1994, publisher TIRR, Houston, Texas, 1994.

INTERVIEWS BY AUTHOR, PERSONAL CORRESPONDENCE AND COMMUNICATIONS TO AUTHOR

Interviews and Other Communications

Henry Betts, M.D. interviews July 29, 2004, October 7, 2004 and October 9, 2004.

Barbara deLatour, M.D. interview November 27, 2007.

John Ditunno, M.D. interviews October 27, 2005.

William Fowler, M.D. interview September 10, 2004.

Bruce Gans, M.D. American Academy of Physical Medicine and Rehabilitation Presidential Address, October 27, 2005

Lynn Gerber, M.D. interview October 9, 2004.

Carl Granger, M.D. interview October 27, 2005.

Ernest Johnson, M.D. interview October 27, 2005.

Dennis Mathews interview October 27, 2005.

Richard Melia interview April 21, 2004.

John Melvin, M.D. interview October 27, 2005.

Joachim Opitz, M.D. interview September 15, 2004.

William Pease, M.D. interview December 18, 2007.

Leon Reinstein, M.D. interview October 7, 2004.

Elizabeth Sandel, M.D. interview October 8, 2004.

Carolyn Zollar, J.D. interview December 22, 2006.

Correspondence

Henry Betts, M.D. written correspondence to author January 6, 2004 and October 28, 2005.

Randall Braddom, D. M.S. email to author December 17,.2007.

Joel DeLisa, M.D. M.S. email to author August 9, 2007.

John Ditunno, M.D. emails to author December 31, 2003, November 24 and 28, 2006, and December 4, 2006.

Kristjan Ragnarsson, M.D. email to author June 22, 2006.

Leon Reinstein, M.D. email to author April 3, 2004.

Arthur Sherwood, Ph.D. email to author, April 29, 2004.

Index

Abramson, Arthur M.D., 170, 179, 199–200, 242, 251
academic medical centers and rehabilitation, 78–80, 169
Afghanistan war and rehabilitation medicine, 23, 223–24, 255–56
AIDS and ADA, 247
Albee, Frederick M.D., 22, 26–27, 33, 86–87, 111
American Academy of Orthopedic Surgery, 110–12. *See also* American Orthopedic Association
American Academy of Physical Medicine and Rehabilitation [AAPMR], 178–79, 184, 209, 215, 216–17; ADA and, 247, 251; NIH research advocacy of, 235–39; VA Task Force of, 223; wounded warriors Afghanistan and Iraq wars and, 255–56. *See also* Society of Physical Therapy Physicians
American Association of Neuromuscular and Electrodiagnostic Medicine [AANEM], 187–88, 224
American Board of Medical Specialties [ABMS] and rehabilitation, 106–7
American Board of Physical Medicine, 104–7

American Board of Physical Medicine and Rehabilitation, 107–11. *See also* American Board of Physical Medicine
American Coalition of Citizens with Disabilities [ACCD], 198
American College [renamed Congress] of Physical Therapy, 34, 35
American College of Radiology and Physiotherapy, 34
American Congress of Rehabilitation Medicine, 35, 178–79, 184, 190, 194, 200, 209; ADA and, 247, 251; Medicare inpatient and outpatient guidelines and programs, 216–17; rehabilitation research at NIH and advocacy of, 236–239. *See also* American College of Physical Therapy Physicians
American Electro-therapeutic Association, 34
American Hospital Association, 123, 131
American-Korean Foundation and Rusk, 148
American Medical Association [AMA], 25, 37, 44, 67–69, 144, 182; hospital construction and, 131–32; Medicare, Medicaid and, 167–69; national